Solace

Stitches of Comfort

Irina Anikeeva

2025

Table of Contents

Foreword

Knitting has always been more than the creation of fabric. Each stitch is a small act of care, a rhythm of movement that slows the pace of the day, a way of grounding ourselves in a world that too often feels hurried and uncertain. With this book, Solace: Stitches of Comfort, I wanted to celebrate not only the beauty of knitwear but also the calm and healing presence that knitting can bring to our lives.

Inside these pages you will find 22 patterns for garments and accessories. Each one was designed with the idea of comfort at its heart – comfort in the wearing and comfort in the making. Sweaters with easy silhouettes, wraps that envelop the body, hats and cowls that warm against the chill — these are pieces that invite you to linger with the yarn, to let your hands find their rhythm, and to enjoy the simple pleasure of watching fabric grow beneath your needles.

The act of knitting has long been linked to mental well-being. Studies show what knitters have known intuitively for generations: that the steady repetition of stitches can ease stress, lower anxiety, and even help with focus. Knitting is portable meditation. When we pick up our needles, we give ourselves permission to slow down, to breathe, and to be present in the moment. It is in this quiet space that creativity flourishes and worries gently recede.

In today's turbulent world, where news cycles are relentless and our schedules often leave little room for pause, the need for this kind of calming practice is greater than ever. Knitting reminds us that worthwhile things take time — that each stitch contributes to a greater whole, that progress is made little by little, and that beauty often lies in the simplest of repetitions.

In this way, knitting mirrors life itself: the steady accumulation of small moments becomes something lasting and meaningful.

The patterns in Solace were designed to reflect that philosophy. They are engaging yet approachable, with textures that invite your fingers to linger and constructions that encourage mindful progress. Whether it is a sweater worked seamlessly from the top down, a lace shawl that grows organically from a single point, or a textured hat that reveals its rhythm row by row, each project offers both satisfaction in the making and comfort in the wearing.

But more than just a collection of patterns, this book is an invitation. It is an invitation to carve out space for yourself, to find stillness in the click of needles, to rediscover the pleasure of creating something with your own two hands. My hope is that these designs will not only add warmth to your wardrobe but also moments of quiet to your life — that they will remind you, stitch by stitch, of the restorative power of making.

May Solace accompany you in those moments when you need them most: when the world feels noisy, when your mind feels restless, or when you simply want to retreat into the gentle rhythm of yarn and needles. May it offer you not only patterns to knit but also a sense of calm, connection, and comfort that endures long after the last stitch is bound off.

Sincerely yours,
Irina Anikeeva

MISS BABS YARNS

Babs and the Miss Babs Team have been dyeing beautiful yarns in our studio in the mountains of eastern Tennessee since 2005. We love seeing the colors that occur in nature and playing off them to create yarns that evoke the emotional impact of the natural world. We are delighted to work with Irina Anikeeva on this project and have provided some of our favorite yarns in Merino wool as well as wool and silk blends for the book.

Yummy 2-ply

This versatile, 2-ply superwash Merino is wonderful for cowls, scarves, shawls, and lightweight sweaters.

Laurel Falls

Laurel Falls is a sport weight yarn created with soft American Shaniko Merino wool. With a matte finish and a lofty, round 3-ply construction, we think Laurel Falls is a great choice for sport weight sweaters and accessories. This yarn will work well in a variety of textured stitches as well as colorwork.

Caroline

Caroline is lusciously soft, blending super fine merino wool with cashmere and nylon. Colors on Caroline are gentle, and your finished project will have a little bit of halo. You'll love Caroline in textured or lacy accessories like shawls, cowls, hand warmers, and hats.

Intrepid

Intrepid is the non-superwash worsted weight yarn we've been searching for. It is an all-American yarn, from the Targhee sheep, to the processing, to the dyeing. Targhee wool has a great bouncy liveliness while still being soft. Intrepid is a classic 3-ply worsted weight with a lot of body, perfect for warm and cozy textures in sweaters, hats, and more.

Putnam

With a 4-ply construction, Putnam is round and smooth, with the right elasticity and density for socks. Putnam has a smooth matte finish that will show off all your careful stitching.

Tarte

Tarte is smooth and round, with a balanced 4-ply construction. Nylon and Tencel add strength, sheen, and drape to the superwash Merino in this yarn. Tarte is a beautiful choice for many fingering weight projects, including shawlettes and sweaters where you'll enjoy the generous yardage in each skein. It's also great for socks where you'll enjoy its strength and smoothness.

Killington

Killington is a lofty DK weight blend of Polwarth wool and Tussah silk. It has a subtle sheen, a slightly crisp hand, and excellent wearing qualities.

Yowza

You'll be saying "Yowza! These skeins are BIG!" when you see this yarn. Plied from soft superwash Merino wool, Yowza is excellent for sweaters, accessories, and baby items. Yowza has a smooth hand that works well for textured stitching.

Miss Babs
Hand-Dyed Yarns

BASICS AND BEYOND

Knitting language is full of technical terms, abbreviations and familiar words used in particular ways. The section below will help you excel with a better understanding of how to read knitting patterns in general, techniques, and other useful information.

How to understand the size

Most of the garment patterns have multiple sizes, and first of all you need to decide which size to make. In tops and sweaters pattern descriptions you will find the information about Size and Finished Measurements. What is the difference between them? The "size" refers to your actual bust circumference. To measure it, wrap the sewing tape measure around the fullest part of your bust. This number is your actual bust size.

The "finished measurements" of garment patterns show the bust circumference of the actual knitted sweater. It can be larger than the body bust size ("positive ease") to have a relaxed fit, or smaller ("negative ease"). All the tops from this book are designed to fit somewhat loosely, with 2"/5 cm to 12"/30 cm of positive ease.

The Finished Measurements description also contains the information about the size worn by the model, e.g., "shown in size M (39½"/99 cm) on 38"/95 cm bust with 1½"/4 cm of positive ease". That means if your bust circumference is 34"/85 cm and you are making the size with final bust size of the garment 36"/90 cm you will achieve the fit close to that shown on the model in photo.

If your bust size falls between the measurements listed, you can decide if you want a garment a bit looser or tighter than shown in the photo. Another tool that will help you with your size decision is the schematics. Compare your upper-arm or hips measurements to the schematics to choose the size which seems to be best on you and for your desired fit and ease.

Gauge and swatch

All patterns list a gauge, the measurement of how many stitches and rows you should achieve over certain distance (usually per 4"/10 cm). This information helps to choose the yarn and the needles size and it is provided to ensure the final knitted piece is the correct size.
To check the gauge, we need to knit a swatch. It doesn't need to be a chore. Swatching is a great way to get to know your yarn, to decide how it feels, behaves and if you like the knitted fabric it produces.

The needle size listed in a pattern is the size I used to make the project. Since every knitter knits differently you may need to use different-size needles to achieve required gauge.

I always prefer to make nice, large swatches – at least 8"/20 cm square, but with simple stockinette you may knit smaller, 4"/10 cm square swatch. First, use the needles listed in the pattern and work until your piece is about 5"/12.5 cm long. If gauge is listed in rows, work the piece flat; if gauge is listed in rounds, work in the round. Bind off all stitches.

Now wash your swatch in the same way you'll wash a finished project and lay it flat to dry. Don't pin or stretch it unless you plan to pin the finished piece. Basically, don't pin a garment swatch but do pin a swatch for a lace shawl. Use the ruler to carefully measure 4"/10 cm across and count the stitches, and then measure same distance up and down and count the rows/rounds. The number of stitches and rows/rounds need to match the numbers listed in pattern.

If you see too many stitches, that means your stitches are too small and you need try again with larger needles; too few stitches mean that your stitches are too big, and you need to use smaller needles to achieve the correct gauge.

Counting the rows is really important. When a pattern says "work until piece reaches 10 inches from, *say*, underarms," it refers to *your* row gauge. If your blocked swatch measures 8 rows per inch, that means you'll need to knit 10 x 8 = 80 rows. Counting rows ensures accuracy and fit, while measuring fabric directly can lead to distortion and errors due to the difference between gauge of unblocked and blocked fabric.

Left or right?

In some patterns you will see the parts of it, named "Right Back" or "Left Front". These directions always refer to wearer's left or right, rather than the piece in relation to you when knitting.
"Right side" (or RS) is the side of knitted piece is to be shown on the outside, the other side is the "wrong side" (or WS).

How to read a pattern?

Knitting patterns use a kind of shorthand: symbols like asterisks or brackets are there to break instructions into smaller, repeatable parts. Understanding how they work is an essential step in learning to read patterns with confidence.

Asterisks

An asterisk (*) marks the beginning of a repeat. When a pattern tells you to "repeat from *," it means to go back to that point and work the sequence again, usually until the end of a row, round, or a specified marker.

For example:
Row 1: P2TOG, *k1, p1; repeat from * to end.
This means purl two together, then alternate knit one, purl one until the end of the row.

Sometimes, asterisks define a repeat that ends before the row does:

Row 1: *K1, p1; repeat from * to last stitch, k1.
Here, you'll repeat k1, p1 until 1 stitch remain, then finish with k1.

Brackets

Brackets [ ] also group stitches, but they usually indicate a sequence to be repeated a specific number of times.

For example:
Row 1: [K1, p1] 3 times, knit to end.
This means sequence of knit 1 and purl 1 three times total, then knit all stitches to the end of the row.

Brackets are also used to show the stitch count after a row or round, especially when shaping has changed it:

Round 1: K2, P2TOG; repeat from * to end.
[2 (3, 4, 5, 8, 9), {11, 12, 15, 17} stitches]

The numbers in parentheses show stitch counts for different sizes.

Blocking

Every pattern instructs to "block item to measurements". It is a crucial step and it allow you to finally see your knitted piece in its full glory. Textured stitch patterns, such as cables, lace need to lie flat, relaxed and opened. There are several methods for doing this, but I usually prefer to wet block the garments.

To do that, fill the basin or tub with lukewarm water with a drop of no-rinse wool wash, submerge your knit and leave it for 10 minutes so the fibers become fully saturated. Drain the water and gently press the knit against the side of the basin, then transfer it to a towel. Roll the towel with the wet knit inside and press down to squeeze out the remaining water.
Lay the piece flat on the blocking mats, shape it to the measurements on the schematic using pins, if needed, to hold it in place. Let the knitting dry completely and remove pins.
Sometimes I steam-block parts of the garment after that to remove any creases if they appear.

Bess

This pullover is a celebration of texture and geometry, worked in an allover lace and knit-purl motif that creates a richly sculpted fabric. Horizontal bands of chevrons, diamonds, and eyelets alternate to form a rhythm of patterning that feels both modern and timeless.

The silhouette of this top-down pullover is relaxed yet refined, with a round yoke, straight body, and slightly tapered sleeves finished with deep ribbed cuffs. A simple ribbed hem and neckline provide clean framing that balances the ornate fabric.

Sizes
XS (S, M, L, XL, 2XL), {3XL, 4XL, 5XL, 6XL}: to fit bust 28-30 (32-34, 36-38, 40-42, 44-46, 48-50), {52-54, 56-58, 60-62, 64-66}"/70-75 (80-85, 90-95, 100-105, 110-115, 120-125), {130-135, 140-145, 150-155, 160-165} cm.

Finished Measurements
37 (40, 46¼, 49¼, 52½, 58½), {61½, 64½, 67¾, 70¾}"/ 92.5 (100, 115.5, 123, 131.5, 146.5), {154, 161.5, 169.5, 177} cm bust circumference.
Pullover shown measures 46¼"/115.5 cm on 38"/95 cm bust with 8¼"/20.5 cm of positive ease.

Yarn
Fingering weight yarn (approximate amounts): 1240 (1350, 1550, 1660, 1760, 1970), {2070, 2180, 2280, 2380} yards/1128 (1228, 1411, 1511, 1601, 1793), {1884, 1984, 2075, 2166} m.

Miss Babs Tarte (75% Superwash Merino Wool, 15% Nylon, 10% Tencel; 500 yds/457 m in 4.3 oz/ 122 gr), Dark Adobe: 3 (3, 4, 4, 4, 4), {5, 5, 5, 5} skeins.

Needles
Size US 3/3.25 mm: 16"/40 cm, 24"/60 cm circular and set of double-pointed needles.
Adjust needle size if necessary to obtain the correct gauge.

Notions
Stitch markers, stitch holders or waste yarn, tapestry needle.

Gauge
26 stitches and 34 rows = 4"/10 cm in charted pattern, after blocking.

Notes
- This pullover is worked in one piece from the top down with round yoke shaping.

DIRECTIONS

01 YOKE

With US 3/3.25 mm 16"/40 cm needle cast on 96 (108, 120, 120, 126, 126), {135, 140, 140, 140} stitches. Place marker for beginning of the round (BOR), join in the round.

Knit all stitches in the next 4 rounds.

Ribbing Round: *K1, p1; repeat to end.
Repeat Ribbing Round another 7 times.

Sizes XS (S, M, _, _, _), {3XL, 4XL, 5XL, 6XL} only:
Next Round: Knit.

Size _ (_, _, L, _, _), {_, _, _, _} only:
Increase Round: K5, [M1L, k10] 11 times, M1L, k5.

Sizes _ (_, _, _, XL, _), {_, _, _, _} only:
Increase Round: K5, [M1L, k11] 3 times, [M1L, k10] 5 times, [M1L, k11] 3 times, M1L, k5.

Size _ (_, _, _, _, 2XL), {_, _, _, _} only:
Increase Round: K3, [M1L, k7] 17 times, M1L, k4.

[96 (108, 120, 132, 138, 144), {135, 140, 140, 140} stitches on the needle]

Purl all stitches for the next 2 rounds.

Shape back neck with German Short-Rows (see Special Techniques, page 226):
Short-Row 1 (RS): K14 (15, 16, 17, 18, 18), {18, 18, 18, 18}, turn work.
Short-Row 2 (WS): Make double stitch, purl to BOR, p14 (15, 16, 17, 18, 18), {18, 18, 18, 18}, turn work.
Short-Row 3 (RS): Make double stitch, knit to double stitch on previous row, work double stitch as a single stitch, k4 (4, 4, 4, 5, 5), {5, 5, 5, 5}, turn work.
Short-Row 4 (WS): Make double stitch, purl to double stitch on previous row, work double stitch as a single stitch, p4 (4, 4, 4, 5, 5), {5, 5, 5, 5}, turn work.

Short-Rows 5-8: Repeat Short-rows 3 and 4 two more times.

Short-Row 9 (RS): Make DS, knit to BOR. Continue working in the round.

Next Round: Knit all stitches, working double stitches as single stitches when you come to them.

Chart Set-Up Round: Work Row 1 of Yoke Chart for your size.

NOTE: While following the chart, change to US 3/3.25 cm 24"/60 cm circular needle when needed.

TIP: To eliminate the "jog" when working the two Reverse Stockinette rounds, slip purlwise the first stitch on the first round after the purl rounds from left to right needle, without working it.

Continue following Yoke Chart through Row 54 (54, 54, 65, 65, 65), {68, 68, 76, 76}.
[352, (396, 440, 484, 506, 528), {594, 616, 672, 672} stitches on the needle]

Next Round: Purl.

Size _ (S, _, _, _, _), {_, _, _, _} only:
Increase Round: P12, [M1P, p25] 6 times, [M1P, p24] 3 times, [M1P, p25] 6 times, M1P, p12. [412 stitches]

Size _ (_, M, _, _, _), {_, _, _, _} only:
Increase Round: P18, [M1P, p37] 4 times, [M1P, p36] 3 times, [M1P, p37] 4 times, M1P, p18. [452 stitches]

Size _ (_, _, L, _, _), {_, _, _, _} only:
Increase Round: P12, [M1P, p25] 2 times, [M1P, p24] 15 times, [M1P, p25] 2 times, M1P, p12. [504 stitches]

Size _ (_, _, _, XL, _), {_, _, _, _} only:
Increase Round: P14, M1P, p29, [M1P, p28] 15 times, M1P, p29, M1P, p14. [524 stitches]

Size _ (_, _, _, _, 2XL), {_, _, _, _} only:
Increase Round: P13, [M1P, p27] 4 times, [M1P, p26] 11 times, [M1P, p27] 4 times, M1P, p13. [548 stitches]

Size _ (_, _, _, _, _), {3XL, _, _, _} only:
Increase Round: P49, [M1P, p99] 5 times, M1P, p50. [600 stitches]

Size _ (_, _, _, _, _), {_, 4XL, _, _} only:
Increase Round: P77, [M1P, p154] 3 times, M1P, p77. [620 stitches]

Size _ (_, _, _, _, _), {_, _, _, 6XL} only:
Increase Round: P17, [M1P, p33] 4 times, [M1P, p34] 11 times, [M1P, p33] 4 times, M1P, p17. [692 stitches]

All sizes:
[352 (412, 452, 504, 524, 548), {600, 620, 672, 692} stitches on the needle]

Divide for Body and Sleeves
Division Round: K54 (59, 69, 73, 78, 86), {90, 95, 99, 104}, place next 68 (88, 88, 106, 106, 102), {120, 120, 138, 138} stitches on hold for Right Sleeve, cast on 12 (12, 12, 14, 14, 18), {20, 20, 22, 22} stitches for right underarm, k108 (118, 138, 146, 156, 172), {180, 190, 198, 208}, place next 68 (88, 88, 106, 106, 102), {120, 120, 138, 138} stitches on hold for Left Sleeve, cast on 12 (12, 12, 14, 14, 18), {20, 20, 22, 22} stitches for left underarm, k54 (59, 69, 73, 78, 86), {90, 95, 99, 104} to end.
[240 (260, 300, 320, 340, 380), {400, 420, 440, 460} stitches on the needle for Body]

Continue working on Body stitches..

02 BODY

Next Round: Knit all stitches.

Chart-Set-Up Round: Work Row 1 of Main Chart. Continue following Main Chart through Round 55, then work Rounds 1-43 (1-43, 1-43, 1-43, 1-43, 1-55), {1-55, 1-55, 1-55, 1-55} of Main Chart.

Sizes _ (_, _, _, _, 2XL), {3XL, 4XL, 5XL, 6XL} only:
Next Round: Knit all stitches.

All sizes:
Ribbing Round: *K1, p1; repeat from * to end.
Repeat Ribbing Round until ribbing measures 2"/5 cm.

Bind off all stitches in pattern or use Tubular Bind Off method for k1, p1 rib (see Special Techniques, page 226).

03 SLEEVES

With US 3/3.25 mm double-pointed needles, beginning at the center of the underarm, pick up and knit 6 (6, 6, 7, 7, 9), {10, 10, 11, 11} stitches along the underarm, knit held 68 (88, 88, 106, 106, 102), {120, 120, 138, 138} Sleeve stitches, pick up and knit 6 (6, 6, 7, 7, 9), {10, 10, 11, 11} stitches along the underarm. [80 (100, 100, 120, 120, 120), {140, 140, 160, 160} stitches on the needle]

Place marker for the beginning of the round and join in the round.

Chart-Set-Up Round: Work Row 1 of Main Chart. Continue following Main Chart through Round 55, then work Rounds 1-55 of Main Chart once more.

Next Round: Knit all stitches.

Cuff
Size XS (_, _, _, _, _), {_, _, _, _} only:
Decrease Round: K2TOG, k38, K2TOG, knit to end. [78 stitches]

Sizes _ (S, M, _, _, _), {_, _, _, _} only:
Decrease Round: K2, [K2TOG, k3] 7 times, [K2TOG, k4] 4 times, [K2TOG, k3] 7 times, K2TOG, k2. [81 stitches]

Size _ (_, _, L, _, _), {_, _, _, _} only:
Decrease Round: K1, [K2TOG, k1] 18 times, [K2TOG, k2] 2 times, [K2TOG, k1] 18 times, K2TOG, k1. [81 stitches]

Sizes _ (_, _, _, XL, 2XL), {_, _, _, _} only:
Decrease Round: K1, [K2TOG, k2] 29 times, K2TOG, k1. [90 stitches]

Sizes _ (_, _, _, _, _), {3XL, 4XL, _, _} only:
Decrease Round: K1, [K2TOG, k1] 17 times, [K2TOG, k2] 4 times, [K2TOG, k1] 18 times, [K2TOG, k2] 4 times, K2TOG. [96 stitches]

Sizes _ (_, _, _, _, _), {_, _, 5XL, 6XL} only:
Decrease Round: K1, [K2TOG, k1] 23 times, [K2TOG, k2] 2 times, [K2TOG, k1] 24 times, [K2TOG, k2] 2 times, K2TOG. [108 stitches]

All sizes:
[78 (81, 81, 81, 90, 90), {96, 96, 108, 108} stitches on the needle]

Ribbing Round 1: *K1, p2; repeat from * to end. Repeat last round until cuff measures 2"/5 cm.

Decrease Round: *K1, P2TOG; repeat from * to end. [52 (54, 54, 54, 60, 60), {64, 64, 72, 72} stitches]

Ribbing Round 2: *K1, p1; repeat from * to end. Repeat Ribbing Round 2 for 3"/7.5 cm more, until cuff measures 5"/12.5 cm.

Bind off all stitches in pattern or use Tubular Bind Off method for k1, p1 rib (see Special Techniques, page 226).

04 FINISHING

Block to measurements. Weave in ends.

CHARTS

YOKE CHART (SIZES XS, S AND M ONLY)

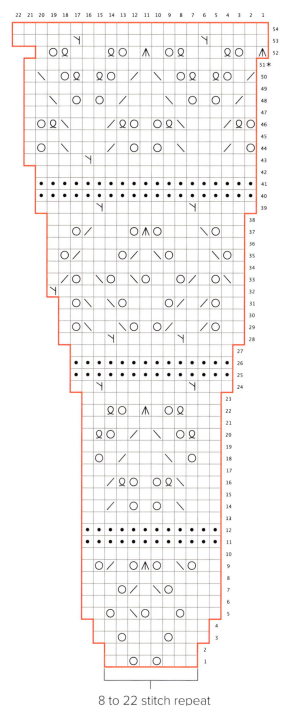

8 to 22 stitch repeat

LEGEND

☐ **K**: Knit stitch

• **P**: Purl stitch

Ⓠ **K1 tbl**: Knit stitch through back loop

◯ **YO**: Yarn over

⅄ **M1L**: With left needle tip, pick up the thread between stitches from front to back. Knit lifted loop through the backloop – 1 stitch increased

╱ **K2TOG**: Knit 2 stitches together – 1 stitch decreased with right slant.

╲ **SSK**: Slip 1 stitch knitwise, slip 1 stitch knitwise, return 2 slipped stitches back to left needle and knit them together through back loops – 1 stitch decreased with left slant

⋀ **CDD** (central double decrease): Slip 2 stitches as if to K2TOG, k1, pass 2 slipped stitches over knit stitch – 2 stitches decreased.

☐ Pattern repeat

* Follow Chart Written Instructions

YOKE CHART
(SIZES L, XL AND 2XL ONLY)

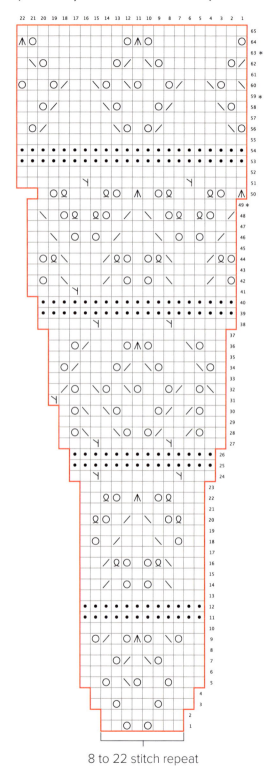

8 to 22 stitch repeat

YOKE CHART
(SIZES 3XL AND 4XL ONLY)

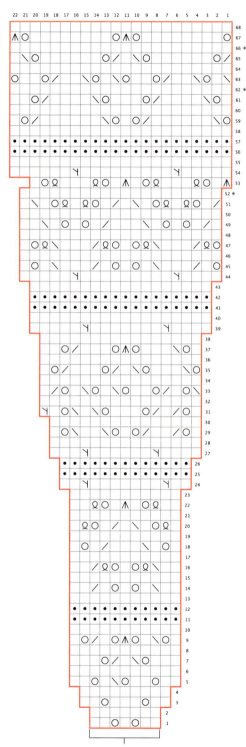

7 to 22 stitch repeat

YOKE CHART
(SIZES 5XL AND 6XL ONLY)

MAIN CHART

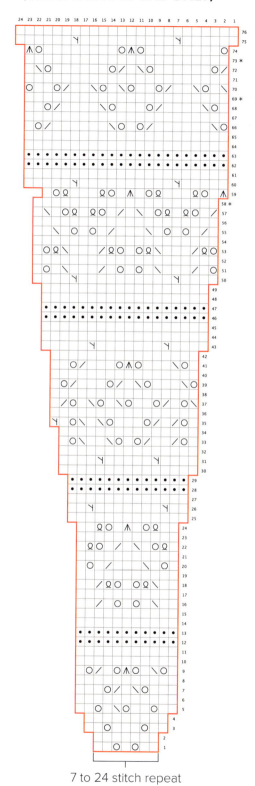

7 to 24 stitch repeat

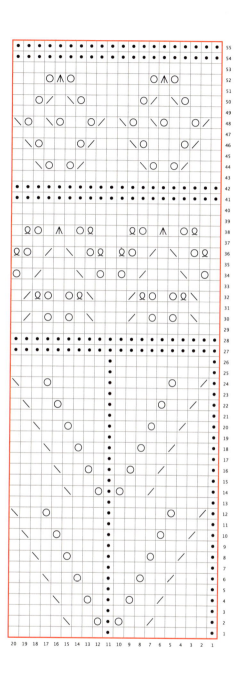

Written instructions for Yoke Chart
(sizes XS, S and M only)
.. – pattern repeat
Note: See Chart Legend for special abbreviations.

Round 1: *K3, YO, k1, YO, k2*
Round 2: Knit.
Round 3: *[K3, YO] 2 times, k2*
Round 4: Knit.
Round 5: *K3, YO, k2, YO, SSK, k1, YO, k2*
Round 6: Knit.
Round 7: *K4, YO, SSK, k1, K2TOG, YO, k3*
Round 8: Knit.
Round 9: *K2, YO, SSK, k1, YO, CDD, YO, k1, K2TOG, YO, k1*
Round 10: Knit.
Rounds 11 - 12: Purl.
Round 13: Knit.
Round 14: *K3, SSK, [k1, YO] 2 times, k1, K2TOG, k2*
Round 15: Knit.
Round 16: *K3, SSK, k1 tbl, YO, k1, YO, k1 tbl, K2TOG, k2*
Round 17: Knit.
Round 18: *K2, YO, k1, SSK, k3, K2TOG, k1, YO, k1*
Round 19: Knit.
Round 20: *K2, k1 tbl, YO, k1, SSK, k1, K2TOG, k1, YO, k1 tbl, k1*
Round 21: Knit.
Round 22: *K3, k1 tbl, YO, k1, CDD, k1, YO, k1 tbl, k2*
Round 23: Knit.
Round 24: *K3, M1L, k7, M1L, k2*
Rounds 25 - 26: Purl.
Round 27: Knit.
Round 28: *[K5, M1L] 2 times, k4*
Round 29: *K2, YO, K2TOG, k2, K2TOG, YO, k1, YO, SSK, k2, SSK, YO, k1*
Round 30: Knit.
Round 31: *K2, YO, K2TOG, k1, K2TOG, YO, k3, YO, SSK, k1, SSK, YO, k1*
Round 32: *K16, M1L*
Round 33: *K1, SSK, YO, k1, K2TOG, YO, k2, [YO, SSK, k1] 2 times, YO, K2TOG, k1*
Round 34: Knit.
Round 35: *K1, YO, SSK, k3, YO, SSK, k1, K2TOG, YO, k3, K2TOG, YO, k1*
Round 36: Knit.

Round 37: *K2, YO, SSK, k3, YO, CDD, YO, k3, K2TOG, YO, k2*
Round 38: Knit.
Round 39: *K5, M1L, k7, M1L, k5*
Rounds 40 - 41: Purl.
Round 42: Knit.
Round 43: *K14, M1L, k5*
Round 44: *YO, k1, K2TOG, k3, SSK, k1, YO, k1*
Round 45: Knit.
Round 46: *YO, k1 tbl, K2TOG, k3, SSK, k1 tbl, YO, k1*
Round 47: Knit.
Round 48: *K1, K2TOG, [k1, YO] 2 times, k1, SSK, k3, K2TOG, [k1, YO] 2 times, k1, SSK, k2*
Round 49: Knit.
Round 50: *[K2TOG, k1, YO, k1 tbl, k1, k1 tbl, YO, k1, SSK, k1] 2 times*
* Round 51 (Shift Marker): Knit to last 2 stitches of the round, slip next 2 stitches to right needle, remove BOR, place just slipped 2 stitches from right to left needle, replace BOR.
Round 52: *CDD, k1, YO, k1 tbl, k3, k1 tbl, YO, k1*
Round 53: *K5, M1L, k10, M1L, k5*
Round 54: Knit.

Written instructions for Yoke Chart
(sizes L, XL and 2XL only)
.. – pattern repeat

Round 1: *K3, YO, k1, YO, k2*
Round 2: Knit.
Round 3: *[K3, YO] 2 times, k2*
Round 4: Knit.
Round 5: *K3, YO, k2, YO, SSK, k1, YO, k2*
Round 6: Knit.
Round 7: *K4, YO, SSK, k1, K2TOG, YO, k3*
Round 8: Knit.
Round 9: *K2, YO, SSK, k1, YO, CDD, YO, k1, K2TOG, YO, k1*
Round 10: Knit.
Rounds 11 - 12: Purl.
Round 13: Knit.
Round 14: *K3, SSK, [k1, YO] 2 times, k1, K2TOG, k2*
Round 15: Knit.
Round 16: *K3, SSK, k1 tbl, YO, k1, YO, k1 tbl, K2TOG, k2*
Round 17: Knit.

Round 18: *K2, YO, k1, SSK, k3, K2TOG, k1, YO, k1*
Round 19: Knit.
Round 20: *K2, k1 tbl, YO, k1, SSK, k1, K2TOG, k1, YO, k1 tbl, k1*
Round 21: Knit.
Round 22: *K3, k1 tbl, YO, k1, CDD, k1, YO, k1 tbl, k2*
Round 23: Knit.
Round 24: *K3, M1L, k7, M1L, k2*
Rounds 25 - 26: Purl.
Round 27: *K5, M1L, k6, M1L, k3*
Round 28: *K2, YO, K2TOG, k2, K2TOG, YO, k1, YO, SSK, k2, SSK, YO, k1*
Round 29: Knit.
Round 30: *K2, YO, K2TOG, k1, K2TOG, YO, k3, YO, SSK, k1, SSK, YO, k1*
Round 31: *K16, M1L*
Round 32: *K1, SSK, YO, k1, K2TOG, YO, k2, [YO, SSK, k1] 2 times, YO, K2TOG, k1*
Round 33: Knit.
Round 34: *K1, YO, SSK, k3, YO, SSK, k1, K2TOG, YO, k3, K2TOG, YO, k1*
Round 35: Knit.
Round 36: *K2, YO, SSK, k3, YO, CDD, YO, k3, K2TOG, YO, k2*
Round 37: Knit.
Round 38: *[K6, M1L] 2 times, k5*
Rounds 39 - 40: Purl.
Round 41: *K15, M1L, k4*
Round 42: *YO, k1, K2TOG, k3, SSK, k1, YO, k1*
Round 43: Knit.
Round 44: *YO, k1 tbl, K2TOG, k3, SSK, k1 tbl, YO, k1*
Round 45: Knit.
Round 46: *K1, K2TOG, [k1, YO] 2 times, k1, SSK, k3, K2TOG, [k1, YO] 2 times, k1, SSK, k2*
Round 47: Knit.
Round 48: *K2TOG, k1, YO, k1 tbl, k1, k1 tbl, YO, k1, SSK, k1*
* Round 49 (Shift Marker): Knit to last 2 stitches of the round, slip next 2 stitches to right needle, remove BOR, place just slipped 2 stitches from right to left needle, replace BOR.
Round 50: *CDD, k1, YO, k1 tbl, k3, k1 tbl, YO, k1*
Round 51: *K5, M1L, k9, M1L, k6*
Round 52: Knit.
Rounds 53 - 54: Purl.
Round 55: Knit.

Round 56: *YO, SSK, k6, K2TOG, YO, k1, YO, SSK, k6, K2TOG, YO, k1*
Round 57: Knit.
Round 58: *K1, YO, SSK, k4, K2TOG, YO, k3, YO, SSK, k4, K2TOG, YO, k2*
* Round 59 (Shift Marker): Knit to last stitch of the round, slip next stitch to right needle, remove BOR, place just slipped stitch from right to left needle, replace BOR.
Round 60: *SSK, k1, YO, SSK, k2, K2TOG, YO, k2, YO*
Round 61: Knit.
Round 62: *K2TOG, YO, k6, YO, SSK, k1*
* Round 63 (Shift Marker): Knit to end the round, remove BOR, slip 1 stitch to right needle, replace BOR, place just slipped stitch from right to left needle.
Round 64: *YO, k8, YO, CDD*
Round 65: Knit.

Written instructions for Yoke Chart
(sizes 3XL and 4XL only)
.. – pattern repeat

Round 1: *K2, YO, k1, YO, k2*
Round 2: Knit.
Round 3: *K2, YO, k3, YO, k2*
Round 4: Knit.
Round 5: *[K2, YO] 2 times, SSK, k1, YO, k2*
Round 6: Knit.
Round 7: *K3, YO, SSK, k1, K2TOG, YO, k3*
Round 8: Knit.
Round 9: *K1, YO, SSK, k1, YO, CDD, YO, k1, K2TOG, YO, k1*
Round 10: Knit.
Rounds 11 - 12: Purl.
Round 13: Knit.
Round 14: *K2, SSK, [k1, YO] 2 times, k1, K2TOG, k2*
Round 15: Knit.
Round 16: *K2, SSK, k1 tbl, YO, k1, YO, k1 tbl, K2TOG, k2*
Round 17: Knit.
Round 18: *K1, YO, k1, SSK, k3, K2TOG, k1, YO, k1*
Round 19: Knit.
Round 20: *K1, k1 tbl, YO, k1, SSK, k1, K2TOG, k1, YO, k1 tbl, k1*
Round 21: Knit.
Round 22: *K2, k1 tbl, YO, k1, CDD, k1, YO, k1 tbl, k2*

Round 23: Knit.
Round 24: *K2, M1L, k7, M1L, k2*
Rounds 25 - 26: Purl.
Round 27: *K4, M1L, k6, M1L, k3*
Round 28: Knit.
Round 29: *K1, YO, K2TOG, k2, K2TOG, YO, k1, YO, SSK, k2, SSK, YO, k1*
Round 30: Knit.
Round 31: *K1, YO, K2TOG, k1, K2TOG, YO, k3, YO, SSK, k1, SSK, YO, k1, M1L*
Round 32: Knit.
Round 33: *SSK, YO, k1, K2TOG, YO, k2, [YO, SSK, k1] 2 times, YO, K2TOG, k1*
Round 34: Knit.
Round 35: *YO, SSK, k3, YO, SSK, k1, K2TOG, YO, k3, K2TOG, YO, k1*
Round 36: Knit.
Round 37: *K1, YO, SSK, k3, YO, CDD, YO, k3, K2TOG, YO, k2*
Round 38: Knit.
Round 39: *K4, M1L, k7, M1L, k5*
Round 40: Knit.
Rounds 41 - 42: Purl.
Round 43: Knit.
Round 44: *K4, M1L, k9, M1L, k5*
Round 45: *YO, k1, K2TOG, k3, SSK, k1, YO, k1*
Round 46: Knit.
Round 47: *YO, k1 tbl, K2TOG, k3, SSK, k1 tbl, YO, k1*
Round 48: Knit.
Round 49: *K1, K2TOG, [k1, YO] 2 times, k1, SSK, k3, K2TOG, [k1, YO] 2 times, k1, SSK, k2*
Round 50: Knit.
Round 51: *K2TOG, k1, YO, k1 tbl, k1, k1 tbl, YO, k1, SSK, k1*
* Round 52 (Shift Marker): Knit to last 2 stitches of the round, slip next 2 stitches to right needle, remove BOR, place just slipped 2 stitches from right to left needle, replace BOR.
Round 53: *CDD, k1, YO, k1 tbl, k3, k1 tbl, YO, k1*
Round 54: *K5, M1L, k9, M1L, k6*
Round 55: Knit.
Rounds 56 - 57: Purl.
Round 58: Knit.
Round 59: *YO, SSK, k6, K2TOG, YO, k1, YO, SSK, k6, K2TOG, YO, k1*
Round 60: Knit.

Round 61: *K1, YO, SSK, k4, K2TOG, YO, k3, YO, SSK, k4, K2TOG, YO, k2*
*Round 62 (Shift Marker): Knit to last stitch of the round, slip next stitch to right needle, remove BOR, place just slipped stitch from right to left needle, replace BOR.
Round 63: *SSK, k1, YO, SSK, k2, K2TOG, YO, k2, YO*
Round 64: Knit.
Round 65: *K2TOG, YO, k6, YO, SSK, k1*
* Round 66 (Shift Marker): Knit to end the round, remove BOR, slip 1 stitch to right needle, replace BOR, place just slipped stitch from right to left needle.
Round 67: *YO, k8, YO, CDD*
Round 68: Knit.

Written instructions for Yoke Chart
(sizes 5XL and 6XL only)
.. – pattern repeat

Round 1: *K2, YO, k1, YO, k2*
Round 2: Knit.
Round 3: *K2, YO, k3, YO, k2*
Round 4: Knit.
Round 5: *[K2, YO] 2 times, SSK, k1, YO, k2*
Round 6: Knit.
Round 7: *K3, YO, SSK, k1, K2TOG, YO, k3*
Round 8: Knit.
Round 9: *K1, YO, SSK, k1, YO, CDD, YO, k1, K2TOG, YO, k1*
Rounds 10 - 11: Knit.
Rounds 12 - 13: Purl.
Rounds 14 - 15: Knit.
Round 16: *K2, SSK, [k1, YO] 2 times, k1, K2TOG, k2*
Round 17: Knit.
Round 18: *K2, SSK, k1 tbl, YO, k1, YO, k1 tbl, K2TOG, k2*
Round 19: Knit.
Round 20: *K1, YO, k1, SSK, k3, K2TOG, k1, YO, k1*
Round 21: Knit.
Round 22: *K1, k1 tbl, YO, k1, SSK, k1, K2TOG, k1, YO, k1 tbl, k1*
Round 23: Knit.
Round 24: *K2, k1 tbl, YO, k1, CDD, k1, YO, k1 tbl, k2*
Round 25: Knit.
Round 26: *K2, M1L, k7, M1L, k2*
Round 27: Knit.

Rounds 28 - 29: Purl.
Round 30: Knit.
Round 31: *K4, M1L, k5, M1L, k4*
Round 32: Knit.
Round 33: *K1, YO, K2TOG, k2, K2TOG, YO, k1, YO, SSK, k2, SSK, YO, k1*
Round 34: Knit.
Round 35: *K1, YO, K2TOG, k1, K2TOG, YO, k3, YO, SSK, k1, SSK, YO, k1, M1L*
Round 36: Knit.
Round 37: *SSK, YO, k1, K2TOG, YO, k2, [YO, SSK, k1] 2 times, YO, K2TOG, k1*
Round 38: Knit.
Round 39: *YO, SSK, k3, YO, SSK, k1, K2TOG, YO, k3, K2TOG, YO, k1*
Round 40: Knit.
Round 41: *K1, YO, SSK, k3, YO, CDD, YO, k3, K2TOG, YO, k2*
Round 42: Knit.
Round 43: *K4, M1L, k7, M1L, k5*
Rounds 44 - 45: Knit.
Rounds 46 - 47: Purl.
Rounds 48 - 49: Knit.
Round 50: *K4, M1L, k10, M1L, k4*
Round 51: *YO, k1, K2TOG, k3, SSK, k1, YO, k1*
Round 52: Knit.
Round 53: *YO, k1 tbl, K2TOG, k3, SSK, k1 tbl, YO, k1*
Round 54: Knit.
Round 55: *K1, K2TOG, [k1, YO] 2 times, k1, SSK, k3, K2TOG, [k1, YO] 2 times, k1, SSK, k2*
Round 56: Knit.
Round 57: *K2TOG, k1, YO, k1 tbl, k1, k1 tbl, YO, k1, SSK, k1*
* Round 58 (Shift Marker): Knit to last 2 stitches of the round, slip next 2 stitches to right needle, remove BOR, place just slipped 2 stitches from right to left needle, replace BOR.
Round 59: *CDD, k1, YO, k1 tbl, k3, k1 tbl, YO, k1*
Round 60: *K5, M1L, k10, M1L, k5*
Round 61: Knit.
Rounds 62 - 63: Purl.
Rounds 64 - 65: Knit.
Round 66: *YO, SSK, k6, K2TOG, YO, k1, YO, SSK, k6, K2TOG, YO, k1*
Round 67: Knit.
Round 68: *K1, YO, SSK, k4, K2TOG, YO, k3, YO, SSK, k4, K2TOG, YO, k2*

* Round 69 (Shift Marker): Knit to last stitch of the round, slip next stitch to right needle, remove BOR, place just slipped stitch from right to left needle, replace BOR.
Round 70: *SSK, k1, YO, SSK, k2, K2TOG, YO, k2, YO*
Round 71: Knit.
Round 72: *K2TOG, YO, k6, YO, SSK, k1*
* Round 73 (Shift Marker): Knit to end the round, remove BOR, slip 1 stitch to right needle, replace BOR, place just slipped stitch from right to left needle.
Round 74: *YO, k8, YO, CDD*
Round 75: *K6, M1L, k10, M1L, k6*
Round 76: Knit.

Written instructions for Main Chart
.. – pattern repeat

Round 1: *P1, k9*
Round 2: *P1, k5, K2TOG, k2, YO, p1, YO, k2, SSK, k5*
Round 3: Repeat round 1.
Round 4: *P1, k4, K2TOG, k2, YO, k1, p1, k1, YO, k2, SSK, k4*
Round 5: *P1, k9*
Round 6: *P1, k3, K2TOG, k2, YO, k2, p1, k2, YO, k2, SSK, k3*
Round 7: *P1, k9*
Round 8: *P1, k2, K2TOG, k2, YO, k3, p1, k3, YO, k2, SSK, k2*
Round 9: *P1, k9*
Round 10: *P1, k1, K2TOG, k2, YO, k4, p1, k4, YO, k2, SSK, k1*
Round 11: *P1, k9*
Round 12: *P1, K2TOG, k2, YO, k5, p1, k5, YO, k2, SSK*
Round 13: Repeat round 1.
Rounds 14 - 25: Repeat rounds 2 - 13.
Round 26: *P1, k9*
Rounds 27 - 28: Purl.
Round 29: Knit.
Round 30: *K2, SSK, [k1, YO] 2 times, k1, K2TOG, k3, SSK, [k1, YO] 2 times, k1, K2TOG, k1*
Round 31: Knit.
Round 32: *K2, SSK, k1 tbl, YO, k1, YO, k1 tbl, K2TOG, k3, SSK, k1 tbl, YO, k1, YO, k1 tbl, K2TOG, k1*
Round 33: Knit.
Round 34: *K1, YO, k1, SSK, k3, K2TOG, k1, YO*
Round 35: Knit.

Round 36: *K1, k1 tbl, YO, k1, SSK, k1, K2TOG, k1, YO, k1 tbl*

Round 37: Knit.

Round 38: *K2, k1 tbl, YO, k1, CDD, k1, YO, k1 tbl, k3, k1 tbl, YO, k1, CDD, k1, YO, k1 tbl, k1*

Rounds 39 - 40: Knit.

Rounds 41 - 42: Purl.

Round 43: Knit.

Round 44: *K3, K2TOG, YO, k1, YO, SSK, k5, K2TOG, YO, k1, YO, SSK, k2*

Round 45: Knit.

Round 46: *K2, K2TOG, YO, k3, YO, SSK, k3, K2TOG, YO, k3, YO, SSK, k1*

Round 47: Knit.

Round 48: *K1, K2TOG, YO, k2, YO, SSK, k1, YO, SSK*

Round 49: Knit.

Round 50: *K3, YO, SSK, k1, K2TOG, YO, k5, YO, SSK, k1, K2TOG, YO, k2*

Round 51: Knit.

Round 52: *K4, YO, CDD, YO, k7, YO, CDD, YO, k3*

Round 53: Knit.

Rounds 54 - 55: Purl.

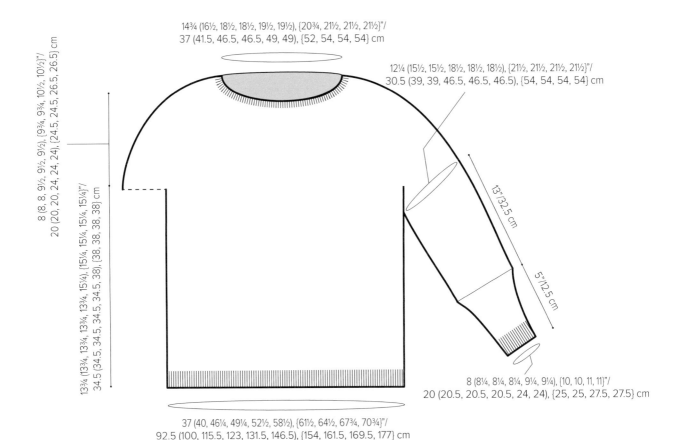

14¾ (16½, 18½, 18½, 19½, 19½), {20¾, 21½, 21½, 21½}"/
37 (41.5, 46.5, 46.5, 49, 49), {52, 54, 54, 54} cm

12¼ (15½, 15½, 18½, 18½, 18½), {21½, 21½, 21½, 21½}"/
30.5 (39, 39, 46.5, 46.5, 46.5), {54, 54, 54, 54} cm

8 (8, 8, 9½, 9½, 9½), {9¾, 9¾, 10½, 10½}"/
20 (20, 20, 24, 24, 24), {24.5, 24.5, 26.5, 26.5} cm

13"/32.5 cm

5"/12.5 cm

13¾ (13¾, 13¾, 13¾, 15¼), {15¼, 15¼, 15¼, 15¼}"/
34.5 (34.5, 34.5, 34.5, 34.5, 38), {38, 38, 38, 38} cm

8 (8¼, 8¼, 8¼, 9¼, 9¼), {10, 10, 11, 11}"/
20 (20.5, 20.5, 20.5, 24, 24), {25, 25, 27.5, 27.5} cm

37 (40, 46¼, 49¼, 52½, 58½), {61½, 64½, 67¾, 70¾}"/
92.5 (100, 115.5, 123, 131.5, 146.5), {154, 161.5, 169.5, 177} cm

Apato

The Apato Pullover is a modern top-down sweater that blends clean Stockinette fabric with striking twisted stitch cable panels. The design features bold vertical motifs on the front, back and sleeves, framed by simple lines that keep the look balanced and wearable. Worked seamlessly from the neckline down, Apato allows easy customization of body and sleeve length while maintaining a polished finish. With its flowing cables and versatile silhouette, this pullover is both engaging to knit and effortless to wear. The suggested yarn provides an exceptional stitch definition and is perfectly soft against the skin.

Sizes
XS (S, M, L, XL, 2XL), {3XL, 4XL, 5XL, 6XL}: to fit bust 28-30 (32-34, 36-38, 40-42, 44-46, 48-50), {52-54, 56-58, 60-62, 64-66}"/70-75 (80-85, 90-95, 100-105, 110-115, 120-125), {130-135, 140-145, 150-155, 160-165} cm.

Finished Measurements
36 (41, 45, 49, 53, 57), {61, 65, 69, 73}"/90 (102.5, 112.5, 122.5, 132.5, 142.5), {152.5, 162.5, 172.5, 182.5} cm bust circumference.
Shown in size M (45"/112.5 cm) on 38"/95 cm bust with 7"/17.5 cm of positive ease.

Yarn
Sport weight yarn (approximate amounts): 1160 (1320, 1450, 1580, 1710, 1840), {1970, 2100, 2230, 2360} yds/ 1060 (1207, 1325, 1444, 1563, 1682), {1801, 1919, 2038, 2157} m.

Miss Babs Laurel Falls (100% Superwash Shaniko Merino Wool; 300 yards/275 m in 3.5 oz/100 g), Milk Chocolate: 4 (5, 5, 6, 6, 7), {7, 7, 8, 8} skeins.

Needles
Size US 4/3.5 mm: 24-32"/60-80 cm circular and set of double-pointed.
Sizes US 3/3.25 mm: 24-32"/60-80 cm circular, 16"/40 cm circular and set of double-pointed.
Optional: second US 3/3.25 mm 24-32"/60-80 cm circular for the Tubular Bind Off.
Adjust needle size if necessary to obtain gauge.

Notions
Stitch markers, waste yarn, tapestry needle, cable needle.

Gauge
23 stitches and 34 rows = 4"/10 cm in Stockinette Stitch on size US 4/3.5 mm needle, after blocking.
28 stitches and 34 rows = 4"/10 cm in charted pattern or k1 tbl, p1 rib on size US 4/3.5 mm needle, after blocking.

Notes
- This pullover is worked from the top down. The top back is worked back and forth to underarms, then stitches for front are picked up at the shoulders and worked back and forth to the underarm. The back and front then joined and the lower body is worked in the round to the lower edge.
- Stitches for the sleeves are picked up around the armhole and the sleeves are worked from the top down in the round.
- The Body Chart is worked in the round and in rows. When working flat in rows, read odd-numbered chart rows from right to left, and even-numbered rows from left to right.

Stitch Guide

Stockinette stitch
RS rows and all rounds: Knit.
WS rows: Purl.

Knot Stitch: Insert right needle into the 3rd stitch on the left needle; lift it over stitches 1 and 2 and let it drop.
Knit stitch 1, yarn over, knit stitch 2.

Chain pattern (in rows):
Row 1 (RS): P1, Knot Stitch (see above), p1.
Row 2 (WS): K1, p3, k1.
Row 3 (RS): P1, k3, p1.
Row 4 (WS): K1, p3, k1.
Repeat Rows 1-4 for pattern.

Chain pattern (in the round):
Round 1: P1, Knot Stitch, p1.
Round 2 - 4: P1, k3, p1.
Repeat Rounds 1-4 for pattern.

DIRECTIONS

01 NECK

With US 3/3.25 mm 16"/40 cm circular needle, cast on 98 (98, 106, 106, 114, 114), {114, 114, 126, 126} stitches. Join for working in the round.

Knit all stitches in the next 4 rounds.

02 BACK

With working yarn, US 4/3.5 mm 32"/80 cm circular needle, using Backward Loop method (see Special Techniques, page 226), cast on 33 (41, 45, 51, 55, 61), {67, 73, 76, 82} stitches for the Left Shoulder, knit first 49 (49, 53, 53, 56, 56), {56, 56, 63, 63} held Neck stitches from US 3/3.25 mm 16"/40 cm needle; then, with the same working yarn, using Backward Loop method, cast on 33 (41, 45, 51, 55, 61), {67, 73, 76, 82} stitches for the Right Shoulder.

The remaining 49 (49, 53, 53, 56, 56), {56, 56, 63, 63} Front Neck stitches will be left on 16"/40 cm circular needle until we start working on the Front (knitters may want to put stoppers on the tips of the 16"/40 cm circular needle). [115 (131, 143, 155, 167, 179), {191, 203, 215, 227} stitches on the US 4/3.5 mm needle for the Back]

Continue working on Back stitches back and forth in rows.
Next Row (WS): P1, place marker, k1, p3, k1, place marker, p17 (23, 27, 33, 37, 43), {45, 51, 55, 59}, place chart marker #2, [k1, p1] over next 68 (72, 76, 76, 80, 80), {88, 88, 92, 96} stitches, k1, place chart marker #1, p17 (23, 27, 33, 37, 43), {45, 51, 55, 59}, place marker, k1, p3, k1, place marker, p1.

Start shaping shoulders, using German Short-Rows (see Special Techniques, page 226), as follows:
Short-Row 1 (RS): K1, slip marker, p1, k3, p1, slip marker, knit to chart marker #1, slip chart marker #1, [p1, k1 tbl] to 1 stitch before chart marker #2, p1, slip chart marker #2, k3 (3, 5, 6, 7, 7), {7, 8, 9, 9}, turn work.
Short-Row 2 (WS): Make double stitch, purl to chart marker #2, slip marker, [k1, p1 tbl] to 1 stitch before chart marker #1, k1, slip chart marker #1, p3 (3, 5, 6, 7, 7), {7, 8, 9, 9}, turn work.
Short-Row 3 (RS): Make double stitch, work in established pattern, slipping markers, to double stitch, work double stitch as regular stitch, k2 (3, 3, 4, 4, 5), {6, 6, 7, 8}, turn work.
Short-Row 4 (WS): Make double stitch, work in established pattern, slipping markers, to double stitch, work double stitch as regular stitch, p2 (3, 3, 4, 4, 5), {6, 6, 7, 8}, turn work.

Short-Rows 5-14: Repeat Short-Rows 3 and 4 another 5 times.

Next Row (RS): Make double stitch, work in established pattern to double stitch, working double stitch as regular stitch, knit to next marker, slip marker, p1, k3, p1, slip marker, k1.

Next Row (WS): P1, slip marker, k1, p3, k1, slip marker, purl to chart marker #2, slip marker #2, [k1, p1 tbl] to 1 stitch before chart marker #1, k1, slip chart marker #1, purl to marker, slip marker, k1, p3, k1, slip marker, p1.

Start working on Body Chart:
Chart Set-Up Row 1 (RS): K1, slip marker, work Row 1 of Chain pattern (see Stitch Guide), slip marker, knit to chart marker #1, slip chart marker #1, [p1, k1 tbl] 5 (6, 1, 1, 2, 2), {4, 4, 5, 6} time(s), work Row 1 of Body Chart over 49 (49, 73, 73, 73, 73), {73, 73, 73, 73} stitches, working 24-stitch pattern repeat 1 (1, 2, 2, 2, 2), {2, 2, 2, 2} times, [k1 tbl, p1] 5 (6, 1, 1, 2, 2), {4, 4, 5, 6} time(s), slip chart marker #2, knit to marker, slip marker, work Row 1 of Chain pattern, slip marker, k1.

Chart Set-Up Row 2 (WS): P1, slip marker, work Row 2 of Chain pattern, slip marker, purl to chart marker #2, slip chart marker #2, [k1, p1 tbl] 5 (6, 1, 1, 2, 2), {4, 4, 5, 6} times, work Row 2 of Body Chart over 49 (49, 73, 73, 73, 73), {73, 73, 73, 73} stitches, working 24-stitch pattern repeat 1 (1, 2, 2, 2, 2), {2, 2, 2, 2} times, [p1 tbl, k1] 5 (6, 1, 1, 2, 2), {4, 4, 5, 6} times, slip chart marker #1, knit to marker, slip marker, work Row 2 of Chain pattern, slip marker, p1.

Continue working in established pattern and follow Chain pattern and Body Chart through row 44, then repeat Rows 17-44, until Back measures 6½ (7, 7, 7½, 8, 8), {9, 10, 10, 11}"/16.5 (17.5, 17.5, 19, 20, 20), {22.5, 25, 25, 27.5} cm, measured along the armhole from the cast-on row, ending with WS row.

Break yarn and place Back stitches on hold. Make a note of the last Chart Row worked.

03 FRONT

With US 4/3.5 mm 32"/80 cm needle and RS facing, join yarn at the armhole edge of the right shoulder and pick up and knit directly into 33 (41, 45, 51, 55, 61), {67, 73, 76, 82} stitches of Right Shoulder, knit held 49 (49, 53, 53, 56, 56), {56, 56, 63, 63} Front Neck stitches from 16"/40 cm circular needle, pick up and knit directly into 33 (41, 45, 51, 55, 61), {67, 73, 76, 82} stitches of Left Shoulder. [115 (131, 143, 155, 167, 179), {191, 203, 215, 227} stitches on the working needle for the Front]

Continue working on Front stitches back and forth in rows.
Next Row (WS): P1, place marker, k1, p3, k1, place marker, p17 (23, 27, 33, 37, 43), {45, 51, 55, 59}, place chart marker #2, [k1, p1 tbl] over next 68 (72, 76, 76, 80, 80), {88, 88, 92, 96} stitches, k1, place chart marker #1, p17 (23, 27, 33, 37, 43), {45, 51, 55, 59}, place marker, k1, p3, k1, place marker, p1.

Shape Right Neck and Shoulder:
Short-Row 1 (RS): K1, slip marker, p1, k3, p1, slip marker, knit to chart marker #1, slip marker, [p1, k1 tbl] 5 (6, 6, 6, 6, 6), {8, 8, 8, 8} times, turn work.
Short-Row 2 (WS): Make double stitch, work stitches as they appear (knit as knits and purl as p1 tbl) to chart marker #1, slip marker, p3 (3, 5, 6, 7, 7), {7, 8, 9, 9}, turn work.
Short-Row 3 (RS): Make double stitch, knit to chart marker #1, slip marker, work stitches as they appear (purl as purls and knits as k1 tbl) to double stitch, work double stitch as regular stitch, work next stitch as it appears, turn work.

Short-Row 4 (WS): Make double stitch, work stitches as they appear to chart marker #1, slip marker, purl to double stitch, work double stitch as regular stitch, p2 (3, 3, 4, 4, 5), {6, 6, 7, 8}, turn work.
Short-Rows 5-14: Repeat Short-Rows 3 and 4 another 5 times.

Shape Left Neck and Shoulder:

Short-Row 15 (RS): Make double stitch, knit to chart marker #1, slip marker, work stitches as they appear to double stitch, work double stitch as regular stitch, work to chart marker #2, slip marker, k3 (3, 5, 6, 7, 7), {7, 8, 9, 9}, turn work.

Short-Row 16 (WS): Make double stitch, purl to chart marker #2, slip marker, [k1, p1 tbl] 5 (6, 6, 6, 6, 6), {8, 8, 8, 8} times, turn work.

Short-Row 17 (RS): Make double stitch, work stitches as they appear to chart marker #2, slip marker, knit to double stitch, work double stitch as regular stitch, k2 (3, 3, 4, 4, 5), {6, 6, 7, 8}, turn work.

Short-Row 18 (WS): Make double stitch, purl to chart marker #2, slip marker, work stitches as they appear to double stitch, work double stitch as regular stitch, work next stitch as it appears, turn work.

Short-Rows 19-28: Repeat Short-Rows 17 and 18 another 5 times.

Short-Row 29 (RS): Make double stitch, work stitches as they appear to chart marker #2, slip marker, knit to double stitch, work double stitch as regular stitch, knit to marker, slip marker, p1, k3, p1, slip marker, k1.

Next Row (WS): P1, slip marker, k1, p3, k1, slip marker, purl to chart marker #2, slip marker, work stitches as they appear to double stitch, work double stitch as regular stitch, work to chart marker #1, slip marker, purl to marker, slip marker, k1, p3, k1, slip marker, p1.

Start working on Body Chart:

Body Chart Set-Up Row 1 (RS): K1, slip marker, work Row 1 of Chain pattern (see Stitch Guide), slip marker, knit to chart marker #1, slip chart marker #1, [p1, k1 tbl] 5 (6, 1, 1, 2, 2), {4, 4, 5, 6} times, work Row 1 of Body Chart over 49 (49, 73, 73, 73, 73), {73, 73, 73, 73} stitches, working 24-stitch pattern repeat 1 (1, 2, 2, 2, 2), {2, 2, 2, 2} times, [k1 tbl, p1] 5 (6, 1, 1, 2, 2), {4, 4, 5, 6} times, slip chart marker #2, knit to marker, slip marker, work Row 1 of Chain pattern, slip marker, k1.

Body Chart Set-Up Row 2 (WS): P1, slip marker, work Row 2 of Chain pattern, slip marker, purl to chart marker #2, slip chart marker #2, [k1, p1 tbl] 5 (6, 1, 1, 2, 2), {4, 4, 5, 6} times, work Row 2 of Body Chart over 49 (49, 73, 73, 73, 73), {73, 73, 73, 73} stitches, working 24-stitch pattern repeat 1 (1, 2, 2, 2, 2), {2, 2, 2, 2} times, [p1 tbl, k1] 5 (6, 1, 1, 2, 2), {4, 4, 5, 6} times, slip chart marker #1, knit to marker, slip marker, work Row 2 of Chain pattern, slip marker, p1.

Continue working in established pattern and follow Chain pattern and Body Chart through row 44, then repeat Rows 17-44, until Back measures 6½ (7, 7, 7½, 8, 8), {9, 10, 10, 11}"/16.5 (17.5, 17.5, 19, 20, 20), {22.5, 25, 25, 27.5} cm, measured along the armhole from the cast-on row, ending with the same WS row as Back. Do not break yarn.

Join Front and Back

Joining Row (RS): *K1, slip marker, work next Row of Chain pattern, slip marker, knit to chart marker #1, slip chart marker #1, [p1, k1] 5 (6, 1, 1, 2, 2), {4, 4, 5, 6} times, work next Row of Body Chart, [k1, p1] 5 (6, 1, 1, 2, 2), {4, 4, 5, 6} times, slip chart marker #2, knit to marker, slip marker, work next Row of Chain pattern, slip marker, k1*; place held Back stitches onto a spare needle and repeat from * to * once more, working Back stitches.

Place marker for the beginning of the round (BOR) and join for working in round. [230 (262, 286, 310, 334, 358), {382, 406, 430, 454} stitches for the Body]

04 BODY

Next Round: *K1, slip marker, work next Row of Chain pattern, slip marker, knit to chart marker #1, slip chart marker #1, [p1, k1] 5 (6, 1, 1, 2, 2), {4, 4, 5, 6} times, work next Row of Body Chart, [k1, p1] 5 (6, 1, 1, 2, 2), {4, 4, 5, 6} times, slip chart marker #2, knit to marker, slip marker, work next Row of Chain pattern, slip marker, k1*, slip side marker, repeat from * to * once more.

Continue working in established pattern, following Chain pattern and Body Chart in the round, until Body measures approximately 10½ (10½, 10½, 10½, 11½, 11½), {11½, 11½, 11½, 11½}"/26.5 (26.5, 26.5, 26.5, 29, 29), {29, 29, 29, 29} cm from underarm, ending with either Round 30 or 44 of Body Chart.

NOTE: If your last Body Chart Round is Round 30, continue working as instructed below, working the Border Chart B.
If your last Body Chart Round is Round 44, continue working as instructed below, working the Border Chart A.

Body Chart Set-Up Round: * P1, slip marker, work next round of Chain pattern, slip marker, knit to chart marker #1, slip chart marker #1, [p1, k1 tbl] 5 (6, 1, 1, 2, 2), {4, 4, 5, 6} times, work Round 1 of Border Chart A or B (depending on your last Body Chart round) over 49 (49, 73, 73, 73, 73), {73, 73, 73, 73} stitches, working 24-stitch pattern repeat 1 (1, 2, 2, 2, 2), {2, 2, 2, 2} times, [k1 tbl, p1] 5 (6, 1, 1, 2, 2), {4, 4, 5, 6} times, slip chart marker #2, knit to marker, slip marker, work next round of Chain pattern, slip marker, k1.

Continue working in established pattern, following Border Chart A or B through Round 11.

Decrease Round: Work in established pattern, working Round 12 of Border Chart A or B to 1 stitch before side marker, slip next stitch to right needle, remove side marker, replace slipped stitch to left needle, K2TOG, work to 1 stitch before BOR, place new BOR, K2TOG, removing old BOR.
[228 (260, 284, 308, 332, 356), {380, 404, 428, 452} stitches for the Body]

Change to US 3/3.25 mm 32"/80 cm needle.

Ribbing Round: *K1 tbl, p1; repeat from * to end. Make sure that the ribbing lines up with the ribbing in the middle of Front and Back.
Repeat Ribbing Round for 2"/5 cm. Bind off all stitches in pattern.

05 SLEEVES

With size US 4/3.5 mm double-pointed needles and RS facing, beginning at the center of underarm, pick up and knit 40 (43, 43, 46, 49, 49), {54, 60, 60, 66} stitches along armhole to the top of the shoulder, pick up and knit 1 stitch in the shoulder "seam", pick up and knit 40 (43, 43, 46, 49, 49), {54, 60, 60, 66} stitches down to center of underarm. [81 (87, 87, 93, 99, 99), {109, 121, 121, 133} stitches total]

Place BOR and join for working in the round.

Set-Up Round 1: K26 (29, 29, 32, 35, 35), {40, 46, 46, 52}, place marker, work Round 1 of Sleeve Chart over next 29 stitches, place marker, k26 (29, 29, 32, 35, 35), {40, 46, 46, 52} to end.
Set-Up Round 2: Knit to marker, slip marker, work Round 2 of Sleeve Chart to marker, slip marker, knit to end.

Continue working in established pattern, following the Sleeve Chart for 4 rounds (Round 6 of Sleeve Chart is worked).

NOTE: While shaping the sleeve as instructed below, follow the Sleeve Chart through Round 30, then repeat rounds 3-30 throughout.

Decrease Round: K1, SSK, work in established pattern to last 3 stitches, K2TOG, k1. [2 stitches decreased]
Repeat Decrease Round another 10 (13, 12, 15, 17, 17), {19, 25, 22, 28} times in every 10 (8, 8, 7, 6, 6), {5, 4, 4, 4}th round. [59 (59, 61, 61, 63, 63), {69, 69, 75, 75} stitches]
Continue working without decreases, if necessary, until sleeve measures 14"/35 cm, preferably ending with Round 6, 10, 14, 16, 20, 24, 28 or 30 of Sleeve Chart.

Decrease Round: Work all stitches as they appear to last 2 stitches, SSK. [58 (58, 60, 60, 62, 62), {68, 68, 74, 74} stitches]

Change to US 3/3.25 mm double-pointed needles.

Ribbing Round: *P1, k1 tbl; repeat from * to the end of the round.
Repeat Ribbing Round until ribbing measures 3"/7.5 cm.

Knit all stitches in the next 3 rounds.
Bind off all stitches.

06 FINISHING

Block to measurements. Weave in ends.

CHARTS

BODY CHART

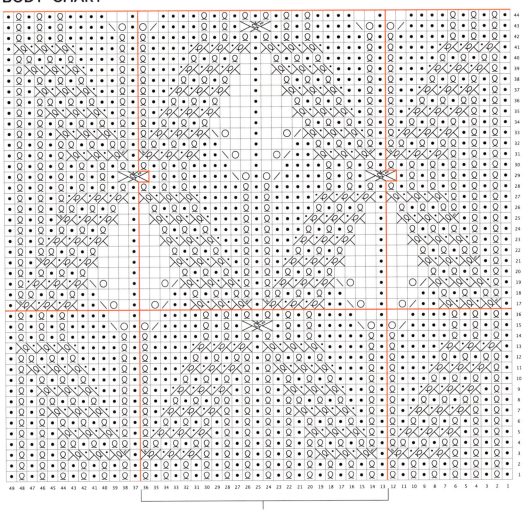

24-stitch repeat

LEGEND

☐ **K:** Knit stitch on RS rows and all rounds; purl stitch on WS

▪ **P:** Purl stitch on RS rows and all rounds; knit stitch on WS

Q **K1 tbl:** Knit stitch through back loop on RS
P1 tbl: Purl stitch through back loop on WS

O **YO:** Yarn over

╱ **K2TOG:** Knit 2 stitches together – 1 stitch decreased with right slant.

╲ **SSK:** Slip 1 stitch knitwise, slip 1 stitch knitwise, return 2 slipped stitches back to left needle and knit them together through back loops – 1 stitch decreased with left slant

1/1 RT: Slip 1 stitch to cable needle, hold in back, k1 tbl, k1 tbl from cable needle

1/1 LT: Slip 1 stitch to cable needle, hold in front, k1 tbl, k1 tbl from cable needle

1/1 RPT: Slip 1 stitch to cable needle, hold in back, k1 tbl, p1 from cable needle

1/1 LPT: Slip 1 stitch to cable needle, hold in front, p1, k1 tbl from cable needle

1/1/1 LPT: Slip 1 stitch to cable needle and hold in front; slip 1 stitch to 2nd cable needle and hold in back, k1 tbl; p1 from back cable needle, k1 tbl from front cable needle

☐ Pattern repeat

BORDER CHART A

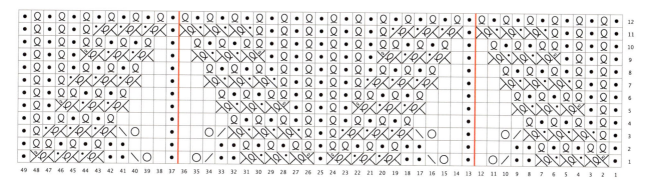

BORDER CHART B

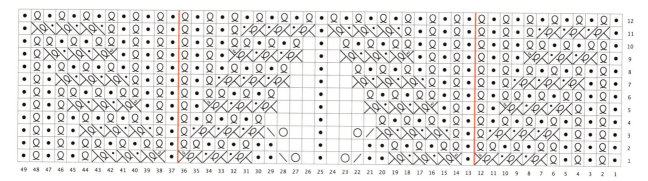

SLEEVE CHART

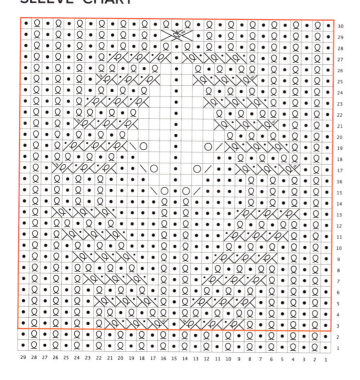

Written instructions for Body Chart (worked in rows)
... – *pattern repeat*
Note: See Chart Legend for special abbreviations.

Row 1 (RS): [P1, k1 tbl] to last stitch, p1.
Row 2 (WS): [K1, p1 tbl] to last stitch, k1.
Row 3 (RS): [P1, k1 tbl] 3 times, [1/1 RPT] 2 times, 1/1 RT, *p1, 1/1 LT, [1/1 LPT] 2 times, [k1 tbl, p1] 5 times, k1 tbl, [1/1 RPT] 2 times, 1/1 RT*, p1, 1/1 LT, [1/1 LPT] 2 times, [k1 tbl, p1] 3 times.
Row 4 (WS): K1, p1 tbl, [k1, p1 tbl, k1, [p1 tbl] 2 times] 2 times, k1, *[[p1 tbl] 2 times, k1, p1 tbl, k1] 2 times, p1 tbl, k1, p1 tbl, [k1, p1 tbl, k1, [p1 tbl] 2 times] 2 times, k1*, [[p1 tbl] 2 times, k1, p1 tbl, k1] 2 times, p1 tbl, k1.
Row 5 (RS): [P1, k1 tbl] 2 times, p1, [1/1 RPT] 3 times, k1 tbl, *p1, k1 tbl, [1/1 LPT] 3 times, [p1, k1 tbl] 4 times, p1, [1/1 RPT] 3 times, k1 tbl*, p1, k1 tbl, [1/1 LPT] 3 times, [p1, k1 tbl] 2 times, p1.
Row 6 (WS): [K1, p1 tbl] to last stitch, k1.
Row 7 (RS): [P1, k1 tbl] 2 times, [1/1 RPT] 3 times, p1, k1 tbl, *p1, k1 tbl, p1, [1/1 LPT] 3 times, [k1 tbl, p1] 3 times, k1 tbl, [1/1 RPT] 3 times, p1, k1 tbl*, p1, k1 tbl, p1, [1/1 LPT] 3 times, [k1 tbl, p1] 2 times.
Row 8 (WS): K1, p1 tbl, k1, [p1 tbl] 2 times, [k1, p1 tbl] 2 times, k2, p1 tbl, k1, *p1 tbl, k2, [[p1 tbl, k1] 2 times, [p1 tbl] 2 times, k1] 2 times, p1 tbl, k1, p1 tbl, k2, p1 tbl, k1*, p1 tbl, k2, [p1 tbl, k1] 2 times, [p1 tbl] 2 times, k1, p1 tbl, k1.
Row 9 (RS): P1, k1 tbl, p1, [1/1 RPT] 3 times, p2, k1 tbl, *p1, k1 tbl, p2, [1/1 LPT] 3 times, [p1, k1 tbl] 2 times, p1, [1/1 RPT] 3 times, p2, k1 tbl*, p1, k1 tbl, p2, [1/1 LPT] 3 times, p1, k1 tbl, p1.
Row 10 (WS): [K1, p1 tbl] 4 times, k3, p1 tbl, k1, *p1 tbl, k3, [p1 tbl, k1] 7 times, p1 tbl, k3, p1 tbl, k1*, p1 tbl, k3, [p1 tbl, k1] 4 times.
Row 11 (RS): P1, k1 tbl, [1/1 RPT] 3 times, p3, k1 tbl, *p1, k1 tbl, p3, [1/1 LPT] 3 times, k1 tbl, p1, k1 tbl, [1/1 RPT] 3 times, p3, k1 tbl*, p1, k1 tbl, p3, [1/1 LPT] 3 times, k1 tbl, p1.
Row 12 (WS): K1, [p1 tbl] 2 times, [k1, p1 tbl] 2 times, k4, p1 tbl, k1, *p1 tbl, k4, [p1 tbl, k1] 2 times, [[p1 tbl] 2 times, k1] 2 times, p1 tbl, k1, p1 tbl, k4, p1 tbl, k1*, p1 tbl, k4, [p1 tbl, k1] 2 times, [p1 tbl] 2 times, k1.
Row 13 (RS): P1, [1/1 RPT] 3 times, p4, k1 tbl, *p1, k1 tbl, p4, [1/1 LPT] 3 times, p1, [1/1 RPT] 3 times, p4, k1 tbl*, p1, k1 tbl, p4, [1/1 LPT] 3 times, p1.

Row 14 (WS): [K1, p1 tbl] 3 times, k5, p1 tbl, k1, *p1 tbl, k5, [p1 tbl, k1] 5 times, p1 tbl, k5, p1 tbl, k1*, p1 tbl, k5, [p1 tbl, k1] 3 times.
Row 15 (RS): [P1, k1 tbl] 3 times, p4, K2TOG, YO, *p1, YO, SSK, p4, [k1, p1 tbl] 2 times, 1/1/1 LPT, [p1, k1 tbl] 2 times, p4, K2TOG, YO*, p1, YO, SSK, p4, [k1 tbl, p1] 3 times.
Row 16 (WS): [K1, p1 tbl] 3 times, k4, p2, k1, *p2, k4, [p1 tbl, k1] 5 times, p1 tbl, k4, p2, k1*, p2, k4, [p1 tbl, k1] 3 times.
Row 17 (RS): P1, 1/1 LT, [1/1 LPT] 2 times, p2, K2TOG, YO, k1, *p1, k1, YO, SSK, p2, [1/1 RPT] 2 times, 1/1 RT, p1, 1/1 LT, [1/1 LPT] 2 times, p2, K2TOG, YO, k1*, p1, k1, YO, SSK, p2, [1/1 RPT] 2 times, 1/1 RT, p1.
Row 18 (WS): K1, [p1 tbl] 2 times, [k1, p1 tbl] 2 times, k2, p3, k1, *p3, k2, [p1 tbl, k1] 2 times, [[p1 tbl] 2 times, k1] 2 times, p1 tbl, k1, p1 tbl, k2, p3, k1*, p3, k2, [p1 tbl, k1] 2 times, [p1 tbl] 2 times, k1.
Row 19 (RS): P1, k1 tbl, [1/1 LPT] 3 times, K2TOG, YO, k2, *p1, k2, YO, SSK, [1/1 RPT] 3 times, k1 tbl, p1, k1 tbl, [1/1 LPT] 3 times, K2TOG, YO, k2*, p1, k2, YO, SSK, [1/1 RPT] 3 times, k1 tbl, p1.
Row 20 (WS): [K1, p1 tbl] 4 times, p4, k1, *p4, [p1 tbl, k1] 7 times, p1 tbl, p4, k1*, p4, [p1 tbl, k1] 4 times.
Row 21 (RS): P1, k1 tbl, p1, 1/1 LT, [1/1 LPT] 2 times, k3, *p1, k3, [1/1 RPT] 3 times, [p1, k1 tbl] 2 times, p1, [1/1 LPT] 3 times, k3*, p1, k3, [1/1 RPT] 2 times, 1/1 RT, p1, k1 tbl, p1.
Row 22 (WS): K1, p1 tbl, k1, [p1 tbl] 2 times, [k1, p1 tbl] 2 times, p3, k1, *p3, p1 tbl, k1, [p1 tbl, k1, p1 tbl, k2] 2 times, [p1 tbl, k1] 2 times, p1 tbl, p3, k1*, p3, [p1 tbl, k1] 2 times, [p1 tbl] 2 times, k1, p1 tbl, k1.
Row 23 (RS): [P1, k1 tbl] 2 times, [1/1 LPT] 3 times, k2, *p1, k2, [1/1 RPT] 3 times, p2, k1 tbl, p1, k1 tbl, p2, [1/1 LPT] 3 times, k2*, p1, k2, [1/1 RPT] 3 times, [k1 tbl, p1] 2 times.
Row 24 (WS): [K1, p1 tbl] 5 times, p2, k1, *p2, p1 tbl, k1, [p1 tbl, k1, p1 tbl, k3] 2 times, [p1 tbl, k1] 2 times, p1 tbl, p2, k1*, p2, [p1 tbl, k1] 5 times.
Row 25 (RS): [P1, k1 tbl] 2 times, p1, 1/1 LT, [1/1 LPT] 2 times, k1, *p1, k1, [1/1 RPT] 3 times, p3, k1 tbl, p1, k1 tbl, p3, [1/1 LPT] 3 times, k1*, p1, k1, [1/1 RPT] 2 times, 1/1 RT, [p1, k1 tbl] 2 times, p1.
Row 26 (WS): [K1, p1 tbl] 2 times, k1, [p1 tbl] 2 times, [k1, p1 tbl] 2 times, p1, k1, *p1, p1 tbl, k1, [p1 tbl, k1, p1 tbl, k4] 2 times, [p1 tbl, k1] 2 times, p1 tbl, p1, k1*, p1, [p1 tbl, k1] 2 times, [p1 tbl] 2 times, [k1, p1 tbl] 2 times, k1.

Row 27 (RS): [P1, k1 tbl] 3 times, [1/1 LPT] 3 times, *p1, [1/1 RPT] 3 times, p4, k1 tbl, p1, k1 tbl, p4, [1/1 LPT] 3 times*, p1, [1/1 RPT] 3 times, [k1 tbl, p1] 3 times.

Row 28 (WS): [K1, p1 tbl] 6 times, k1, *p1 tbl, k1, [p1 tbl, k1, p1 tbl, k5] 2 times, [p1 tbl, k1] 3 times*, [p1 tbl, k1] 6 times.

Row 29 (RS): [P1, k1 tbl] 5 times, p1, *1/1/1 LPT, [p1, k1 tbl] 2 times, p4, K2TOG, YO, p1, YO, SSK, p4, [k1 tbl, p1] 2 times*, 1/1/1 LPT, [p1, k1 tbl] 5 times, p1.

Row 30 (WS): [K1, p1 tbl] 6 times, k1, *[p1 tbl, k1] 2 times, p1 tbl, k4, p2, k1, p2, k4, [p1 tbl, k1] 3 times*, [p1 tbl, k1] 6 times.

Row 31 (RS): [P1, k1 tbl] 3 times, [1/1 RPT] 2 times, 1/1 RT, *p1, 1/1 LT, [1/1 LPT] 2 times, p2, K2TOG, YO, k1, p1, k1, YO, SSK, p2, [1/1 RPT] 2 times, 1/1 RT*, p1, 1/1 LT, [1/1 LPT] 2 times, [k1 tbl, p1] 3 times.

Row 32 (WS): K1, p1 tbl, [k1, p1 tbl, k1, [p1 tbl] 2 times] 2 times, k1, *[p1 tbl] 2 times, [k1, p1 tbl] 2 times, k2, p3, k1, p3, k2, [p1 tbl, k1] 2 times, [p1 tbl] 2 times, k1*, [[p1 tbl]
2 times, k1, p1 tbl, k1] 2 times, p1 tbl, k1.

Row 33 (RS): [P1, k1 tbl] 2 times, p1, [1/1 RPT] 3 times, k1 tbl, *p1, k1 tbl, [1/1 LPT] 3 times, K2TOG, YO, k2, p1, k2, YO, SSK, [1/1 RPT] 3 times, k1 tbl*, p1, k1 tbl, [1/1 LPT] 3 times, [p1, k1 tbl] 2 times, p1.

Row 34 (WS): [K1, p1 tbl] 6 times, k1, *[p1 tbl, k1] 3 times, p1 tbl, p4, k1, p4, [p1 tbl, k1] 4 times*, [p1 tbl, k1] 6 times.

Row 35 (RS): [P1, k1 tbl] 2 times, [1/1 RPT] 3 times, p1, k1 tbl, *k1 tbl, p1, [1/1 LPT] 3 times, k3, p1, k3, [1/1 RPT] 3 times, p1, k1 tbl*, p1, k1 tbl, p1, [1/1 LPT] 3 times, [k1 tbl, p1] 2 times.

Row 36 (WS): K1, p1 tbl, k1, [p1 tbl] 2 times, [k1, p1 tbl] 2 times, k2, p1 tbl, k1, *p1 tbl, k2, [p1 tbl, k1] 2 times, p1 tbl, p3, k1, p3, [p1 tbl, k1] 2 times, p1 tbl, k2, p1 tbl, k1*, p1 tbl, k2, [p1 tbl, k1] 2 times, [p1 tbl] 2 times, k1, p1 tbl, k1.

Row 37 (RS): P1, k1 tbl, p1, [1/1 RPT] 3 times, p2, k1 tbl, *p1, k1 tbl, p2, [1/1 LPT] 3 times, k2, p1, k2, [1/1 RPT] 3 times, p2, k1 tbl*, p1, k1 tbl, p2, [1/1 LPT] 3 times, p1, k1 tbl, p1.

Row 38 (WS): [K1, p1 tbl] 4 times, k3, p1 tbl, k1, *p1 tbl, k3, [p1 tbl, k1] 2 times, p1 tbl, p2, k1, p2, [p1 tbl, k1] 2 times, p1 tbl, k3, p1 tbl, k1*, p1 tbl, k3, [p1 tbl, k1] 4 times.

Row 39 (RS): P1, k1 tbl, [1/1 RPT] 3 times, p3, k1 tbl, *p1, k1 tbl, p3, [1/1 LPT] 3 times, k1, p1, k1, [1/1 RPT] 3 times, p3, k1 tbl*, p1, k1 tbl, p3, [1/1 LPT] 3 times, k1 tbl, p1.

Row 40 (WS): K1, [p1 tbl] 2 times, [k1, p1 tbl] 2 times, k4, p1 tbl, k1, *p1 tbl, k4, [p1 tbl, k1] 2 times, p1 tbl, p1, k1, p1, [p1 tbl, k1] 2 times, p1 tbl, k4, p1 tbl, k1*, p1 tbl, k4, [p1 tbl, k1] 2 times, [p1 tbl] 2 times, k1.

Rows 41-44: Repeat row 13-16.

Written instructions for Body Chart (worked in the round)

... – *pattern repeat*

Rounds 1 - 2: [P1, k1 tbl] to last stitch, p1.

Round 3: [P1, k1 tbl] 3 times, [1/1 RPT] 2 times, 1/1 RT, *p1, 1/1 LT, [1/1 LPT] 2 times, [k1 tbl, p1] 5 times, k1 tbl, [1/1 RPT] 2 times, 1/1 RT*, p1, 1/1 LT, [1/1 LPT] 2 times, [k1 tbl, p1] 3 times.

Round 4: P1, k1 tbl, [p1, k1 tbl, p1, [k1 tbl] 2 times] 2 times, *[p1, [k1 tbl] 2 times, p1, k1 tbl] 2 times, [p1, k1 tbl, p1, [k1 tbl] 2 times] 2 times*, [p1, [k1 tbl] 2 times, p1, k1 tbl] 2 times, p1, k1 tbl, p1.

Round 5: [P1, k1 tbl] 2 times, p1, [1/1 RPT] 3 times, k1 tbl, *p1, k1 tbl, [1/1 LPT] 3 times, [p1, k1 tbl] 4 times, p1, [1/1 RPT] 3 times, k1 tbl*, p1, k1 tbl, [1/1 LPT] 3 times, [p1, k1 tbl] 2 times, p1.

Round 6: Repeat round 1.

Round 7: [P1, k1 tbl] 2 times, [1/1 RPT] 3 times, p1, k1 tbl, *p1, k1 tbl, p1, [1/1 LPT] 3 times, [k1 tbl, p1] 3 times, k1 tbl, [1/1 RPT] 3 times, p1, k1 tbl*, p1, k1 tbl, p1, [1/1 LPT] 3 times, [k1 tbl, p1] 2 times.

Round 8: P1, k1 tbl, p1, [k1 tbl] 2 times, [p1, k1 tbl] 2 times, p2, k1 tbl, *k1 tbl, p2, [[k1 tbl, p1] 2 times, [k1 tbl] 2 times, p1] 2 times, k1 tbl, p1, k1 tbl, p2, k1 tbl*, p1, k1 tbl, p2, [k1 tbl, p1] 2 times, [k1 tbl] 2 times, p1, k1 tbl, p1.

Round 9: P1, k1 tbl, p1, [1/1 RPT] 3 times, p2, k1 tbl, *p1, k1 tbl, p2, [1/1 LPT] 3 times, [p1, k1 tbl] 2 times, p1, [1/1 RPT] 3 times, p2, k1 tbl*, p1, k1 tbl, p2, [1/1 LPT] 3 times, p1, k1 tbl, p1.

Round 10: [P1, k1 tbl] 4 times, p3, k1 tbl, *p1, k1 tbl, p3, [k1 tbl, p1] 7 times, k1 tbl, p3, k1 tbl*, p1, k1 tbl, p3, [k1 tbl, p1] 4 times.

Round 11: P1, k1 tbl, [1/1 RPT] 3 times, p3, k1 tbl, *p1, k1 tbl, p3, [1/1 LPT] 3 times, k1 tbl, p1, k1 tbl, [1/1 RPT] 3 times, p3, k1 tbl*, p1, k1 tbl, p3, [1/1 LPT] 3 times, k1 tbl, p1.

Round 12: P1, [k1 tbl] 2 times, [p1, k1 tbl] 2 times, p4, k1 tbl, *p1, k1 tbl, p4, [k1 tbl, p1] 2 times, [[(k1 tbl) 2 times, p1] 2 times, k1 tbl, p1, k1 tbl, p4, k1 tbl*, p1, k1 tbl, p4, [k1 tbl, p1] 2 times, [k1 tbl] 2 times, p1.

Round 13: P1, [1/1 RPT] 3 times, p4, k1 tbl, *p1, k1 tbl, p4, [1/1 LPT] 3 times, p1, [1/1 RPT] 3 times, p4, k1 tbl*, p1, k1 tbl, p4, [1/1 LPT] 3 times, p1.

Round 14: [P1, k1 tbl] 3 times, p5, k1 tbl, *p1, k1 tbl, p5, [k1 tbl, p1] 5 times, k1 tbl, p5, k1 tbl*, p1, k1 tbl, p5, [k1 tbl, p1] 3 times.

Round 15: [P1, k1 tbl] 3 times, p4, K2TOG, YO, *p1, YO, SSK, p4, [k1 tbl, p1] 2 times, 1/1/1 LPT, [k1 tbl, p1] 2 times, p4, K2TOG, YO*, p1, YO, SSK, p4, [k1 tbl, p1] 3 times.

Round 16: [P1, k1 tbl] 3 times, p4, k2, *p1, k2, p4, [k1 tbl, p1] 5 times, k1 tbl, p4, k2*, p1, k2, p4, [k1 tbl, p1] 3 times.

Round 17: P1, 1/1 LT, [1/1 LPT] 2 times, p2, K2TOG, YO, k1, *p1, k1, YO, SSK, p2, [1/1 RPT] 2 times, 1/1 RT, p1, 1/1 LT, [1/1 LPT] 2 times, p2, K2TOG, YO, k1*, p1, k1, YO, SSK, p2, [1/1 RPT] 2 times, 1/1 RT, p1.

Round 18: P1, [k1 tbl] 2 times, [p1, k1 tbl] 2 times, p2, k3, *p1, k3, p2, [k1 tbl, p1] 2 times, [[k1 tbl] 2 times, p1] 2 times, k1 tbl, p1, k1 tbl, p2, k3*, p1, k3, p2, [k1 tbl, p1] 2 times, [k1 tbl] 2 times, p1.

Round 19: P1, k1 tbl, [1/1 LPT] 3 times, K2TOG, YO, k2, *p1, k2, YO, SSK, [1/1 RPT] 3 times, k1 tbl, p1, k1 tbl, [1/1 LPT] 3 times, K2TOG, YO, k2*, p1, k2, YO, SSK, [1/1 RPT] 3 times, k1 tbl, p1.

Round 20: [P1, k1 tbl] 4 times, k4, *p1, k4, [k1 tbl, p1] 7 times, k1 tbl, k4*, p1, k4, [k1 tbl, p1] 4 times.

Round 21: P1, k1 tbl, p1, 1/1 LT, [1/1 LPT] 2 times, k3, *p1, k3, [1/1 RPT] 3 times, [p1, k1 tbl] 2 times, p1, [1/1 LPT] 3 times, k3*, p1, k3, [1/1 RPT] 2 times, 1/1 RT, p1, k1 tbl, p1.

Round 22: P1, k1 tbl, p1, [k1 tbl] 2 times, [p1, k1 tbl] 2 times, k3, *p1, k3, k1 tbl, p1, [k1 tbl, p1, k1 tbl, p2] 2 times, [k1 tbl, p1] 2 times, k1 tbl, k3*, p1, k3, [k1 tbl, p1] 2 times, [k1 tbl] 2 times, p1, k1 tbl, p1.

Round 23: [P1, k1 tbl] 2 times, [1/1 LPT] 3 times, k2, *p1, k2, [1/1 RPT] 3 times, p2, k1 tbl, p1, k1 tbl, p2, [1/1 LPT] 3 times, k2*, p1, k2, [1/1 RPT] 3 times, [k1 tbl, p1] 2 times.

Round 24: [P1, k1 tbl] 5 times, k2, *p1, k2, k1 tbl, p1, [k1 tbl, p1, k1 tbl, p3] 2 times, [k1 tbl, p1] 2 times, k1 tbl, k2*, p1, k2, [k1 tbl, p1] 5 times.

Round 25: [P1, k1 tbl] 2 times, p1, 1/1 LT, [1/1 LPT] 2 times, k1, *p1, k1, [1/1 RPT] 3 times, p3, k1 tbl, p1, k1 tbl, p3, [1/1 LPT] 3 times, k1*, p1, k1, [1/1 RPT] 2 times, 1/1 RT, [p1, k1 tbl] 2 times, p1.

Round 26: [P1, k1 tbl] 2 times, p1, [k1 tbl] 2 times, [p1, k1 tbl] 2 times, k1, *p1, k1, k1 tbl, p1, [k1 tbl, p1, k1 tbl, p4] 2 times, [k1 tbl, p1] 2 times, k1 tbl, k1*, p1, k1, [k1 tbl, p1] 2 times, [k1 tbl] 2 times, [p1, k1 tbl] 2 times, p1.

Round 27: [P1, k1 tbl] 3 times, [1/1 LPT] 3 times, *p1, [1/1 RPT] 3 times, p4, k1 tbl, p1, k1 tbl, p4, [1/1 LPT] 3 times*, p1, [1/1 RPT] 3 times, [k1 tbl, p1] 3 times.

Round 28: [P1, k1 tbl] 6 times, *p1, k1 tbl, p1, [k1 tbl, p1, k1 tbl, p5] 2 times, [k1 tbl, p1] 2 times, k1 tbl*, [p1, k1 tbl] 6 times, p1.

Round 29: [P1, k1 tbl] 5 times, p1, *1/1/1 LPT, [p1, k1 tbl] 2 times, p4, K2TOG, YO, p1, YO, SSK, p4, [k1 tbl, p1] 2 times*, 1/1/1 LPT, [p1, k1 tbl] 5 times, p1.

Round 30: [P1, k1 tbl] 6 times, *[p1, k1 tbl] 3 times, p4, k2, p1, k2, p4, [k1 tbl, p1] 2 times, k1 tbl*, [p1, k1 tbl] 6 times, p1.

Round 31: [P1, k1 tbl] 3 times, [1/1 RPT] 2 times, 1/1 RT, *p1, 1/1 LT, [1/1 LPT] 2 times, p2, K2TOG, YO, k1, p1, k1, YO, SSK, p2, [1/1 RPT] 2 times, 1/1 RT*, p1, 1/1 LT, [1/1 LPT] 2 times, [k1 tbl, p1] 3 times.

Round 32: P1, k1 tbl, [p1, k1 tbl, p1, [k1 tbl] 2 times] 2 times, *p1, [k1 tbl] 2 times, [p1, k1 tbl] 2 times, p2, k3, p1, k3, p2, [k1 tbl, p1] 2 times, [k1 tbl] 2 times*, [p1, [k1 tbl] 2 times, p1, k1 tbl] 2 times, p1, k1 tbl, p1.

Round 33: [P1, k1 tbl] 2 times, p1, [1/1 RPT] 3 times, k1 tbl, *p1, k1 tbl, [1/1 LPT] 3 times, K2TOG, YO, k2, p1, k2, YO, SSK, [1/1 RPT] 3 times, k1 tbl*, p1, k1 tbl, [1/1 LPT] 3 times, [p1, k1 tbl] 2 times, p1.

Round 34: [P1, k1 tbl] 6 times, *[p1, k1 tbl] 4 times, k4, p1, k4, [k1 tbl, p1] 3 times, k1 tbl*, [p1, k1 tbl] 6 times, p1.

Round 35: [P1, k1 tbl] 2 times, [1/1 RPT] 3 times, p1, k1 tbl, *p1, k1 tbl, p1, [1/1 LPT] 3 times, k3, p1, k3, [1/1 RPT] 3 times, p1, k1 tbl*, p1, k1 tbl, p1, [1/1 LPT] 3 times, [k1 tbl, p1] 2 times.

Round 36: P1, k1 tbl, p1, [k1 tbl] 2 times, [p1, k1 tbl] 2 times, p2, k1 tbl, *p1, k1 tbl, p2, [k1 tbl, p1] 2 times, k1 tbl, k3, p1, k3, [k1 tbl, p1] 2 times, k1 tbl, p2, k1 tbl*, p1, k1 tbl, p2, [k1 tbl, p1] 2 times, [k1 tbl] 2 times, p1, k1 tbl, p1.

Round 37: P1, k1 tbl, p1, [1/1 RPT] 3 times, p2, k1 tbl, *p1, k1 tbl, p2, [1/1 LPT] 3 times, k2, p1, k2, [1/1 RPT] 3 times, p2, k1 tbl*, p1, k1 tbl, p2, [1/1 LPT] 3 times, p1, k1 tbl, p1.

Round 38: [P1, k1 tbl] 4 times, p3, k1 tbl, *p1, k1 tbl, p3, [k1 tbl, p1] 2 times, k1 tbl, k2, p1, k2, [k1 tbl, p1] 2 times, k1 tbl, p3, k1 tbl*, p1, k1 tbl, p3, [k1 tbl, p1] 4 times.

Round 39: P1, k1 tbl, [1/1 RPT] 3 times, p3, k1 tbl, *p1, k1 tbl, p3, [1/1 LPT] 3 times, k1, p1, k1, [1/1 RPT] 3 times, p3, k1 tbl*, p1, k1 tbl, p3, [1/1 LPT] 3 times, k1 tbl, p1.

Round 40: P1, [k1 tbl] 2 times, [p1, k1 tbl] 2 times, p4, k1 tbl, *p1, k1 tbl, p4, [k1 tbl, p1] 2 times, k1 tbl, k1, p1, k1, [k1 tbl, p1] 2 times, k1 tbl, p4, k1 tbl*, p1, k1 tbl, p4, [k1 tbl, p1] 2 times, [k1 tbl] 2 times, p1.

Rounds 41-44: Repeat rounds 13-16.

Written instructions for Border Chart A
... – pattern repeat

Round 1: P1, 1/1 LT, [1/1 LPT] 2 times, p2, K2TOG, YO, k1, *p1, k1, YO, SSK, p2, [1/1 RPT] 2 times, 1/1 RT, p1, 1/1 LT, [1/1 LPT] 2 times, p2, K2TOG, YO, k1*, p1, k1, YO, SSK, p2, [1/1 RPT] 2 times, 1/1 RT, p1.

Round 2: P1, [k1 tbl] 2 times, [p1, k1 tbl] 2 times, p2, k3, *p1, k3, p2, [k1 tbl, p1] 2 times, [[k1 tbl] 2 times, p1] 2 times, k1 tbl, p1, k1 tbl, p2, k3*, p1, k3, p2, [k1 tbl, p1] 2 times, [k1 tbl] 2 times, p1.

Round 3: P1, k1 tbl, [1/1 LPT] 3 times, K2TOG, YO, k2, *p1, k2, YO, SSK, [1/1 RPT] 3 times, k1 tbl, p1, k1 tbl, [1/1 LPT] 3 times, K2TOG, YO, k2*, p1, k2, YO, SSK, [1/1 RPT] 3 times, k1 tbl, p1.

Round 4: [P1, k1 tbl] 4 times, k4, *p1, k4, [k1 tbl, p1] 7 times, k1 tbl, k4*, p1, k4, [k1 tbl, p1] 4 times.

Round 5: P1, k1 tbl, p1, 1/1 LT, [1/1 LPT] 2 times, k3, *p1, k3, [1/1 RPT] 2 times, 1/1 RT, [p1, k1 tbl] 2 times, p1, 1/1 LT, [1/1 LPT] 2 times, k3*, p1, k3, [1/1 RPT] 2 times, 1/1 RT, p1, k1 tbl, p1.

Round 6: P1, k1 tbl, p1, [k1 tbl] 2 times, [p1, k1 tbl] 2 times, k3, *p1, k3, [[k1 tbl, p1] 2 times, [k1 tbl] 2 times, p1] 2 times, k1 tbl, p1, k1 tbl, k3*, p1, k3, [k1 tbl, p1] 2 times, [k1 tbl] 2 times, p1, k1 tbl, p1.

Round 7: [P1, k1 tbl] 2 times, [1/1 LPT] 3 times, k2, *p1, k2, [1/1 RPT] 3 times, [k1 tbl, p1] 3 times, k1 tbl, [1/1 LPT] 3 times, k2*, p1, k2, [1/1 RPT] 3 times, [k1 tbl, p1] 2 times.

Round 8: [P1, k1 tbl] 5 times, k2, *p1, k2, [k1 tbl, p1] 9 times, k1 tbl, k2*, p1, k2, [k1 tbl, p1] 5 times.

Round 9: [P1, k1 tbl] 2 times, p1, 1/1 LT, [1/1 LPT] 2 times, k1, *p1, k1, [1/1 RPT] 2 times, 1/1 RT, [p1, k1 tbl] 4 times, p1, 1/1 LT, [1/1 LPT] 2 times, k1*, p1, k1, [1/1 RPT] 2 times, 1/1 RT, [p1, k1 tbl] 2 times, p1.

Round 10: [P1, k1 tbl] 2 times, p1, [k1 tbl] 2 times, [p1, k1 tbl] 2 times, k1, *p1, k1, [k1 tbl, p1] 2 times, [k1 tbl] 2 times, [p1, k1 tbl] 4 times, p1, [k1 tbl] 2 times, [p1, k1 tbl] 2 times, k1*, p1, k1, [k1 tbl, p1] 2 times, [k1 tbl] 2 times, [p1, k1 tbl] 2 times, p1.

Round 11: [P1, k1 tbl] 3 times, [1/1 LPT] 3 times, *p1, [1/1 RPT] 3 times, [k1 tbl, p1] 5 times, k1 tbl, [1/1 LPT] 3 times*, p1, [1/1 RPT] 3 times, [k1 tbl, p1] 3 times.

Round 12: [P1, k1 tbl] to last stitch, p1.

Written instructions for Border Chart B
... – pattern repeat

Round 1: [P1, k1 tbl] 3 times, [1/1 RPT] 2 times, 1/1 RT, *p1, 1/1 LT, [1/1 LPT] 2 times, p2, K2TOG, YO, k1, p1, k1, YO, SSK, p2, [1/1 RPT] 2 times, 1/1 RT*, p1, 1/1 LT, [1/1 LPT] 2 times, [k1 tbl, p1] 3 times.

Round 2: P1, k1 tbl, [p1, k1 tbl, p1, [k1 tbl] 2 times] 2 times, *p1, [k1 tbl] 2 times, [p1, k1 tbl] 2 times, p2, k3, p1, k3, p2, [k1 tbl, p1] 2 times, [k1 tbl] 2 times*, [p1, (k1 tbl) 2 times, p1, k1 tbl] 2 times, p1, k1 tbl, p1.

Round 3: [P1, k1 tbl] 2 times, p1, [1/1 RPT] 3 times, k1 tbl, *p1, k1 tbl, [1/1 LPT] 3 times, K2TOG, YO, k2, p1, k2, YO, SSK, [1/1 RPT] 3 times, k1 tbl*, p1, k1 tbl, [1/1 LPT] 3 times, [p1, k1 tbl] 2 times, p1.

Round 4: [P1, k1 tbl] 6 times, *[p1, k1 tbl] 4 times, k4, p1, k4, [k1 tbl, p1] 3 times, k1 tbl*, [p1, k1 tbl] 6 times, p1.

Round 5: [P1, k1 tbl] 2 times, [1/1 RPT] 2 times, 1/1 RT, p1, k1 tbl, *p1, k1 tbl, p1, 1/1 LT, [1/1 LPT] 2 times, k3, p1, k3, [1/1 RPT] 2 times, 1/1 RT, p1, k1 tbl*, p1, k1 tbl, p1, 1/1 LT, [1/1 LPT] 2 times, [k1 tbl, p1] 2 times.

Round 6: [P1, k1 tbl, p1, [k1 tbl] 2 times] 2 times, p1, k1 tbl, *p1, k1 tbl, p1, [k1 tbl] 2 times, [p1, k1 tbl] 2 times, k3, p1, k3, [k1 tbl, p1] 2 times, [k1 tbl] 2 times, p1, k1 tbl*, [p1, k1 tbl, p1, [k1 tbl] 2 times] 2 times, p1, k1 tbl, p1.

Round 7: P1, k1 tbl, p1, [1/1 RPT] 3 times, k1 tbl, p1, k1 tbl, *[p1, k1 tbl] 2 times, [1/1 LPT] 3 times, k2, p1, k2, [1/1 RPT] 3 times, k1 tbl, p1, k1 tbl*, [p1, k1 tbl] 2 times, [1/1 LPT] 3 times, p1, k1 tbl, p1.

Round 8: [P1, k1 tbl] 6 times, *[p1, k1 tbl] 5 times, k2, p1, k2, [k1 tbl, p1] 4 times, k1 tbl*, [p1, k1 tbl] 6 times, p1.

Round 9: P1, k1 tbl, [1/1 RPT] 2 times, 1/1 RT, [p1, k1 tbl] 2 times, *[p1, k1 tbl] 2 times, p1, 1/1 LT, [1/1 LPT] 2 times, k1, p1, k1, [1/1 RPT] 2 times, 1/1 RT, [p1, k1 tbl] 2 times*, [p1, k1 tbl] 2 times, p1, 1/1 LT, [1/1 LPT] 2 times, k1 tbl, p1.

Round 10: [P1, [k1 tbl] 2 times, p1, k1 tbl] 2 times, p1, k1 tbl, *[p1, k1 tbl] 2 times, p1, [k1 tbl] 2 times, [p1, k1 tbl] 2 times, k1, p1, k1, [k1 tbl, p1] 2 times, [k1 tbl] 2 times, [p1, k1 tbl] 2 times*, p1, k1 tbl, [p1, k1 tbl, p1, [k1 tbl] 2 times]] 2 times, p1.

Round 11: P1, [1/1 RPT] 3 times, [k1 tbl, p1] 2 times, k1 tbl, *[p1, k1 tbl] 3 times, [1/1 LPT] 3 times, p1, [1/1 RPT] 3 times, [k1 tbl, p1] 2 times, k1 tbl*, [p1, k1 tbl] 3 times, [1/1 LPT] 3 times, p1.

Round 12: [P1, k1 tbl] to last stitch, p1.

Written instructions for Sleeve Chart

Rounds 1 - 2: [P1, k1 tbl] to last stitch, p1.

Round 3: [P1, k1 tbl] 4 times, [1/1 RPT] 2 times, 1/1 RT, p1, 1/1 LT, [1/1 LPT] 2 times, [k1 tbl, p1] 4 times.

Round 4: [P1, k1 tbl] 3 times, [p1, [k1 tbl] 2 times, p1, k1 tbl, p1, [k1 tbl] 2 times] 2 times, [p1, k1 tbl] 3 times, p1.

Round 5: [P1, k1 tbl] 3 times, p1, [1/1 RPT] 3 times, k1 tbl, p1, k1 tbl, [1/1 LPT] 3 times, [p1, k1 tbl] 3 times, p1.

Round 6: [P1, k1 tbl] to last stitch, p1.

Round 7: [P1, k1 tbl] 3 times, [1/1 RPT] 3 times, [p1, k1 tbl] 2 times, p1, [1/1 LPT] 3 times, [k1 tbl, p1] 3 times.

Round 8: [P1, k1 tbl] 2 times, p1, [k1 tbl] 2 times, p1, [k1 tbl, p1, k1 tbl, p2] 2 times, [k1 tbl, p1] 2 times, [k1 tbl] 2 times, [p1, k1 tbl] 2 times, p1.

Round 9: [P1, k1 tbl] 2 times, p1, [1/1 RPT] 3 times, p2, k1 tbl, p1, k1 tbl, p2, [1/1 LPT] 3 times, [p1, k1 tbl] 2 times, p1.

Round 10: [P1, k1 tbl] 5 times, p3, k1 tbl, p1, k1 tbl, p3, [k1 tbl, p1] 5 times.

Round 11: [P1, k1 tbl] 2 times, [1/1 RPT] 3 times, p3, k1 tbl, p1, k1 tbl, p3, [1/1 LPT] 3 times, [k1 tbl, p1] 2 times.

Round 12: *P1, k1 tbl, p1, [k1 tbl] 2 times, p1, [k1 tbl, p1, k1 tbl, p4] 2 times, [k1 tbl, p1] 2 times, [k1 tbl] 2 times, p1, k1 tbl, p1.

Round 13: *P1, k1 tbl, p1, [1/1 RPT] 3 times, p4, k1 tbl, p1, k1 tbl, p4, [1/1 LPT] 3 times, p1, k1 tbl, p1.

Round 14: [P1, k1 tbl] 4 times, [p5, k1 tbl, p1, k1 tbl] 2 times, [p1, k1 tbl] 2 times, p1.

Round 15: [P1, k1 tbl] 4 times, p4, K2TOG, YO, p1, YO, SSK, p4, [k1 tbl, p1] 4 times.

Round 16: [P1, k1 tbl] 4 times, p4, k2, p1, k2, p4, [k1 tbl, p1] 4 times.

Round 17: *P1, k1 tbl, p1, 1/1 LT, [1/1 LPT] 2 times, p2, K2TOG, YO, k1, p1, k1, YO, SSK, p2, [1/1 RPT] 2 times, 1/1 RT, p1, k1 tbl, p1.

Round 18: *P1, k1 tbl, p1, [k1 tbl] 2 times, [p1, k1 tbl] 2 times, p2, k3, p1, k3, p2, [k1 tbl, p1] 2 times, [k1 tbl] 2 times, p1, k1 tbl, p1.

Round 19: [P1, k1 tbl] 2 times, [1/1 LPT] 3 times, K2TOG, YO, k2, p1, k2, YO, SSK, [1/1 RPT] 3 times, [k1 tbl, p1] 2 times.

Round 20: [P1, k1 tbl] 5 times, k4, p1, k4, [k1 tbl, p1] 5 times.

Round 21: [P1, k1 tbl] 2 times, p1, 1/1 LT, [1/1 LPT] 2 times, k3, p1, k3, [1/1 RPT] 2 times, 1/1 RT, [p1, k1 tbl] 2 times, p1.

Round 22: [P1, k1 tbl] 2 times, p1, [k1 tbl] 2 times, [p1, k1 tbl] 2 times, k3, p1, k3, [k1 tbl, p1] 2 times, [k1 tbl] 2 times, [p1, k1 tbl] 2 times, p1.

Round 23: [P1, k1 tbl] 3 times, [1/1 LPT] 3 times, k2, p1, k2, [1/1 RPT] 3 times, [k1 tbl, p1] 3 times.

Round 24: [P1, k1 tbl] 6 times, k2, p1, k2, [k1 tbl, p1] 6 times.

Round 25: [P1, k1 tbl] 3 times, p1, 1/1 LT, [1/1 LPT] 2 times, k1, p1, k1, [1/1 RPT] 2 times, 1/1 RT, [p1, k1 tbl] 3 times, p1.

Round 26: [P1, k1 tbl] 3 times, p1, [k1 tbl] 2 times, [p1, k1 tbl] 2 times, k1, p1, k1, [k1 tbl, p1] 2 times, [k1 tbl] 2 times, [p1, k1 tbl] 3 times, p1.

Round 27: [P1, k1 tbl] 4 times, [1/1 LPT] 3 times, p1, [1/1 RPT] 3 times, [k1 tbl, p1] 4 times.

Round 28: [P1, k1 tbl] to last stitch, p1.

Round 29: [P1, k1 tbl] 6 times, p1, 1/1/1 LPT, [p1, k1 tbl] 6 times, p1.

Round 30: [P1, k1 tbl] to last stitch, p1.

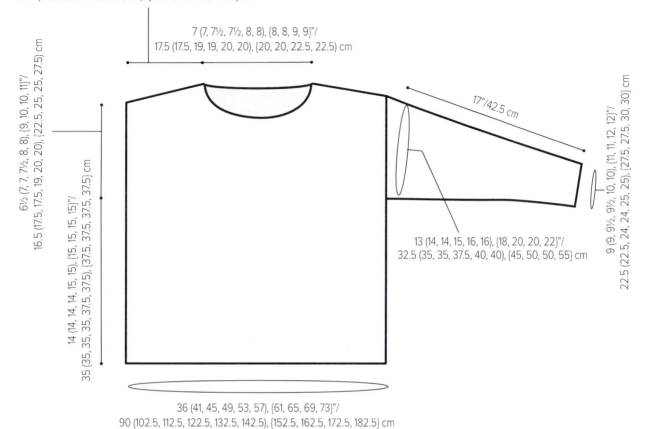

6¼ (7¼, 8, 9, 9¾, 10¾), {11¾, 12¾, 13¼, 14¼)"/
15.5 (18, 20, 22.5, 24.5, 27), {29.5, 32, 33, 35.5} cm

7 (7, 7½, 7½, 8, 8), {8, 8, 9, 9}"/
17.5 (17.5, 19, 19, 20, 20), {20, 20, 22.5, 22.5} cm

17"/42.5 cm

6½ (7, 7, 7½, 8, 8), {9, 10, 10, 11}"/
16.5 (17.5, 17.5, 19, 20, 20), {22.5, 25, 25, 27.5} cm

14 (14, 14, 14, 15, 15), {15, 15, 15, 15}"/
35 (35, 35, 35, 37.5, 37.5), {37.5, 37.5, 37.5, 37.5} cm

9 (9, 9½, 9½, 10, 10), {11, 11, 12, 12}"/
22.5 (22.5, 24, 24, 25, 25), {27.5, 27.5, 30, 30} cm

13 (14, 14, 15, 16, 16), {18, 20, 20, 22}"/
32.5 (35, 35, 37.5, 40, 40), {45, 50, 50, 55} cm

36 (41, 45, 49, 53, 57), {61, 65, 69, 73}"/
90 (102.5, 112.5, 122.5, 132.5, 142.5), {152.5, 162.5, 172.5, 182.5} cm

Cadmus

This versatile accessory blends the coziness of a cowl with the elegance of a lace shawl. Worked in a rich, textured lace motif, it drapes beautifully around the neck and tapers to a soft point in front, creating both warmth and a flattering silhouette.

The cowl is worked flat and sideways. Live stitches at the beginning and the end of the cowl are joined with Kitchener Stitch. The compact size of Cadmus makes it an engaging project for lace lovers and an excellent gift knit.

Finished Measurements
19"/47.5 cm neck opening circumference.
14"/35 cm tall.
Measurements are taken after blocking.

Yarn
Fingering weight yarn (approximate amount): 320 yards/291 m.

Miss Babs Tarte (75% superwash Merino wool, 15% Nylon, 10% Tencel; 500 yds/457 m in 122 g); Wolfsbane, 1 skein.

Needles
Size US 4/3.5 mm: straight or circular 24"/60 cm.
Optional: spare needle of the same size.
Size US 4/3.5 mm: set of double pointed needles.
Adjust needle size if necessary to obtain the correct gauge.

Notions
Stitch markers, waste yarn, tapestry needle.

Gauge
24 stitches and 36 rows = 4"/10 cm in Garter stitch on US 4/3.5 mm needle.
25 stitches and 32 rows = 4"/10 cm in Lace pattern on US 4/3.5 mm needle.

Notes
- This cowl is worked flat and sideways. Live stitches at the beginning and the end of the cowl are joined with Kitchener Stitch.
- Knitters may consider placing markers between chart repetitions

DIRECTIONS

01 COWL

With waste yarn and your favorite provisional cast-on method, cast on 42 stitches. Place on hold and set aside.
Using working yarn and Long Tail cast on (see Special Techniques, page 226), cast on 63 stitches, place marker; with the same needle, knit held 42 provisionally cast-on stitches - 105 stitches on the needle.

Next Row (WS): Knit all stitches.
Next Row (RS): K2, K2TOG, knit to marker, M1R, slip marker, k1, M1L, knit to last 3 stitches, SSK, k1.
Next Row (WS): Knit to end.

Chart Set-Up Row 1 (RS): Work Row 1 of Chart A, working 10-stitch chart repeat 5 times total, to marker, slip marker, k1, M1L, knit to last 4 stitches, SSK, slip 1 stitch with yarn in back, p1.

Work in established pattern through row 16 of Chart A.

Continue working as established, working Chart B, Chart C, Chart D and Chart E respectively.

Work Charts A–D once more.

Next Row (RS): K2, K2TOG, knit to marker, M1R, slip marker, k1, M1L, knit to last 3 stitches, SSK, k1.
Next Row (WS): Knit to end.

Next Row (RS): Loosely bind off 63 stitches.

Place remaining 42 stitches on hold.
Break yarn, leaving 30"/75 cm tail.

Carefully unravel provisional cast on and place released 42 stitches onto spare needle. Graft live and stitches from provisional cast on together, using Kitchener Stitch.

02 FINISHING

Work Applied I-cord top neck edging:

With double-pointed needle, and using a provisional method of your choice, cast on 3 stitches.
With RS facing and beginning at the "seam", work applied I-cord as follows: *K2, slip 1 stitch purlwise with yarn in back, yarn over, pick up and knit 1 stitch from top selvedge of the cowl, pass yarn over and slip stitch over, slide stitches to opposite end of double-pointed needle; repeat from * around the circumference of the neck opening, picking up 1 stitch into each garter ridge.
Remove waste yarn from provisional cast on and place first 3 stitches on another double-pointed needle.
With tail threaded on a tapestry needle, graft first 3 and last 3 I-cord stitches together using Kitchener Stitch (see Special Techniques, page 226).
Block to measurements, accentuating the scalloped edge of lace pattern.

Weave in ends.

CHARTS

CHART A

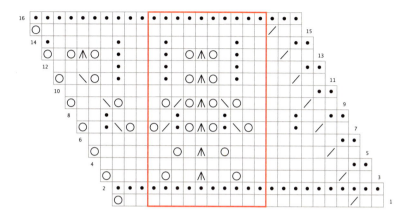

CHART B

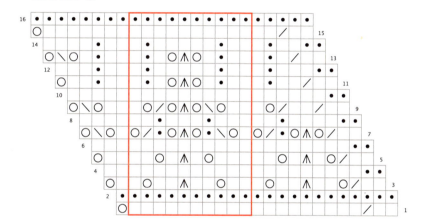

LEGEND

☐ **K**: Knit stitch on RS; purl stitch on WS

• **P**: Purl stitch on RS; knit stitch on WS

Ⓞ **YO**: Yarn over

╱ **K2TOG**: Knit 2 stitches together – 1 stitch decreased with right slant.

╲ **SSK**: Slip 1 stitch knitwise, slip 1 stitch knitwise, return 2 slipped stitches back to left needle and knit them together through back loops – 1 stitch decreased with left slant

⋀ **CDD** (central double decrease): Slip 2 stitches as if to K2TOG, k1, pass 2 slipped stitches over knit stitch – 2 stitches decreased.

☐ Pattern repeat

CHART C

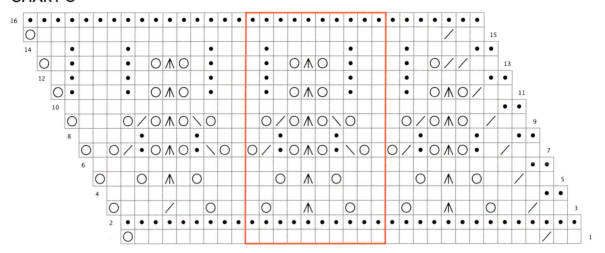

CHART D

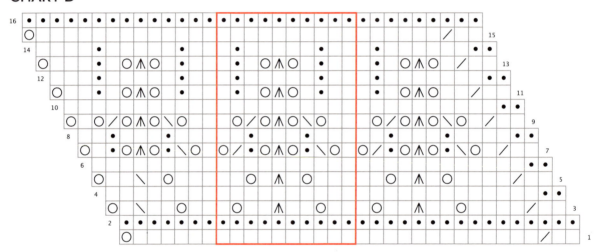

CHART E

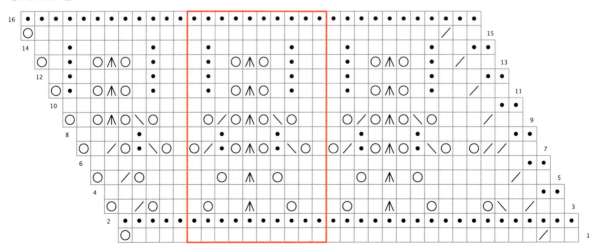

LEGEND

☐ **K**: Knit stitch on RS; purl stitch on WS

⊡ **P**: Purl stitch on RS; knit stitch on WS

◯ **YO**: Yarn over

◺ **K2TOG**: Knit 2 stitches together – 1 stitch decreased with right slant.

◺ **SSK**: Slip 1 stitch knitwise, slip 1 stitch knitwise, return 2 slipped stitches back to left needle and knit them together through back loops – 1 stitch decreased with left slant

◮ **CDD** (central double decrease): Slip 2 stitches as if to K2TOG, k1, pass 2 slipped stitches over knit stitch – 2 stitches decreased.

☐ Pattern repeat

Written instructions for Chart A

... – pattern repeat

Note: See Chart Legend for special abbreviations.

Row 1 (RS): K2, K2TOG, k7, *k10*, k2, YO.
Row 2 (WS): Knit.
Row 3 (RS): K2, K2TOG, k6, *k2, YO, k2, CDD, k2, YO, k1*, k3, YO.
Row 4 (WS): Purl to last 2 stitches, k2.
Row 5 (RS): K2, K2TOG, k5, *k3, YO, k1, CDD, k1, YO, k2*, k4, YO.
Row 6 (WS): Purl to last 2 stitches, k2.
Row 7 (RS): K2, K2TOG, k1, p1, k2, *k1, YO, SSK, p1, YO, CDD, YO, p1, K2TOG, YO*, k1, YO, SSK, p1, k1, YO.
Row 8 (WS): P2, k1, p3, *p2, [k1, p3] 2 times*, p2, k1, p2, k2.
Row 9 (RS): K2, K2TOG, k3, *k2, YO, SSK, YO, CDD, YO, K2TOG, YO, k1*, k2, YO, SSK, k2, YO.
Row 10 (WS): Purl to last 2 stitches, k2.
Row 11 (RS): K2, K2TOG, k2, *k2, p1, k1, YO, CDD, YO, k1, p1, k1*, k2, p1, k1, YO, SSK, k1, YO.
Row 12 (WS): P5, k1, p2, *p1, k1, p5, k1, p2*, p3, k2.
Row 13 (RS): K2, K2TOG, k1, *k2, p1, k1, YO, CDD, YO, k1, p1, k1*, k2, p1, k1, YO, CDD, YO, k1, YO.
Row 14 (WS): K1, p5, k1, p2, *p1, k1, p5, k1, p2*, p2, k2.
Row 15 (RS): K2, K2TOG, *k10*, k9, YO.
Row 16 (WS): Knit.

Written instructions for Chart B

... – pattern repeat

Row 1 (RS): K2, K2TOG, k9, *k10*, YO.
Row 2 (WS): Knit.
Row 3 (RS): K2, K2TOG, YO, k2, CDD, k2, YO, k1, *k2, YO, k2, CDD, k2, YO, k1*, k1, YO.

Row 4 (WS): Purl to last 2 stitches, k2.
Row 5 (RS): K2, K2TOG, YO, k1, CDD, k1, YO, k2, *k3, YO, k1, CDD, k1, YO, k2*, k2, YO.
Row 6 (WS): Purl to last 2 stitches, k2.
Row 7 (RS): K2, K2TOG, YO, CDD, YO, p1, K2TOG, YO, *k1, YO, SSK, p1, YO, CDD, YO, p1, K2TOG, YO*, k1, YO, SSK, YO.
Row 8 (WS): P4, *p2, [k1, p3] 2 times*, p2, k1, p4, k2.
Row 9 (RS): [K2, K2TOG] 2 times, YO, k1, *k2, YO, SSK, YO, CDD, YO, K2TOG, YO, k1*, k2, YO, SSK, YO.
Row 10 (WS): Purl to last 2 stitches, k2.
Row 11 (RS): K2, K2TOG, k2, p1, k1, *k2, p1, k1, YO, CDD, YO, k1, p1, k1*, k2, p1, k2, YO.
Row 12 (WS): P3, k1, p2, *p1, k1, p5, k1, p2*, p1, k1, p3, k2.
Row 13 (RS): K2, K2TOG, k1, p1, k1, *k2, p1, k1, YO, CDD, YO, k1, p1, k1*, k2, p1, k1, YO, SSK, YO.
Row 14 (WS): P4, k1, p2, *p1, k1, p5, k1, p2*, p1, k1, p2, k2.
Row 15 (RS): K2, K2TOG, k2, *k10*, k7, YO.
Row 16 (WS): Knit.

Written instructions for Chart C

... – pattern repeat

Row 1 (RS): K2, K2TOG, k11, *k10*, k8, YO.
Row 2 (WS): Knit.
Row 3 (RS): K2, K2TOG, k2, YO, k2, CDD, k2, YO, k1, *k2, YO, k2, CDD, k2, YO, k1*, k2, YO, k2, K2TOG, k3, YO.
Row 4 (WS): Purl to last 2 stitches, k2.
Row 5 (RS): K2, K2TOG, k2, YO, k1, CDD, k1, YO, k2, *k3, YO, k1, CDD, k1, YO, k2*, k3, YO, k1, CDD, k1, YO, k2, YO.
Row 6 (WS): Purl to last 2 stitches, k2.

Row 7 (RS): K2, K2TOG, k1, p1, YO, CDD, YO, p1, K2TOG, YO, *k1, YO, SSK, p1, YO, CDD, YO, p1, K2TOG, YO*, k1, YO, SSK, p1, YO, CDD, YO, p1, K2TOG, YO, k1, YO.

Row 8 (WS): P4, [k1, p3] 2 times, *p2, [k1, p3] 2 times*, p2, k1, p3, k1, p2, k2.

Row 9 (RS): K2, K2TOG, k1, YO, CDD, YO, K2TOG, YO, k1, *k2, YO, SSK, YO, CDD, YO, K2TOG, YO, k1*, k2, YO, SSK, YO, CDD, YO, K2TOG, YO, k3, YO.

Row 10 (WS): Purl to last 2 stitches, k2.

Row 11 (RS): K2, K2TOG, YO, CDD, YO, k1, p1, k1, *k2, p1, k1, YO, CDD, YO, k1, p1, k1*, k2, p1, k1, YO, CDD, YO, k1, p1, k3, p1, YO.

Row 12 (WS): P1, k1, p3, k1, p5, k1, p2, *p1, k1, p5, k1, p2*, p1, k1, p5, k2.

Row 13 (RS): K2, K2TOG 2 times, YO, k1, p1, k1, *k2, p1, k1, YO, CDD, YO, k1, p1, k1*, k2, p1, k1, YO, CDD, YO, k1, p1, k3, p1, k1, YO.

Row 14 (WS): P2, k1, p3, k1, p5, k1, p2, *p1, k1, p5, k1, p2*, p1, k1, p4, k2.

Row 15 (RS): K2, K2TOG, k4, *k10*, k15, YO.

Row 16 (WS): Knit.

Written instructions for Chart D

... – pattern repeat

Row 1 (RS): K2, K2TOG, k13, *k10*, k6, YO.

Row 2 (WS): Knit.

Row 3 (RS): K2, K2TOG, k4, YO, k2, CDD, k2, YO, k1, *k2, YO, k2, CDD, k2, YO, k1*, k2, YO, k2, SSK, k1, YO.

Row 4 (WS): Purl to last 2 stitches, k2.

Row 5 (RS): K2, K2TOG, k4, YO, k1, CDD, k1, YO, k2, *k3, YO, k1, CDD, k1, YO, k2*, k3, YO, k1, SSK, k2, YO.

Row 6 (WS): Purl to last 2 stitches, k2.

Row 7 (RS): K2, K2TOG, k1, YO, SSK, p1, YO, CDD, YO, p1, K2TOG, YO, *k1, YO, SSK, p1, YO, CDD, YO, p1, K2TOG, YO*, k1, YO, SSK, p1, YO, CDD, YO, p1, k1, YO.

Row 8 (WS): P2, [k1, p3] 2 times, *p2, [k1, p3] 2 times*, p2, k1, p3, k1, p4, k2.

Row 9 (RS): K2, K2TOG, k1, YO, SSK, YO, CDD, YO, K2TOG, YO, k1, *k2, YO, SSK, YO, CDD, YO, K2TOG, YO, k1*, k2, YO, SSK, YO, CDD, YO, K2TOG, YO, k1, YO.

Row 10 (WS): Purl to last 2 stitches, k2.

Row 11 (RS): K2, K2TOG, k2, YO, CDD, YO, k1, p1, k1, *k2, p1, k1, YO, CDD, YO, k1, p1, k1*, k2, p1, k1, YO, CDD, YO, k1, p1, k2, YO.

Row 12 (WS): P3, k1, p5, k1, p2, *p1, k1, p5, k1, p2*, p1, k1, p7, k2.

Row 13 (RS): K2, K2TOG, k1, YO, CDD, YO, k1, p1, k1, *k2, p1, k1, YO, CDD, YO, k1, p1, k1*, k2, p1, k1, YO, CDD, YO, k1, p1, k3, YO.

Row 14 (WS): P4, k1, p5, k1, p2, *p1, k1, p5, k1, p2*, p1, k1, p6, k2.

Row 15 (RS): K2, K2TOG, k6, *k10*, k13, YO.

Row 16 (WS): Knit.

Written instructions for Chart E

... – pattern repeat

Row 1 (RS): K2, K2TOG, k15, *k10*, k4, YO.

Row 2 (WS): Knit.

Row 3 (RS): K2, K2TOG, k1, SSK, YO, k3, YO, k2, CDD, k2, YO, k1, *k2, YO, k2, CDD, k2, YO, k1*, k2, YO, K2TOG, k1, YO.

Row 4 (WS): Purl to last 2 stitches, k2.

Row 5 (RS): K2, K2TOG, k6, YO, k1, CDD, k1, YO, k2, *k3, YO, k1, CDD, k1, YO, k2*, k3, YO, K2TOG, k1, YO.

Row 6 (WS): Purl to last 2 stitches, k2.

Row 7 (RS): K2, [K2TOG] 2 times, YO, k1, YO, SSK, p1, YO, CDD, YO, p1, K2TOG, YO, *k1, YO, SSK, p1, YO, CDD, YO, p1, K2TOG, YO*, k1, YO, SSK, p1, YO, K2TOG, k1, YO.

Row 8 (WS): P4, k1, p3, *p2, [k1, p3] 2 times*, p2, k1, p3, k1, p6, k2.

Row 9 (RS): K2, K2TOG, k3, YO, SSK, YO, CDD, YO, K2TOG, YO, k1, *k2, YO, SSK, YO, CDD, YO, K2TOG, YO, k1*, k2, YO, SSK, YO, CDD, YO, k1, YO.

Row 10 (WS): Purl to last 2 stitches, k2.

Row 11 (RS): K2, K2TOG, k2, p1, k1, YO, CDD, YO, k1, p1, k1, *k2, p1, k1, YO, CDD, YO, k1, p1, k1*, k2, p1, k1, YO, CDD, YO, k1, p1, YO.

Row 12 (WS): P1, k1, p5, k1, p2, *p1, k1, p5, k1, p2*, p1, k1, p5, k1, p3, k2.

Row 13 (RS): K2, K2TOG, k1, p1, k1, YO, CDD, YO, k1, p1, k1, *k2, p1, k1, YO, CDD, YO, k1, p1, k1*, k2, p1, k1, YO, CDD, YO, k1, p1, k1, YO.

Row 14 (WS): P2, k1, p5, k1, p2, *p1, k1, p5, k1, p2*, p1, k1, p5, k1, p2, k2.

Row 15 (RS): K2, K2TOG, k8, *k10*, k11, YO.

Row 16 (WS): Knit.

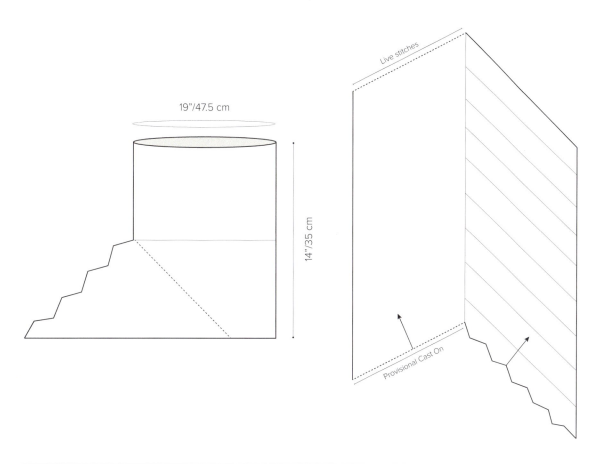

19"/47.5 cm

14"/35 cm

Live stitches

Provisional Cast On

Gond

Saddle sleeves meet sculptural cables in a pullover that balances structure and ease. Modified drop shoulders create a relaxed silhouette, while slip-stitch cables bring a sense of movement and depth to the fabric.

The texture on the body is framed with classic ribbing at the neckline, cuffs, and hem. At the bottom edge, deep ribbing is finished with small side slits for comfort and a contemporary look. The mix of smooth stockinette on the top and sleeves with the bold texture of the lower body creates a clean contrast that highlights the stitchwork.

Sizes

XS (S, M, L, XL, 2XL), {3XL, 4XL, 5XL, 6XL}: to fit bust 28-30 (32-34, 36-38, 40-42, 44-46, 48-50), {52-54, 56-58, 60-62, 64-66}"/70-75 (80-85, 90-95, 100-105, 110-115, 120-125), {130-135, 140-145, 150-155, 160-165} cm.

Finished Measurements

36¼ (40½, 45¼, 49½, 53½, 58½), {62½, 67½, 72, 76½}"/90.5 (101.5, 113, 124, 134, 146.5), {156.5, 169, 180, 146.5} cm bust circumference.

Shown in size M (45¼"/113 cm) on 38"/95 cm bust with 7¼"/18 cm of positive ease.

Yarn

Sport weight yarn (approximate amounts): 1190 (1320, 1440, 1570, 1690, 1800), {1940, 2070, 2190, 2320} yds/1083 (1201, 1310, 1429, 1538, 1638), {1765, 1884, 1993, 2111} m.

Miss Babs Laurel Falls (100% Superwash Shaniko Merino Wool; 300 yards/275 m in 3.5 oz/100 g), Blue Slate: 4 (5, 5, 6, 6, 6), {7, 7, 8, 8} skeins.

Needles

Size US 4/3.5 mm: 24-32"/60-80 cm circular and set of double-pointed.

Sizes US 3/3.25 mm: 24-32"/60-80 cm circular, 16"/40 cm circular and set of double-pointed.

Optional: second US 3/3.25 mm 24-32"/60-80 cm circular for the Tubular Bind Off.

Adjust needle size if necessary to obtain gauge.

Notions

Stitch markers, waste yarn, tapestry needle, cable needle.

Gauge

23 stitches and 34 rows = 4"/10 cm in Stockinette Stitch on size US 4/3.5 mm needle, after blocking.

28 stitches and 38 rows = 4"/10 cm in charted pattern on size US 4/3.5 mm needle, after blocking.

21 stitches and 34 rows = 4"/10 cm in Seed Stitch on size US 4/3.5 mm needle, after blocking.

Notes

- This pullover is worked from the top down. The saddle shoulders are worked back and forth from the neckline edge towards the armhole edge, then stitches for the back and fronts are picked up along the long sides of the saddles and worked back and forth to the underarm. The pieces then joined and the lower body is worked in the round to the lower edge.

- Stitches for the sleeves are picked up around the armhole and the sleeves are worked from the top down in the round.

Stitch Guide

Seed stitch (worked in rows on even number of stitches):
Row 1 (RS): *K1, p1; repeat from * to end.
Row 2 (WS): *P1, k1; repeat from * to end.
Repeat Rows 1 and 2 for pattern.

Seed stitch (worked in the round on even number of stitches):
Round 1: *K1, p1; repeat from * to end.
Round 2: *P1, k1; repeat from * to end.
Repeat Rounds 1 and 2 for pattern.

DIRECTIONS

01 RIGHT SADDLE

With US 4/3.5 mm 24-32"/60-80 cm circular needle, cast on 14 stitches.
Set-Up Row 1 (RS): K2, p1, place marker, work Row 1 of Seed stitch over next 8 stitches, place marker, p1, k2.
Set-Up row 2 (WS): P2, k1, slip marker, work Row 2 of Seed to marker, slip marker, k1, p2.

Repeat last 2 rows another 23 (27, 31, 35, 40, 44) {48, 53, 55, 61} times, slipping markers. Saddle measures approx. 5¾ (6½, 7½, 8½, 9¾, 10½), {11½, 13, 13½, 14½}"/14.5 (16.5, 19, 21.5, 24.5, 26.5), {29, 32.5, 34, 36.5} cm. Place all stitches on hold, break yarn. Leave markers at their places.
The cast-on short edge will be the neck opening edge and the edge with live stitches will be the armhole edge.

02 LEFT SADDLE

Work as Right Saddle.
Do not break yarn.

03 BACK

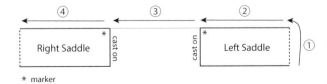

* marker

Next Row (RS): Work 14 Left Saddle stitches in established pattern ①, working Row 1 of Seed stitch, place just worked 14 stitches on hold.
Turn the Left Saddle 90 degrees clockwise and, with yarn attached to Left Saddle, beginning at the live stitches end (that will be the armhole end), pick up and knit 33 (38, 44, 50, 56, 61), {67, 74, 77, 84} stitches evenly along the long edge of the Left Saddle ②, place marker. With the same yarn, using the Backward Loop method (see Special Techniques, page 226), cast on 38 (40, 42, 42, 42, 46), {46, 46, 52, 52} stitches for back neck ③; place marker, then, with the same yarn, pick up and knit 33 (38, 44, 50, 56, 61), {67, 74, 77, 84} stitches evenly along the long edge of the Right Saddle ④, beginning at the neck opening and end with armhole edge.
[104 (116, 130, 142, 154, 168), {180, 194, 206, 220} stitches for Back]

Shape shoulders with German short-rows (see Special Techniques, page 226) as follows:
Short-Row 1 (WS): Purl to marker, slip marker, purl cast-on stitches, slip marker, p4 (4, 4, 5, 6, 6), {7, 8, 8, 9}, turn work.
Short-Row 2 (RS): Make double stitch, [knit to marker, slip marker] 2 times, k4 (4, 4, 5, 6, 6), {7, 8, 8, 9}, turn work.
Short-Row 3 (WS): Make double stitch, purl to double stitch, removing markers, work double stitch as single stitch, p4 (4, 4, 5, 6, 6), {7, 8, 8, 9}, turn work.
Short-Row 4 (RS): Make double stitch, knit to double stitch, work double stitch as single stitch, k4 (4, 4, 5, 6, 6), {7, 8, 8, 9}, turn work.

Short-Rows 5-14: Repeat last 2 short-rows 5 more times.

Next Row (WS): Make double stitch, purl to end, working double stitch as single stitch.
Next Row (RS): Knit to end, working double stitch as single stitch and removing markers.

Continue working in Stockinette stitch in rows until armhole measures 5½ (6, 6, 6½, 7, 7), {8, 9, 9, 10}"/ 14 (15, 15, 16.5, 17.5, 17.5), {20, 22.5, 22.5, 25} cm from the pick-up row, ending with WS row. Break yarn, place all stitches on hold.

04 FRONT

04a. Left Front
With US 4/3.5 mm 24-32"/60-80 cm circular needle, beginning at the neck opening, pick up and knit 33 (38, 44, 50, 56, 61), {67, 74, 77, 84} stitches evenly along the long edge of the Left Saddle.
Next Row (WS): Purl all stitches.

Shape left shoulder
Short-Row 1 (RS): K4 (4, 4, 5, 6, 6), {7, 8, 8, 9}, turn work.
Short-Row 2 (WS): Make double stitch, purl to end.
Short-Row 3 (RS): Knit to double stitch, work double stitch as single stitch, k4 (4, 4, 5, 6, 6), {7, 8, 8, 9}, turn work.
Short-Row 4 (WS): Make double stitch, purl to end.
Short-Rows 5-14: Repeat last 2 short-rows 5 more times.

Next Row (RS): Knit to end, working double stitch as single stitch.
Next Row (WS): Purl to end.

Shape the left neckline
Increase Row (RS): K2, M1L, knit to end. [1 stitch increased].
Next Row (WS): Purl to end.
Repeat last 2 rows another 3 times. [37 (42, 48, 54, 60, 65), {71, 78, 81, 88} stitches]

Break yarn, place all Left Front stitches on hold.

04b. Right Front
With US 4/3.5 mm 24-32"/60-80 cm circular needle, beginning at the armhole, pick up and knit 33 (38, 44, 50, 56, 61), {67, 74, 77, 84} stitches evenly along the long edge of the Right Saddle.

Shape the left shoulder
Short-Row 1 (WS): P4 (4, 4, 5, 6, 6), {7, 8, 8, 9}, turn work.
Short-Row 2 (RS): Make double stitch, knit to end.
Short-Row 3 (WS): Purl to double stitch, work double stitch as single stitch, p4 (4, 4, 5, 6, 6), {7, 8, 8, 9}, turn work.
Short-Row 4 (RS): Make double stitch, knit to end.

Short-Rows 5-14: Repeat last 2 short-rows 5 more times.

Next Row (WS): Purl to end, working double stitch as single stitch.

Work next 2 rows in Stockinette stitch.

Shape the right neckline
Increase Row (RS): Knit to last 2 stitches, M1R, k2. [1 stitch increased].
Next Row (WS): Purl to end.
Repeat last 2 rows another 3 times. [37 (42, 48, 54, 60, 65), {71, 78, 81, 88} stitches]

Join fronts
Joining Row (RS): Knit 37 (42, 48, 54, 60, 65), {71, 78, 81, 88} Right Front stitches, cast on 30 (32, 34, 34, 34, 38), {38, 38, 44, 44} stitches for the front neck, knit 37 (42, 48, 54, 60, 65), {71, 78, 81, 88} held Left Front stitches. [104 (116, 130, 142, 154, 168), {180, 194, 206, 220} stitches]

Continue working in Stockinette stitch in rows until armhole measures 5½ (6, 6, 6½, 7, 7), {8, 9, 9, 10}"/ 14 (15, 15, 16.5, 17.5, 17.5), {20, 22.5, 22.5, 25} cm from the pick-up row, ending with WS row.

05 BODY

Join Front and Back

Joining Row (RS): Knit 104 (116, 130, 142, 154, 168), {180, 194, 206, 220} Front stitches, place side marker, knit 104 (116, 130, 142, 154, 168), {180, 194, 206, 220} held Back stitches. Join in the round, place marker for the beginning of the round (BOR).
[208 (232, 260, 284, 308, 336), {360, 388, 412, 440} stitches]

Knit all stitches in the next 2 rounds.

Increase Round: K2, [M1L, k5] 8 (4, 10, 6, 2, 8), {4, 10, 6, 12} times, [M1L, k4] 15 (23, 19, 27, 35, 31), {39, 35, 43, 39} times, [M1L, k5] 8 (4, 10, 6, 2, 8), {4, 10, 6, 12} times, [M1L, k4] 16 (24, 20, 28, 36, 32), {40, 36, 44, 40} times, M1L, k2. [256 (288, 320, 352, 384, 416), {448, 480, 512, 544} stitches]

Next Round: Purl all stitches.
Next Round: Knit all stitches.

*** Chart Set-Up Round:** Work Row 1 of Cable Chart, working 16-stitch chart repeat 16 (18, 20, 22, 24, 26), {28, 30, 32, 34} times.
Continue following Cable Chart through Row 30.

Next Round: Knit all stitches.
Next Round: Purl all stitches.
Next Round: Knit all stitches. *

Repeat last 33 rows (from * to *) two more times.

Decrease Round: K2, [K2TOG, k4] 8 (4, 10, 6, 2, 8), {4, 10, 6, 12} times, [K2TOG, k3] 15 (23, 19, 27, 35, 31), {39, 35, 43, 39} times, [K2TOG, k4] 8 (4, 10, 6, 2, 8), {4, 10, 6, 12} times, [K2TOG, k3] 16 (24, 20, 28, 36, 32), {40, 36, 44, 40} times, K2TOG, k1.
[208 (232, 260, 284, 308, 336), {360, 388, 412, 440} stitches]

Continue working in Stockinette stitch in the round for 2"/5 cm.

Purl all stitches in the next 2 rounds.

Divide Front and Back as follows:
Division/Increase Round: Knit 104 (116, 130, 142, 154, 168), {180, 194, 206, 220} Front stitches to side marker, M1L, slip side marker, place just worked stitches on hold for the Front; knit 104 (116, 130, 142, 154, 168), {180, 194, 206, 220} Back stitches to BOR, M1L. [105 (117, 131, 143, 155, 167), {181, 195, 207, 221} for each Front and Back]

Change to US 3/3.25 mm 24-32"/60-80 cm circular needle and continue working on Back stitches.

Ribbing Row 1 (WS): P2, *k1, p1; repeat from * to last stitch, p1.
Ribbing Row 2 (RS): K2, *p1, k1; repeat from * to last stitch, k1.

Repeat Ribbing Rows 1 and 2 until Back ribbing measures 3"/7.5 cm, ending with RS row.

Bind off all stitches in pattern.
If you prefer using the Tubular method, work as follows:

Decrease Row (WS): Work in established pattern to last 2 stitches, P2TOG. [1 stitch decreased]

Work the Tubular Bind Off for k1, p1 rib (see Special Techniques, page 226).

Place Front stitches onto US 4/3.5 mm 24-32"/60-80 cm circular needle. Join yarn at the beginning of WS row and continue working as Back ribbing until Front ribbing measures 1½"/4 cm, ending with RS row.

Bind off all stitches in pattern.
If you prefer using the Tubular method, work as follows:

Decrease Row (WS): Work in established pattern to last 2 stitches, P2TOG. [1 stitch decreased]

Work the Tubular Bind Off for k1, p1 rib.

06 SLEEVES

With size US 4/3.5 mm double-pointed needles and RS facing, beginning at the center of underarm, pick up and knit 30 (33, 33, 35, 38, 38), {43, 48, 54, 57} stitches along armhole edge to held saddle stitches, place marker, work 14 held saddle stitches as follows: p1, k1, p1, work Row 2 of Seed Stitch in rows over next 8 stitches, p1, k1, p1, place marker, pick up and knit 30 (33, 33, 35, 38, 38), {43, 48, 54, 57} stitches to center of underarm cast on stitches.
[74 (80, 80, 84, 90, 90), {100, 110, 122, 128} stitches total]
Place BOR and join for working in the round.

Set-Up Round 1: Knit to marker, slip marker, p1, k1, p1, work Round 1 of Seed Stitch in the round over next 8 saddle stitches, p1, k1, p1, slip marker, knit to end.

Set-Up Round 2: Knit to marker, slip marker, p1, k1, p1, work Round 2 of Seed Stitch in the round over next 8 saddle stitches, p1, k1, p1, slip marker, knit to end.

Continue working in established pattern until sleeve measures 1"/2.5 cm.

Decrease Round: K1, SSK, work in established pattern to last 3 stitches, K2TOG, k1. [2 stitches decreased]

Repeat Decrease Round another 10 (13, 12, 14, 16, 16), {18, 23, 26, 28} times in every 11 (8, 9, 8, 7, 7), {6, 5, 4, 4}th round.
[52 (52, 54, 54, 56, 56), {62, 62, 68, 70} stitches]

Continue working without decreases, if necessary, until sleeve measures 14½"/36.5 cm.

Change to US 3/3.25 mm 24-32"/60-80 cm circular needle.

Ribbing Round: *K1, p1; repeat from * to the end of the round.
Repeat Ribbing Round until ribbing measures 3"/7.5 cm.

Knit all stitches in the next 3 rounds.
Bind off all stitches.

07 FINISHING

Neckband
With size US 3/3.25 mm double-pointed needles and RS facing, pick up and knit each of the 12 visible Right Saddle stitches, pick up and knit 36 (38, 40, 40, 40, 44), {44, 44, 50, 50} stitches along the Back neck, pick up and knit each of the 12 visible Left Saddle stitches, pick up and knit 56 (58, 60, 60, 60, 64), {64, 64, 70, 70} stitches along the Front neck.
[116 (120, 124, 124, 124, 132), {132, 132, 144, 144} stitches]
Place marker, join in the round.

Purl all stitches in the next 2 rounds.
Knit all stitches in the next round.

Ribbing Round: *K1, p1; repeat from * to the end.
Repeat Ribbing Round another 5 times.

Knit all stitches in the next 3 rounds.
Bind off all stitches.

Weave in ends. Block to measurements.

CHARTS

CABLE CHART

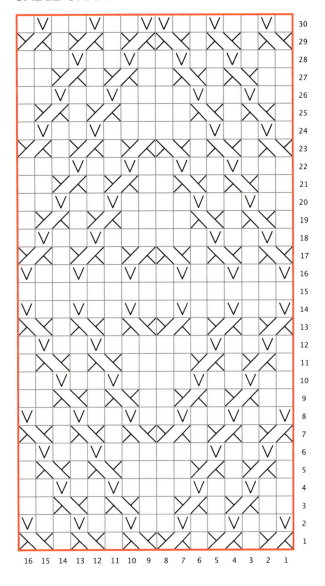

Written instructions for Slip Stitch Chart

... – pattern repeat

Note: See Chart Legend for special abbreviations.

Round 1: *[1/1 RC, k1] 2 times, 1/1 RC, [1/1 LC, k1] 2 times, 1/1 LC*.

Round 2: *[Slip 1 wyib, k2] 5 times, slip 1 wyib*.

Round 3: *K2, 1/1 RC, k1, 1/1 RC, k2, 1/1 LC, k1, 1/1 LC, k2*.

Round 4: *[K2, slip 1 wyib] 2 times, k4, [slip 1 wyib, k2] 2 times*.

Round 5: *[K1, 1/1 RC] 2 times, k4, [1/1 LC, k1] 2 times*.

Round 6: *K1, slip 1 wyib, k2, slip 1 wyib, k6, slip 1 wyib, k2, slip 1 wyib, k1*.

Rounds 7 - 12: Repeat rounds 1 - 6.

Rounds 13 - 14: Repeat rounds 1 - 2.

Round 15: Knit.

Round 16: *[Slip 1 wyib, k2] 5 times, slip 1 wyib*.

Round 17: *[1/1 LC, k1] 2 times, 1/1 LC, [1/1 RC, k1] 2 times, 1/1 RC*.

Round 18: *K1, slip 1 wyib, k2, slip 1 wyib, k6, slip 1 wyib, k2, slip 1 wyib, k1*.

Round 19: *[K1, 1/1 LC] 2 times, k4, [1/1 RC, k1] 2 times*.

Round 20: *[K2, slip 1 wyib] 2 times, k4, [slip 1 wyib, k2] 2 times*.

Round 21: *K2, 1/1 LC, k1, 1/1 LC, k2, 1/1 RC, k1, 1/1 RC, k2*.

Round 22: *K3, [slip 1 wyib, k2] 3 times, slip 1 wyib, k3*.

Rounds 23 - 28: Repeat round 17 - 22.

Round 29: *[1/1 LC, k1] 2 times, 1/1 LC, [1/1 RC, k1] 2 times, 1/1 RC*.

Round 30: *K1, [slip 1 wyib, k2] 2 times, slip 1 wyib 2 times, [k2, slip 1 wyib] 2 times, k1*.

LEGEND

☐ **K:** Knit stitch

▽ **Slip 1 wyib:** Slip 1 stitch purlwise with yarn in back

◨ **1/1 RC:** Slip 1 stitch to cable needle, hold in back, k1, k1 from cable needle

◨ **1/1 LC:** Slip 1 stitch to cable needle, hold in front, k1, k1 from cable needle

☐ Pattern repeat

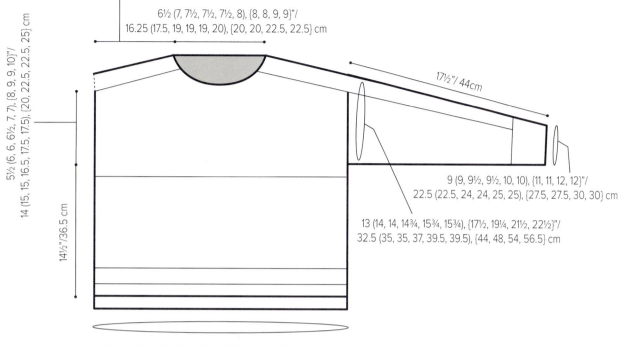

5¾ (6½, 7½, 8¾, 9¾, 10½), {11½, 13, 13½, 14½}"/
14.5 (16.5, 19, 22, 24.5, 26.5), {29, 32.5, 34, 36.5} cm

6½ (7, 7½, 7½, 7½, 8), {8, 8, 9, 9}"/
16.25 (17.5, 19, 19, 19, 20), {20, 20, 22.5, 22.5} cm

5½ (6, 6, 6½, 7, 7), {8, 9, 9, 10}"/
14 (15, 15, 16.5, 17.5, 17.5), {20, 22.5, 22.5, 25} cm

17½"/ 44cm

14½"/36.5 cm

9 (9, 9½, 9½, 10, 10), {11, 11, 12, 12}"/
22.5 (22.5, 24, 24, 25, 25), {27.5, 27.5, 30, 30} cm

13 (14, 14, 14¾, 15¾, 15¾), {17½, 19¼, 21½, 22½}"/
32.5 (35, 35, 37, 39.5, 39.5), {44, 48, 54, 56.5} cm

36¼ (40½, 45¼, 49½, 53½, 58½), {62½, 67½, 72, 76½}"/
90.5 (101.5, 113, 124, 134, 146.5), {156.5, 169, 180, 191.5} cm

Lyg

Richly textured cables bring warmth and character to this button-front cardigan. Worked in an engaging allover cable motif, the fabric has depth and dimension while maintaining a comfortable drape. The V-neckline and classic button band frame the design, giving it a versatile style that layers easily over casual or dressier outfits.

Stockinette sleeves provide contrast to the heavily patterned body, letting the cablework stand out while ensuring a smooth, easy fit through the arms. Ribbing at the hem, cuffs, and button band ties the design together with a neat finish.

Sizes

XS (S, M, L, XL, 2XL), {3XL, 4XL, 5XL, 6XL}: to fit bust 28-30 (32-34, 36-38, 40-42, 44-46, 48-50), {52-54, 56-58, 60-62, 64-66}"/70-75 (80-85, 90-95, 100-105, 110-115, 120-125), {130-135, 140-145, 150-155, 160-165} cm.

Finished Measurements

41 (45½, 50, 54½, 59, 63½), {68, 72½, 77, 81¼}"/ 102.5 (114, 125, 136.5, 147.5, 159), {170, 181.5, 192.5, 203.5} cm bust circumference, buttoned.
Intended Ease: +10–15"/25–37.5 cm.
Sample shown measures 50"/125 cm on 38"/95 cm bust with 12"/30 cm ease on model.

Yarn

DK weight yarn (approximate amounts): 1330 (1480, 1620, 1770, 1910, 2060), {2200, 2350, 2500, 2630} yards/1210 (1347, 1474, 1611, 1738, 1875), {2002, 2139, 2275, 2393} m.
Miss Babs Yowza (100% Superwash Merino Wool, 560 yds/512 m in 8 oz/225 gr), Cygnus: 3 (3, 3, 4, 4, 4), {4, 5, 5, 5} skeins.

Needles

Size US 6/4 mm: 32"/80 cm circular and set of double-pointed needles.
Size US 5/3.75 mm: 32"/80 cm circular and set of double-pointed needles.
Optional: spare size US 5/3.75 mm 32"/80 cm circular needle for Tubular Bind Off.
Adjust needle size if necessary to obtain the correct gauge.

Notions

Stitch markers, cable needle, stitch holders, waste yarn, tapestry needle, 5 buttons ⅞"/22 mm in diameter.

Gauge

22 stitches and 30 rows = 4"/10 cm in Stockinette stitch, on larger needles, after blocking.
25 stitches and 30 rows = 4"/10 cm in charted pattern, on larger needles, after blocking.

Notes

- The cardigan is worked in one piece from the bottom up to underarms; then fronts and back are worked separately. Stitches for sleeves are picked up along the armholes and sleeves are worked in the round from the top down.
- A circular needle is used to accommodate the large number of stitches.
- Read RS (odd-numbered) chart rows from right to left; read WS (even-numbered) chart rows from left to right.
- During shaping, if there are not enough stitches to work a complete cable crossing, work the stitches of the partial cable as they appear.

DIRECTIONS

01 BODY

NOTE: If you do not wish to work a Tubular Cast On, cast on 256 (284, 312, 340, 368, 396), {424, 452, 480, 508} stitches using US 5/3.75 mm 32"/80 cm circular needle, working yarn, and your preferred method, then proceed to the Ribbing Row 1.

Tubular Cast On (see Special Techniques, page 226)

With US 5/3.75 mm 32"/80 cm circular needle and waste yarn, cast on 128 (142, 156, 170, 184, 198), {212, 226, 240, 254} stitches with your preferred method.

Foundation Row (RS): Knit all stitches in row. This row is worked directly into your waste yarn stitches.
Row 1 (WS): Purl to end.
Row 2 (RS): Knit to end.
Row 3 (WS): Purl to end.

Carefully snip and remove the waste yarn from the cast-edge, placing the stitches onto the second US 5/3.75 mm 32"/80 cm circular needle as you go, and ending with the half-loop at the edge of the fabric. Make sure you have the same number of stitches on each needle. Bring the needle with the cast-on stitches up behind the working needle, wrong sides together.
Now we have 128 (142, 156, 170, 184, 198), {212, 226, 240, 254} stitches on first needle and 128 (142, 156, 170, 184, 198), {212, 226, 240, 254} cast-on stitches on the spare needle.

Next Row (RS): Purl 1 from back needle, *knit 2 from front needle, purl 2 from back needle; repeat from * to last 3 stitches, knit 2 from front needle, purl 1 from back needle. [256 (284, 312, 340, 368, 396), {424, 452, 480, 508} stitches on the needle]

Next Row (WS): K1, *p2, k2; repeat from * to last 3 stitches, p2, k1.

Ribbing Row 1 (RS): P1, *k2, p2; repeat from * to last 3 stitches, k2, p1.
Ribbing Row 2 (WS): K1, *p2, k2; repeat from * to last 3 stitches, p2, k1.
Work even in established pattern until piece measures 1¾"/4.5 cm from cast-on edge, ending with a WS row.

Change to US 6/4 mm 32"/80 cm circular needle.

Next Row (RS): K2, place marker, work Row 1 of Body Chart to last 2 stitches, place marker, k2.
Next Row (WS): P2, slip marker, work Row 2 of Body Chart to last 2 stitches, slip marker, p2.
Work even in established pattern until piece measures 12½ (12½, 12½, 12½, 12½, 12½), {13½, 13½, 13½, 13½}"/31.5 (31.5, 31.5, 31.5, 31.5, 31.5), {34, 34, 34, 34} cm from cast-on edge, ending with a WS row.

Shape Front Neck

Neck Decrease Row (RS): K2, slip marker, P2TOG, work as established to last 4 stitches, P2TOG, slip marker, k2. [2 stitches decreased]
Next Row (WS): P2, slip marker, work as established to last 2 stitches, slip marker, p2.

Repeat last 2 rows 6 more times. [242 (270, 298, 326, 354, 382), {410, 438, 466, 494} stitches remain]

Divide Fronts and Back

Division/Neck Decrease Row (RS): K2, slip marker, P2TOG, work next 52 (59, 66, 73, 80, 87), {94, 101, 108, 115} stitches in established pattern, place the last 55 (62, 69, 76, 83, 90), {97, 104, 111, 118} on hold for Right Front, bind off next 2 stitches, work next 126 (140, 154, 168, 182, 196), {210, 224, 238, 252} stitches and place them on hold for Back, bind off next 2 stitches, work in established pattern to last 4 stitches, P2TOG, slip marker, k2. [55 (62, 69, 76, 83, 90), {97, 104, 111, 118} stitches on the needle for Left Front]

Make note of last row of chart worked.
Continue working on Left Front stitches.

02 LEFT FRONT

Next Row (WS): P2, slip marker, work in established pattern to last 2 stitches, place marker, p2.

Shape Left Front Neck
Neck Decrease Row (RS): K2, slip marker, work in established pattern to last 4 stitches, P2TOG, slip marker, k2. [1 stitch decreased]

Continuing to work first and last stitches in stockinette stitch as established, repeat Neck Decrease Row every 2nd row 7 (6, 3, 3, 1, 3), {4, 3, 8, 4} more time(s), then every 4th row 4 (7, 10, 11, 13, 13), {13, 14, 12, 15} times.
[43 (48, 55, 61, 68, 73), {79, 86, 90, 98} stitches remain]

Work without decreases until Front measures 5½ (6¾, 7½, 8, 8½, 9), {9¼, 9½, 10, 10½}"/14 (17, 19, 20, 21.5, 22.5), {23, 24, 25, 26.5} cm from the Division Row, ending with WS row.

Make note of last row of chart worked.

Shape Left Shoulder
Note: Use the Sloped Bind Off (see Special Techniques, page 226) in this section for best results.

Bind off 6 (7, 8, 9, 10, 10), {11, 12, 13, 14} stitches at the beginning of the next 6 RS rows. [7 (6, 7, 7, 8, 13), {13, 14, 12, 14} stitches remain]

Work 1 WS row even.

Bind off remaining Left Front stitches.

03 RIGHT FRONT

Place 55 (62, 69, 76, 83, 90), {97, 104, 111, 118} held Right Front stitches on US 6/4 mm 32"/80 cm circular needle and join yarn with WS facing.

Next Row (WS): P2, place marker, work as established to last 2 stitches, slip marker, p2.

Shape Right Front Neck
Neck Decrease Row (RS): K2, slip marker, P2TOG, work in pattern to last 2 stitches, slip marker, k2. [1 stitch decreased]
Continuing to work first and last stitches in stockinette stitch as established, repeat Neck Decrease Row every 2nd row 7 (6, 3, 3, 1, 3), {4, 3, 8, 4} more time(s), then every 4th row 4 (7, 10, 11, 13, 13), {13, 14, 12, 15} times.
[43 (48, 55, 61, 68, 73), {79, 86, 90, 98} stitches remain]

Work without decreases until Front measures 5½ (6¾, 7½, 8, 8½, 9), {9¼, 9½, 10, 10½}"/14 (17, 19, 20, 21.5, 22.5), {23, 24, 25, 26.5} cm from the Division Row, ending with WS row.

Make note of last row of chart worked.

Shape Right Shoulder
NOTE: Use the Sloped Bind Off in this section for best results. Discontinue selvedge stitches at bind-off edge.

Bind off 6 (7, 8, 9, 10, 10), {11, 12, 13, 14} stitches at the beginning of the next 6 WS rows.
[7 (6, 7, 7, 8, 13), {13, 14, 12, 14} stitches remain]

Work 1 RS row even.

Bind off remaining Right Front stitches.

04 BACK

Place 126 (140, 154, 168, 182, 196), {210, 224, 238, 252} held Back stitches on US 6/4 mm 32"/80 cm circular needle and join yarn with WS facing.

Next Row (WS): P2, place marker, work in established pattern to last 2 stitches, place marker, p2.
Next Row (RS): K2, slip marker, work in established pattern to last 2 stitches, slip marker, k2.

Work even in established pattern until piece measures 5½ (6¾, 7½, 8, 8½, 9), {9¼, 9½, 10, 10½}"/ 14 (17, 19, 20, 21.5, 22.5), {23, 24, 25, 26.5} cm from the Division Row, ending with the same WS row of Chart as for Left Front.

Shape Back Shoulders

NOTE: Use the Sloped Bind Off in this section for best results. Discontinue selvedge stitches at bind-off edges.

Bind off 6 (7, 8, 9, 10, 10), {11, 12, 13, 14} stitches at the beginning of the next 12 rows, then 7 (6, 7, 7, 8, 13), {13, 14, 12, 14} stitches at the beginning of the next 2 rows.
Bind off remaining 40 (44, 44, 46, 46, 50), {52, 52, 58, 56} Back neck stitches.

05 SLEEVES

Sew shoulder seams.

With US 6/4 mm needles in preferred style for working small circumferences in the round, RS facing, and beginning at center of underarm, pick up and knit 60 (74, 82, 88, 94, 100), {102, 104, 110, 116} stitches around armhole. Place marker for beginning of the round and join for working in the round.

Work even in stockinette stitch (knit every round) for 1"/2.5 cm.

Decrease Round: K1, K2TOG, knit to last 3 stitches, SSK, k1. [2 stitches decreased]

Repeat Decrease Round every 18th (7th, 5th, 5th, 4th, 4th), {4th, 4th, 4th, 3rd} round 5 (12, 16, 17, 20, 21), {22, 21, 24, 27} more times. [48 (48, 48, 52, 52, 56), {56, 60, 60, 60} stitches remain]

Work even until sleeve measures 14¼"/35.5 cm from underarm.

Change to US 5/3.75 mm needles.

Next Round: K1, *p2, k2; repeat from * to last 3 stitches, p2, k1.
Work even until ribbing measures 1¾"/4.5 cm.

Bind off all stitches in pattern or using the Tubular Bind Off for k2, p2 ribbing in rounds (see Special Techniques, page 226).

06 FINISHING

Collar and Front Bands

NOTE: The ribbing pick-up ratio is approx. 5 stitches per 6 rows. If you're changing the number of pick-up stitches, make sure that the total number of stitches is divisible by 4.

With US 5/3.75 mm: 32"/80 cm circular needle and RS facing, beginning at hem edge, pick up and knit 72 stitches to the beginning of the neckline decreases, place marker, pick up and knit 58 (64, 70, 72, 76, 78), {86, 88, 90, 94} stitches along the neckline to the shoulder seam, 36 (40, 40, 44, 44, 48), {48, 48, 52, 52} stitches across back neck, 58 (64, 70, 72, 76, 78), {86, 88, 90, 94} stitches down the neckline to the beginning of the neckline decreases, place marker, pick up and knit 72 stitches down the left front edge. [296 (312, 324, 332, 340, 348), {364, 368, 376, 384} stitches]

Next Row (WS): P3, *k2, p2; repeat from * to last stitch, p1.
Next Row (RS): K3, *p2, k2; repeat from * to last stitch, k1.
Next Row (WS): Slip 1 purlwise with yarn in front, p2, *k2, p2; repeat from * to last stitch, slip 1 purlwise with yarn in front.
Repeat the last two rows one more time.

Buttonhole Row (RS): Work 6 stitches as established, SSK, [YO] 2 times, *work 14 stitches as established, SSK, [YO] 2 times; repeat from * 3 more times, work in pattern to end.
Next Row (WS): [Work to double YO, knit 1 dropping extra wrap] 5 times, work to end.

Work 4 rows even.

Bind off all stitches in pattern or using the Tubular Bind Off for k2, p2 ribbing in rows (see Special Techniques, page 226).

Weave in ends, block to measurements.
Sew on buttons to correspond to buttonholes.

CHARTS

BODY CHART

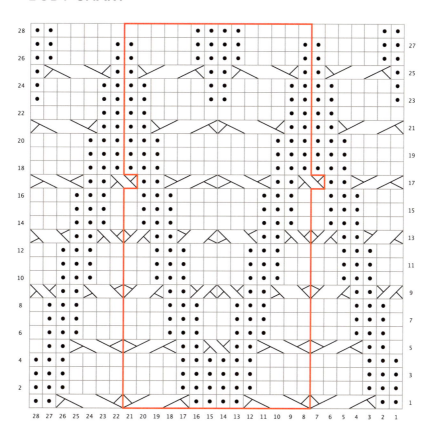

LEGEND

 K: Knit stitch on RS; purl stitch on WS

• P: Purl stitch on RS; knit stitch on WS

1/1 RC: Slip 1 stitch to cable needle, hold in back, k1, k1 from cable needle

1/1 LC: Slip 1 stitch to cable needle, hold in front, k1, k1 from cable needle

2/1 RC: Slip 1 stitch to cable needle, hold in back, k2, k1 from cable needle

2/1 LC: Slip 2 stitches to cable needle, hold in front, k1, k2 from cable needle

2/2 RC: Slip 2 stitches to cable needle, hold in back, knit 2, knit 2 from cable needle

2/2 LC: Slip 2 stitches to cable needle, hold in front, knit 2, knit 2 from cable needle

3/2 RC: Slip 2 stitches to cable needle, hold in back, knit 3, knit 2 from cable needle

3/2 LC: Slip 3 stitches to cable needle, hold in front, knit 2, knit 3 from cable needle

☐ Pattern repeat

Written instructions for Body Chart

Note: See Chart Legend for special abbreviations.
... - pattern repeat

Row 1 (RS): P2, 3/2 RC, *3/2 LC, p4, 3/2 RC*, 3/2 LC, p2.
Row 2 (WS): K3, p4, *p4, k6, p4*, p4, k3.
Row 3 (RS): P3, k4, *k4, p6, k4*, k4, p3.
Row 4 (WS): K3, p4, *p4, k6, p4*, p4, k3.
Row 5 (RS): K1, p2, 2/2 RC, *2/2 LC, p2, 1/1 LC, p2, 2/2 RC*, 2/2 LC, p2, k1.
Row 6 (WS): P1, k3, p3, *p3, k3, p2, k3, p3*, p3, k3, p1.
Row 7 (RS): K1, p3, k3, *k3, p3, k2, p3, k3*, k3, p3, k1.
Row 8 (WS): P1, k3, p3, *p3, k3, p2, k3, p3*, p3, k3, p1.
Row 9 (RS): 1/1 RC, p2, 2/1 RC, *2/1 LC, p2, 1/1 LC, 1/1 RC, p2, 2/1 RC*, 2/1 LC, p2, 1/1 LC.
Row 10 (WS): P2, k3, p2, *p2, k3, p4, k3, p2*, p2, k3, p2.
Row 11 (RS): K2, p3, k2, *k2, p3, k4, p3, k2*, k2, p3, k2.
Row 12 (WS): P2, k3, p2, *p2, k3, p4, k3, p2*, p2, k3, p2.

Row 13 (RS): 2/1 RC, p2, 1/1 RC, *1/1 LC, p2, 2/1 LC, 2/1 RC, p2, 1/1 RC*, 1/1 LC, p2, 2/1 LC.
Row 14 (WS): P3, k3, p1, *p1, k3, p6, k3, p1*, p1, k3, p3.
Row 15 (RS): K3, p3, k1, *k1, p3, k6, p3, k1*, k1, p3, k3.
Row 16 (WS): P3, k3, p1, *p1, k3, p6, k3, p1*, p1, k3, p3.
Row 17 (RS): 2/2 RC, p2, *1/1 LC, p2, 2/2 LC, 2/2 RC, p2*, 1/1 LC, p2, 2/2 LC.
Row 18 (WS): P4, k3, *k3, p8, k3*, k3, p4.
Row 19 (RS): K4, p3, *p3, k8, p3*, p3, k4.
Row 20 (WS): P4, k3, *k3, p8, k3*, k3, p4.
Row 21 (RS): 3/2 RC, p2, *p2, 3/2 LC, 3/2 RC, p2*, p2, 3/2 LC.
Row 22 (WS): P5, k2, *k2, p10, k2*, k2, p5.
Row 23 (RS): P1, k4, p2, *(p2, k4) × 2, p2*, p2, k4, p1.
Row 24 (WS): K1, p4, k2, *(k2, p4) × 2, k2*, k2, p4, k1.
Row 25 (RS): P1, 3/2 RC, p1, *p1, 3/2 LC, p2, 3/2 RC, p1*, p1, 3/2 LC, p1.
Row 26 (WS): K2, p4, k1, *k1, p4, k4, p4, k1*, k1, p4, k2.
Row 27 (RS): P2, k4, p1, *p1, k4, p4, k4, p1*, p1, k4, p2.
Row 28 (WS): K2, p5, *p5, k4, p5*, p5, k2.

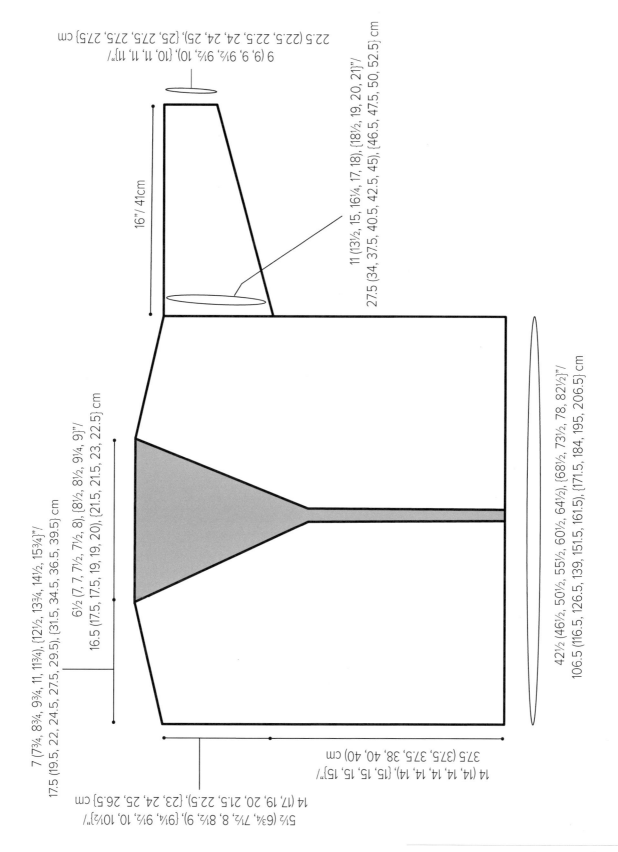

22.5 (22.5, 22.5, 24, 25), {25, 27.5, 27.5, 27.5} cm
9 (9, 9, 9½, 10), {10, 11, 11, 11}"/

16" / 41cm

27.5 (34, 37.5, 40.5, 42.5, 45), {46.5, 47.5, 50, 52.5} cm
11 (13½, 15, 16¼, 17, 18), {18½, 19, 20, 21}"/

106.5 (116.5, 126.5, 139, 151.5, 161.5), {171.5, 184, 195, 206.5} cm
42½ (46½, 50½, 55½, 60½, 64½), {68½, 73½, 78, 82½}"/

17.5 (19.5, 22, 24.5, 27.5, 29.5), {31.5, 34.5, 36.5, 39.5} cm
7 (7¾, 8¾, 9¾, 11, 11¾), {12½, 13¾, 14½, 15¾}"/

16.5 (17.5, 17.5, 19, 19, 20), {21.5, 21.5, 23, 22.5} cm
6½ (7, 7, 7½, 7½, 8), {8½, 8½, 9¼, 9}"/

37.5 (37.5, 37.5, 37.5, 38, 40), {40} cm
14 (14, 14, 14, 14), {15, 15, 15, 15}"/

14 (17, 19, 20, 21.5, 22.5), {23, 24, 25, 26.5} cm
5½ (6¾, 7½, 8, 8½, 9), {9¼, 9½, 10, 10½}"/

Elbrus

Inspired by the dramatic ridges and sharp contours of Mount Elbrus in the Caucasus, this pullover showcases bold geometric colorwork that echoes the mountain's angular slopes. The two-tone motif is worked in stranded knitting across the body, with mirrored lines that create depth and movement. Solid stockinette at the yoke, sleeves, and hem provides balance, letting the striking patterning take center stage.

The sweater features a straight body and set-in style sleeves for a comfortable fit. Worked seamlessly, the design highlights the rhythm of the charted motif while keeping construction approachable.

Sizes
XS (S, M, L, XL, 2XL), {3XL, 4XL, 5XL, 6XL}: to fit bust 28-30 (32-34, 36-38, 40-42, 44-46, 48-50), {52-54, 56-58, 60-62, 64-66}"/70-75 (80-85, 90-95, 100-105, 110-115, 120-125), {130-135, 140-145, 150-155, 160-165} cm.

Finished Measurements
37½ (41¼, 45, 49¼, 52½, 56½), {60¼, 64, 67¾, 70¾}"/94 (103, 112.5, 123, 131.5, 141.5), {150.5, 160, 169.5, 177} cm bust circumference.
Shown in size M (45"/112.5 cm) on 38"/95 cm bust with 7"/17.5 cm of positive ease.

Yarn
Fingering weight yarn (approximate amounts):
1300 (1430, 1560, 1700, 1820, 1960), {2090, 2220, 2350, 2450} yards/1183 (1301, 1420, 1547, 1656, 1784), {1902, 2020, 2139, 2230} m.

Color A (blue): 890 (975, 1070, 1160, 1240, 1340), {1430, 1520, 1610, 1670} yards/810 (887, 974, 1056, 1128, 1219), {1301, 1383, 1465, 1520} m.
Color B (off-white): 410 (455, 490, 540, 580, 620), {660, 700, 740, 780} yards/373 (414, 446, 491, 528, 564), {601, 637, 673, 710} m.

Miss Babs Putnam (75% Superwash Merino Wool, 25% Nylon; 400 yards/365 m in 3.9 oz/110 g),
Color A (blue): Pathway, 3 (3, 3, 3, 4, 4), {4, 4, 4, 5} skeins.
Color B (off-white): White Peppercorn, 2 skeins.

Needles
Sizes US 4/3.5 mm: 24-32"/60-80 cm circular.
Size US 3/3.25 mm: 24-32"/60-80 cm circular and 16"/40 cm. (Optional: spare needles of same size).
Set of double-pointed needles of the same sizes.
Adjust needle size if necessary to obtain gauge.

Notions
Stitch markers, removable stitch markers or safety pins, waste yarn, tapestry needle.

Gauge
26 stitches and 32 rounds = 4"/10 cm in Stockinette Stitch or charted pattern on size US 4/3.5 mm needle, after blocking.
28 stitches and 32 rounds = 4"/10 cm in charted pattern on size US 4/3.5 mm needle, after blocking.

Notes
- This pullover is worked from the top down in rows to underarms, then front and back are joined and body is worked in the round.
- Stitches for sleeves are picked up along the armholes and sleeves are worked in the round from the top down.

DIRECTIONS

01 BACK

With waste yarn, US 4/3.5 mm circular needle, cast on 88 (94, 98, 100, 108, 108), {110, 118, 130, 130} stitches.

Next Row (RS): With color A working yarn, knit all waste yarn stitches.
Next Row (WS): P22 (24, 26, 26, 30, 30), {30, 32, 36, 36}, place marker, p44 (46, 46, 48, 48, 48), {50, 54, 58, 58}, place marker, p22 (24, 26, 26, 30, 30), {30, 32, 36, 36} to end.

Shape Back shoulders, using German Short-Rows (see Special Techniques, page 226):
Short-Row 1 (RS): [Knit to marker, slip marker] 2 times, k4 (4, 5, 5, 5, 6), {7, 8, 8, 8}, turn.
Short-Row 2 (WS): Make double stitch, [purl to marker, slip marker] 2 times, p4 (4, 5, 5, 5, 6), {7, 8, 8, 8}, turn.
Short-Row 3 (RS): Make double stitch, knit to double stitch, work it as a single stitch, k4 (4, 5, 5, 5, 6), {7, 8, 8, 8}, turn.
Short-Row 4 (WS): Make double stitch, purl to double stitch, work it as a single stitch, p4 (4, 5, 5, 5, 6), {7, 8, 8, 8}, turn.
Short-Rows 5-6: Repeat Short-Rows 3 and 4 once.

Next Row (RS): Make double stitch, knit to end, working double stitch as a single stitch. Remove markers as you go.
Next Row (WS): Purl to end, working double stitch as a single stitch.

Continue working in Stockinette stitch in rows for 5 (4½, 4, 3½, 3¾, 5), {4½, 4¼, 5½, 4½}"/12.5 (11.5, 10, 9, 9.5, 12.5), {11.5, 10.5, 14, 11.5} cm from cast-on row, measured along the armhole edge, ending with WS row.

Shape armholes:
Increase Row (RS): K2, M1L, knit to last 2 stitches, M1R, k2. [2 stitches increased]
Next Row (WS): Purl.
Repeat last 2 rows another 1 (3, 7, 11, 12, 7), {11, 12, 11, 15} times. [92 (102, 114, 124, 134, 124), {134, 144, 154, 162} stitches]

Sizes XS (S, M, L, XL, _), {_, _, _, _} only:
Using Backward Loop method (see Special Techniques, page 226), cast on 2 stitches at the end of the next 6 rows.
[104 (114, 126, 136, 146, _), {_, _, _, _} stitches]
Using Backward Loop method, cast on 3 stitches at the end of the next 2 rows.
[110 (120, 132, 142, 152, _), {_, _, _, _} stitches]
Using Backward Loop method, cast on 6 (7, 7, 9, 9, _), {_, _, _, _} stitches at the end of the next 2 rows.
[122 (134, 146, 160, 170, _), {_, _, _, _} stitches]

Sizes _ (_, _, _, _, 2XL), {3XL, 4XL, 5XL, 6XL} only:
Using Backward Loop method (see Special Techniques, page 226), cast on 2 stitches at the end of the next 2 rows.
[_ (_, _, _, _, 128), {138, 148, 158, 166} stitches]
Using Backward Loop method, cast on 3 stitches at the end of the next 4 rows.
[_ (_, _, _, _, 140), {150, 160, 170, 178} stitches]
Using Backward Loop method, cast on 4 stitches at the end of the next 6 rows.
[_ (_, _, _, _, 164), {174, 184, 194, 202} stitches]
Using Backward Loop method, cast on _ (_, _, _, _, 10), {11, 12, 13, 14} stitches at the end of the next 2 rows.
[_ (_, _, _, _, 184), {196, 208, 220, 230} stitches]

All sizes:
Break yarn, place all 122 (134, 146, 160, 170, 184), {196, 208, 220, 230} Back stitches on hold.

02 FRONT

02a. Left Front
Beginning at the armhole edge of Left Shoulder, carefully unravel last 22 (24, 26, 26, 30, 30), {30, 32, 36, 36} provisionally cast-on stitches of the row and place these stitches on US 4/3.5 mm circular needle for Left Front. Do not remove waste yarn from remaining stitches. Join color A yarn with RS facing at the neck opening and continue working on Left Front stitches in rows.

Shape Left Front Shoulder, using German Short-Rows:

Short-Row 1 (RS): K4 (4, 5, 5, 5, 6), {7, 8, 8, 8}, turn.
Short-Row 2 (WS): Make double stitch, purl to end.
Short-Row 3 (RS): Knit to double stitch, work it as a single stitch, k4 (4, 5, 5, 5, 6), {7, 8, 8, 8}, turn.
Short-Row 4 (WS): Make double stitch, purl to end.
Short-Rows 5-6: Repeat Short-Rows 3 and 4 once.

Next Row (RS): Knit to end, working double stitch as a single stitch.
Next Row (WS): Purl.
Work even in Stockinette Stitch for 2 (2, 4, 4, 4, 4), {4, 4, 4, 4} rows.

Shape Left Front neckline

Increase Row (RS): K2, M1L, knit to end.
[1 stitch increased]
Next Row (WS): Purl.
Repeat last 2 rows another 4 (4, 4, 5, 5, 5), {6, 6, 6, 6} times. [27 (29, 31, 32, 36, 36), {37, 39, 43, 43} stitches]

Break yarn, place Left Front stitches on hold.

02b. Right Front

Beginning at the armhole edge of Right Shoulder, carefully unravel first 22 (24, 26, 26, 30, 30), {30, 32, 36, 36} provisionally cast-on stitches of the row and place these stitches on US 4/3.5 mm circular needle for Right Front. Do not remove waste yarn from remaining stitches. Join color A yarn at the neck opening with WS facing and continue working on Right Front stitches in rows.

Shape Right Front Shoulder

Short-Row 1 (WS): P4 (4, 5, 5, 5, 6), {7, 8, 8, 8}, turn.
Short-Row 2 (RS): Make double stitch, knit to end.
Short-Row 3 (WS): Purl to double stitch, work it as a single stitch, p4 (4, 5, 5, 5, 6), {7, 8, 8, 8}, wrap next stitch and turn.
Short-Row 4 (RS): Make double stitch, knit to end.
Short-Rows 5-6: Repeat Short-Rows 3 and 4 once.
Next Row (WS): Purl to end, working double stitch as a single stitch.
Work even in Stockinette Stitch for 2 (2, 4, 4, 4, 4), {4, 4, 4, 4} rows.

Shape Right Front neckline

Increase Row (RS): Knit to last 2 stitches, M1R, k2.
[1 stitch increased]
Next Row (WS): Purl.
Repeat last 2 rows another 4 (4, 4, 5, 5, 5), {6, 6, 6, 6} times. [27 (29, 31, 32, 36, 36), {37, 39, 43, 43} stitches]
Do not break yarn.

02c. Lower Front

Join Right and Left Fronts

Joining Row (RS): Knit 27 (29, 31, 32, 36, 36), {37, 39, 43, 43} Right Front stitches to end, then, using Backward Loop method, cast on 34 (36, 36, 36, 36), {36, 40, 44, 44} stitches, knit held 27 (29, 31, 32, 36, 36), {37, 39, 43, 43} Left Front stitches to end.
[88 (94, 98, 100, 108, 108), {110, 118, 130, 130} stitches]
Next Row (WS): Purl.

Continue working in Stockinette stitch in rows for 5 (4½, 4, 3½, 3¾, 5), {4½, 4¼, 5½, 4½}"/12.5 (11.5, 10, 9, 9.5, 12.5), {11.5, 10.5, 14, 11.5} cm from cast-on row, measured along the armhole edge, ending with WS row.
Work armhole shaping as for Back but do NOT break yarn at the end. [122 (134, 146, 160, 170, 184), {196, 208, 220, 230} on the needle for Front]

03 BODY

Join Back and Front

Joining Row (RS): With color A, knit across 122 (134, 146, 160, 170, 184), {196, 208, 220, 230} Front stitches, place marker for left side, knit across held 122 (134, 146, 160, 170, 184), {196, 208, 220, 230} Back stitches, place marker for the Beginning of the Round (BOR). Join for working in the round. [244 (268, 292, 320, 340, 368), {392, 416, 440, 460} stitches for Body]

Work in Stockinette stitch in the round for 1 (1, 1, 1, 4, 4), {4, 4, 4, 4} rounds.

Size XS only:

Increase Round: [M1L, k16] 2 times, [M1L, k15] 6 times, [M1L, k16] 2 times, [M1L, k15] 6 times. [260 stitches]

Size S only:
Increase Round: M1L, k14, [M1L, k15] 8 times, M1L, k14, [M1L, k15] 8 times. [286 stitches]

Size M only:
Increase Round: [M1L, k14] 4 times, [M1L, k15] 6 times, [M1L, k14] 4 times, [M1L, k15] 6 times. [312 stitches]

Size L only:
Increase Round: [M1L, k18] 7 times, [M1L, k17] 2 times, [M1L, k18] 7 times, [M1L, k17] 2 times. [338 stitches]

Size XL only:
Increase Round: [M1L, k14] 10 times, [M1L, k15] 2 times, [M1L, k14] 10 times, [M1L, k15] 2 times. [364 stitches]

Size 2XL only:
Increase Round: [M1L, k16] 3 times, [M1L, k17] 8 times, [M1L, k16] 3 times, [M1L, k17] 8 times. [390 stitches]

Size 3XL only:
Increase Round: [M1L, k16] 8 times, [M1L, k17] 4 times, [M1L, k16] 8 times, [M1L, k17] 4 times. [416 stitches]

Size 4XL only:
Increase Round: [M1L, k16] 26 times. [442 stitches]

Size 5XL only:
Increase Round: [M1L, k16] 10 times, [M1L, k15] 4 times, [M1L, k16] 10 times, [M1L, k15] 4 times. [468 stitches]

Size 6XL only:
Increase Round: [M1L, k14] 9 times, [M1L, k13] 8 times, [M1L, k14] 9 times, [M1L, k13] 8 times. [494 stitches]

All sizes:
Next Round: Knit.
Chart-Set-Up Round: Work Row 1 of Body Chart, working 26-stitch pattern repeat 10 (11, 12, 13, 14, 15), {16, 17, 18, 19} times around.
Work Body Chart through Row 48, then work rows 1-48 once more. Continue working with color A.

Size XS only:
Decrease Round: [K2TOG, k15] 2 times, [K2TOG, k14] 6 times, [K2TOG, k15] 2 times, [K2TOG, k14] 6 times. [244 stitches]

Size S only:
Decrease Round: K2TOG, k13, [K2TOG, k14] 8 times, K2TOG, k13, [K2TOG, k14] 8 times. [268 stitches]

Size M only:
Decrease Round: [K2TOG, k13] 4 times, [K2TOG, k14] 6 times, [K2TOG, k13] 4 times, [K2TOG, k14] 6 times. [292 stitches]

Size L only:
Decrease Round: [K2TOG, k17] 7 times, [K2TOG, k16] 2 times, [K2TOG, k17] 7 times, [K2TOG, k16] 2 times. [320 stitches]

Size XL only:
Decrease Round: [K2TOG, k13] 10 times, [K2TOG, k14] 2 times, [K2TOG, k13] 10 times, [K2TOG, k14] 2 times. [340 stitches]

Size 2XL only:
Decrease Round: [K2TOG, k15] 3 times, [K2TOG, k16] 8 times, [K2TOG, k15] 3 times, [K2TOG, k16] 8 times. [368 stitches]

Size 3XL only:
Decrease Round: [K2TOG, k15] 8 times, [K2TOG, k16] 4 times, [K2TOG, k15] 8 times, [K2TOG, k16] 4 times. [392 stitches]

Size 4XL only:
Decrease Round: [K2TOG, k15] 26 times. [416 stitches]

Size 5XL only:
Decrease Round: [K2TOG, k15] 10 times, [K2TOG, k14] 4 times, [K2TOG, k15] 10 times, [K2TOG, k14] 4 times. [440 stitches]

Size 6XL only:
Decrease Round: [K2TOG, k13] 9 times, [K2TOG, k12] 8 times, [K2TOG, k13] 9 times, [K2TOG, k12] 8 times. [460 stitches]
All sizes:
Knit all stitches in the next 2 rounds.

Change to US 3/3.25 mm 24-32"/60-80 cm circular needle.

Ribbing Round: K1, *p2, k2; repeat from * to last 3 stitches, p2, k1.
Repeat Ribbing Round until ribbing measures 2"/5 cm. Bind off all stitches in pattern of using Tubular bind off for k2, p2 rib in the round (see Special Techniques, page 226).

04 SLEEVES

Shape Cap
NOTE: Pick up stitches using US 3/3.25 mm double-pointed needles, then transfer them to US 4/3.5 mm double-pointed needles before beginning to work sleeve cap.

Place a removable stitch marker on front and back 1¼ (1¼, 1½, 1½, 1¾, 1¾), {2, 2, 2, 2}"/3 (3, 4, 4, 4.5, 4.5), {5, 5, 5, 5} cm down from the shoulder seam. Place a third marker at the center of the underarm. The marker to the left of the shoulder seam is M-1, to the right of shoulder is M-2, at underarm is M-3.

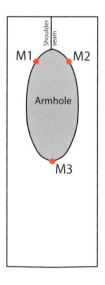

Begin at M-1. With color A, working just inside the column of knit stitches on the edge of armhole, pick up and knit 22 (22, 22, 26, 28, 30), {34, 34, 36, 36} stitches between M-1 and M-2, pick up and knit 28 (31, 35, 37, 38, 43), {45, 48, 50, 54} stitches between M-2 and M-3, place unique marker for beginning of round (BOR), pick up and knit 28 (31, 35, 37, 38, 43), {45, 48, 50, 54} more stitches, ending at M-1. [78 (84, 92, 100, 104, 116), {124, 130, 136, 144} stitches]

Remove M-1, M-2 and M-3.
Transfer stitches to US 4/3.5 mm double-pointed needles.

NOTE: Do not work wraps together with their wrapped stitches; the slipped stitches help reduce the size of the holes at the turning points, and the slip-stitch floats and wraps create a decorative effect along the cap edge.

Short-Row 1 (RS): K22 (22, 22, 26, 28, 30), {34, 34, 36, 36}, wrap next stitch and turn.
Short-Row 2 (WS): P22 (22, 22, 26, 28, 30), {34, 34, 36, 36}, wrap next stitch and turn.
Short-Row 3 (RS): Knit to wrapped stitch, knit wrapped stitch, slip 1 stitch with yarn in front, shift yarn to back, wrap next stitch and turn.
Short-Row 4 (WS): Purl to wrapped stitch, purl wrapped stitch, slip 1 stitch with yarn in back, bring yarn to front, wrap next stitch and turn.
Short-Rows 5-8: Repeat last 2 rows 2 more times.
Short-Row 9 (RS): Knit to wrapped stitch, knit wrapped stitch, wrap next stitch and turn.
Short-Row 10 (WS): Purl to wrapped stitch, purl wrapped stitch, wrap next stitch and turn.
Repeat last 2 rows 17 (18, 18, 19, 20, 21), {23, 23, 23, 23} more times.

Next Row (RS): Knit to wrapped stitch, knit wrapped stitch, knit to BOR.
Resume working in the round.

Shape Sleeve
Next Round: Knit to next wrapped stitch, knit wrapped stitch, knit to BOR.

Decrease Round: K1, K2TOG, knit to 3 stitches before the BOR, SSK, k1. [2 stitches decreased]
Repeat Decrease Round another 5 (3, 8, 9, 9, 16), {12, 13, 10, 6} times in every 12th (12th, 8th, 6th, 6th, 4th), {4th, 4th, 4th, 4th} round, then 1 (4, 1, 4, 4, 3), {11, 9, 15, 23} time(s) in every 10th (8th, 6th, 4th, 4th, 2nd), {2nd, 2nd, 2nd, 2nd} round [64 (68, 72, 72, 76, 76), {76, 84, 84, 84} stitches]

Continue working in Stockinette stitch in the round even, without decreases, if needed, until Sleeve measures 10"/25 cm from underarm.

Change to US 3/3.25 mm double-pointed needles.

Ribbing Round: K1, *p2, k2; repeat from * to last 3 stitches, p2, k1.
Repeat Ribbing Round until ribbing measures 2"/5 cm. Bind off all stitches in pattern of using Tubular bind off for k2, p2 rib in the round.

05 FINISHING

Carefully remove yarn from provisionally cast-on 44 (46, 46, 48, 48, 48), {50, 54, 58, 58} Back neck stitches, place them on US 3/3.25 mm 16"/40 cm circular needle.

Join color A yarn, and, with RS facing, knit these held stitches; with the same needle, pick up and knit 16 stitches evenly along left side of front neck, 28 (30, 30, 36, 36, 36), {38, 38, 42, 42} stitches evenly along center of front neck, 16 stitches evenly along right side of front neck. [104 (108, 108, 116, 116, 116), {120, 124, 132, 132} stitches now on needle]
Place the marker, join for working in the round.

Ribbing Round: K1, *p2, k2; repeat from * to last 3 stitches, p2, k1.
Repeat Ribbing Round until ribbing measures 1"/2.5 cm. Bind off all stitches in pattern of using Tubular bind off for k2, p2 rib.
Weave in ends. Block to measurements.

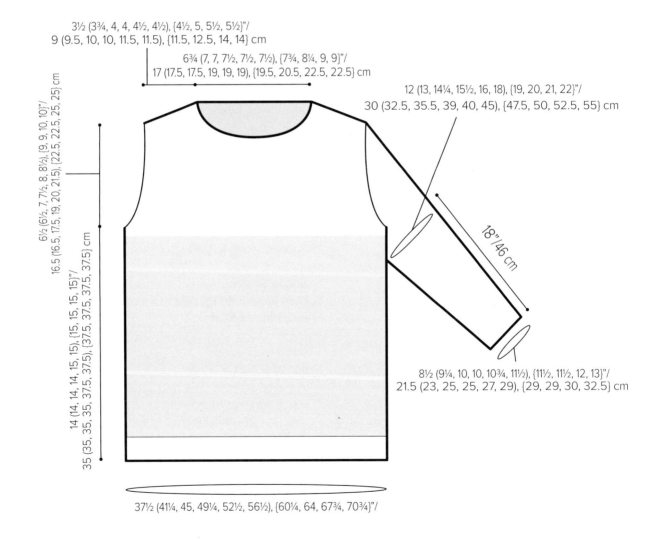

3½ (3¾, 4, 4, 4½, 4½), {4½, 5, 5½, 5½}"/
9 (9.5, 10, 10, 11.5, 11.5), {11.5, 12.5, 14, 14} cm

6¾ (7, 7, 7½, 7½, 7½), {7¾, 8¼, 9, 9}"/
17 (17.5, 17.5, 19, 19, 19), {19.5, 20.5, 22.5, 22.5} cm

12 (13, 14¼, 15½, 16, 18), {19, 20, 21, 22}"/
30 (32.5, 35.5, 39, 40, 45), {47.5, 50, 52.5, 55} cm

6½ (6½, 7, 7½, 8, 8½), {9, 9, 10, 10}"/
16.5 (16.5, 17.5, 19, 20, 21.5), {22.5, 22.5, 25, 25} cm

18"/46 cm

14 (14, 14, 14, 15, 15), {15, 15, 15, 15}"/
35 (35, 35, 35, 37.5, 37.5), {37.5, 37.5, 37.5, 37.5} cm

8½ (9¼, 10, 10, 10¾, 11½), {11½, 11½, 12, 13}"/
21.5 (23, 25, 25, 27, 29), {29, 29, 30, 32.5} cm

37½ (41¼, 45, 49¼, 52½, 56½), {60¼, 64, 67¾, 70¾}"/

CHARTS

BODY CHART

LEGEND

- ⬛ Knit with color A
- ⬜ Knit with color B
- ☐ Pattern repeat

Silvanus

Named after Silvanus, the Roman deity of woods and forests, this beret draws its inspiration from the natural rhythms of trees and leaves. It is worked in an organic lace-and-cables pattern that ripples outward like branches spreading through a canopy, creating a fabric full of movement and lightness. A snug ribbed band anchors the fit, while the body of the hat expands gracefully into the classic beret silhouette.

Finished Measurements

17½"/44 cm brim circumference.
8½"/21.5 cm height from base of ribbing to top center of crown.
Measurements are taken after blocking.
Fits average adult head sizes 20-21"/51-53 cm.

Yarn

Fingering weight yarn (appoximate amount):
200 yds/182 m.

Miss Babs Caroline (70% Superwash Merino Wool, 20% Cashmere, 10% Nylon; 400 yards/365 m in 3.3 oz/95 g): Old Gold - 1 skein.

Needles

Size US 3/3.25 mm circular 16"/40 cm long and set of double-pointed.
Size US 2/2.75 mm: 16"/40 cm long circular.
Adjust needle size if necessary to obtain gauge.

Notions

Stitch markers, cable needle, tapestry needle.

Gauge

22 stitches and 38 rounds = 4"/10 cm on size US 3/3.25 mm needles in charted pattern after blocking.

Notes

- This beret is worked from brim to crown in the round.
- All chart rounds are read from right to left.
- Knitters may consider placing markers between the chart repetitions.

DIRECTIONS

01 BRIM

With US 2/2.75 mm 16"/40 cm circular needle cast on 120 stitches. Join for working in the round, being careful not to twist stitches, place beginning-of-the round marker.

Ribbing Round: *K1 through back loop, p1; repeat from * to the end of the round.
Repeat Ribbing Round until brim measures 1¼"/3 cm in height.

02 BODY

Change to US 3/3.25 mm circular 16"/40 cm circular needle as you work the next round.
Next Round: Purl all stitches.

Increase Round: Work Round 1 of Body Chart. [150 stitches]
Next Round: Work Round 2 of Body Chart.

Work Rounds 3-18 of Body Chart 3 times total.

03 CROWN

Work rounds 1-21 of Crown Chart, changing to US 3/3.25 mm double-pointed needles when necessary. [10 stitches]

04 FINISHING

Cut yarn, leaving an 8"/20 cm tail. Using a tapestry needle, thread yarn tail through remaining stitches two times, then pull tightly. Weave in yarn ends.

Blocking Recommendations

Soak the beret in lukewarm water with a small amount of wool wash for 20 minutes. Lift the beret from the water and gently squeeze the excess water out of it. Lay it flat on a towel and roll the beret in the towel, gently squeezing more moisture out.
Lightly stretch the beret over the bottom of a 10-11"/25-27.5 cm dinner plate.
Carefully thread the waste yarn through the full circumference of the brim's top and gently tighten it to the required size.
Place the plate on a jar or something similar while it dries for maximum air circulation. Once it is completely dry, carefully remove the waste yarn. Remove the beret from the plate.
You can also block your finished project without a plate, just laying the beret flat on an appropriate blocking surface.

CHARTS

BODY CHART

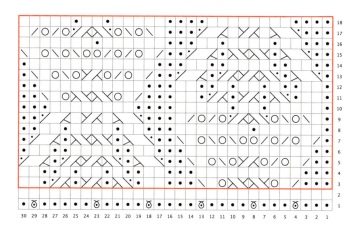

CROWN CHART

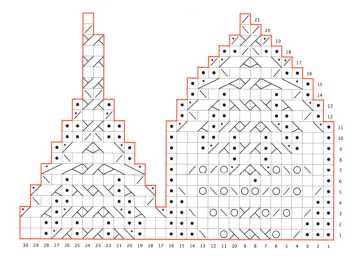

LEGEND

☐ K: Knit stitch

• P: Purl stitch

Ⓞ YO: Yarn over

Ⓞ M1P: With left needle tip, pick up the thread between stitches from back to front. Purl lifted loop through the front loop – 1 stitch increased

╱ K2TOG: Knit 2 stitches together – 1 stitch decreased with right slant

╲ SSK: Slip 1 stitch knitwise, slip 1 stitch knitwise, return 2 slipped stitches back to left needle and knit them through back loops – 1 stitch decreased with left slant

╱ P2TOG: Purl 2 stitches together – 1 stitch decreased

1/1 RC: Slip 1 stitch to cable needle, hold in back, knit 1, knit 1 from cable needle

1/1 LC: Slip 1 stitch to cable needle, hold in front, knit 1, knit 1 from cable needle

1/1 RPC: Slip 1 stitch to cable needle, hold in back, knit 1, purl 1 from cable needle

1/1 LPC: Slip 1 stitch to cable needle, hold in front, purl 1, knit 1 from cable needle

2/1 RPC: Slip 1 stitch to cable needle, hold in back, knit 2, purl 1 from cable needle

2/1 LPC: Slip 2 stitches to cable needle, hold in front, purl 1, knit 2 from cable needle

2/2 RPC: Slip 2 stitches to cable needle, hold in back, knit 2, purl 2 from cable needle

2/2 LPC: Slip 2 stitches to cable needle, hold in front, purl 2, knit 2 from cable needle

☐ Pattern repeat

Written instructions for Body Chart

... – pattern repeat

Note: See Chart Legend for special abbreviations.

Round 1: *P3, M1P, p3, [M1P, p4] 3 times, M1P, p5, M1P, p1* [150 stitches]

Round 2: Knit all stitches.

Round 3: *P3, K2TOG, k1, YO, [1/1 LC] twice, YO, k1, SSK, p3, k2, p1, 1/1 LPC, p1, 1/1 RC, p1, 1/1 RPC, p1, k2*

Round 4: *P3, k10, p3, k2, p2, k1, p1, k2, p1, k1, p2, k2*

Round 5: *P2, K2TOG, k1, YO, K2TOG, YO, 1/1 RC, YO, SSK, YO, k1, SSK, p2, 2/1 LPC, p1, 1/1 LPC, 1/1 RC, 1/1 RPC, p1, 2/1 RPC*

Round 6: *P2, k12, p3, k2, p2, k4, p2, k2, p1*

Round 7: *P1, K2TOG, k1, [YO, K2TOG] 2 times, [YO] 2 times, [SSK, YO] 2 times, k1, SSK, p2, 2/1 LPC, p1, [1/1 LC] 2 times, p1, 2/1 RPC, p1*

Round 8: *P1, k6, p1, k7, p3, k2, p1, k4, p1, k2, p2*

Round 9: *P1, k1, [SSK, YO] 2 times, 1/1 LPC, 1/1 RPC, [YO, K2TOG] 2 times, k1, p3, 2/1 LPC, k1, 1/1 RC, k1, 2/1 RPC, p2*

Round 10: *P1, k5, p1, k2, p1, k5, p4, k8, p3*

Round 11: *P1, k2, p1, 1/1 LPC, p1, 1/1 RC, p1, 1/1 RPC, p1, k2, p3, K2TOG, k1, YO, [1/1 LC] 2 times, YO, k1, SSK, p2*

Round 12: *P1, k2, p2, k1, p1, k2, p1, k1, p2, k2, p3, k10, p2*

Round 13: *P1, 2/1 LPC, p1, 1/1 LPC, 1/1 RC, 1/1 RPC, p1, 2/1 RPC, p2, K2TOG, k1, YO, K2TOG, YO, 1/1 RC, YO, SSK, YO, k1, SSK, p1*

Round 14: *P2, k2, p2, k4, p2, k2, p3, k12, p1*

Round 15: *P2, 2/1 LPC, p1, [1/1 LC] 2 times, p1, 2/1 RPC, p2, K2TOG, k1, [YO, K2TOG] 2 times, [YO] 2 times, [SSK, YO] 2 times, k1, SSK*

Round 16: *P3, k2, p1, k4, p1, k2, p3, k6, p1, k7*

Round 17: *P3, 2/1 LPC, k1, 1/1 RC, k1, 2/1 RPC, p3, k1, [SSK, YO] 2 times, 1/1 LPC, 1/1 RPC, [YO, K2TOG] 2 times, k1*

Round 18: *P4, k8, p4, k5, p1, k2, p1, k5*

Written instructions for Crown Chart

... – pattern repeat

Round 1: *P3, K2TOG, k1, YO, [1/1 LC] 2 times, YO, k1, SSK, p3, k2, p1, 1/1 LPC, p1, 1/1 RC, p1, 1/1 RPC, p1, k2*

Round 2: *P3, k10, p3, k2, p2, k1, p1, k2, p1, k1, p2, k2*

Round 3: *P2, K2TOG, k1, YO, K2TOG, YO, 1/1 RC, YO, SSK, YO, k1, SSK, p2, 2/1 LPC, p1, 1/1 LPC, 1/1 RC, 1/1 RPC, p1, 2/1 RPC*

Round 4: *P2, k12, p2, K2TOG, k1, p2, k4, p2, k1, SSK* [140 stitches]

Round 5: *P1, K2TOG, k1, [YO, K2TOG] 2 times, [YO] 2 times, [SSK, YO] 2 times, k1, SSK, p1, 2/1 LPC, p1, [1/1 LC] 2 times, p1, 2/1 RPC*

Round 6: *P1, k6, p1, k7, p1, K2TOG, k1, p1, k4, p1, k1, SSK* [130 stitches]

Round 7: *P1, k1, [SSK, YO] 2 times, 1/1 LPC, 1/1 RPC, [YO, K2TOG] 2 times, k1, p1, 2/2 LPC, 1/1 RC, 2/2 RPC*

Round 8: *P1, k5, p1, k2, p1, k5, p2, K2TOG, k4, SSK, p1* [120 stitches]

Round 9: *P1, k2, p1, 1/1 LPC, p1, 1/1 RC, p1, 1/1 RPC, p1, k2, p2, 2/1 LPC, 2/1 RPC, p1*

Round 10: *P1, k2, p2, k1, p1, k2, p1, k1, p2, k2, p3, SSK, K2TOG, p2* [110 stitches]

Round 11: *P1, 2/1 LPC, p1, 1/1 LPC, 1/1 RC, 1/1 RPC, p1, 2/1 RPC, p3, 1/1 RC, p2*

Round 12: *P1, K2TOG, k1, p2, k4, p2, k1, SSK, p1, P2TOG, k2, P2TOG* [90 stitches]

Round 13: *P1, 2/1 LPC, p1, [1/1 LC] 2 times, p1, 2/1 RPC, p2, 1/1 RC, p1*

Round 14: *P1, K2TOG, k1, p1, k4, p1, k1, SSK, p1, K2TOG, SSK* [70 stitches]

Round 15: *P1, 2/2 LPC, 1/1 RC, 2/2 RPC, p1, 1/1 RC*

Round 16: *P2, K2TOG, k4, SSK, p2, k2* [60 stitches]

Round 17: *P2TOG, 2/1 LPC, 2/1 RPC, P2TOG, 1/1 RC* [50 stitches]

Round 18: *P2, SSK, K2TOG, p2, k2* [40 stitches]

Round 19: *[P2TOG, 1/1 RC] 2 times* [30 stitches]

Round 20: *K2TOG, SSK, K2TOG* [15 stitches]

Round 21: *K2TOG, k1* [10 stitches]

Topology

Geometric order and optical play define this cardigan, where the stitchwork is inspired by Escher's mathematical art. Lines of textured knit and purl create shifting planes across the body, suggesting depth and layered surfaces that change with movement and light. The cardigan is worked flat and features a classic button band and crew neckline, giving a structured frame to the dynamic patterning. Drop-shoulder sleeves keep the silhouette relaxed. Minimalist yet full of intrigue, the design invites knitters to engage with structure as much as surface. The result is a cardigan that feels at once contemporary and artful, bringing mathematical inspiration into everyday wear.

Sizes

XS (S, M, L, XL, 2XL), {3XL, 4XL, 5XL, 6XL}: to fit bust 28-30 (32-34, 36-38, 40-42, 44-46, 48-50), {52-54, 56-58, 60-62, 64-66}"/70-75 (80-85, 90-95, 100-105, 110-115, 120-125), {130-135, 140-145, 150-155, 160-165} cm.

Finished Measurements

37¼ (41¼, 43½, 47½, 51¾, 55¾), {59¾, 64, 68½, 72½}"/93 (103, 109, 119, 129.5, 139.5), {149.5, 160, 171.5, 181.5) cm circumference at chest.
Intended Ease: + 5–10"/12.5–25 cm.
Sample shown is size 47½"/119 cm with 8½"/21.5 cm ease on model.

Yarn

Fingering weight yarn (approximate amounts):
1180 (1330, 1400, 1530, 1670, 1800), {1930, 2060, 2200, 2330} yards/1074 (1210, 1274, 1392, 1520, 1638), {1756, 1875, 2002, 2120} m.

Miss Babs Putnam (400 yds/365 m in 3.9 oz/110 gr), Dark Parchment: 3 (4, 4, 4, 5, 5), {5, 6, 6, 6} skeins.

Needles

Size US 3/3.25 mm: 24-32"/60-80 cm circular and set of double-pointed needles.
Size US 2/2.75 mm: 24-32"/60-80 cm circular, 16"/40 cm circular, and set of double-pointed needles.
Adjust needle size if necessary to obtain gauge.

Notions

Stitch markers, stitch holders, tapestry needle, 7 buttons ⅝"/16 mm.

Gauge

26 stitches and 34 rows = 4"/10 cm in Stockinette stitch or charted pattern on larger needles, after blocking.

Notes

- The cardigan is worked in one piece from the bottom up to underarms; then fronts and back are worked separately. Stitches for sleeves are picked up along the armholes and sleeves are worked in the round from the top down.
- A circular needle is used to accommodate the large number of stitches.
- Read RS (odd-numbered) chart rows from right to left; read WS (even-numbered) chart rows from left to right.

Stitch Guide

Garter Stitch (in rows)
Row 1 (RS): Knit.
Row 2 (WS): Knit.
Repeat last 2 rows for pattern.

Garter Stitch (in the round)
Round 1: Knit.
Round 2: Purl.
Repeat last 2 rounds for pattern.

Stockinette Stitch
RS rows and all rounds: Knit.
WS rows: Purl.

Reverse Stockinette Stitch
RS rows and all rounds: Purl.
WS rows: Knit.

DIRECTIONS

01 BODY

With US 2/2.75 circular needle 32"/80 cm long, cast on 236 (262, 276, 302, 330, 356), {382, 410, 438, 464} stitches [suggested: Old Norwegian method (see Special Techniques, page 226)].

Work in Garter stitch in rows until piece measures 2"/5 cm from the cast-on edge, ending with WS row.

Change to US 3/3.25 circular needle 32"/80 cm long.

Next Row (RS): K114 (127, 134, 147, 161, 174), {187, 201, 215, 228}, place marker, p8, place marker, knit 114 (127, 134, 147, 161, 174), {187, 201, 215, 228} stitches to end.
Next Row (WS): Work all stitches as they appear (purl the purl stitches and knit the knit stitches) to end.

Repeat last 2 rows another 4 times, slipping markers [Total of 10 rows]

Chart Set-Up Row 1 (RS): K7, place marker, work Row 1 of Chart A over 36 stitches, place marker, work Row 1 of Chart C over 29 (42, 49, 62, 76, 89), {102, 116, 130, 143} stitches, place marker, work Row 1 of Chart B over 36 stitches, place marker, k6 to marker, slip marker, p8, slip marker, k6, place marker, work Row 1 of Chart A over 36 stitches, place marker, work Row 1 of Chart C over 29 (42, 49, 62, 76, 89), {102, 116, 130, 143} stitches, place marker, work Row 1 of Chart B over 36 stitches, place marker, k7.

Chart Set-Up Row 2 (WS): Purl to marker, slip marker, work Row 2 of Chart B, slip marker, work Row 2 of Chart C to marker, slip marker, work Row 2 of Chart A, slip marker, purl to marker, slip marker, knit to marker, slip marker, purl to marker, slip marker, work Row 2 of Chart B, slip marker, work Row 2 of Chart C to marker, slip marker, work Row 2 of Chart A, slip marker, purl to end.

Continue working in established pattern through Row 48 of charts, then work Rows 47 and 48 of charts until Body measures 12 (12, 13, 13, 13, 13), {14, 14, 14, 14}"/30 (30, 32.5, 32.5, 32.5, 32.5), {35, 35, 35, 35} cm from the cast on edge, ending with WS row.

Divide for fronts and back

Division Row (RS): Work in established pattern 58 (64, 68, 74, 82, 88), [94, 102, 108, 114] stitches, place just worked stitches on hold for right front, work next 120 (134, 140, 154, 166, 180), [194, 206, 222, 236] stitches and place them on hold for back, work to end – 58 (64, 68, 74, 82, 88), {94, 102, 108, 114} stitches on the needle for left front.

Continue working on left front stitches.

02 LEFT FRONT

Work in rows in established pattern on 58 (64, 68, 74, 82, 88), [94, 102, 108, 114] left front stitches until front measures 5, (5, 5½, 5½, 6, 6), {6½, 7, 8, 8½}"/12.5 (12.5, 14, 14, 15, 15), {16.5, 17.5, 20, 21.5} cm from Division Row, ending with RS row.

Shape neckline

At the beginning of WS rows, bind off 10 (9, 10, 10, 13, 12), {12, 16, 16, 16} stitches once, 3 stitches once, 2 stitches once and 1 stitch 3 times. [40 (47, 50, 56, 61, 68), {74, 78, 84, 90} stitches on the needle]
Next Row (RS): Work all stitches in pattern.

Shape left shoulder, using the German Short-Rows (see Special Techniques, page 226):
Short-Row 1 (WS): Work in pattern to last 4 (4, 4, 5, 6, 6), {7, 8, 8, 9} stitches, turn work.
Short-Row 2 (RS): Make double stitch, work in pattern to end.
Short-Row 3 (WS): Work in pattern to 3 (3, 3, 4, 5, 5), {6, 7, 7, 8} stitches before double stitch, turn work.
Short-Row 4 (RS): Make double stitch, work in pattern to end.

Short-Rows 5-18: Repeat last 2 rows 7 more times.

Next Row (WS): Work all left shoulder stitches in pattern to end, working double stitches as single stitches.
Place all stitches on hold. Break yarn, leaving long tail for 3-Needle Bind Off.

03 BACK

Place held 120 (134, 140, 154, 166, 180), [194, 206, 222, 236] Back stitches onto US 3/3.25 mm needle. Join yarn, ready to work WS row.
Work in rows in established pattern until Back measures 6½, (6½, 7, 7, 7½, 7½), [8, 8½, 9½, 10]"/ 16.5 (16.5, 17.5, 17.5, 19, 19), {20, 21.5, 24, 25} cm from Division Row, ending with WS row.

Start shaping shoulders:
Short-Row 1 (RS): Work in pattern to last 4 (4, 4, 5, 6, 6), {7, 8, 8, 9} stitches, turn work.
Short-Row 2 (WS): Make double stitch, work in pattern to last 4 (4, 4, 5, 6, 6), {7, 8, 8, 9} stitches, turn work.
Short-Row 3 (RS): Make double stitch, work in pattern to 3 (3, 3, 4, 5, 5), {6, 7, 7, 8} stitches before double stitch, turn work.
Short-Row 4 (WS): Make double stitch, work in pattern to 3 (3, 3, 4, 5, 5), {6, 7, 7, 8} stitches before double stitch, turn work.

Short-Rows 5-18: Repeat last 2 rows 7 more times.
Next Row (RS): Make double stitch, work all stitches in pattern to end, working double stitches as single stitches.
Next Row (WS): Work 40 (47, 50, 56, 61, 68), {74, 78, 84, 90} left shoulder stitches in pattern and place them on hold, bind off next 40 (40, 40, 42, 44, 44), {46, 50, 54, 56} stitches for back neck, work last 40 (47, 50, 56, 61, 68), {74, 78, 84, 90} right shoulder stitches in pattern, working DS as single stitches.

Place right shoulder stitches on hold.

04 RIGHT FRONT

Place held 58 (64, 68, 74, 82, 88), {94, 102, 108, 114} right front stitches onto US 3/3.25 mm needle. Join yarn from WS row.
Work in rows in established pattern until front measures 5, (5, 5½, 5½, 6, 6), [6½, 7, 8, 8½]"/12.5 (12.5, 14, 14, 15, 15), {16.5, 17.5, 20, 21.5} cm from Division Row, ending with WS row.

Shape neckline

At the beginning of RS rows, bind off 10 (9, 10, 10, 13, 12), {12, 16, 16, 16} stitches once, 3 stitches once, 2 stitches once and 1 stitch 3 times. [40 (47, 50, 56, 61, 68), {74, 78, 84, 90} stitches on the needle]
Next Row (WS): Work all stitches in pattern.

Start shaping right shoulder:
Short-Row 1 (RS): Work in pattern to last 4 (4, 4, 5, 6, 6), {7, 8, 8, 9} stitches, turn work.
Short-Row 2 (WS): Make double stitch, work in pattern to end.
Short-Row 3 (RS): Work in pattern to 3 (3, 3, 4, 5, 5), {6, 7, 7, 8} stitches before double stitch, turn work.
Short-Row 4 (WS): Make double stitch, work in pattern to end.

Short-Rows 5-18: Repeat last 2 rows 7 more times.
Next Row (RS): Work all right shoulder stitches in pattern to end, working double stitches as single stitches.
Place all stitches on hold. Do not break yarn.
Join live shoulder stitches with 3-Needle Bind Off (see Special Techniques, page 226).

05 SLEEVES

With US 3/3.25 mm double-pointed needles, pick up and knit 88 (88, 94, 94, 102, 102), {108, 114, 128, 136} stitches along the armhole, beginning at underarm. Join in the round.

Knit all stitches for 2 rounds.

NOTE: The sleeve stitch pattern and the shaping occur at the same time. Please read the following section through.

Continue working in Stockinette stitch in the round for 9½"/24 cm, then work:
8 rounds in Reverse stockinette stitch in the round,
6 rounds in Stockinette stitch in the round.
Repeat last 14 rounds once more.

Work 8 rounds in Reverse stockinette stitch in the round. Continue work in Stockinette stitch in the round.

AT THE SAME TIME (in 2 rows after picking up Sleeve stitches) shape the sleeves as follows:
Decrease Round: Work 1 stitch, K2TOG (or P2TOG, to keep in pattern), work to last 3 stitches, SSK (or P2TOG), work last stitch.

Repeat Decrease Round 13 (13, 16, 14, 18, 18), {19, 21, 26, 30} more times in every 10 (10, 8, 8, 7, 7), {7, 6, 4, 4}th round. [60 (60, 60, 64, 64, 64), {68, 70, 74, 74} stitches]

Continue working in pattern until sleeve measures 16 (16, 16, 16, 16, 16), {16, 15½, 15½, 15}"/40 (40, 40, 40, 40, 40), {40, 39, 39, 37.5} cm.

Change to US 2/2.75 mm double-pointed needles.

Start working the cuff:
Next Round: K1, purl to end.
Next Round: Knit to end.
Repeat last 2 rounds until cuff measures 1½"/4 cm.
Next Round: K1, purl to end.

Bind off all stitches.

06 FINISHING

Neckband
With US 2/2.75 mm circular needle and RS facing, pick up and knit 114 (114, 114, 116, 118, 118), {120, 122, 124, 126} stitches evenly around neck edge.

Next Row (WS): Knit to end.
Next Row (RS): Knit to end.
Repeat last 2 rows 5 more times, then work one more WS row. Bind off all stitches.

Button band
NOTE: The pick-up ratio on bands is 5 stitches per 6 rows.

With US 2/2.75 mm circular needle and RS facing, pick up and knit 116 (116, 126, 126, 132, 132), {140, 142, 150, 152} stitches along left front edge, starting with the collar. Begin working in rows.
Next Row (WS): Knit.
Next Row (RS): Knit.
Repeat last 2 rows 5 more times, then work one more WS row. Bind off all stitches.

Buttonhole band
With US 2/2.75 mm circular needle and RS facing, starting at the lower edge of the right front, pick up and knit 116 (116, 126, 126, 132, 132), {140, 142, 150, 152} stitches along the right front.

Next Row (WS): Knit.
Next Row (RS): Knit.
Repeat last 2 rows one more time.

Next Row (WS): Knit.
Buttonhole row (RS): K6 (6, 5, 5, 5, 5), {6, 4, 5, 6}, *SSK, YO, k15 (15, 17, 17, 18, 18), {19, 20, 21, 21}; repeat from * 5 more times, SSK, YO, k6 (6, 5, 5, 5, 5), {6, 4, 5, 6} stitches to end.
Next Row (WS): Knit all stitches, knitting each YO.
Next Row (RS): Knit.
Next Row (WS): Knit.
Repeat last 2 rows twice more. Bind off all stitches.

Weave in ends, block to measurements. Sew on buttons.

CHARTS

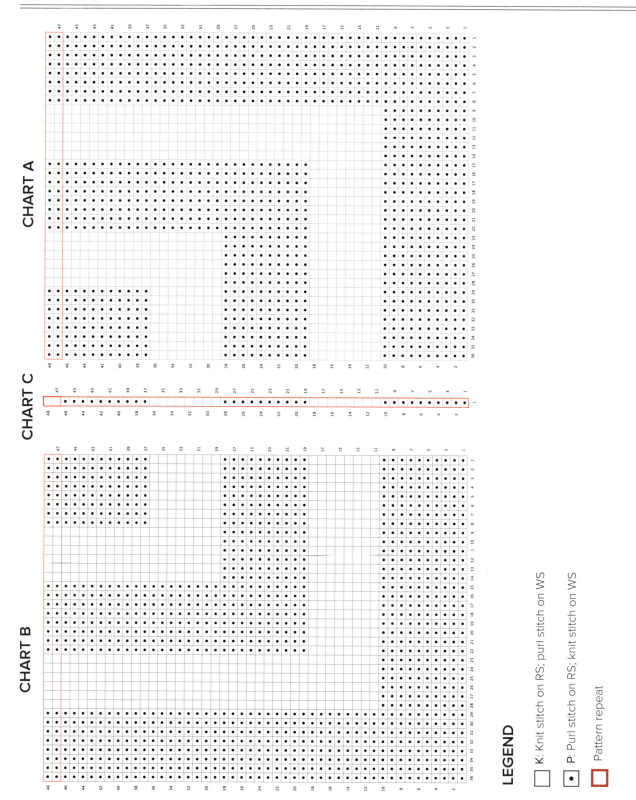

LEGEND

☐ K: Knit stitch on RS; purl stitch on WS

▣ P: Purl stitch on RS; knit stitch on WS

▢ Pattern repeat

Written instructions for Chart A

Note: See Chart Legend for special abbreviations.

Row 1 (RS): Purl.
Row 2 (WS): Knit.
Rows 3 - 10: Repeat rows 1 - 2.
Row 11 (RS): P8, k28.
Row 12 (WS): P28, k8.
Rows 13 - 18: Repeat rows 11 - 12.
Row 19 (RS): P8, k6, p22.
Row 20 (WS): K22, p6, k8.
Rows 21 - 28: Repeat rows 19 - 20.
Row 29 (RS): P8, k6, p8, k14.
Row 30 (WS): P14, k8, p6, k8.
Rows 31 - 36: Repeat rows 29 - 30.
Row 37 (RS): [P8, k6] 2 times, p8.
Row 38 (WS): [K8, p6] 2 times, k8.
Rows 39 - 48: Repeat rows 37 - 38.

Written instructions for Chart B

Row 1 (RS): Purl.
Row 2 (WS): Knit.
Rows 3 - 10: Repeat rows 1 - 2.
Row 11 (RS): K28, p8.
Row 12 (WS): K8, p28.
Rows 13 - 18: Repeat rows 11 - 12.
Row 19 (RS): P22, k6, p8.
Row 20 (WS): K8, p6, k22.
Rows 21 - 28: Repeat rows 19 - 20.
Row 29 (RS): K14, p8, k6, p8.
Row 30 (WS): K8, p6, k8, p14.
Rows 31 - 36: Repeat rows 29 - 30.
Row 37 (RS): [P8, k6] 2 times, p8.
Row 38 (WS): [K8, p6] 2 times, k8.
Rows 39 - 48: Repeat rows 37 - 38.

Written instructions for Chart C

Row 1 (RS): Purl.
Row 2 (WS): Knit.
Rows 3 - 10: Repeat rows 1 - 2.
Row 11 (RS): Knit.
Row 12 (WS): Purl.
Rows 13 - 18: Repeat rows 11 - 12.
Row 19 (RS): Purl.
Rows 20 - 37: Repeat rows 2 - 19.
Row 38 (WS): Knit.
Row 39 (RS): Purl.
Rows 40 - 45: Repeat rows 38 - 39.
Rows 46 (WS): Knit.

Row 47 (RS): Knit.
Row 48 (WS): Purl.

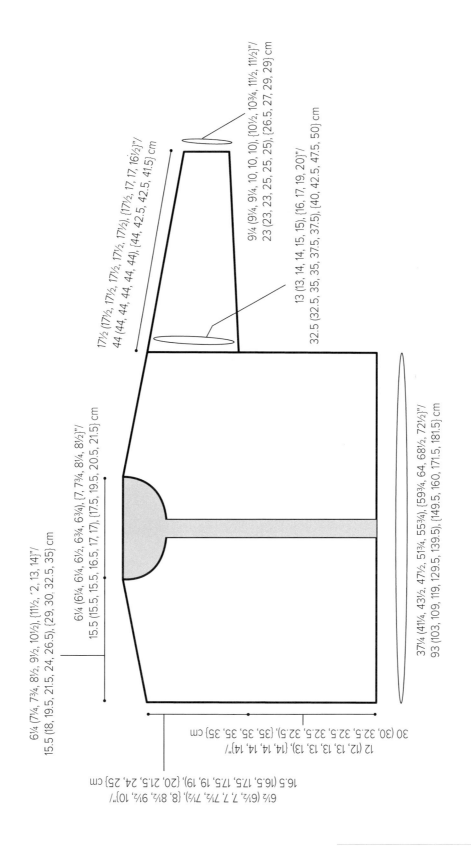

17½ (17½, 17½, 17½, 17½, 17½), [17½, 17, 17, 16½)]" /
44 (44, 44, 44, 44, 44), [44, 42.5, 42.5, 41.5] cm

9¼ (9¼, 9¼, 10, 10, 10), [10½, 10¾, 11½, 11½)]" /
23 (23, 23, 25, 25, 25), [26.5, 27, 29, 29] cm

13 (13, 14, 14, 15, 15), [16, 17, 19, 20]" /
32.5 (32.5, 35, 35, 37.5, 37.5), [40, 42.5, 47.5, 50] cm

6¼ (7¼, 7¾, 8½, 9½, 10½), [11½, ʼ2, 13, 14]" /
15.5 (18, 19.5, 21.5, 24, 26.5), [29, 30, 32.5, 35] cm

6¼ (6¼, 6¼, 6½, 6¾, 6¾), [7, 7¾, 8¼, 8½)]" /
15.5 (15.5, 15.5, 16.5, 17, 17), [17.5, 19.5, 20.5, 21.5] cm

37¼ (41¼, 43½, 47½, 51¾, 55¾), [59¾, 64, 68½, 72½)]" /
93 (103, 109, 119, 129.5, 139.5), [149.5, 160, 171.5, 181.5] cm

30 (30, 32.5, 32.5, 32.5), [35, 35, 35, 35] cm
12 (12, 13, 13, 13), [14, 14, 14, 14]" /

16.5 (16.5, 17.5, 19, 19), [20, 21.5, 24, 25] cm
6½ (6½, 7, 7, 7½, 7½), [8, 8½, 9½, 10]" /

Dorabella

Delicate lace motifs crown the yoke of this top-down pullover, flowing into columns of purl stitches that travel down the body and sleeves. The textured vertical lines add rhythm to the smooth stockinette background, creating visual interest while letting the yoke remain the focal point.

Voluminous sleeves taper gently into fitted cuffs, giving the sweater a soft, modern silhouette that balances ease with refinement. Worked seamlessly from the neckline down, the pullover offers straightforward construction with easy opportunities to adjust sleeve or body length.

Sizes
XS (S, M, L, XL, 2XL), {3XL, 4XL, 5XL, 6XL}: to fit bust 28-30 (32-34, 36-38, 40-42, 44-46, 48-50), {52-54, 56-58, 60-62, 64-66}"/70-75 (80-85, 90-95, 100-105, 110-115, 120-125), {130-135, 140-145, 150-155, 160-165} cm.

Finished Measurements
33¼ (37¼, 41¼, 44½, 48½, 53½), {56½, 60, 63, 66}"/83 (93, 103, 111.5, 121.5, 134), {141.5, 150, 157.5, 165} cm bust circumference.
Pullover shown measures M (41¼"/103 cm) on 38"/95 cm bust with 3¼"/8 cm of positive ease.

Yarn
Fingering weight yarn (approximate amounts):
1190 (1330, 1470, 1580, 1760, 1905), {2050, 2150, 2270, 2380} yards/1083 (1210, 1338, 1438, 1602, 1734), {1866, 1957, 2066, 2166} m.

Miss Babs Caroline (70% Superwash Merino Wool, 20% Cashmere, 10% Nylon; 400 yards/ 365 m in 95 g), Roasted Pumpkin: 3 (4, 4, 4, 4, 5), {5, 6, 6, 6} skeins.

Needles
Size US 3/3.25 mm: 24-32"/60-80 cm circular, 16"/40 cm circular and set of double-pointed.
Size US 2/2.75 mm: 24-32"/60-80 cm circular (optional: spare needle of same size), 16"/40 cm circular and set of double-pointed.
Adjust needle size if necessary to obtain gauge.

Notions
Stitch markers, stitch holders or waste yarn, tapestry needle, cable needle.

Gauge
28 stitches and 34 rows = 4"/10 cm in Stockinette stitch, after blocking.

Notes
- This pullover is worked in one piece from the top down with round yoke shaping.

DIRECTIONS

01 YOKE

With US 3/3.25 mm circular needle 16"/40 cm long, cast on 108 (114, 108, 114, 120, 150), {156, 168, 186, 186} stitches. Place beginning-of-the round marker (BOR) and join for working in the round, being careful not to twist stitches.

Knit all stitches for the next 4 rounds.

Work Rounds 1-46 of Chart A, working chart repeat 18 (19, 18, 19, 20, 25), {26, 28, 31, 31} times around. [324 (342, 324, 342, 360, 450), {468, 504, 558, 558} stitches]

Work Rounds 1-14 of Chart B (C, E, E, E, D), {D, D, C, D}. [324 (380, 432, 456, 480, 550), {572, 616, 620, 682} stitches]

NOTE: Continue working all stitches as they appear: knit the knit stitches and purl the purls in all rounds.

Next Round: *K8 (9, 11, 11, 9, 10), {10, 10, 9, 10}, p1; repeat from * to end.

Shape back neck using German Short-Rows (see Special Techniques, page 226):

Short-Row 1 (RS): Work 108 (126, 144, 152, 160, 182), {190, 205, 206, 227} stitches in pattern, turn work.

Short-Row 2 (WS): Make double stitch, work in pattern to BOR, slip marker, work in pattern 108 (126, 144, 152, 160, 182), {190, 205, 206, 227}, turn work.

Short-Row 3 (RS): Make double stitch, work in pattern to double stitch, work double stitch as a single stitch, work next 5 stitches, turn work.

Short-Row 4 (WS): Make double stitch, work in pattern to double stitch, work double stitch as a single stitch, work next 5 stitches, turn work.

Short-Rows 5-10: Repeat Short-Rows 3 and 4 another 3 times.

Next Round: Make double stitch, work in pattern to double stitch, work double stitch as a single stitch, work to BOR.

Resume working in the round for the next 0 (2, 5, 9, 16, 21), {25, 25, 30, 30} rounds, working double stitch as a single stitch in the next round.

Divide for Body and Sleeves

Division Round: Work in pattern 48 (55, 64, 69, 73, 83), {88, 95, 96, 104}, place next 66 (80, 88, 90, 94, 108), {110, 118, 118, 132} stitches on hold for Right Sleeve, with Backward-Loop method (see Special Techniques, page 226), cast on 20 (20, (16, 18, 24, 20), {22, 20, 28, 22} stitches for underarm, work in pattern 96 (110, 128, 138, 146, 167), {176, 190, 192, 209} Front stitches, place next 66 (80, 88, 90, 94, 108), {110, 118, 118, 132} stitches on hold for Left Sleeve, cast on 20 (20, (16, 18, 24, 20), {22, 20, 28, 22} stitches for underarm, work in pattern 48 (55, 64, 69, 73, 84), {88, 95, 96, 105} to BOR.

[232 (260, 288, 312, 340, 374), {396, 420, 440, 462) stitches on the needle for Body]

Continue working in the round on Body stitches.

02 BODY

Size XS only:

Set-Up Round: [K8, p1] 5 times, k3; work 20 underarm stitches as follows: k5, p1, k7, p1, k6; continue working 96 front stitches as follows: k2, p1, [k8, p1] 10 times, k3; work 20 underarm stitches as follows: k5, p1, k7, p1, k6; work remaining 48 stitches as follows: k2, p1, [k8, p1] 5 times.

Next Round: Work all stitches in pattern (knit the knit stitches and purl the purls).

Size S only:

Next Round: [K9, p1] to the end of the round.

Size M only:

Next Round: [K11, p1] to the end of the round.

Size L only:

Next Round: [K11, p1] to the end of the round.

Size XL only:

Next Round: [K9, p1] to the end of the round.

Size 2XL only:

Next Round: [K10, p1] to the end of the round.

Size 3XL only:
Next Round: [K10, p1] to the end of the round.

Size 4XL only:
Set-Up Round: [K10, p1] 8 times, k7; work 20 underarm stitches as follows: k3, p1, k11, p1, k4; continue working 190 front stitches as follows: k6, p1, [k10, p1] 16 times, k7; work 20 underarm stitches as follows: k3, p1, k11, p1, k4; work remaining 95 stitches as follows: k6, p1, [k10, p1] 8 times.
Next Round: Work all stitches in pattern (knit the knit stitches and purl the purls).

Size 5XL only:
Next Round: [K9, p1] to the end of the round.

Size 6XL only:
Next Round: [K10, p1] to the end of the round.

All sizes:
Work all stitches in pattern (knit the knit stitches and purl the purls) until Body reaches 12½"/31 cm from underarm or 1½"/4 cm shorter than desired length.
Change to US 2/2.75 mm 24-32"/60-80 cm circular needles.

Ribbing Round: *K1 tbl, p1; repeat to end.
Repeat last round 11 more times.
Bind off all stitches in pattern or using Tubular Bind Off method (see Special Techniques, page 226).

03 SLEEVES

With US 3/3.25 mm double-pointed needles and RS facing, pick up and knit 20 (20, 16, 18, 24, 20), {22, 20, 28, 22} underarm stitches, work 66 (80, 88, 90, 94, 108), {110, 118, 118, 132} held Sleeve stitches in pattern. [86 (100, 104, 108, 118, 128), {132, 138, 146, 154} stitches] Place BOR and join in the round.

Next Round: Work in pattern to the end of round, working the underarm stitches in Stockinette stitch in the round.
Work in established pattern until sleeve measures 16"/40 cm.

Sizes XS:
Decrease Round: K1, [K2TOG] 2 times, [K2TOG, k1] 25 times, [K2TOG] 3 times. [56 stitches]

Size S:
Decrease Round: K1, [K2TOG, k1] 5 times, [K2TOG] 16 times, [K2TOG, k1] 6 times, [K2TOG] 17 times. [56 stitches]

Size M:
Decrease Round: K1, [K2TOG, k1] 3 times, [K2TOG] 20 times, [K2TOG, k1] 4 times, [K2TOG] 21 times. [56 stitches]

Size L:
Decrease Round: K1, [K2TOG] 12 times, [K2TOG, k1] 9 times, [K2TOG] 12 times, [K2TOG, k1] 10 times, K2TOG. [64 stitches]

Size XL:
Decrease Round: K1, [K2TOG] 22 times, [K2TOG, k1] 4 times, [K2TOG] 22 times, [K2TOG, k1] 5 times, K2TOG. [64 stitches]

Size 2XL:
Decrease Round: K1, [K2TOG] 29 times, [K2TOG, k1] 3 times, [K2TOG] 29 times, K2TOG. [66 stitches]

Sizes 3XL and 4XL:
Decrease Round: K1, [K2TOG] to last stitch, k1. [70 stitches]

Size 5XL and 6XL:
Decrease Round: K1, [K2TOG] to last stitch, k1. [73 (78) stitches]

All sizes:
Next Round: Knit all stitches.
Switch to US 2/2.75 mm double-pointed needles.
Ribbing Round: *K1 tbl, p1; repeat from * to end.
Repeat Ribbing Round for 7 rounds.
Bind off all stitches in pattern or using Tubular Bind Off method.

04 FINISHING

Block to measurements. Weave in ends.

15½ (16¼, 15½, 16¼, 17¼, 21½), {22¼, 24, 26½, 26½}"/
39 (40.5, 39, 40.5, 43, 54), {55.5, 60, 66.5, 6.5} cm

12¼ (14¼, 15, 15½, 17, 18¼), {19, 19¾, 21, 22}"/
30.5 (35.5, 37.5, 39, 42.5, 45.5), {47.5, 49.5, 52.5, 55} cm

7 (7¼, 7½, 8, 9, 9½), {10, 10, 10½, 10½}"/
17.5 (18, 19, 20, 22.5, 24), {25, 25, 26.5, 26.5} cm

14½"/36.5 cm

17"/42.5 cm

8 (8, 8, 9, 9, 9¼), {10, 10, 10½, 11}"/
20 (20, 20, 22.5, 22.5, 23), {25, 25, 26.5, 27.5} cm

33¼ (37¼, 41¼, 44½, 48½, 53½), {56½, 60, 63, 66}"/
83 (93, 103, 111.5, 121.5, 134), {141.5, 150, 157.5, 165} cm

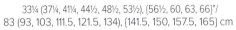

CHARTS

CHART A

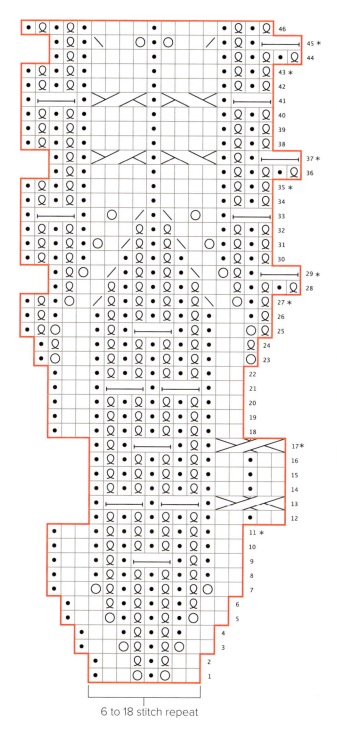

6 to 18 stitch repeat

LEGEND

☐ **K:** Knit stitch

• **P:** Purl stitch

Ω **K1 tbl:** Knit stitch through back loop

O **YO:** Yarn over

⊠ **P3TOG:** Purl 3 stitches together – 2 stitches decreased

⁄ **K2TOG:** Knit 2 stitches together – 1 stitch decreased with right slant.

\ **SSK:** Slip 1 stitch knitwise, slip 1 stitch knitwise, return 2 slipped stitches back to left needle and knit them together through back loops – 1 stitch decreased with left slant

⊐ **3-stitch cluster:** Slip 3 stitches to cable needle, wrap yarn 3 times around these 3 stitches in a counter-clockwise direction, (k1 tbl, p1, k1 tbl) from cable needle

⧄ **2/2 RC:** Slip 2 stitches to cable needle, hold in back, knit 2, knit 2 from cable needle

⧅ **2/2 LC:** Slip 2 stitches to cable needle, hold in front, knit 2, knit 2 from cable needle

⧄ **2/1/2 RPC:** Slip next 2 stitches to cable needle #1 and hold in back, slip next stitch onto cable needle #2 and hold in back, k2 from left needle, p1 from cable needle #2, k2 from cable needle #1

☐ Pattern repeat

* Follow the Written Chart Instructions

CHART B

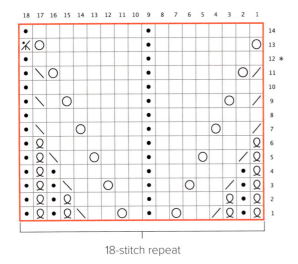

18-stitch repeat

CHART C

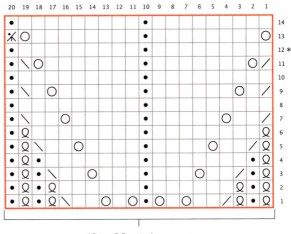

18 to 20-stitch repeat

CHART D

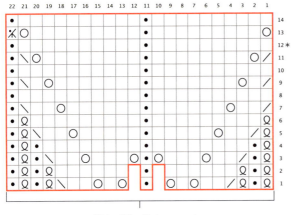

18 to 22-stitch repeat

CHART E

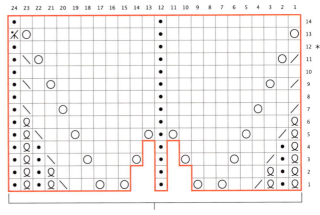

18 to 24-stitch repeat

* Follow the Written Chart Instructions

Written instructions for Chart A

.. – *pattern repeat*

Note: See Chart Legend for special abbreviations.

Round 1: *K2, YO, p1, YO, k2, p1*
Round 2: *K2, k1 tbl, p1, k1 tbl, k2, p1*
Round 3: *K2, YO, k1 tbl, p1, k1 tbl, YO, k2, p1*
Round 4: *K2, [p1, k1 tbl] 2 times, p1, k2, p1*
Round 5: *K2, YO, [p1, k1 tbl] 2 times, p1, YO, k2, p1*
Round 6: *K2, [k1 tbl, p1] 3 times, k1 tbl, k2, p1*
Round 7: *K2, YO, [k1 tbl, p1] 3 times, k1 tbl, YO, k2, p1*
Round 8: *K2, [p1, k1 tbl] 4 times, p1, k2, p1*
Round 9: *K2, p1, k1 tbl, p1, 3-stitch cluster, p1, k1 tbl, p1, k2, p1*
Rounds 10: *K2, [p1, k1 tbl] 4 times, p1, k2, p1*
* Round 11 (Shift marker): *K2, [p1, k1 tbl] 4 times, p1, k2, p1; repeat from * to last 3 stitches of the round, slip 3 stitches purlwise to right needle, remove marker, slip 3 stitches back to left needle, replace marker.
Round 12: *K2, p1, k2, [p1, k1 tbl] 4 times, p1*
Round 13: *2/1/2 RPC, [p1, 3-stitch cluster] 2 times, p1*
Rounds 14 - 16: *K2, p1, k2, [p1, k1 tbl] 4 times, p1*
* Round 17 (Shift marker): *2/1/2 RPC, p1, k1 tbl, p1, 3-stitch cluster, p1, k1 tbl, p1; repeat from * around. Remove marker, k2, p1, replace marker.
Rounds 18 - 20: *K2, [p1, k1 tbl] 4 times, p1, k2, p1*
Round 21: *K2, [p1, 3-stitch cluster] 2 times, p1, k2, p1*
Round 22: *K2, [p1, k1 tbl] 4 times, p1, k2, p1*
Round 23: *YO, k2, [p1, k1 tbl] 4 times, p1, k2, YO, p1*
Round 24: *K1 tbl, k2, [p1, k1 tbl] 4 times, p1, k2, k1 tbl, p1*
Round 25: *K1 tbl, YO, k2, p1, k1 tbl, p1, 3-stitch cluster, p1, k1 tbl, p1, k2, YO, k1 tbl, p1*
Round 26: *K1 tbl, p1, k2, [p1, k1 tbl] 4 times, p1, k2, p1, k1 tbl, p1*
* Round 27 (Shift marker): *K1 tbl, p1, YO, k1, SSK, [k1 tbl, p1] 3 times, k1 tbl, K2TOG, k1, YO, p1, k1 tbl, p1; repeat from * to last 2 stitches of the round, slip 2 stitches purlwise to right needle, remove marker, slip 2 stitches back to left needle, replace marker.
Round 28: *[K1 tbl, p1] 2 times, k1 tbl, k2, [k1 tbl, p1] 3 times, k1 tbl, k2, k1tbl, p1*
* Round 29 (Shift marker): *3-stitch cluster, p1, k1 tbl, YO, k1, SSK, [p1, k1 tbl] 2 times, p1, K2TOG, k1, YO, k1 tbl, p1; repeat from * around. Remove marker, k1 tbl, p1, replace marker.

Round 30: *[K1 tbl, p1] 2 times, k2, [p1, k1 tbl] 2 times, p1, k2, [p1, k1 tbl] 2 times, p1*
Round 31: *[K1 tbl, p1] 2 times, YO, k1, SSK, k1 tbl, p1, k1 tbl, K2TOG, k1, YO, [p1, k1 tbl] 2 times, p1*
Round 32: *[K1 tbl, p1] 2 times, k3, k1 tbl, p1, k1 tbl, k3, [p1, k1 tbl] 2 times, p1*
 Round 33: *3-stitch cluster, p1, k1, YO, k1, SSK, p1, K2TOG, k1, YO, k1, p1, 3-stitch cluster, p1*
Rounds 34: *[K1 tbl, p1] 2 times, [k4, p1] 2 times, [k1 tbl, p1] 2 times*
* Rounds 35 (Shift marker): *[K1 tbl, p1] 2 times, [k4, p1] 2 times, [k1 tbl, p1] 2 times; repeat from * to last 2 stitches of the round, slip 2 stitches purlwise to right needle, remove marker, slip 2 stitches back to left needle, replace marker.
Round 36: *[K1 tbl, p1] 3 times, [k4, p1] 2 times, k1 tbl, p1*
* Round 37 (Shift marker): *3-stitch cluster, p1, k1 tbl, p1, 2/2 LC, p1, 2/2 RC, p1, k1 tbl, p1; repeat from * around. Remove marker, k1 tbl, p1, replace marker.
Rounds 38 - 40: *[K1 tbl, p1] 2 times, [k4, p1] 2 times, [k1 tbl, p1] 2 times*
Round 41: *3-stitch cluster, p1, 2/2 LC, p1, 2/2 RC, p1, 3-stitch cluster, p1*
Rounds 42: *[K1 tbl, p1] 2 times, [k4, p1] 2 times, [k1 tbl, p1] 2 times*
* Rounds 43 (Shift marker): *[K1 tbl, p1] 2 times, [k4, p1] 2 times, [k1 tbl, p1] 2 times; repeat from * to last 2 stitches of the round, slip 2 stitches purlwise to right needle, remove marker, slip 2 stitches back to left needle, replace marker.
Round 44: *[K1 tbl, p1] 3 times, [k4, p1] 2 times, k1 tbl, p1*
* Round 45 (Shift marker): *3-stitch cluster, p1, k1 tbl, p1, K2TOG, k2, YO, p1, YO, k2, SSK, p1, k1 tbl, p1; repeat from * around. Remove marker, k1 tbl, p1, replace marker.
Round 46: *[K1 tbl, p1] 2 times, [k4, p1] 2 times, [k1 tbl, p1] 2 times*

Written instructions for Chart B

.. – *pattern repeat*

Round 1: *K1 tbl, p1, k1 tbl, K2TOG, k2, YO, k1, p1, k1, YO, k2, SSK, [k1 tbl, p1] 2 times*
Round 2: *K1 tbl, p1, k1 tbl, k5, p1, k5, [k1 tbl, p1] 2 times*
Round 3: *K1 tbl, p1, K2TOG, k2, YO, k2, p1, k2, YO, k2, SSK, p1, k1 tbl, p1*
Round 4: *K1 tbl, [p1, k6] 2 times, p1, k1 tbl, p1*

Round 5: *K1 tbl, K2TOG, k2, YO, k3, p1, k3, YO, k2, SSK, k1 tbl, p1*
Round 6: *K1 tbl, k7, p1, k7, k1 tbl, p1*
Round 7: *K2TOG, k2, YO, k4, p1, k4, YO, k2, SSK, p1*
Round 8: *K8, p1*
Round 9: *K2TOG, k1, YO, k5, p1, k5, YO, k1, SSK, p1*
Round 10: *K8, p1*
Round 11: *K2TOG, YO, k6, p1, k6, YO, SSK, p1*
* **Round 12 (Shift Marker):** *K8, p1; repeat from * around. Remove marker, k1, replace marker.
Round 13: *YO, k7, p1, k7, YO, P3TOG*
Round 14: *K8, p1*

Written instructions for Chart C
.. – pattern repeat

Round 1: *K1 tbl, p1, k1 tbl, K2TOG, k2, YO, k1, YO, p1, YO, k1, YO, k2, SSK, [k1 tbl, p1] 2 times*
Round 2: *K1 tbl, p1, k1 tbl, k6, p1, k6, [k1 tbl, p1] 2 times*
Round 3: *K1 tbl, p1, K2TOG, k2, YO, k3, p1, k3, YO, k2, SSK, p1, k1 tbl, p1*
Round 4: *K1 tbl, [p1, k7] 2 times, p1, k1 tbl, p1*
Round 5: *K1 tbl, K2TOG, k2, YO, k4, p1, k4, YO, k2, SSK, k1 tbl, p1*
Round 6: *K1 tbl, k8, p1, k8, k1 tbl, p1*
Round 7: *K2TOG, k2, YO, k5, p1, k5, YO, k2, SSK, p1*
Round 8: *K9, p1*
Round 9: *K2TOG, k1, YO, k6, p1, k6, YO, k1, SSK, p1*
Round 10: *K9, p1*
Round 11: *K2TOG, YO, k7, p1, k7, YO, SSK, p1*
* **Round 12 (Shift Marker):** *K9, p1; repeat from * around. Remove marker, k1, replace marker.
Round 13: *YO, k8, p1, k8, YO, P3TOG*
Round 14: *K9, p1*

Written instructions for Chart D
.. – pattern repeat

Round 1: *K1 tbl, p1, k1 tbl, K2TOG, k2, YO, k1, YO, p1, YO, k1, YO, k2, SSK, [k1 tbl, p1] 2 times*
Round 2: *K1 tbl, p1, k1 tbl, k6, p1, k6, [k1 tbl, p1] 2 times*
Round 3: *K1 tbl, p1, K2TOG, k2, YO, k3, YO, p1, YO, k3,

YO, k2, SSK, p1, k1 tbl, p1*
Round 4: *K1 tbl, [p1, k8] 2 times, p1, k1 tbl, p1*
Round 5: *K1 tbl, K2TOG, k2, YO, k5, p1, k5, YO, k2, SSK, k1 tbl, p1*
Round 6: *K1 tbl, k9, p1, k9, k1 tbl, p1*
Round 7: *K2TOG, k2, YO, k6, p1, k6, YO, k2, SSK, p1*
Round 8: *K10, p1*
Round 9: *K2TOG, k1, YO, k7, p1, k7, YO, k1, SSK, p1*
Round 10: *K10, p1*
Round 11: *K2TOG, YO, k8, p1, k8, YO, SSK, p1*
* **Round 12 (Shift Marker):** *K10, p1; repeat from * around. Remove marker, k1, replace marker.
Round 13: *YO, k9, p1, k9, YO, P3TOG*
Round 14: *K10, p1*

Written instructions for Chart E
.. – pattern repeat

Round 1: *K1 tbl, p1, k1 tbl, K2TOG, k2, YO, k1, YO, p1, YO, k1, YO, k2, SSK, [k1 tbl, p1] 2 times*
Round 2: *K1 tbl, p1, k1 tbl, k6, p1, k6, [k1 tbl, p1] 2 times*
Round 3: *K1 tbl, p1, K2TOG, k2, YO, k3, YO, p1, YO, k3, YO, k2, SSK, p1, k1 tbl, p1*
Round 4: *K1 tbl, [p1, k8] 2 times, p1, k1 tbl, p1*
Round 5: *K1 tbl, K2TOG, k2, YO, k5, YO, p1, YO, k5, YO, k2, SSK, k1 tbl, p1*
Round 6: *K1 tbl, k10, p1, k10, k1 tbl, p1*
Round 7: *K2TOG, k2, YO, k7, p1, k7, YO, k2, SSK, p1*
Round 8: *K11, p1*
Round 9: *K2TOG, k1, YO, k8, p1, k8, YO, k1, SSK, p1*
Round 10: *K11, p1*
Round 11: *K2TOG, YO, k9, p1, k9, YO, SSK, p1*
* **Round 12 (Shift Marker):** *K11, p1; repeat from * around. Remove marker, k1, replace marker.
Round 13: *YO, k10, p1, k10, YO, P3TOG*
Round 14: *K11, p1*

Stairs

A bold chevron motif makes this shawl a striking accessory, with angled lines that create movement and visual energy. A wide textured border provides balance and weight to mosaic zigzag pattern, worked in two contrasting colors.
The generous wingspan and asymmetrical shaping allow the shawl to drape effortlessly over the shoulders or wrap warmly around the neck. Slip-stitch colorwork keeps the knitting approachable while producing a dramatic graphic effect.

Finished Measurements
Approximately 50"/125 cm height; 47¾"/119.5 cm depth.
Measurements taken from relaxed fabric after blocking.

Yarn
Sport weight yarn (approximate amount):
1190 yds/1088 m.
Color C1 (off-white): 420 yards/384 m.
Color C2 (brown-red): 770 yards/704 m

C1: Miss Babs Laurel Falls (100% Superwash Shaniko Merino Wool; 300 yards/275 m in 13.5 oz/100 g), Plover: 2 skeins.
C2: Laurel Falls (100% Superwash Shaniko Merino Wool; 300 yards/275 m in 13.5 oz/100 g), Dark Chocolate: 3 skeins.

Needles
Size US 6/4 mm: 24-32"/60-80 cm straight or circular.
2 double-pointed needles of the same size.
Adjust needle size if necessary to obtain gauge.

Notions
Tapestry needle.

Gauge
22 stitches and 43 rows = 4"/10 cm in charted pattern, after blocking.
22 stitches and 30 rows = 4"/10 cm in garter stitch pattern, after blocking.

Notes
- This shawl is worked back and forth from side to side, beginning at the narrow tip and ending at the wide edge.
- A circular needle is used to accommodate the large number of stitches.

Notes on Slipped Stitch Pattern
This is a slip-stitch pattern. Each row is worked using only one color, and by slipping a stitch without working it, a stitch from the row below brings a new color into the working row. Every Right Side row is followed by a Wrong Side row of the same color. The colors change every two rows.
To work a slip stitch, move it to the right needle without knitting or purling it, purlwise. On all Right Side rows slip all of the slipped stitches with yarn in back. On all wrong side rows slip all the slipped stitches with yarn in front.
When changing colors, always drop the C1 yarn in front and pick up the C2 yarn behind it.

DIRECTIONS

01 BODY

With C1, cast on 2 stitches.

Work Rows 1-2 of Stairs Chart, join C2 and continue following the chart through Row 52, then work Rows 29-52 a total of 18 times. [244 stitches]

Break C1, continue working with C2.

02 BORDER

With C2, work Garter border as follows:
Next Row (RS): K2, KFB, knit to the end of the row. [1 stitch increased]
Next Row (WS): Knit.
Work last 2 rows another 17 times. [262 stitches; 18 ridges of Garter stitch pattern]

Do not break yarn.

03 FINISHING

Work **I-cord Bind Off** as follows:
Step 1: At the end of the row just worked, cast on 2 stitches using provisional method of your choice.
Step 2: Turn work to RS and knit 3 stitches. Slip 3 just worked stitches back to left needle.
Step 3: K2, K2TOG tbl.
Step 4: Return 3 just worked stitches back to left needle.

Repeat steps 3 and 4 to the end of live stitches – 3 stitches on the needle.
Work extra row of I-cord for turning corner as follows: Knit 3 stitches, place 3 stitches just worked back to left-hand needle.

Change to double-pointed needles and work the **I-cord edging** along straight edge of the shawl as follows:
*K2, slip stitch 1 purlwise with yarn in back, YO, pick up and knit 1 stitch from the edge, pass YO and slipped stitch over, slide stitches to opposite end of double-pointed needle; repeat from *, picking up 1 stitch in every garter ridge along the shawl edge.

Work I-cord edging to the narrow point of the shawl. Work extra row of I-cord for turning corner as follows: Knit 3 stitches, place 3 stitches just worked back to left-hand needle.
Work the I-cord edging along sloped edge of the shawl as instructed before – 3 stitches on the needle.

Remove waste yarn from provisional cast on and place stitches on the other double-pointed needle. With tail threaded on a tapestry needle, graft stitches together.

Weave in ends, block to measurements.

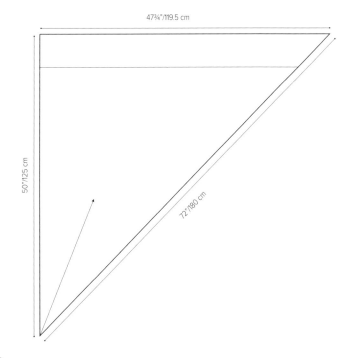

47¾"/119.5 cm

50"/125 cm

72"/180 cm

CHARTS

STAIRS CHART

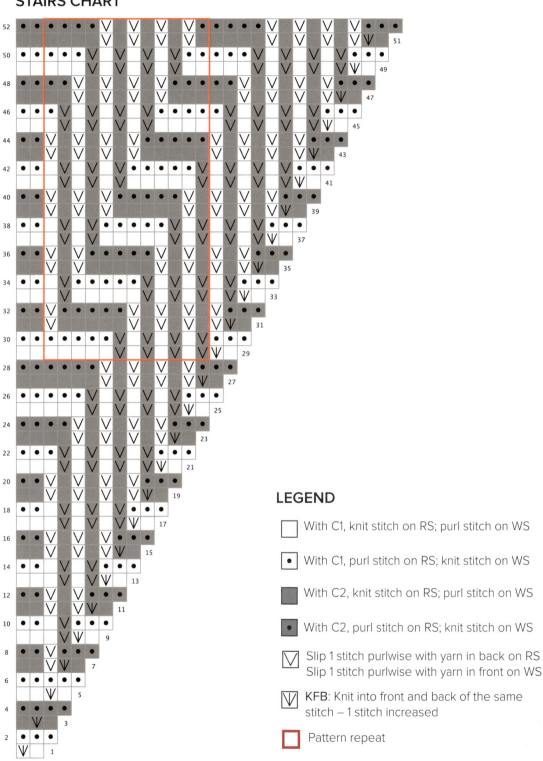

LEGEND

☐	With C1, knit stitch on RS; purl stitch on WS
☐•	With C1, purl stitch on RS; knit stitch on WS
▨	With C2, knit stitch on RS; purl stitch on WS
▨•	With C2, purl stitch on RS; knit stitch on WS
⩔	Slip 1 stitch purlwise with yarn in back on RS Slip 1 stitch purlwise with yarn in front on WS
⩔	KFB: Knit into front and back of the same stitch – 1 stitch increased
☐	Pattern repeat

Blocks

A richly cabled pullover that is coziness itself, with a lot of style. The modular construction begins with the yoke worked flat from armhole to armhole with shoulder and neck shaping. Stitches for the lower body are picked up for the body, knit seamlessly in the round from the top down. Relaxed in fit yet rich in detail, the pullover features dropped shoulders, voluminous sleeves tapering into deep ribbed cuffs, and matching ribbing at the hem and neckline.

Sizes

XS (S, M, L, XL, 2XL), {3XL, 4XL, 5XL, 6XL}: to fit bust 28-30 (32-34, 36-38, 40-42, 44-46, 48-50), {52-54, 56-58, 60-62, 64-66}"/70-75 (80-85, 90-95, 100-105, 110-115, 120-125), {130-135, 140-145, 150-155, 160-165} cm.

Finished Measurements

38½ (44, 48, 53, 57, 60), {62, 66, 72, 75½}"/96.5 (110, 120, 132.5, 142.5, 150), {155, 165, 180, 189} cm bust circumference.
Shown in size M (48"/120 cm) on 38"/95 cm bust with 10"/25 cm of positive ease.

Yarn

DK weight yarn (approximate amounts): 1340 (1520, 1660, 1840, 1980, 2080), {2150, 2290, 2490, 2620} yds/1220 (1383, 1510, 1674, 1802, 1893), {1957, 2084, 2266, 2384} m.

Miss Babs Killington (85% Polwarth Wool, 15% Tussah Silk; 350 yards/320 m in 4.2 oz/120 g), Parchment: 4 (5, 5, 6, 6, 6), {7, 7, 8, 8} skeins.

Needles

Size US 7/4.5 mm: 24-32"/60-80 cm circular.
Sizes US 6/4 mm: 24-32"/60-80 cm circular, 16"/40 cm circular and set of double-pointed.
Optional: spare US 6/4 mm 24-32"/60-80 cm circular for Tubular Bind Off.
Adjust needle size if necessary to obtain gauge.

Notions

Stitch markers, stitch holders or waste yarn, cable needle, tapestry needle.

Gauge

18 stitches and 28 rows = 4"/10 cm in Stockinette Stitch on US 7/4.5 mm needle, after blocking.
24 stitches and 28 rows = 4"/10 cm in Body Chart on US 7/4.5 mm needle, after blocking.
21 stitches and 28 rows = 4"/10 cm in k2, p2 rib on US 7/4.5 mm needle, after blocking.
32 stitches of Lattice Chart = 4½"/11.5 cm in charted pattern on US 7/4.5 mm needle, after blocking.

Notes

- The yoke is worked flat, side-to-side, from the right armhole to the neck hole with right shoulder shaping. At the beginning of the neck opening, the yoke is separated into back and front pieces and worked separately to the opposite side of the neck. Then both back and front yokes are joined, and yoke is worked as one piece again to the left armhole with left shoulder shaping.
- Stitches for the body are picked up from the yoke's lower edges and worked in the round from the top down.

DIRECTIONS

01 YOKE

01a. Right Yoke

With US 7/4.5 mm circular needle, cast on 98 (98, 102, 102, 106, 106), {114, 114, 118, 118} stitches [see Diagram 1 (page 106)].

Sizes XS (S, _, _, _, _), {_, _, _, _} only:
Set-Up Row 1 (RS): K3, p2, k2, p2, place chart marker, work Row 1 of Lattice Chart over next 32 stitches, place chart marker, [p2, k2] 2 times, place marker for shoulder, [k2, p2] 2 times, place chart marker, work Row 1 of Lattice Chart over next 32 stitches, place chart marker, p2, k2, p2, k3.
Set-Up Row 2 (WS): P3, k2, p2, k2, slip chart marker, work Row 2 of Lattice Chart, slip chart marker, [k2, p2] 2 times, slip shoulder marker, [p2, k2] 2 times, slip chart marker, work Row 2 of Lattice Chart, slip chart marker, k2, p2, k2, p3.

Continue in established pattern and follow Lattice Chart through Row 4.

Sizes _ (_, M, L, _, _), {_, _, _, _} only:
Set-Up Row 1 (RS): K3, p2, k2, p3, place chart marker, work Row 1 of Lattice Chart over next 32 stitches, place chart marker, p3, k2, p2, k2, place marker for shoulder, k2, p2, k2, p3, place chart marker, work Row 1 of Lattice Chart over next 32 stitches, place chart marker, p3, k2, p2, k3.
Set-Up Row 2 (WS): P3, k2, p2, k3, slip chart marker, work Row 2 of Lattice Chart, slip chart marker, k3, p2, k2, p2, slip shoulder marker, p2, k2, p2, k3, slip chart marker, work Row 2 of Lattice Chart, slip chart marker, k3, p2, k2, p3.

Continue in established pattern and follow Lattice Chart through Row 4.

Sizes _ (_, _, _, XL, 2X), {_, _, _, _} only:
Set-Up Row 1 (RS): K3, p3, k2, p3, place chart marker, work Row 1 of Lattice Chart over next 32 stitches, place chart marker, [p3, k2] 2 times, place marker for shoulder, [k2, p3] 2 times, place chart marker, work Row 1 of Lattice Chart over next 32 stitches, place chart marker, p3, k2, p3, k3.

Set-Up Row 2 (WS): P3, k3, p2, k3, slip chart marker, work Row 2 of Lattice Chart, slip chart marker, [k3, p2] 2 times, slip shoulder marker, [p2, k3] 2 times, slip chart marker, work Row 2 of Lattice Chart, slip chart marker, k3, p2, k3, p3.

Continue in established pattern and follow Lattice Chart through Row 4.

Sizes _ (_, _, _, _, _), {3X, 4X _, _} only:
Set-Up Row 1 (RS): K3, p2, [k2, p2] 2 times, place chart marker, work Row 1 of Lattice Chart over next 32 stitches, place chart marker, [p2, k2] 3 times, place marker for shoulder, [k2, p2] 3 times, place chart marker, work Row 1 of Lattice Chart over next 32 stitches, place chart marker, [p2, k2] 2 times, p2, k3.
Set-Up Row 2 (WS): P3, k2, [p2, k2] 2 times, slip chart marker, work Row 2 of Lattice Chart, slip chart marker, [k2, p2] 3 times, slip shoulder marker, [p2, k2] 3 times, slip chart marker, work Row 2 of Lattice Chart, slip chart marker, [k2, p2] 2 times, k2, p3.

Continue in established pattern and follow Lattice Chart through Row 4, then repeat last 4 rows, slipping markers and working Lattice Chart Rows 1-4 once more.

Sizes _ (_, _, _, _, _), {_, _, 5X, 6X} only:
Set-Up Row 1 (RS): K3, [p2, k2] 2 times, p3, place chart marker, work Row 1 of Lattice Chart over next 32 stitches, place chart marker, p3, k2, [p2, k2] 2 times, place marker for shoulder, [k2, p2] 2 times, k2, p3, place chart marker, work Row 1 of Lattice Chart over next 32 stitches, place chart marker, p3, [k2, p2] 2 times, k3.
Set-Up Row 2 (WS): P3, [k2, p2] 2 times, k3, slip chart marker, work Row 2 of Lattice Chart, slip chart marker, k3, p2, [k2, p2] 2 times, slip shoulder marker, [p2, k2] 2 times, p2, k3, slip chart marker, work Row 2 of Lattice Chart, slip chart marker, k3, [p2, k2] 2 times, p3.

Continue in established pattern and follow Lattice Chart through Row 4, then repeat last 2 rows, slipping markers and working Lattice Chart Rows 1-2 once more.

All sizes:
NOTE: While working the yoke, continue following the established pattern and repeat Rows 5-20 of Lattice Chart throughout. Work all increase stitches in Stockinette stitch pattern.

Shape Right Shoulder
Sizes XS (S, _, _, _, _), {_, _, _, _} only:
Increase Row (RS): Work to 1 stitch before shoulder marker, M1R, k1, slip marker, k1, M1L, work to end of row. [2 stitches increased]
Next Row (WS): Work all stitches in established pattern.

Repeat last 2 rows 4 (1, _, _, _, _), {_, _, _, _} more times. [108 (102, _, _, _, _), {_, _, _, _} stitches]

Repeat Increase Row [2 stitches increased]
Work next 3 rows in established pattern without increases.
Repeat last 4 rows 7 (10, _, _, _, _), {_, _, _, _} more times. [124 stitches]

Last Lattice Chart row worked: Row 14 (20, _, _, _, _), {_, _, _, _}.

Size _ (_, M, _, _, _), {_, _, _, _} only:
Increase Row (RS): Work to 1 stitch before shoulder marker, M1R, k1, slip marker, k1, M1L, work to end of row. [2 stitches increased]
Work next 3 rows in established pattern without increases.

Repeat last 4 rows 12 more times. [128 stitches]
Last Lattice Chart row worked: Row 8.

Sizes _ (_, _, L, XL, 2X), {3X, _, _, _} only:
Increase Row (RS): Work to 1 stitch before shoulder marker, M1R, k1, slip marker, k1, M1L, work to end of row. [2 stitches increased]
Work next 3 rows in established pattern without increases.

Repeat last 4 rows _ (_, _, 9, 6, 3), {2, _, _, _} more times. [_ (_, _, 122, 120, 114), {120, _, _, _} stitches]

Repeat Increase Row [2 stitches increased]
Work next 5 rows in established pattern without increases.
Repeat last 6 rows _ (_, _, 2, 5, 8), {9, _, _, _} more time(s). [_ (_, _, 128, 132, 132), {140, _, _, _} stitches]
Last Lattice Chart row worked: Row _ (_, _, 14, 20, 10), {12, _, _, _}.

Sizes _ (_, _, _, _, _), {_, 4X, 5X, 6X} only:
Increase Row (RS): Work to 1 stitch before shoulder marker, M1R, k1, slip marker, k1, M1L, work to end of row. [2 stitches increased]
Work next 5 rows in established pattern without increases.
Repeat last 6 rows _ (_, _, _, _, _), {_, 11, 8, 4} more time(s). [_ (_, _, _, _, _), {_, 138, 136, 128} stitches]

Repeat Increase Row [2 stitches increased]
Work next 7 rows in established pattern without increases.
Repeat last 8 rows _ (_, _, _, _, _), {_, 0, 3, 7} more time(s). [_ (_, _, _, _, _), {_, 140, 144, 144} stitches]

Last Lattice Chart row worked: Row _ (_, _, _, _, _), {_, 20, 10, 18}.

All sizes:
124 (124, 128, 128, 132, 132), {140, 140, 144, 144} stitches on the needles.

Last Lattice Chart row worked: Row 14 (20, 8, 14, 20, 10), {12, 20, 10, 18}.

Start shaping neckline as follows:
Decrease Row (RS): Work in established pattern to 7 stitches before shoulder marker, place just worked 55 (55, 57, 57, 59, 59), {63, 63, 65, 65} stitches on hold for Front Yoke; bind off next 7 stitches, remove shoulder marker, bind off 2 stitches, work to end in established pattern. [60 (60, 62, 62, 64, 64), {68, 68, 70, 70} Back Yoke stitches]

01b. Back Yoke

Continue working on Back Yoke stitches in rows.
Next Row (WS): Work in established pattern to neck opening.

Last Lattice Chart row worked: Row 16 (6, 10, 16, 6, 12), {14, 6, 12, 20}.

Work even without decreases 42 (46, 54, 58, 62, 66), {62, 62, 66, 66} more rows.

Last Lattice Chart row worked: Row 10 (20, 16, 10, 20, 14), {12, 20, 14, 6}.

Place just worked Back Yoke stitches on hold.

01c. Front Yoke

Place 55 (55, 57, 57, 59, 59), {63, 63, 65, 65} held Front Yoke stitches onto US 7/4.5 mm circular needle. Join yarn at the neck opening, ready to begin the WS row.

Continue shaping the neckline as follows:
Decrease Row 1 (WS): Bind off 2 stitches, work in established pattern to end. [53 (53, 55, 55, 57, 57), {61, 61, 63, 63} stitches]
Next Row (RS): Work in established pattern.

Decrease Row 2 (WS): Bind off 1 stitch, work in established pattern to end.
Next Row (RS): Work in established pattern.

Repeat last 2 rows. [51 (51, 53, 53, 55, 55), {59, 59, 61, 61} stitches]

Next Row (WS): Work in established pattern.
Last Lattice Chart row worked: Row 6 (12, 16, 6, 12, 18), {20, 12, 18, 10}.

Work even without decrease 30 (34, 42, 46, 50, 54), {50, 50, 54, 54} more rows.

Last Lattice Chart row worked: Row 20 (14, 10, 20, 14, 8), {6, 14, 8, 16}.

Increase Row 1 (RS): Work in established pattern to end, cast on 1 stitch. [1 stitch increased]

Next Row (WS): Work in established pattern, including cast-on stitches in Stockinette stitch.

Repeat last 2 rows. [53 (53, 55, 55, 57, 57), {61, 61, 63, 63} stitches]

Increase Row 2 (RS): Work in established pattern to end, cast on 2 stitches. [55 (55, 57, 57, 59, 59), {63, 63, 65, 65} stitches]
Next Row (WS): Work in established pattern, including cast-on stitches in Stockinette stitch.

Last Lattice Chart row worked: Row 10 (20, 16, 10, 20, 14), {12, 20, 14, 6}.

01d. Left Yoke

Join Front and Back Yoke as follows:
Joining Row (RS): Work 55 (55, 57, 57, 59, 59), {63, 63, 65, 65} Front Yoke stitches in established pattern, cast on 7 stitches, place shoulder marker; cast on 2 stitches, work held 60 (60, 62, 62, 64, 64), {68, 68, 70, 70} Back Yoke stitches in established pattern to end. [124 (124, 128, 128, 132, 132), {140, 140, 144, 144} stitches]

Last Lattice Chart row worked: Row 11 (5, 17, 11, 5, 15), {13, 5, 15, 7}.

Work in established pattern, including cast-on stitches in Stockinette stitch, for 3 (3, 3, 5, 5, 5), {5, 7, 7, 7} rows.

Last Lattice Chart row worked: Row 14 (8, 20, 16, 10, 20), {18, 12, 6, 14}.

Shape left shoulder as follows:
Sizes XS (S, _, _, _, _), {_, _, _, _} only:
Decrease Row (RS): Work in established pattern to 3 stitches before shoulder marker, SSK, k1, slip shoulder marker, k1, K2TOG, work in established pattern to end. [2 stitches decreased]
Work next 3 rows in established pattern without increases.
Repeat last 4 rows 6 (9, _, _, _, _), {_, _, _, _} more times. [110 (104, _, _, _, _), {_, _, _, _} stitches]

Decrease Row (RS): Work in established pattern to 3 stitches before shoulder marker, SSK, k1, slip shoulder marker, k1, K2TOG, work in established pattern to end. [2 stitches decreased]

Next Row (WS): Work all stitches in established pattern.

Repeat last 2 rows 4 (1, _, _, _, _), {_, _, _, _} more times. [100 stitches]

Decrease Row (RS): Work in established pattern to 3 stitches before shoulder marker, SSK, k1, slip shoulder marker, k1, K2TOG, work in established pattern to end. [98 stitches]

Last row of Lattice Chart worked: Row 5.

Work in established pattern for 3 more rows, working rows 22-24 of Lattice Chart.

Size _ (_, M, _, _, _), {_, _, _, _} only:
Decrease Row (RS): Work in established pattern to 3 stitches before shoulder marker, SSK, k1, slip shoulder marker, k1, K2TOG, work in established pattern to end. [2 stitches decreased]

Work next 3 rows in established pattern without increases.

Repeat last 4 rows 11 more times. [104 stitches]

Decrease Row (RS): Work in established pattern to 3 stitches before shoulder marker, SSK, k1, slip shoulder marker, k1, K2TOG, work in established pattern to end. [102 stitches]

Last row of Lattice Chart worked: Row 5.

Work in established pattern for 3 more rows, working rows 22-24 of Lattice Chart.

Sizes _ (_, _, L, XL, 2X), {_, _, _, _} only:
Decrease Row (RS): Work in established pattern to 3 stitches before shoulder marker, SSK, k1, slip shoulder marker, k1, K2TOG, work in established pattern to end. [2 stitches decreased]

Work next 5 rows in established pattern without increases.

Repeat last 6 rows _ (_, _, 1, 4, 7), {_, _, _, _} more time(s). [_ (_, _, 124, 122, 116), {_, _, _, _} stitches]

Decrease Row (RS): Work in established pattern to 3 stitches before shoulder marker, SSK, k1, slip shoulder marker, k1, K2TOG, work in established pattern to end. [2 stitches decreased]

Work next 3 rows in established pattern without increases.

Repeat last 4 rows _ (_, _, 9, 6, 3), {_, _, _, _} more times. [_ (_, _, 104, 108, 108), {_, _, _, _} stitches]

Decrease Row (RS): Work in established pattern to 3 stitches before shoulder marker, SSK, k1, slip shoulder marker, k1, K2TOG, work in established pattern to end. [_ (_, _, 102, 106, 106), {_, _, _, _} stitches]

Last row of Lattice Chart worked: Row 5.

Work in established pattern for 3 more rows, working rows 22-24 of Lattice Chart.

Sizes _ (_, _, _, _, _), {3X, _, _, _} only:
Decrease Row (RS): Work in established pattern to 3 stitches before shoulder marker, SSK, k1, slip shoulder marker, k1, K2TOG, work in established pattern to end. [2 stitches decreased]

Work next 5 rows in established pattern without increases.

Repeat last 6 rows 8 more times. [122 stitches]

Decrease Row (RS): Work in established pattern to 3 stitches before shoulder marker, SSK, k1, slip shoulder marker, k1, K2TOG, work in established pattern to end. [2 stitches decreased]

Work next 3 rows in established pattern without increases.

Repeat last 4 rows 2 more times. [116 stitches]

Decrease Row (RS): Work in established pattern to 3 stitches before shoulder marker, SSK, k1, slip shoulder marker, k1, K2TOG, work in established pattern to end. [114 stitches]

Last row of Lattice Chart worked: Row 5.

Work in established pattern for 3 more rows, working rows 22-24 of Lattice Chart, then work 4 more rows, working Rows 23-24 of Lattice Chart twice.

Decrease Row (RS): Work in established pattern to 3 stitches before shoulder marker, SSK, k1, slip shoulder marker, k1, K2TOG, work in established pattern to end. [2 stitches decreased]
Work next 5 rows in established pattern without increases.
Repeat last 6 rows 11 more times. [116 stitches]

Decrease Row (RS): Work in established pattern to 3 stitches before shoulder marker, SSK, k1, slip shoulder marker, k1, K2TOG, work in established pattern to end. [114 stitches]

Last row of Lattice Chart worked: Row 5.

Work in established pattern for 3 more rows, working rows 22-24 of Lattice Chart, then work 4 more rows, working Rows 23-24 of Lattice Chart twice.

Sizes _ (_, _, _, _, _), {_, _, 5X, 6X} only:
Decrease Row (RS): Work in established pattern to 3 stitches before shoulder marker, SSK, k1, slip shoulder marker, k1, K2TOG, work in established pattern to end. [2 stitches decreased]
Work next 7 rows in established pattern without increases.
Repeat last 8 rows _ (_, _, _, _, _), {_, _, 2, 6} more time(s). [_ (_, _, _, _, _), {_, _, 138, 130} stitches]

Decrease Row (RS): Work in established pattern to 3 stitches before shoulder marker, SSK, k1, slip shoulder marker, k1, K2TOG, work in established pattern to end. [2 stitches decreased]
Work next 5 rows in established pattern without increases.
Repeat last 6 rows _ (_, _, _, _, _), {_, _, 8, 4} more time(s). [120 stitches]

Decrease Row (RS): Work in established pattern to 3 stitches before shoulder marker, SSK, k1, slip shoulder marker, k1, K2TOG, work in established pattern to end. [118 stitches]

Last row of Lattice Chart worked: Row 5.
Work in established pattern for 3 more rows, working rows 22-24 of Lattice Chart, then work 2 more rows, working Rows 23-24 of Lattice Chart.

All sizes:
Bind off all stitches in pattern.

02 BODY

With US 7/4.5 mm circular needle and RS facing, pick up and knit 122 (132, 144, 152, 166, 188), {192, 210, 216, 232} stitches evenly across longer edge of the Front Yoke [see Diagram 2, (page 106)]. Place side marker, then, with the same yarn, pick up and knit 122 (132, 144, 152, 166, 188), {192, 210, 216, 232} stitches evenly across longer edge of the Back Yoke. Place beginning of the round marker (BOR) and join in the round.

Continue working in the round on 244 (264, 288, 304, 332, 376), {384, 420, 432, 464} Body stitches.

Sizes XS (S, M, L, XL, 2X), {3X, 4X, _, 6X} only:
Chart Set-Up Round 1: *K1, work first 10 stitches of Round 1 of Body Chart for your size, then work 22 (20, 22, 20, 22, 22), {20, 22, _, 22}-stitch Body Chart repeat 5 (6, 6, 7, 7, 8), {9, 9, _, 10} times, k1*, slip side marker, repeat from * to * once more.
Chart Set-Up Round 2: *K1, work first 10 stitches of Round 2 of Body Chart for your size, then work 22 (20, 22, 20, 22, 22), {20, 22, _, 22}-stitch Body Chart repeat 5 (6, 6, 7, 7, 8), {9, 9, _, 10} times, k1*, slip side marker, repeat from * to * once more.

Size _ (_, _, _, _, _), {_, _, 5X, _} only:
Chart Set-Up Round 1: *K1, p2, work first 10 stitches of Round 1 of Body Chart for your size, then work 20-stitch Body Chart repeat 10 times, p2, k1*, slip side marker, repeat from * to * once more.
Chart Set-Up Round 2: *K1, p2, work first 10 stitches of Round 2 of Body Chart for your size, then work 20-stitch Body Chart repeat 10 times, p2, k1*, slip side marker, repeat from * to * once more.

All sizes:
Continue working in established pattern, repeating Rounds 3-10 of Body Chart for your size, until Body measures 9½ (9½, 10½, 10½, 10½, 10½), {11½, 11½, 11½, 11½}"/24 (24, 26.5, 26.5, 26.5, 26.5), {29, 29, 29, 29} cm.

Next Round: K1, purl to last stitch before side marker, k1, slip side marker, k1, purl to last stitch before BOR, k1.
Repeat last round once.

Change to US 6/4 mm 24-32"/60-80 cm circular needle.
Ribbing Round: K1, *p2, k2; repeat from * to last 3 stitches, p2, k1. Repeat Ribbing Round until ribbing measures 2½"/6.5 cm.

Bind off all stitches in pattern or using Tubular method for k2, p2 rib in the round (see Special Techniques, page 226).

03 SLEEVES (make 2)

With US 7/4.5 mm circular needle and your preferred Provisional method, cast on 52 stitches [see Diagram 3, (page 106)].

Next Row (WS): Purl all stitches.

Chart Set-Up Row 1 (RS): K3, p2, k2, p3, place chart marker, work Row 1 of Lattice Chart, place chart marker, p3, k2, p2, k3.
Chart Set-Up Row 2 (WS): P3, k2, p2, k3, slip chart marker, work Row 2 of Lattice Chart, slip chart marker, k3, p2, k2, p3.

Sizes XS (S, _, _, XL, 2X), {_, _, 5X, 6X} only:
Continue following the Lattice Chart and work rows 3-4 twice, then work rows 5-20 six (6, _, _, 7, 7), {_, _, 8, 8} times, then work rows 21-24 once, then work rows 23-24 once.

Sizes _ (_, M, L, _, _), {2X, 3X, _, _} only:
Continue following the Lattice Chart and work rows 3-4 once, then work rows 5-20 _ (_, 7, 7, _, _), {8, 8, _, _} times, then work rows 21-24 once.

All sizes:
Place live stitches of the last row on hold. Block sleeve to measurements.

Transfer live stitches from cast on to circular needle and live stitches from last row to the second circular needle [see Diagram 4, (page 106)]. With right sides held together and wrong side out, join ends together, using 3-Needle Bind Off (see Special Techniques, page 226) to create the tube. Turn the tube to right side.

Cuff
With RS facing and US 6/4 mm double-pointed needles, beginning at the seam, pick up and knit 72 (72, 76, 76, 80, 80), {88, 88, 92, 92} stitches evenly along the right sleeve selvage [see Diagram 5, (page 106)]. Place marker and join in the round.

Ribbing Round: K1, *p2, k2; repeat from * to last 3 stitches, p2, k1. Repeat Ribbing Round until cuff measures 8 (8, 8, 8, 8, 8), {7½, 7½, 7, 7}"/20 (20, 20, 20, 20, 20), {19, 19, 17.5, 17.5} cm.

Bind off all stitches in pattern or using Tubular method for k2, p2 rib in the round (see Special Techniques, page 226).

04 FINISHING

Sew both sleeves into armholes.

Neckband
With US 6/4 mm 16"/40 cm circular needle, beginning at the center of Right Shoulder, pick up and knit 38 (40, 50, 50, 54, 56), {54, 54, 60, 60} stitches along the back neck, 8 stitches along left side of front neck, 26 (28, 34, 34, 38, 40), {38, 38, 40, 40} stitches evenly along center of the front neck, 8 stitches along the right side of the front neck. [80 (84, 100, 100, 108, 112), {108, 108, 116, 116} stitches]

Ribbing Round: K1, *p2, k2; repeat from * to last 3 stitches, p2, k1.
Repeat Ribbing Round until neckband measures 1"/2.5 cm.

Bind off all stitches in pattern or using Tubular method for k2, p2 rib in the round. Weave in ends. Block to measurements.

DIAGRAM

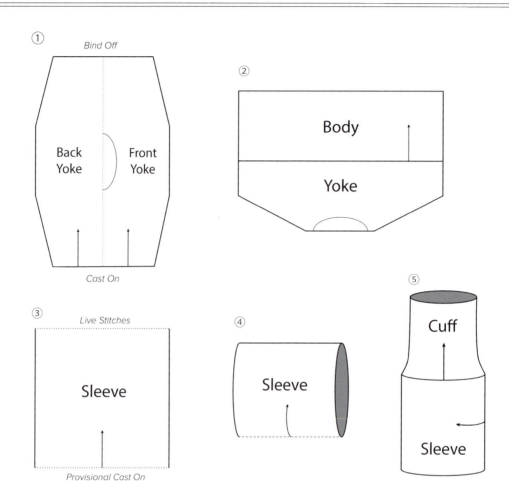

① Bind Off

Back Yoke   Front Yoke

Cast On

② Body

Yoke

③ Live Stitches

Sleeve

Provisional Cast On

④ Sleeve

⑤ Cuff

Sleeve

LEGEND

☐ **K**: Knit stitch on RS rows and all rounds; purl stitch on WS rows

⊡ **P**: Purl stitch on RS rows and all rounds; knit stitch on WS rows

1/1 RC: Slip 1 stitch to cable needle, hold in back, k1, k1 from cable needle

2/2 RC: Slip 2 stitches to cable needle, hold in back, knit 2, knit 2 from cable needle

2/2 LC: Slip 2 stitches to cable needle, hold in front, knit 2, knit 2 from cable needle

2/2 RPC: Slip 2 stitches to cable needle, hold in back, k2, p2 from cable needle

2/2 LPC: Slip 2 stitches to cable needle, hold in front, p2, k2 from cable needle

6/6 RC: Slip 6 stitches to cable needle, hold in back, k2, p2, k2, (k2, p2, k2) from cable needle

6/6 LC: Slip 6 stitches to cable needle, hold in front, k2, p2, k2, (k2, p2, k2) from cable needle

☐ Pattern repeat

CHARTS

LATTICE CHART

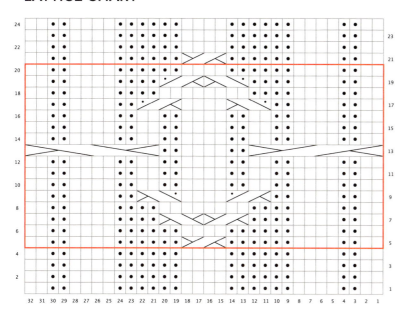

BODY CHART (SIZES XS (_, M, _, XL, 2XL), {_, 4XL, _, 6XL} ONLY)

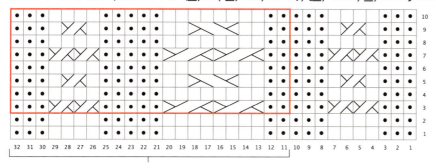

22-stitch repeat

BODY CHART (SIZES _ (S, _, L, _, _), {3XL, _, 5XL, _} ONLY)

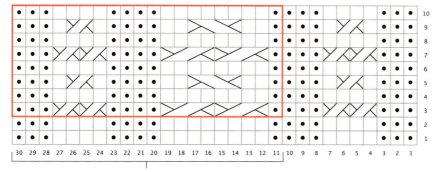

20-stitch repeat

Row 12 (WS): [P2, k2, p4, k2] 3 times, p2.
Row 13 (RS): 6/6 RC, p2, k4, p2, 6/6 LC.
Row 14 (WS): [P2, k2, p4, k2] 3 times, p2.
Row 15 (RS): [K2, p2, k4, p2] 3 times, k2.
Row 16 (WS): [P2, k2, p4, k2] 3 times, p2.
Row 17 (RS): K2, p2, k4, p2, 2/2 LPC, k4, 2/2 RPC, p2, k4, p2, k2.
Row 18 (WS): P2, k2, p4, k4, p8, k4, p4, k2, p2.
Row 19 (RS): K2, p2, k4, p4, 2/2 LPC, 2/2 RPC, p4, k4, p2, k2.
Row 20 (WS): P2, k2, [p4, k6] 2 times, p4, k2, p2.
Row 21 (RS): K2, p2, k4, p6, 2/2 RC, p6, k4, p2, k2.
Row 22 (WS): P2, k2, [p4, k6] 2 times, p4, k2, p2.
Rows 23-24: Repeat rows 1-2.

Written instructions for Body Chart
(sizes XS (_, M, _, XL, 2XL), {_, 4XL, _, 6XL} only)
.. – pattern repeat

Rounds 1-2: P3, k4, p3, *p2, k8, p5, k4, p3*
Round 3: P3, [1/1 RC] 2 times, p3, *p2, [2/2 RC] 2 times, p5, [1/1 RC] 2 time, p3*
Round 4: P3, k4, p3, *p2, k8, p5, k4, p3*
Round 5: P3, k1, 1/1 RC, k1, p3, *p2, k2, 2/2 LC, k2, p5, k1, 1/1 RC, k1, p3*.
Rounds 6-9: Repeat rounds 2-5.
Round 10: P3, k4, p3, *p2, k8, p5, k4, p3*

Written instructions for Yoke Chart
(sizes _ (S, _, L, _, _), {3XL, _, 5XL, _} only)
.. – pattern repeat

Rounds 1 - 2: P3, k4, p3, *p1, k8, p4, k4, p3*
Round 3: P3, [1/1 RC] 2 times, p3, *p1, [2/2 RC] 2 times, p4, [1/1 RC] 2 times, p3*
Round 4: P3, k4, p3, *p1, k8, p4, k4, p3*
Round 5: P3, k1, 1/1 RC, k1, p3, *p1, k2, 2/2 LC, k2, p4, k1, 1/1 RC, k1, p3*.
Rounds 6-9: Repeat rounds 2-5.
Round 10: P3, k4, p3, *p1, k8, p4, k4, p3*

Written instructions for Lattice Chart
Note: See Chart Legend for special abbreviations.

Row 1 (RS): K2, p2, [k4, p6] 2 times, k4, p2, k2.
Row 2 (WS): P2, k2, [p4, k6] 2 times, p4, k2, p2.
Rows 3-4: Repeat rows 1-2.
Row 5 (RS): K2, p2, k4, p6, 2/2 RC, p6, k4, p2, k2.
Row 6 (WS): P2, k2, [p4, k6] 2 times, p4, k2, p2.
Row 7 (RS): K2, p2, k4, p4, 2/2 RC, 2/2 LC, p4, k4, p2, k2.
Row 8 (WS): P2, k2, p4, k4, p8, k4, p4, k2, p2.
Row 9 (RS): K2, p2, k4, p2, 2/2 RPC, k4, 2/2 LPC, p2, k4, p2, k2.
Row 10 (WS): [P2, k2, p4, k2] 3 times, p2.
Row 11 (RS): [K2, p2, k4, p2] 3 times, k2.

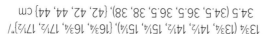

13¾ (13¾, 14½, 14½, 15¼, 15¼), {16¾, 16¾, 17½, 17½}"/
34.5 (34.5, 36.5, 36.5, 38, 38), {42, 42, 44, 44} cm
8 (8, 8, 8, 8, 8), {7½, 7½, 7, 7}"/
20 (20, 20, 20, 20, 20), {19, 19, 17.5, 17.5} cm
8¼"/ 20.5cm
16 (16, 17, 17, 18, 18), {20, 20, 21, 21}"/
40 (40, 42.5, 42.5, 45, 45), {50, 50, 52.5, 52.5} cm
6½ (7, 8¼, 8¾, 9¼, 9¾), {9¼, 9¼, 9¾, 9¾}"/
16.5 (17.5, 20.5, 22, 23, 24.5), {23, 23, 24.5, 24.5} cm
20¼ (22, 24, 25¼, 27¾, 31¼), {32, 35, 36, 38¾}"/
50.5 (55, 60, 63, 69.5, 78), {80, 87.5, 90, 97} cm
40½ (44, 48, 50½, 55½, 62½), {64, 70, 72, 77½}"/
101.5 (110, 120, 126.5, 139, 156.5), {160, 175, 180, 194} cm
6½ (7½, 8, 8¾, 9¾, 10½), {11½, 12½, 13¼, 14¼}"/
16.5 (19, 20, 22, 24.5, 26.5), {29, 31.5, 33, 35.5} cm
12¼ (12¼, 13¼, 13¼, 13¼, 13¼), {14¼, 14¼, 14¼, 14¼}"/
30.5 (30.5, 33, 33, 33, 33), {35.5, 35.5, 35.5, 35.5} cm
7¾ (7¾, 8¼, 8¼, 8½, 8½), {9¼, 9¼, 9¾, 9¾}"/
19.5 (19.5, 20.5, 20.5, 21.5, 21.5), {23, 23, 24.5, 24.5} cm

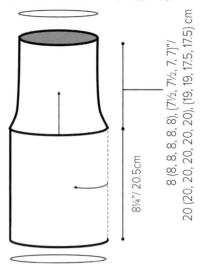

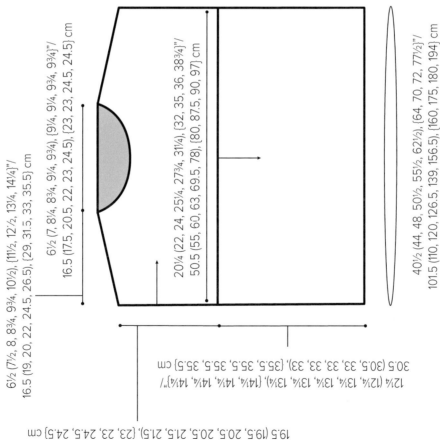

Narn

An allover leaf-inspired motif gives this pullover a rich surface texture, with repeating shapes that feel organic and sculptural. The patterning is created with strategically placed increases and decreases, forming raised leaves that play beautifully with light and shadow across the fabric.

Worked seamlessly from the bottom up, the design features a relaxed fit, short sleeves, and a clean crew neckline. Narn is a versatile layering piece, equally suited for warm-weather wear or transitional seasons.

Sizes

XS (S, M, L, XL, 2XL), {3XL, 4XL, 5XL, 6XL}: to fit bust 28-30 (32-34, 36-38, 40-42, 44-46, 48-50), {52-54, 56-58, 60-62, 64-66}"/70-75 (80-85, 90-95, 100-105, 110-115, 120-125), {130-135, 140-145, 150-155, 160-165} cm.

Finished Measurements

35¼ (40¼, 45½, 50½, 55½, 56¼), {62, 65½, 70½, 75½}"/88 (100.5, 114, 126.5, 139, 140.5), {155, 164, 176.5, 189} cm bust circumference.
Intended ease: +5-9"/12.5-22.5 cm
Shown in size M (45½"/114 cm) on 38"/95 cm bust with 7½"/19 cm of positive ease.

Yarn

Sport weight yarn (approximate amounts):
930 (1060, 1190, 1330, 1460, 1480), {1630, 1730, 1860, 2000} yds/846 (965, 1083, 1210, 1329, 1347), {1483, 1574, 1693, 1820} m.

Miss Babs Laurel Falls (100% Superwash Shaniko Merino Wool; 300 yards/275 m in 100 g),
Cedar – 4 (4, 4, 5, 5, 5), {6, 6, 7, 7} skeins.

Needles

Size US 4/3.5 mm: 24-32"/60-80 cm circular, 16"/40 cm circular.
Size US 3/3.25 mm: 24-32"/60-80 cm circular, 16"/40 cm circular. Optional: spare US 3/3.25 mm 24-32"/60-80 cm circular needle for Tubular cast on and bind off.
Adjust needle size if necessary to obtain gauge.

Notions

Stitch markers, stitch holders, tapestry needle.

Gauge

27 stitches and 34 rounds = 4"/10 cm in charted pattern on size US 4/3.5 mm needle, after blocking.
23 stitches and 34 rounds = 4"/10 cm in Stockinette Stitch on size US 4/3.5 mm needle, after blocking.

Notes

- This top is worked from the bottom up in the round to underarms, then front and back are worked separately.
- Stitches for the sleeves are picked up around the armholes and sleeves are worked in the round from the top down..
- The Body Chart is worked in the round and in rows. When working flat in rows, read odd-numbered chart rows from right to left, and even-numbered rows from left to right.

DIRECTIONS

01 BODY

NOTE: If you do not wish to work a Tubular Cast On, cast on 238 (272, 306, 340, 374, 380), {418, 442, 476, 510} stitches, using US 3/3.25 mm circular needle 24-32"/60-80 cm long, working yarn, and your preferred method for a stretchy cast on. Proceed to the Ribbing Round.

Tubular Cast On (see Special Techniques, page 226)
With waste yarn, US 3/3.25 mm 24-32"/60-80 circular needle and using your preferred method, cast on 173 (194, 217, 232, 250, 268), {280, 289, 301, 313} stitches. Do not join in the round.

Foundation Row (RS): Knit all stitches in row. This row is worked directly into your waste yarn stitches.
Row 1 (WS): Purl to end.
Row 2 (RS): Knit to end.
Row 3 (WS): Purl to end.

Carefully remove waste yarn from cast on and place 119 (136, 153, 170, 187, 190), {209, 221, 238, 255} cast-on stitches onto 2nd US 3/3.25 mm 24-32"/60-80 circular needle. Bring needle with cast-on stitches up behind working needle, with WS together.

Next Row (RS): *K1 from front needle, p1 from back needle; repeat from * to end. [238 (272, 306, 340, 374, 380), {418, 442, 476, 510} stitches on the needle]. Join for working in the round, place beginning-of-the-round marker (BOR).

Ribbing Round: *K1, p1; repeat from * to end.
Repeat Ribbing Round until piece measures 1½"/4 cm from cast on row.

Change to US 4/3.5 mm circular needle 24-32"/60-80 long.

Chart Set-Up Round: *Work Row 1 of Body Chart, working 17 (17, 17, 17, 17, 19), {19, 17, 17, 17}-stitch pattern repeat 7 (8, 9, 10, 11, 10), {11, 13, 14, 15} times*, place side marker, repeat from * to * once.

Continue working in established pattern, following Body Chart and slipping markers, until Body measures 12 (12, 12, 13, 13, 14), {14, 14, 14, 14}"/30 (30, 30, 32.5, 32.5, 35), {35, 35, 35, 35} cm from the cast-on edge, ending with even-numbered chart round.

Division Round: Work next round of Body Chart to side marker, place 119 (136, 153, 170, 187, 190), {209, 221, 238, 255} just worked stitches on hold for Front, work same round of Body Chart to end. [119 (136, 153, 170, 187, 190), {209, 221, 238, 255} on the needle for Back]

Continue working on Back stitches in rows.

02 BACK

Next Row (WS): Work next (even-numbered) row of Body Chart.

Increase Row 1 (RS): K1, place marker, M1P, work next row of Body Chart as follows: work stitches 2-17 (2-17, 2-17, 2-17, 2-17, 2-19), {2-19, 2-19, 2-17, 2-17} of the first chart repeat, then follow the chart to last chart repeat, work stitches 1-16 (1-16, 1-16, 1-16, 1-16, 1-18), {1-18, 1-18, 1-16, 1-16} of last chart repeat, M1P, place marker, k1. [2 stitches increased]
Next Row (WS): P1, slip marker, work next row of Body Chart to marker, slip marker, p1.

Increase Row 2 (RS): K1, M1L, slip marker, work next row of Body Chart to marker, slip marker, M1R, k1. [123 (140, 157, 174, 191, 194), {213, 225, 242, 259} stitches]

Next Row (WS): P2, slip marker, work next row of Body Chart to marker, slip marker, p2.
Next Row (RS): K2, slip marker, work next row of Body Chart to marker, slip marker, k2.

Work in established by the last 2 rows pattern until Back measures 8 (8, 8½, 8½, 9, 9½), {10, 11, 11½, 11½}"/20 (20, 21.5, 21.5, 22.5, 24), {25, 27.5, 29, 29} cm, ending with WS row.

NOTE: When shaping the shoulders, make sure that every increase in pattern has a corresponding decrease. If it is impossible, substitute increase or decrease with knit or purl stitch.

Shape shoulders with German Short-Rows (see Special Techniques, page 226):
Short-Row 1 (RS): Work in established pattern to last 3 (4, 4, 5, 6, 6), {7, 7, 8, 9} stitches, turn work.
Short-Row 2 (WS): Make double stitch, work in established pattern to last 3 (4, 4, 5, 6, 6), {7, 7, 8, 9} stitches, turn work.
Short-Row 3 (RS): Make double stitch, work in established pattern to 3 (4, 4, 5, 6, 6), {7, 7, 8, 9} before double stitch, turn work.
Short-Row 4 (WS): Make double stitch, work in established pattern to 3 (4, 4, 5, 6, 6), {7, 7, 8, 9} before double stitch, turn work.

Short-Rows 5-10: Repeat Short-Rows 3 and 4 another 3 times.

Short-Row 11 (RS): Make double stitch, work all stitches as they present themselves (knit the knits and purl the purls), to end, working double stitches as single stitches.
Break yarn. Turn work so the WS is facing.

Next Row (WS): Place first 38 (46, 52, 60, 69, 70), {78, 84, 91, 99} stitches on hold for Left Shoulder, join working yarn and bind off next 47 (48, 53, 54, 53, 54), {57, 57, 60, 61} stitches; work 38 (46, 52, 60, 69, 70), {78, 84, 91, 99} remaining Right Shoulder stitches as they present themselves (knit the knits and purl the purls), to double stitch, work double stitch as regular stitch, purl to end.

03 FRONT

Place held 119 (136, 153, 170, 187, 190), {209, 221, 238, 255} Front stitches on US 4/3.5 mm circular needle 24-32"/60-80 long and join yarn, ready to work WS row.

Next Row (WS): Work next (even-numbered) row of Body Chart.

Increase Row 1 (RS): K1, place marker, M1P, work next row of Body Chart as follows: work stitches 2-17 (2-17, 2-17, 2-17, 2-17, 2-19), {2-19, 2-19, 2-17, 2-17} of the first chart repeat, then follow the chart to last chart repeat, work stitches 1-16 (1-16, 1-16, 1-16, 1-16, 1-18), {1-18, 1-18, 1-16, 1-16} of last chart repeat, M1P, place marker, k1. [2 stitches increased]
Next Row (WS): P1, slip marker, work next row of Body Chart to marker, slip marker, p1.
Increase Row 2 (RS): K1, M1L, slip marker, work next row of Body Chart to marker, slip marker, M1R, k1. [123 (140, 157, 174, 191, 194), {213, 225, 242, 259} stitches]
Next Row (WS): P2, slip marker, work next row of Body Chart to marker, slip marker, p2.
Next Row (RS): K2, slip marker, work next row of Body Chart to marker, slip marker, k2.

Work in established by the last 2 rows pattern until Back measures 6½ (6½, 7, 7, 7½, 8), {8½, 9½, 10, 10}"/16.5 (16.5, 17.5, 17.5, 19, 20), {21.5, 24, 25, 25} cm, ending with WS row.

Shape Front neck
Next Row (RS): Work in pattern 46 (54, 60, 68, 77, 78), {86, 92, 99, 107} stitches and place them on hold for Left Front, bind off next 31 (32, 37, 38, 37, 38), {41, 41, 44, 45} stitches, work in pattern to end. [46 (54, 60, 68, 77, 78), {86, 92, 99, 107} stitches left for Right Front]

Continue working on Right Front stitches.

03a. Right Front
Next Row (WS): Work in pattern to end.

At the beginning of the next 6 RS rows, bind off 3 stitches once, 2 stitches 2 times, then 1 stitch once. [38 (46, 52, 60, 69, 70), {78, 84, 91, 99} stitches]

Next Row (WS): Work in pattern to end. Continue working even in established pattern even, until Right Front measures 8 (8, 8½, 8½, 9, 9½), {10, 11, 11½, 11½}"/ 20 (20, 21.5, 21.5, 22.5, 24), {25, 27.5, 29, 29} cm from the beginning of the armhole, ending with the same WS row as the Back right before the shoulder shaping.

Shape Right Shoulder, using German Short-Rows:
Short-Row 1 (RS): Work in established pattern to last 3 (4, 4, 5, 6, 6), {7, 7, 8, 9} stitches, turn work.
Short-Row 2 (WS): Make double stitch, work to end.
Short-Row 3 (RS): Work to 3 (4, 4, 5, 6, 6), {7, 7, 8, 9} stitches before double stitch, turn work.
Short-Row 4 (WS): Make double stitch, work to end.

Short-Rows 5-10: Repeat Short-Rows 3 and 4 another 3 times.
Next Row (RS): Work in pattern to end of the row, working double stitch as single stitch.
Next Row (WS): Work in pattern to end.

Place stitches on hold, break yarn, leaving long tail for 3-Needle Bind Off (see Special Techniques, page 226).

03b. Left Front
Place held 46 (54, 60, 68, 77, 78), {86, 92, 99, 107} Left Front stitches onto US 4/3.5 mm circular needle 24-32"/60-80 long and join yarn with WS facing.

Next Row (WS): Work in pattern to end.
Next Row (RS): Work in pattern to end.

At the beginning of the next 6 WS rows, bind off 3 stitches once, 2 stitches 2 times, then 1 stitch once. [38 (46, 52, 60, 69, 70), {78, 84, 91, 99} stitches]

Next Row (RS): Work in pattern to end.
Continue working even in established pattern even until Left Front measures 8 (8, 8½, 8½, 9, 9½), {10, 11, 11½, 11½}"/20 (20, 21.5, 21.5, 22.5, 24), {25, 27.5, 29, 29} cm from the beginning of the armhole, ending with RS row.

Shape Left Shoulder, using German Short-Rows:
Short-Row 1 (WS): Work in established pattern to last 3 (4, 4, 5, 6, 6), {7, 7, 8, 9} stitches, turn work.
Short-Row 2 (RS): Make double stitch, work to end.
Short-Row 3 (WS): Work to 3 (4, 4, 5, 6, 6), {7, 7, 8, 9} stitches before double stitch, turn work.

Short-Rows 4-9: Repeat Short-Rows 2 and 3 another 3 times.
Short-Row 10 (RS): Make double stitch, work to end.

Next Row (WS): Work in pattern to end of the row, working double stitch as single stitch.
Place stitches on hold, break yarn, leaving long tail for 3-Needle Bind Off.
Join shoulders, using 3-needle Bind Off Method.

04 SLEEVES

With US 4/3.5 mm circular needle 16"/40 cm long, with RS facing, beginning at the underarm, pick up and knit 92 (92, 98, 98, 104, 104), {116, 126, 132, 132} stitches around the armhole. Join for working in the round, place beginning-of-the round marker.

Next Round: Knit.

Decrease Round: K1, K2TOG, knit to last 3 stitches, SSK, k1. [2 stitches decreased]
Repeat Decrease Round another 8 times in every 2nd round. [74 (74, 80, 80, 86, 86), {98, 108, 114, 114} stitches]

Change to size US 3/3.25 mm circular needle 16"/40 cm long and work in k1, p1 rib for 1"/2.5 cm.
Bind off all stitches in pattern or using Tubular bind off method for k1, p1 rib (see Special Techniques, page 226).

05 FINISHING

Neckband
With RS facing and US 3/3.25 mm 16"/40 cm circular needle, beginning at the right shoulder seam, pick up and knit 44 (46, 50, 50, 50, 50), {54, 54, 56, 56} stitches evenly along back neck, then pick up and knit 80 (82, 88, 88, 88, 88), {90, 90, 94, 96} stitches along front neck. Place beginning-of-the-round marker. and join for working in the round. [124 (128, 138, 138, 138, 138), {144, 144, 150, 152} stitches]

Ribbing Round: *K1, p1; repeat from * to the end of the round.
Repeat Ribbing Round another 7 times.

Bind off all stitches in pattern or using Tubular bind off method for k1, p1 rib.
Weave in ends. Block to measurements.

CHARTS

BODY CHART
(SIZES XS (S, M, L, XL, _), {_, 4XL, 5XL, 6XL} ONLY)

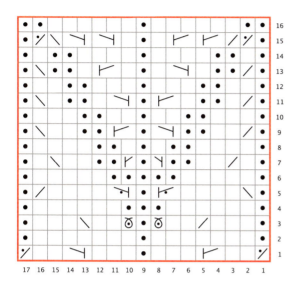

BODY CHART
(SIZES _ (_, _, _, _, 2XL), {3XL, _, _, _} ONLY)

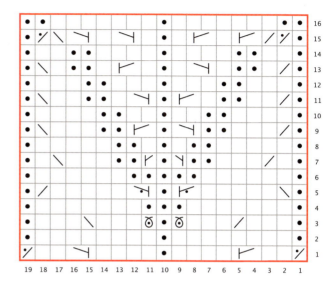

LEGEND

☐ **K:** Knit stitch on RS rows and all rounds; purl stitch on WS

☐ **P:** Purl stitch on RS rows and all rounds; knit stitch on WS

☐ **K2TOG:** Knit 2 stitches together – 1 stitch decreased with right slant.

☐ **SSK:** Slip 1 stitch knitwise, slip 1 stitch knitwise, return 2 slipped stitches back to left needle and knit them together through back loops – 1 stitch decreased with left slant

☐ **P2TOG:** Purl 2 stitches together – 1 stitch decreased

☐ **M1P:** With left needle tip, pick up the thread between stitches from back to front. Purl lifted loop through the front loop – 1 stitch increased

☐ **M1R:** With left needle tip, pick up the thread between stitches from back to front. Knit lifted loop through the front loop – 1 stitch increased with right slant

☐ **M1L:** With left needle tip, pick up the thread between stitches from front to back. Knit lifted loop through the backloop – 1 stitch increased with left slant

☐ **RLI:** Knit into back of the stitch in the row directly below the first stitch on the left needle, then knit the first stitch – 1 stitch increased with right slant

☐ **LLI:** K1, insert the left needle into the back of the first stitch on the right needle just below the stitch just knit, and knit it – 1 stitch increased with left slant

☐ **RLIP:** Purl into back of the stitch in the row directly below the first stitch on the left needle, then purl the first stitch – 1 stitch increased right slant

☐ **LLIP:** P1, insert the left needle into the back of the first stitch on the right needle just below the stitch just purled, and purl it – 1 stitch increased with left slant

☐ Pattern repeat

Written instructions for Body Chart (worked in the round)

(sizes XS (S, M, L, XL, _), {_, 4XL, 5XL, 6XL} only)

... – pattern repeat

Note: See Chart Legend for special abbreviations.

Round 1: *P2TOG, k2, RLI, k3, p1, k3, LLI, k2, P2TOG*
Round 2: *[P1, k7] 2 times, p1*
Round 3: *P1, k3, K2TOG, k2, M1P, p1, M1P, k2, SSK, k3, p1*
Round 4: *P1, k6, p3, k6, p1*
Round 5: *P1, SSK, k4, RLIP, p1, LLIP, k4, K2TOG, p1*
Round 6: *P1, k5, p5, k5, p1*
Round 7: *P1, k1, K2TOG, k2, p2, M1L, p1, M1R, p2, k2, SSK, k1, p1*
Round 8: *P1, k4, p2, k1, p1, k1, p2, k4, p1*
Round 9: *P1, K2TOG, k2, p2, LLI, p1, RLI, p2, k2, SSK, p1*
Round 10: *P1, k3, p2, k2, p1, k2, p2, k3, p1*
Round 11: *P1, K2TOG, k1, p2, k1, RLI, p1, LLI, k1, p2, k1, SSK, p1*
Round 12: *P1, k2, p2, k3, p1, k3, p2, k2, p1*
Round 13: *P1, K2TOG, p2, k1, LLI, k1, p1, k1, RLI, k1, p2, SSK, p1*
Round 14: *P1, k1, p2, k4, p1, k4, p2, k1, p1*
Round 15: *P1, P2TOG, K2TOG, [RLI] 2 times, k1, p1, k1, [LLI] 2 times, SSK, P2TOG, p1*
Round 16: *P2, k6, p1, k6, p2*

Written instructions for Body Chart (worked in rows)

(sizes XS (S, M, L, XL, _), {_, 4XL, 5XL, 6XL} only)

... – pattern repeat

Row 1 (RS): *P2TOG, k2, RLI, k3, p1, k3, LLI, k2, P2TOG* Row 2 (WS): *[K1, p7] 2 times, k1*
Row 3 (RS): *P1, k3, K2TOG, k2, M1P, p1, M1P, k2, SSK, k3, p1*
Row 4 (WS): *K1, p6, k3, p6, k1*
Row 5 (RS): *P1, SSK, k4, RLIP, p1, LLIP, k4, K2TOG, p1*
Row 6 (WS): *K1, p5, k5, p5, k1*
Row 7 (RS): *P1, k1, K2TOG, k2, p2, M1L, p1, M1R, p2, k2, SSK, k1, p1*
Row 8 (WS): *K1, p4, k2, p1, k1, p1, k2, p4, k1*
Row 9 (RS): *P1, K2TOG, k2, p2, LLI, p1, RLI, p2, k2, SSK, p1*
Row 10 (WS): *K1, p3, k2, p2, k1, p2, k2, p3, k1*

Row 11 (RS): *P1, K2TOG, k1, p2, k1, RLI, p1, LLI, k1, p2, k1, SSK, p1*
Row 12 (WS): *K1, p2, k2, p3, k1, p3, k2, p2, k1*
Row 13 (RS): *P1, K2TOG, p2, k1, LLI, k1, p1, k1, RLI, k1, p2, SSK, p1*
Row 14 (WS): *K1, p1, k2, p4, k1, p4, k2, p1, k1*
Row 15 (RS): *P1, P2TOG, K2TOG, [RLI] 2 times, k1, p1, k1, [LLI] 2 times, SSK, P2TOG, p1*
Row 16 (WS): *K2, p6, k1, p6, k2*

Written instructions for Body Chart (worked in the round)

(sizes _ (_, _, _, _, 2XL), {3XL, _, _, _} only)

... – pattern repeat

Round 1: *P2TOG, k2, RLI, k4, p1, k4, LLI, k2, P2TOG*
Round 2: *[P1, k8] 2 times, p1*
Round 3: *P1, k3, K2TOG, k3, M1P, p1, M1P, k3, SSK, k3, p1*
Round 4: *P1, k7, p3, k7, p1*
Round 5: *P1, SSK, k5, RLIP, p1, LLIP, k5, K2TOG, p1*
Round 6: *P1, k6, p5, k6, p1*
Round 7: *P1, k1, K2TOG, k3, p2, M1L, p1, M1R, p2, k3, SSK, k1, p1*
Round 8: *P1, k5, p2, k1, p1, k1, p2, k5, p1*
Round 9: *P1, K2TOG, k3, p2, LLI, p1, RLI, p2, k3, SSK, p1*
Round 10: *P1, k4, p2, k2, p1, k2, p2, k4, p1*
Round 11: *P1, K2TOG, k2, p2, k1, RLI, p1, LLI, k1, p2, k2, SSK, p1*
Round 12: *[P1, k3, p2, k3] 2 times, p1*
Round 13: *P1, K2TOG, k1, p2, k1, LLI, k1, p1, k1, RLI, k1, p2, k1, SSK, p1*
Round 14: *P1, k2, p2, k4, p1, k4, p2, k2, p1*
Round 15: *P1, P2TOG, K2TOG, [RLI, k1] 2 times, p1, [k1, LLI] 2 times, SSK, P2TOG, p1*
Round 16: *P2, k7, p1, k7, p2*

Written instructions for Body Chart (worked in rows)

(sizes _ (_, _, _, _, 2XL), {3XL, _, _, _} only)

... – pattern repeat

Row 1 (RS): *P2TOG, k2, RLI, k4, p1, k4, LLI, k2, P2TOG* Row 2 (WS): *[K1, p8] 2 times, k1*
Row 3 (RS): *P1, k3, K2TOG, k3, M1P, p1, M1P, k3, SSK, k3, p1*

Row 4 (WS): *K1, p7, k3, p7, k1*

Row 5 (RS): *P1, SSK, k5, RLIP, p1, LLIP, k5, K2TOG, p1*

Row 6 (WS): *K1, p6, k5, p6, k1*

Row 7 (RS): *P1, k1, K2TOG, k3, p2, M1L, p1, M1R, p2, k3, SSK, k1, p1*

Row 8 (WS): *K1, p5, k2, p1, k1, p1, k2, p5, k1*

Row 9 (RS): *P1, K2TOG, k3, p2, LLI, p1, RLI, p2, k3, SSK, p1*

Row 10 (WS): *K1, p4, k2, p2, k1, p2, k2, p4, k1*

Row 11 (RS): *P1, K2TOG, k2, p2, k1, RLI, p1, LLI, k1, p2, k2, SSK, p1*

Row 12 (WS): *[K1, p3, k2, p3] 2 times, k1*

Row 13 (RS): *P1, K2TOG, k1, p2, k1, LLI, k1, p1, k1, RLI, k1, p2, k1, SSK, p1*

Row 14 (WS): *K1, p2, k2, p4, k1, p4, k2, p2, k1*

Row 15 (RS): *P1, P2TOG, K2TOG, [RLI, k1] 2 times, p1, [k1, LLI] 2 times, SSK, P2TOG, p1*

Row 16 (WS): *K2, p7, k1, p7, k2*

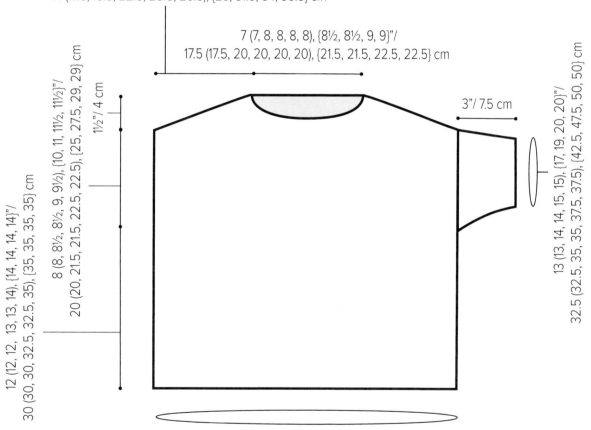

5½ (7, 7¾, 9, 10¼, 10½), {11½, 12½, 13½, 14½}"/
14 (17.5, 19.5, 22.5, 25.5, 26.5), {29, 31.5, 34, 36.5} cm

7 (7, 8, 8, 8, 8), {8½, 8½, 9, 9}"/
17.5 (17.5, 20, 20, 20, 20), {21.5, 21.5, 22.5, 22.5} cm

3"/ 7.5 cm

1½"/ 4 cm

8 (8, 8½, 8½, 9, 9½), {10, 11, 11½, 11½}"/
20 (20, 21.5, 21.5, 22.5, 22.5), {25, 27.5, 29, 29} cm

12 (12, 12, 13, 13, 14), {14, 14, 14, 14}"/
30 (30, 30, 32.5, 32.5, 35), {35, 35, 35, 35} cm

13 (13, 14, 14, 15, 15), {17, 19, 20, 20}"/
32.5 (32.5, 35, 35, 37.5, 37.5), {42.5, 47.5, 50, 50} cm

35¼ (40¼, 45½, 50½, 55½, 56¼), {62, 65½, 70½, 75½}"/
88 (100.5, 114, 126.5, 139, 140.5), {155, 164, 176.5, 189} cm

Barnsley

Flowing lace and rhythmic texture define this triangular shawl, worked from the top down with a central spine that anchors the design. Zig zag lace panels alternate with eyelet ladders and textured ridges, creating a fabric that is both airy and structured. The interplay of openwork and solid stitches forms a bold geometric rhythm, while the scalloped lower edge gives the shawl a graceful finish.

Finished Measurements
72"/180 cm wingspan.
31"/77.5 cm height at center spine.
Measurements are taken after blocking.

Yarn
Fingering weight yarn (approximate amount):
1150 yards/1047 m.
Miss Babs Yummy 2-Ply (100% Superwash Merino Wool; 400 yards/365 m in 110 gr): Fleur de Sel – 3 skeins.

Needles
Size US 3/3.25 mm: 32"/80 cm circular.
Adjust needle size if necessary to obtain the correct gauge.

Notions
Stitch markers, tapestry needle.

Gauge
20 stitches and 34 rows = 4"/10 cm in charted pattern, after blocking.

Notes
- The shawl is worked flat; a circular needle is used to accommodate the large number of stitches.
- Read RS (odd-numbered) chart rows from right to left; read WS (even-numbered) chart rows from left to right.

DIRECTIONS

Knitted Cord Tab
Cast on 2 stitches.

Row 1: K2, slip 2 stitches from right to left needle.
Rows 2–4: Repeat Row 1 three more times.
Row 5 (RS): K2, turn the work 90 degrees clockwise and pick up and knit 3 stitches along left edge of Knitted Tab (picking up from left leg of last Knitted Tab stitch), turn the work 90 degrees clockwise again and pick up and knit 2 stitches from cast-on edge. [7 stitches]
Row 6 (WS): K2, p1, place marker, p1, place marker, p1, k2.
Row 7 (RS): K2, M1L, k1, M1R, slip marker, k1, slip marker, M1L, k1, M1R, k2. [11 stitches]
Row 8 (WS): K2, purl to last 2 stitches, slipping markers, k2.
Row 9 (RS): K2, M1P, k3, M1P, slip marker, k1, slip marker, M1P, k3, M1P, k2. [15 stitches]
Row 10 (WS): K2, place marker, k1, p3, k1, slip marker, p1, slip marker, k1, p3, k1, place marker, k2.

01 SECTION A

Chart A Set-Up Row 1 (RS): K2, slip marker, work Row 1 of Chart A, slip marker, k1, slip marker, work Row 1 of Chart A, slip marker, k2. [19 stitches]
Chart A Set-Up Row 2 (WS): K2, slip marker, work Row 2 of Chart A, slip marker, p1, slip marker, work Row 2 of Chart A, slip marker, k2.

Continue working in established pattern, following Chart A through Row 28. [71 stitches]

02 SECTION B

Chart B Set-Up Row 1 (RS): K2, slip marker, work Row 1 of Chart B, working the 14-stitch chart repeat twice, slip marker, k1, slip marker, work Row 1 of Chart B, working the 14-stitch chart repeat twice, slip marker, k2. [75 stitches]

Chart B Set-Up Row 2 (WS): K2, slip marker, work Row 2 of Chart B, working the 14-stitch chart repeat twice, slip marker, p1, slip marker, work Row 2 of Chart B, working the 14-stitch chart repeat twice, slip marker, k2.

Continue working in established pattern, following Chart B through Row 42. [155 stitches]

03 SECTION C

Chart C Set-Up Row 1 (RS): K2, slip marker, work Row 1 of Chart C, working the 7-stitch chart repeat 10 times, slip marker, k1, slip marker, work Row 1 of Chart C, working the 7-stitch chart repeat 10 times, slip marker, k2. [159 stitches]
Chart C Set-Up Row 2 (WS): K2, slip marker, work Row 2 of Chart C, working the 7-stitch chart repeat 10 times, slip marker, p1, slip marker, work Row 2 of Chart C, working the 7-stitch chart repeat 10 times, slip marker, k2.

Continue working in established pattern, following Chart C through Row 28. [211 stitches]

04 SECTION D

Chart D Set-Up Row 1 (RS): K2, slip marker, work Row 1 of Chart D, working the 14-stitch chart repeat 6 times, slip marker, k1, slip marker, work Row 1 of Chart D, working the 14-stitch chart repeat 6 times, slip marker, k2. [215 stitches]
Chart D Set-Up Row 2 (WS): K2, slip marker, work Row 2 of Chart D, working the 14-stitch chart repeat 6 times, slip marker, p1, slip marker, work Row 2 of Chart D, working the 14-stitch chart repeat 6 times, slip marker, k2.

Continue working in established pattern, following Chart D through Row 26. [263 stitches]

05 SECTION E

Chart E Set-Up Row 1 (RS): K2, slip marker, work Row 1 of Chart E, working the 7-stitch chart repeat 18 times, slip marker, k1, slip marker, work Row 1 of Chart E, working the 7-stitch chart repeat 18 times, slip marker, k2. [267 stitches]

Chart E Set-Up Row 2 (WS): K2, slip marker, work Row 2 of Chart E, working the 7-stitch chart repeat 18 times, slip marker, p1, slip marker, work Row 2 of Chart E, working the 7-stitch chart repeat 18 times, slip marker, k2.

Continue working in established pattern, following Chart E through Row 28. [319 stitches]

06 SECTION F

Chart F Set-Up Row 1 (RS): K2, slip marker, work Row 1 of Chart F, working the 14-stitch chart repeat 10 times, slip marker, k1, slip marker, work Row 1 of Chart F, working the 14-stitch chart repeat 10 times, slip marker, k2. [323 stitches]

Chart F Set-Up Row 2 (WS): K2, slip marker, work Row 2 of Chart F, working the 14-stitch chart repeat 10 times, slip marker, p1, slip marker, work Row 2 of Chart F, working the 14-stitch chart repeat 10 times, slip marker, k2.

Continue working in established pattern, following Chart F through Row 32. [383 stitches]

07 SECTION G

Chart G Set-Up Row 1 (RS): K2, slip marker, work Row 1 of Chart G, working the 7-stitch chart repeat 27 times, slip marker, k1, slip marker, work Row 1 of Chart G, working the 7-stitch chart repeat 27 times, slip marker, k2. [387 stitches]

Chart G Set-Up Row 2 (WS): K2, slip marker, work Row 2 of Chart G, working the 7-stitch chart repeat 27 times, slip marker, p1, slip marker, work Row 2 of Chart G, working the 7-stitch chart repeat 27 times, slip marker, k2.

Continue working in established pattern, following Chart G through Row 20. [423 stitches]

08 BORDER

Border Chart Set-Up Row 1 (RS): K2, slip marker, work Row 1 of Border Chart, working the 14-stitch chart repeat 14 times, slip marker, k1, slip marker, work Row 1 of Border Chart, working the 14-stitch chart repeat 14 times, slip marker, k2. [427 stitches]

Border Chart Set-Up Row 2 (WS): K2, slip marker, work Row 2 of Border Chart, working the 14-stitch chart repeat 14 times, slip marker, p1, slip marker, work Row 2 of Border Chart, working the 14-stitch chart repeat 14 times, slip marker, k2.

Continue working in established pattern, following Border Chart through Row 22. [467 stitches]

Bind off all stitches, using the Elastic method as follows: slip the first stitch, k1 into next stitch, * knit last 2 stitches together through back loop, knit next stitch; repeat from * to end, knit last 2 stitches together through back loop.

09 FINISHING

Weave in ends. Block to measurements.

CHARTS

CHART A

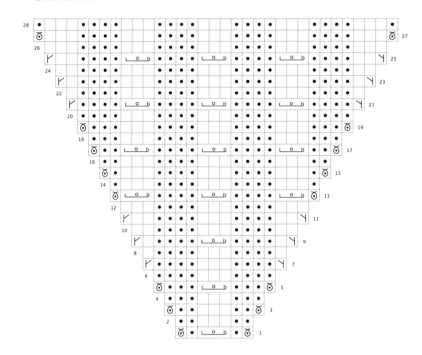

LEGEND

| | K: Knit stitch on RS; purl stitch on WS |
| ☐ | |

| | P: Purl stitch on RS; knit stitch on WS |
| • | |

M1P: With left needle tip, pick up the thread between stitches from back to front. Purl lifted loop through the front loop – 1 stitch increased.

YO: Yarn over

M1R: With left needle tip, pick up the thread between stitches from back to front. Knit lifted loop through the front loop – 1 stitch increased with right slant.

M1L: With left needle tip, pick up the thread between stitches from front to back. Knit lifted loop through the backloop – 1 stitch increased with left slant.

K2TOG: Knit 2 stitches together – 1 stitch decreased with right slant.

SSK: Slip 1 stitch knitwise, slip 1 stitch knitwise, return 2 slipped stitches back to left needle and knit them together through back loops – 1 stitch decreased with left slant.

CDD (central double decrease): Slip 2 stitches as if to K2TOG, k1, pass 2 slipped stitches over knit stitch – 2 stitches decreased.

KS (Knot Stitch): Insert tip of right-hand needle into 3rd stitch on left needle purlwise, lift over stitches 1 and 2 and let it drop. K1, yarn over, k1.

☐ Pattern repeat

CHART B

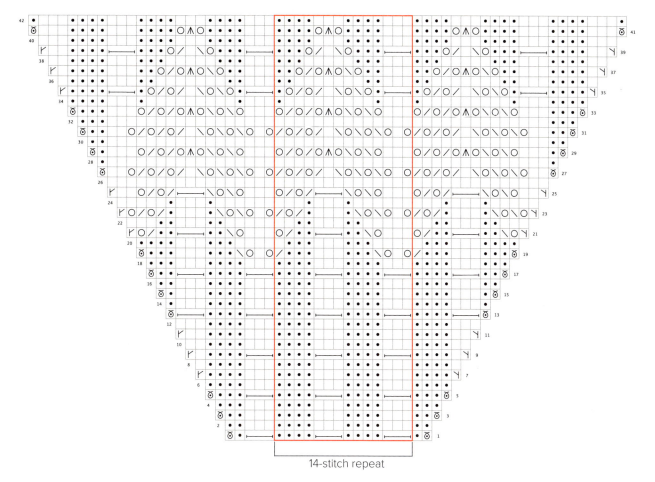

14-stitch repeat

LEGEND

☐ K: Knit stitch on RS; purl stitch on WS

• P: Purl stitch on RS; knit stitch on WS

⊚ M1P: With left needle tip, pick up the thread between stitches from back to front. Purl lifted loop through the front loop – 1 stitch increased.

O YO: Yarn over

⋎ M1R: With left needle tip, pick up the thread between stitches from back to front. Knit lifted loop through the front loop – 1 stitch increased with right slant.

⋏ M1L: With left needle tip, pick up the thread between stitches from front to back. Knit lifted loop through the backloop – 1 stitch increased with left slant.

⧄ K2TOG: Knit 2 stitches together – 1 stitch decreased with right slant.

⧅ SSK: Slip 1 stitch knitwise, slip 1 stitch knitwise, return 2 slipped stitches back to left needle and knit them together through back loops – 1 stitch decreased with left slant.

⧋ CDD (central double decrease): Slip 2 stitches as if to K2TOG, k1, pass 2 slipped stitches over knit stitch – 2 stitches decreased.

⊏⊙⊐ KS (Knot Stitch): Insert tip of right-hand needle into 3rd stitch on left needle purlwise, lift over stitches 1 and 2 and let it drop. K1, yarn over, k1.

☐ Pattern repeat

CHART C

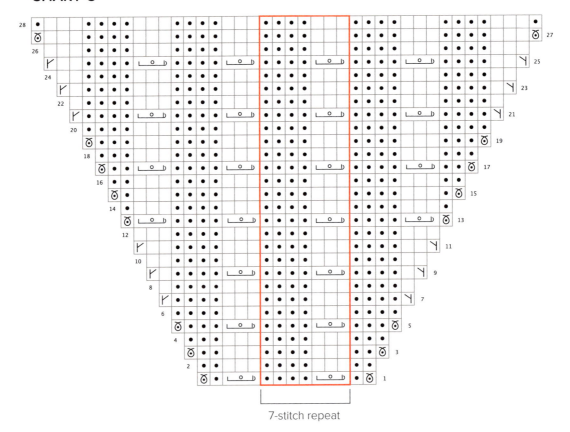

7-stitch repeat

CHART D

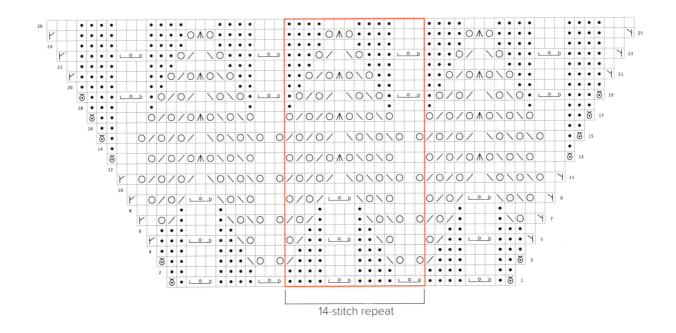

14-stitch repeat

CHART E

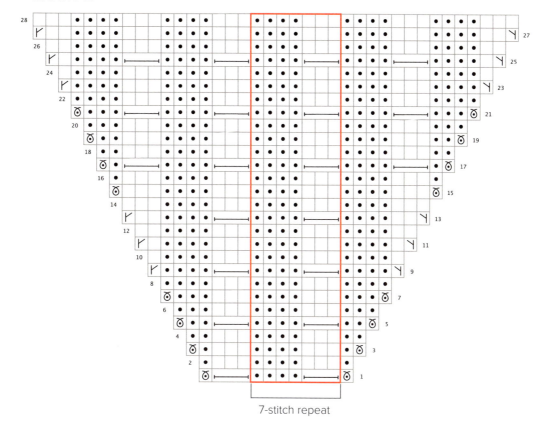

7-stitch repeat

LEGEND

K: Knit stitch on RS; purl stitch on WS

• P: Purl stitch on RS; knit stitch on WS

M1P: With left needle tip, pick up the thread between stitches from back to front. Purl lifted loop through the front loop – 1 stitch increased.

YO: Yarn over

M1R: With left needle tip, pick up the thread between stitches from back to front. Knit lifted loop through the front loop – 1 stitch increased with right slant.

M1L: With left needle tip, pick up the thread between stitches from front to back. Knit lifted loop through the backloop – 1 stitch increased with left slant.

K2TOG: Knit 2 stitches together – 1 stitch decreased with right slant.

SSK: Slip 1 stitch knitwise, slip 1 stitch knitwise, return 2 slipped stitches back to left needle and knit them together through back loops – 1 stitch decreased with left slant.

CDD (central double decrease): Slip 2 stitches as if to K2TOG, k1, pass 2 slipped stitches over knit stitch – 2 stitches decreased.

KS (Knot Stitch): Insert tip of right-hand needle into 3rd stitch on left needle purlwise, lift over stitches 1 and 2 and let it drop. K1, yarn over, k1.

Pattern repeat

CHART F

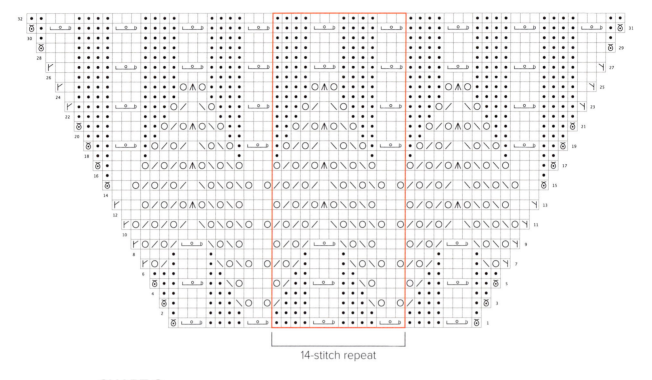

14-stitch repeat

CHART G

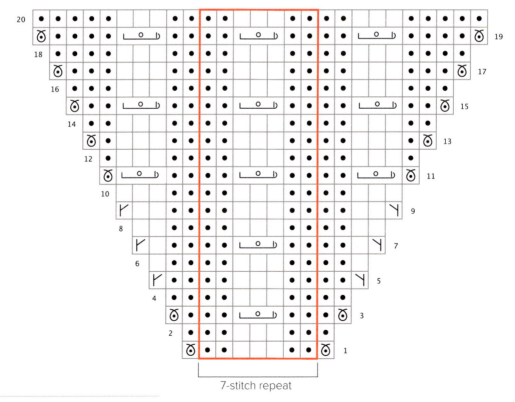

7-stitch repeat

BORDER CHART

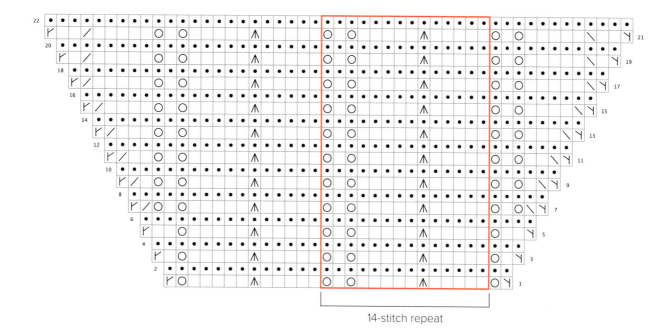

14-stitch repeat

LEGEND

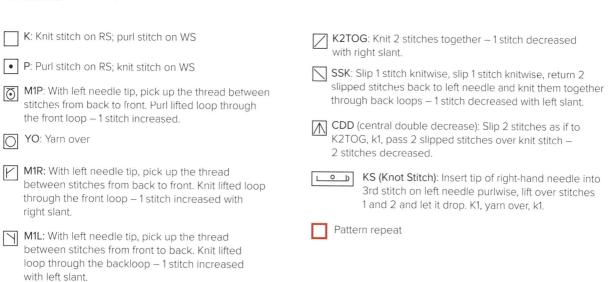

K: Knit stitch on RS; purl stitch on WS

P: Purl stitch on RS; knit stitch on WS

M1P: With left needle tip, pick up the thread between stitches from back to front. Purl lifted loop through the front loop – 1 stitch increased.

YO: Yarn over

M1R: With left needle tip, pick up the thread between stitches from back to front. Knit lifted loop through the front loop – 1 stitch increased with right slant.

M1L: With left needle tip, pick up the thread between stitches from front to back. Knit lifted loop through the backloop – 1 stitch increased with left slant.

K2TOG: Knit 2 stitches together – 1 stitch decreased with right slant.

SSK: Slip 1 stitch knitwise, slip 1 stitch knitwise, return 2 slipped stitches back to left needle and knit them together through back loops – 1 stitch decreased with left slant.

CDD (central double decrease): Slip 2 stitches as if to K2TOG, k1, pass 2 slipped stitches over knit stitch – 2 stitches decreased.

KS (Knot Stitch): Insert tip of right-hand needle into 3rd stitch on left needle purlwise, lift over stitches 1 and 2 and let it drop. K1, yarn over, k1.

Pattern repeat

Written instructions for Chart A

Note: See Chart Legend for special abbreviations.

Row 1 (RS): M1P, p1, KS, p1, M1P.
Row 2 (WS): K2, p3, k2.
Row 3 (RS): M1P, p2, k3, p2, M1P.
Row 4 (WS): K3, p3, k3.
Row 5 (RS): M1P, p3, KS, p3, M1P.
Row 6 (WS): K4, p3, k4.
Row 7 (RS): M1L, p4, k3, p4, M1R.
Row 8 (WS): P1, k4, p3, k4, p1.
Row 9 (RS): M1L, k1, p4, KS, p4, k1, M1R.
Row 10 (WS): P2, k4, p3, k4, p2.
Row 11 (RS): M1L, k2, p4, k3, p4, k2, M1R.
Row 12 (WS): [P3, k4] 2 times, p3.
Row 13 (RS): M1P, [KS, p4] 2 times, KS, M1P.
Row 14 (WS): K1, [p3, k4] 2 times, p3, k1.
Row 15 (RS): M1P, p1, [k3, p4] 2 times, k3, p1, M1P.
Row 16 (WS): K2, [p3, k4] 2 times, p3, k2.
Row 17 (RS): M1P, p2, [KS, p4] 2 times, KS, p2, M1P.
Row 18 (WS): K3, [p3, k4] 2 times, p3, k3.
Row 19 (RS): M1P, p3, [k3, p4] 2 times, k3, p3, M1P.
Row 20 (WS): [K4, p3] 3 times, k4.
Row 21 (RS): M1L, [p4, KS] 3 times, p4, M1R.
Row 22 (WS): P1, [k4, p3] 3 times, k4, p1.
Row 23 (RS): M1L, k1, [p4, k3] 3 times, p4, k1, M1R.
Row 24 (WS): P2, [k4, p3] 3 times, k4, p2.
Row 25 (RS): M1L, k2, [p4, KS] 3 times, p4, k2, M1R.
Row 26 (WS): [P3, k4] 4 times, p3.
Row 27 (RS): M1P, [k3, p4] 4 times, k3, M1P.
Row 28 (WS): K1, [p3, k4] 4 times, p3, k1.

Written instructions for Chart B

... – pattern repeat
Note: See Chart Legend for special abbreviations.

Row 1 (RS): M1P, p1, *[KS, p4] 2 times*, KS, p1, M1P.
Row 2 (WS): K2, p3, *[k4, p3] 2 times*, k2.
Row 3 (RS): M1P, p2, *[k3, p4] 2 times*, k3, p2, M1P.
Row 4 (WS): K3, p3, *[k4, p3] 2 times*, k3.
Row 5 (RS): M1P, p3, *[KS, p4] 2 times*, KS, p3, M1P.
Row 6 (WS): K4, p3, *[k4, p3] 2 times*, k4.
Row 7 (RS): M1L, p4, *[k3, p4] 2 times*, k3, p4, M1R.
Row 8 (WS): P1, k4, p3, *[k4, p3] 2 times*, k4, p1.
Row 9 (RS): M1L, k1, p4, *[KS, p4] 2 times*, KS, p4, k1, M1R.
Row 10 (WS): P2, k4, p3, *[k4, p3] 2 times*, k4, p2.
Row 11 (RS): M1L, k2, p4, *[k3, p4] 2 times*, k3, p4, k2, M1R.

Row 12 (WS): P3, k4, p3, *[k4, p3] 2 times*, k4, p3.
Row 13 (RS): M1P, KS, p4, *[KS, p4] 2 times*, KS, p4, KS, M1P.
Row 14 (WS): K1, p3, k4, p3, *[k4, p3] 2 times*, k4, p3, k1.
Row 15 (RS): M1P, p1, k3, p4, *[k3, p4] 2 times*, k3, p4, k3, p1, M1P.
Row 16 (WS): K2, p3, k4, p3, *[k4, p3] 2 times*, k4, p3, k2.
Row 17 (RS): M1P, p2, KS, p4, *[KS, p4] 2 times*, KS, p4, KS, p2, M1P.
Row 18 (WS): K3, p3, k4, p3, *[k4, p3] 2 times*, k4, p3, k3.
Row 19 (RS): M1P, p3, k3, p3, K2TOG, *YO, k1, YO, SSK, p3, k3, p3, K2TOG*, YO, k1, YO, SSK, p3, k3, p3, M1P.
Row 20 (WS): K4, p3, k3, p4, *p1, k3, p3, k3, p4*, p1, k3, p3, k4.
Row 21 (RS): M1L, YO, SSK, p2, KS, p2, K2TOG, YO, *k3, YO, SSK, p2, KS, p2, K2TOG, YO*, k3, YO, SSK, p2, KS, p2, K2TOG, YO, M1R.
Row 22 (WS): [P3, k2] 2 times, p5, *p2, k2, p3, k2, p5*, p2, [k2, p3] 2 times.
Row 23 (RS): M1L, [YO, SSK] 2 times, p1, k3, p1, K2TOG, YO, K2TOG, *YO, k1, [YO, SSK] 2 times, p1, k3, p1, K2TOG, YO, K2TOG*, YO, k1, [YO, SSK] 2 times, p1, k3, p1, [K2TOG, YO] 2 times, M1R.
Row 24 (WS): P5, k1, p3, k1, p6, *[p3, k1] 2 times, p6*, [p3, k1] 2 times, p5.
Row 25 (RS): M1L, k2, [YO, SSK] 2 times, KS, [K2TOG, YO] 2 times, *k3, [YO, SSK] 2 times, KS, [K2TOG, YO] 2 times*, k3, [YO, SSK] 2 times, KS, [K2TOG, YO] 2 times, k2, M1R.
Row 26 (WS): Purl.
Row 27 (RS): M1P, k2, [YO, SSK] 3 times, k1, [K2TOG, YO] 2 times, K2TOG, *YO, k1, [YO, SSK] 3 times, k1, [K2TOG, YO] 2 times, K2TOG*, YO, k1, [YO, SSK] 3 times, k1, [K2TOG, YO] 3 times, k2, M1P.
Row 28 (WS): K1, purl to last stitch, k1.
Row 29 (RS): M1P, p1, k3, [YO, SSK] 2 times, YO, CDD, [YO, K2TOG] 2 times, YO, *k3, [YO, SSK] 2 times, YO, CDD, [YO, K2TOG] 2 times, YO*, k3, [YO, SSK] 2 times, YO, CDD, [YO, K2TOG] 2 times, YO, k3, p1, M1P.
Row 30 (WS): K2, purl to last 2 stitches, k2.
Row 31 (RS): M1P, p2, k2, [YO, SSK] 3 times, k1, [K2TOG, YO] 2 times, K2TOG, *YO, k1, [YO, SSK] 3 times, k1, [K2TOG, YO] 2 times, K2TOG*, YO, k1, [YO, SSK] 3 times, k1, [K2TOG, YO] 3 times, k2, p2, M1P.
Row 32 (WS): K3, purl to last 3 stitches, k3.

Row 33 (RS): M1P, p3, k3, [YO, SSK] 2 times, YO, CDD, [YO, K2TOG] 2 times, YO, *k3, [YO, SSK] 2 times, YO, CDD, [YO, K2TOG] 2 times, YO*, k3, [YO, SSK] 2 times, YO, CDD, [YO, K2TOG] 2 times, YO, k3, p3, M1P.
Row 34 (WS): K4, p3, k1, p9, k1, p3, *k1, p9, k1, p3*, k1, p9, k1, p3, k4.
Row 35 (RS): M1L, p4, KS, p1, [YO, SSK] 2 times, k1, [K2TOG, YO] 2 times, p1, *KS, p1, [YO, SSK] 2 times, k1, [K2TOG, YO] 2 times, p1*, KS, p1, [YO, SSK] 2 times, k1, [K2TOG, YO] 2 times, p1, KS, p4, M1R.
Row 36 (WS): P1, k4, p3, k2, p7, k2, p3, *k2, p7, k2, p3*, k2, p7, k2, p3, k4, p1.
Row 37 (RS): M1L, k1, p4, k3, p2, YO, SSK, YO, CDD, YO, K2TOG, YO, p2, *k3, p2, YO, SSK, YO, CDD, YO, K2TOG, YO, p2*, k3, p2, YO, SSK, YO, CDD, YO, K2TOG, YO, p2, k3, p4, k1, M1R.
Row 38 (WS): P2, k4, p3, k3, p5, k3, p3, *k3, p5, k3, p3*, k3, p5, k3, p3, k4, p2.
Row 39 (RS): M1L, k2, p4, KS, p3, YO, SSK, k1, K2TOG, YO, p3, *KS, p3, YO, SSK, k1, K2TOG, YO, p3*, KS, p3, YO, SSK, k1, K2TOG, YO, p3, KS, p4, k2, M1R.
Row 40 (WS): [P3, k4] 3 times, p3, *[k4, p3] 2 times*, [k4, p3] 3 times.
Row 41 (RS): M1P, [k3, p4] 2 times, YO, CDD, YO, p4, *k3, p4, YO, CDD, YO, p4*, k3, p4, YO, CDD, YO, [p4, k3] 2 times, M1P.
Row 42 (WS): K1, [p3, k4] 3 times, p3, *[k4, p3] 2 times*, [k4, p3] 3 times, k1.

Written instructions for Chart C
... – pattern repeat

Row 1 (RS): M1P, p1, *KS, p4*, KS, p1, M1P.
Row 2 (WS): K2, p3, *k4, p3*, k2.
Row 3 (RS): M1P, p2, *k3, p4*, k3, p2, M1P.
Row 4 (WS): K3, p3, *k4, p3*, k3.
Row 5 (RS): M1P, p3, *KS, p4*, KS, p3, M1P.
Row 6 (WS): K4, p3, *k4, p3*, k4.
Row 7 (RS): M1L, p4, *k3, p4*, k3, p4, M1R.
Row 8 (WS): P1, k4, p3, *k4, p3*, k4, p1.
Row 9 (RS): M1L, k1, p4, *KS, p4*, KS, p4, k1, M1R.
Row 10 (WS): P2, k4, p3, *k4, p3*, k4, p2.
Row 11 (RS): M1L, k2, p4, *k3, p4*, k3, p4, k2, M1R.
Row 12 (WS): P3, k4, p3, *k4, p3*, k4, p3.
Row 13 (RS): M1P, KS, p4, *KS, p4*, KS, p4, KS, M1P.
Row 14 (WS): K1, p3, k4, p3, *k4, p3*, k4, p3, k1.
Row 15 (RS): M1P, p1, k3, p4, *k3, p4*, k3, p4, k3, p1, M1P.

Row 16 (WS): K2, p3, k4, p3, *k4, p3*, k4, p3, k2.
Row 17 (RS): M1P, p2, KS, p4, *KS, p4*, KS, p4, KS, p2, M1P.
Row 18 (WS): K3, p3, k4, p3, *k4, p3*, k4, p3, k3.
Row 19 (RS): M1P, p3, k3, p4, *k3, p4*, k3, p4, k3, p3, M1P.
Row 20 (WS): [K4, p3] 2 times, *k4, p3*, k4, p3, k4.
Row 21 (RS): M1L, p4, KS, p4, *KS, p4*, [KS, p4] 2 times, M1R.
Row 22 (WS): P1, [k4, p3] 2 times, *k4, p3*, k4, p3, k4, p1.
Row 23 (RS): M1L, k1, p4, k3, p4, *k3, p4*, [k3, p4] 2 times, k1, M1R.
Row 24 (WS): P2, [k4, p3] 2 times, *k4, p3*, k4, p3, k4, p2.
Row 25 (RS): M1L, k2, p4, KS, p4, *KS, p4*, [KS, p4] 2 times, k2, M1R.
Row 26 (WS): [P3, k4] 2 times, p3, *k4, p3*, [k4, p3] 2 times.
Row 27 (RS): M1P, [k3, p4] 2 times, *k3, p4*, [k3, p4] 2 times, k3, M1P.
Row 28 (WS): K1, [p3, k4] 2 times, p3, *k4, p3*, [k4, p3] 2 times, k1.

Written instructions for Chart D
... – pattern repeat

Row 1 (RS): M1P, p1, KS, p4, *[KS, p4] 2 times*, KS, p4, KS, p1, M1P.
Row 2 (WS): K2, p3, k4, p3, *[k4, p3] 2 times*, k4, p3, k2.
Row 3 (RS): M1P, p2, k3, p3, K2TOG, *YO, k1, YO, SSK, p3, k3, p3, K2TOG*, YO, k1, YO, SSK, p3, k3, p2, M1P.
Row 4 (WS): K3, p3, k3, p4, *p1, k3, p3, k3, p4*, p1, k3, p3, k3.
Row 5 (RS): M1L, p3, KS, p2, K2TOG, YO, *k3, YO, SSK, p2, KS, p2, K2TOG, YO*, k3, YO, SSK, p2, KS, p3, M1R.
Row 6 (WS): P1, k3, p3, k2, p5, *p2, k2, p3, k2, p5*, p2, k2, p3, k3, p1.
Row 7 (RS): M1L, k1, YO, SSK, p1, k3, p1, K2TOG, YO, K2TOG, *YO, k1, [YO, SSK] 2 times, p1, k3, p1, K2TOG, YO, K2TOG*, YO, k1, [YO, SSK] 2 times, p1, k3, p1, K2TOG, YO, k1, M1R.
Row 8 (WS): P4, k1, p3, k1, p6, *[p3, k1] 2 times, p6*, [p3, k1] 2 times, p4.
Row 9 (RS): M1L, k1, [YO, SSK] 2 times, KS, [K2TOG, YO] 2 times, *k3, [YO, SSK] 2 times, KS, [K2TOG, YO] 2 times*, k3, [YO, SSK] 2 times, KS, [K2TOG, YO] 2 times, k1, M1R.

Row 10 (WS): Purl.

Row 11 (RS): M1L, k1, [YO, SSK] 3 times, k1, [K2TOG, YO] 2 times, K2TOG, *YO, k1, [YO, SSK] 3 times, k1, [K2TOG, YO] 2 times, K2TOG*, YO, k1, [YO, SSK] 3 times, k1, [K2TOG, YO] 3 times, k1, M1R.

Row 12 (WS): Purl.

Row 13 (RS): M1P, k3, [YO, SSK] 2 times, YO, CDD, [YO, K2TOG] 2 times, YO, *k3, [YO, SSK] 2 times, YO, CDD, [YO, K2TOG] 2 times, YO*, k3, [YO, SSK] 2 times, YO, CDD, [YO, K2TOG] 2 times, YO, k3, M1P.

Row 14 (WS): K1, purl to last stitch, k1.

Row 15 (RS): M1P, p1, k2, [YO, SSK] 3 times, k1, [K2TOG, YO] 2 times, K2TOG, *YO, k1, [YO, SSK] 3 times, k1, [K2TOG, YO] 2 times, K2TOG*, YO, k1, [YO, SSK] 3 times, k1, [K2TOG, YO] 3 times, k2, p1, M1P.

Row 16 (WS): K2, purl to last 2 stitches, k2.

Row 17 (RS): M1P, p2, k3, [YO, SSK] 2 times, YO, CDD, [YO, K2TOG] 2 times, YO, *k3, [YO, SSK] 2 times, YO, CDD, [YO, K2TOG] 2 times, YO*, k3, [YO, SSK] 2 times, YO, CDD, [YO, K2TOG] 2 times, YO, k3, p2, M1P.

Row 18 (WS): K3, p3, k1, p9, k1, p3, *k1, p9, k1, p3*, k1, p9, k1, p3, k3.

Row 19 (RS): M1P, p3, KS, p1, [YO, SSK] 2 times, k1, [K2TOG, YO] 2 times, p1, *KS, p1, [YO, SSK] 2 times, k1, [K2TOG, YO] 2 times, p1*, KS, p1, [YO, SSK] 2 times, k1, [K2TOG, YO] 2 times, p1, KS, p3, M1P.

Row 20 (WS): K4, p3, k2, p7, k2, p3, *k2, p7, k2, p3*, k2, p7, k2, p3, k4.

Row 21 (RS): M1L, p4, k3, p2, YO, SSK, YO, CDD, YO, K2TOG, YO, p2, *k3, p2, YO, SSK, YO, CDD, YO, K2TOG, YO, p2*, k3, p2, YO, SSK, YO, CDD, YO, K2TOG, YO, p2, k3, p4, M1R.

Row 22 (WS): P1, k4, p3, k3, p5, k3, p3, *k3, p5, k3, p3*, k3, p5, k3, p3, k4, p1.

Row 23 (RS): M1L, k1, p4, KS, p3, YO, SSK, k1, K2TOG, YO, p3, *KS, p3, YO, SSK, k1, K2TOG, YO, p3*, KS, p3, YO, SSK, k1, K2TOG, YO, p3, KS, p4, k1, M1R.

Row 24 (WS): P2, [k4, p3] 3 times, *[k4, p3] 2 times*, [k4, p3] 2 times, k4, p2.

Row 25 (RS): M1L, k2, p4, k3, p4, YO, CDD, YO, p4, *k3, p4, YO, CDD, YO, p4*, k3, p4, YO, CDD, YO, p4, k3, p4, k2, M1R.

Row 26 (WS): [P3, k4] 3 times, p3, *[k4, p3] 2 times*, [k4, p3] 3 times.

Written instructions for Chart E

... – pattern repeat

Row 1 (RS): M1P, *KS, p4*, KS, M1P.

Row 2 (WS): K1, p3, *k4, p3*, k1.

Row 3 (RS): M1P, p1, *k3, p4*, k3, p1, M1P.

Row 4 (WS): K2, p3, *k4, p3*, k2.

Row 5 (RS): M1P, p2, *KS, p4*, KS, p2, M1P.

Row 6 (WS): K3, p3, *k4, p3*, k3.

Row 7 (RS): M1P, p3, *k3, p4*, k3, p3, M1P.

Row 8 (WS): K4, p3, *k4, p3*, k4.

Row 9 (RS): M1L, p4, *KS, p4*, KS, p4, M1R.

Row 10 (WS): P1, k4, p3, *k4, p3*, k4, p1.

Row 11 (RS): M1L, k1, p4, *k3, p4*, k3, p4, k1, M1R.

Row 12 (WS): P2, k4, p3, *k4, p3*, k4, p2.

Row 13 (RS): M1L, k2, p4, *KS, p4*, KS, p4, k2, M1R.

Row 14 (WS): P3, k4, p3, *k4, p3*, k4, p3.

Row 15 (RS): M1P, k3, p4, *k3, p4*, k3, p4, k3, M1P.

Row 16 (WS): K1, p3, k4, p3, *k4, p3*, k4, p3, k1.

Row 17 (RS): M1P, p1, KS, p4, *KS, p4*, KS, p4, KS, p1, M1P.

Row 18 (WS): K2, p3, k4, p3, *k4, p3*, k4, p3, k2.

Row 19 (RS): M1P, p2, k3, p4, *k3, p4*, k3, p4, k3, p2, M1P.

Row 20 (WS): K3, p3, k4, p3, *k4, p3*, k4, p3, k3.

Row 21 (RS): M1P, p3, KS, p4, *KS, p4*, KS, p4, KS, p3, M1P.

Row 22 (WS): [K4, p3] 2 times, *k4, p3*, k4, p3, k4.

Row 23 (RS): M1L, p4, k3, p4, *k3, p4*, [k3, p4] 2 times, M1R.

Row 24 (WS): P1, [k4, p3] 2 times, *k4, p3*, k4, p3, k4, p1.

Row 25 (RS): M1L, k1, p4, KS, p4, *KS, p4*, [KS, p4] 2 times, k1, M1R.

Row 26 (WS): P2, [k4, p3] 2 times, *k4, p3*, k4, p3, k4, p2.

Row 27 (RS): M1L, k2, p4, k3, p4, *k3, p4*, [k3, p4] 2 times, k2, M1R.

Row 28 (WS): [P3, k4] 2 times, p3, *k4, p3*, [k4, p3] 2 times.

Written instructions for Chart F
... – pattern repeat

Row 1 (RS): M1P, KS, p4, *[KS, p4] 2 times*, KS, p4, KS, M1P.
Row 2 (WS): K1, p3, k4, p3, *[k4, p3] 2 times*, k4, p3, k1.
Row 3 (RS): M1P, p1, k3, p3, K2TOG, *YO, k1, YO, SSK, p3, k3, p3, K2TOG*, YO, k1, YO, SSK, p3, k3, p1, M1P.
Row 4 (WS): K2, p3, k3, p4, *p1, k3, p3, k3, p4*, p1, k3, p3, k2.
Row 5 (RS): M1P, p2, KS, p2, K2TOG, YO, *k3, YO, SSK, p2, KS, p2, K2TOG, YO*, k3, YO, SSK, p2, KS, p2, M1P.
Row 6 (WS): K3, p3, k2, p5, *p2, k2, p3, k2, p5*, p2, k2, p3, k3.
Row 7 (RS): M1L, YO, SSK, p1, k3, p1, K2TOG, YO, K2TOG, *YO, k1, [YO, SSK] 2 times, p1, k3, p1, K2TOG, YO, K2TOG*, YO, k1, [YO, SSK] 2 times, p1, k3, p1, K2TOG, YO, M1R.
Row 8 (WS): [P3, k1] 2 times, p6, *[p3, k1] 2 times, p6*, [p3, k1] 2 times, p3.
Row 9 (RS): M1L, [YO, SSK] 2 times, KS, [K2TOG, YO] 2 times, *k3, [YO, SSK] 2 times, KS, [K2TOG, YO] 2 times*, k3, [YO, SSK] 2 times, KS, [K2TOG, YO] 2 times, M1R.
Row 10 (WS): Purl.
Row 11 (RS): M1L, [YO, SSK] 3 times, k1, [K2TOG, YO] 2 times, K2TOG, *YO, k1, [YO, SSK] 3 times, k1, [K2TOG, YO] 2 times, K2TOG*, YO, k1, [YO, SSK] 3 times, k1, [K2TOG, YO] 3 times, M1R.
Row 12 (WS): Purl.
Row 13 (RS): M1L, k2, [YO, SSK] 2 times, YO, CDD, [YO, K2TOG] 2 times, YO, *k3, [YO, SSK] 2 times, YO, CDD, [YO, K2TOG] 2 times, YO*, k3, [YO, SSK] 2 times, YO, CDD, [YO, K2TOG] 2 times, YO, k2, M1R.
Row 14 (WS): Purl.
Row 15 (RS): M1P, k2, [YO, SSK] 3 times, k1, [K2TOG, YO] 2 times, K2TOG, *YO, k1, [YO, SSK] 3 times, k1, [K2TOG, YO] 2 times, K2TOG*, YO, k1, [YO, SSK] 3 times, k1, [K2TOG, YO] 3 times, k2, M1P.
Row 16 (WS): K1, purl to last stitch, k1.
Row 17 (RS): M1P, p1, k3, [YO, SSK] 2 times, YO, CDD, [YO, K2TOG] 2 times, YO, *k3, [YO, SSK] 2 times, YO, CDD, [YO, K2TOG] 2 times, YO*, k3, [YO, SSK] 2 times, YO, CDD, [YO, K2TOG] 2 times, YO, k3, p1, M1P.
Row 18 (WS): K2, p3, k1, p9, k1, p3, *k1, p9, k1, p3*, k1, p9, k1, p3, k2.

Row 19 (RS): M1P, p2, KS, p1, [YO, SSK] 2 times, k1, [K2TOG, YO] 2 times, p1, *KS, p1, [YO, SSK] 2 times, k1, [K2TOG, YO] 2 times, p1*, KS, p1, [YO, SSK] 2 times, k1, [K2TOG, YO] 2 times, p1, KS, p2, M1P.
Row 20 (WS): K3, p3, k2, p7, k2, p3, *k2, p7, k2, p3*, k2, p7, k2, p3, k3.
Row 21 (RS): M1P, p3, k3, p2, YO, SSK, YO, CDD, YO, K2TOG, YO, p2, *k3, p2, YO, SSK, YO, CDD, YO, K2TOG, YO, p2*, k3, p2, YO, SSK, YO, CDD, YO, K2TOG, YO, p2, k3, p3, M1P.
Row 22 (WS): K4, p3, k3, p5, k3, p3, *k3, p5, k3, p3*, k3, p5, k3, p3, k4.
Row 23 (RS): M1L, p4, KS, p3, YO, SSK, k1, K2TOG, YO, p3, *KS, p3, YO, SSK, k1, K2TOG, YO, p3*, KS, p3, YO, SSK, k1, K2TOG, YO, p3, KS, p4, M1R.
Row 24 (WS): P1, [k4, p3] 3 times, *[k4, p3] 2 times*, [k4, p3] 2 times, k4, p1.
Row 25 (RS): M1L, k1, p4, k3, p4, YO, CDD, YO, p4, *k3, p4, YO, CDD, YO, p4*, k3, p4, YO, CDD, YO, p4, k3, p4, k1, M1R.
Row 26 (WS): P2, [k4, p3] 3 times, *[k4, p3] 2 times*, [k4, p3] 2 times, k4, p2.
Row 27 (RS): M1L, k2, [p4, KS] 2 times, p4, *[KS, p4] 2 times*, [KS, p4] 3 times, k2, M1R.
Row 28 (WS): [P3, k4] 3 times, p3, *[k4, p3] 2 times*, [k4, p3] 3 times.
Row 29 (RS): M1P, [k3, p4] 3 times, *[k3, p4] 2 times*, [k3, p4] 3 times, k3, M1P.
Row 30 (WS): K1, [p3, k4] 3 times, p3, *[k4, p3] 2 times*, [k4, p3] 3 times, k1.
Row 31 (RS): M1P, p1, [KS, p4] 8 times, KS, p1, M1P.
Row 32 (WS): K2, [p3, k4] 8 times, p3, k2.

Written instructions for Chart G
... – pattern repeat

Row 1 (RS): M1P, *p2, k3, p2*, M1P.
Row 2 (WS): K1, *k2, p3, k2*, k1.
Row 3 (RS): M1P, p1, *p2, KS, p2*, p1, M1P.
Row 4 (WS): K2, *k2, p3, k2*, k2.
Row 5 (RS): M1L, p2, *p2, k3, p2*, p2, M1R.
Row 6 (WS): P1, k2, *k2, p3, k2*, k2, p1.
Row 7 (RS): M1L, k1, p2, *p2, KS, p2*, p2, k1, M1R.
Row 8 (WS): P2, k2, *k2, p3, k2*, k2, p2.
Row 9 (RS): M1L, k2, p2, *p2, k3, p2*, p2, k2, M1R.
Row 10 (WS): P3, k2, *k2, p3, k2*, k2, p3.
Row 11 (RS): M1P, KS, p2, *p2, KS, p2*, p2, KS, M1P.

Row 12 (WS): K1, p3, k2, *k2, p3, k2*, k2, p3, k1.
Row 13 (RS): M1P, p1, [k3, p4] 2 times, k3, p1, M1P.
Row 14 (WS): K2, [p3, k4] 2 times, p3, k2.
Row 15 (RS): M1P, p2, [KS, p4] 2 times, KS, p2, M1P.
Row 16 (WS): K3, [p3, k4] 2 times, p3, k3.
Row 17 (RS): M1P, p3, [k3, p4] 2 times, k3, p3, M1P.
Row 18 (WS): [K4, p3] 3 times, k4.
Row 19 (RS): M1P, [p4, KS] 3 times, p4, M1P.
Row 20 (WS): K5, [p3, k4] 2 times, p3, k5.

Written instructions for Border Chart
... – pattern repeat

Row 1 (RS): M1L, YO, *k5, CDD, k5, YO, k1, YO*, k5, CDD, k5, YO, M1R.
Row 2 and all WS rows: Knit.
Row 3 (RS): M1L, k1, YO, *k5, CDD, k5, YO, k1, YO*, k5, CDD, k5, YO, k1, M1R.
Row 5 (RS): M1L, k2, YO, *k5, CDD, k5, YO, k1, YO*, k5, CDD, k5, YO, k2, M1R.

Row 7 (RS): M1L, SSK, YO, k1, YO, *k5, CDD, k5, YO, k1, YO*, k5, CDD, k5, YO, k1, YO, K2TOG, M1R.
Row 9 (RS): M1L, SSK, [k1, YO] 2 times, *k5, CDD, k5, YO, k1, YO*, k5, CDD, k5, [YO, k1] 2 times, K2TOG, M1R.
Row 11 (RS): M1L, SSK, k2, YO, k1, YO, *k5, CDD, k5, YO, k1, YO*, k5, CDD, k5, YO, k1, YO, k2, K2TOG, M1R.
Row 13 (RS): M1L, SSK, k3, YO, k1, YO, *k5, CDD, k5, YO, k1, YO*, k5, CDD, k5, YO, k1, YO, k3, K2TOG, M1R.
Row 15 (RS): M1L, SSK, k4, YO, k1, YO, *k5, CDD, k5, YO, k1, YO*, k5, CDD, k5, YO, k1, YO, k4, K2TOG, M1R.
Row 17 (RS): M1L, SSK, k5, YO, k1, YO, *k5, CDD, k5, YO, k1, YO*, k5, CDD, k5, YO, k1, YO, k5, K2TOG, M1R.
Row 19 (RS): M1L, k1, SSK, k5, YO, k1, YO, *k5, CDD, k5, YO, k1, YO*, k5, CDD, k5, YO, k1, YO, k5, K2TOG, k1, M1R.
Row 21 (RS): M1L, p2, SSK, k5, YO, k1, YO, *k5, CDD, k5, YO, k1, YO*, k5, CDD, k5, YO, k1, YO, k5, K2TOG, k2, M1R.
Row 22 (WS): Knit.

Bellwood

Richly textured cables and honeycomb stitches cover this cozy cardigan, creating a fabric that feels as intricate as it looks. Vertical cable panels frame repeating honeycomb motifs, while shaped wedges along the sides add subtle flare and ease to the silhouette. The result is a cardigan with both structure and movement, balancing texture and form.

Worked flat with a classic button band, deep ribbing at the hem and cuffs, and a relaxed fit, this piece layers effortlessly over shirts or dresses. Thoughtful shaping ensures a flattering line, while the bold stitchwork makes the cardigan a true showcase of cable artistry.

Sizes

XS (S, M, L, XL, 2XL), {3XL, 4XL, 5XL, 6XL}: to fit bust 28-30 (32-34, 36-38, 40-42, 44-46, 48-50), {52-54, 56-58, 60-62, 64-66}"/70-75 (80-85, 90-95, 100-105, 110-115, 120-125), {130-135, 140-145, 150-155, 160-165} cm.

Finished Measurements

31¾ (38, 43, 47½, 51¼, 54½), {58, 60¾, 62½, 66}"/79.5 (95, 107.5, 119, 128, 136.5), {145, 152, 156.5, 165} cm bust circumference, buttoned. Cardigan shown measures 43"/107.5 cm; modeled with 5"/12.5 cm of positive ease.

Yarn

DK weight yarn (approximate amount): 1330 (1580, 1790, 2000, 2130, 2290), {2420, 2540, 2630, 2750} yds/1210 (1438, 1629, 1820, 1938, 2084), {2202, 2311, 2393, 2503} m.

Miss Babs Yowza (100% Superwash Merino wool; 560 yds/512 m in 8 oz/225 g): Calendula, 3 (3, 4, 4, 4, 4), {5, 5, 5, 5} skeins.

Needles

Size US 5/3.75 mm: 32"/80 cm circular and set of double-pointed needles.
Size US 4/3.5 mm: 32"/80 cm circular and set of double-pointed needles.
Optional: spare US 4/3.5 mm 32"/80 cm circular for Tubular Cast On.
Adjust needle size if necessary to obtain the correct gauge.

Notions

Stitch markers, removable stitch markers or safety pins, cable needle, waste yarn, stitch holders, tapestry needle, 6 buttons ⅞"/22 mm in diameter.

Gauge

27 stitches and 32 rows = 4"/10 cm in Honeycomb or Cable Chart on US 5/3.75 mm needle after blocking.

Notes

- The body of this cardigan is worked in one piece to the underarm, then divided for fronts and back and worked separately to shoulders.
- The sleeves are worked in the round from cuff to underarm. Sleeves are sewn into the armholes.
- A circular needle is used to accommodate a large number of stitches.
- The Sleeve chart is worked both in rounds and back and forth in rows. When working in rounds, work all rounds as RS rounds; when working in rows, work every even-numbered row as a wrong-side row.
- The Sleeve Chart and the Cable Chart for the first 2 sizes are the same chart.
- During shaping, if there are not enough stitches to work a complete cable, work the stitches of the partial cable in stockinette stitch.

DIRECTIONS

01 BODY

Note: If you do not wish to work a Tubular Cast On, cast on with 345 (387, 433, 463, 499, 535), {559, 577, 601, 625} stitches, using US 4/3.5 mm 32"/80 cm circular needle, working yarn, and your preferred method for a stretchy cast on. Join for working in the round, being careful not to twist stitches, then proceed to the Ribbing Row 1.

Tubular Cast On (see Special Techniques, page 226)
With waste yarn, US 4/3.5 mm 32"/80 cm circular needle and using your preferred method, cast on 173 (194, 217, 232, 250, 268), {280, 289, 301, 313} stitches. Do not join in the round.

Foundation Row (RS): Knit all stitches in row. This row is worked directly into your waste yarn stitches.

Row 1 (WS): Purl to end.
Row 2 (RS): Knit to end.
Row 3 (WS): Purl to end.

Carefully snip and remove the waste yarn from the cast-on edge, placing the stitches onto the second US 4/3.5 mm 32"/80 cm circular needle as you go. Don't place the last half-loop at the edge of the fabric.

Now we nave 173 (194, 217, 232, 250, 268), {280, 289, 301, 313} stitches on first needle and 172 (193, 216, 231, 249, 267), {279, 288, 300, 312} cast-on stitches on the spare needle. Bring the needle with the cast-on stitches up behind the working needle, wrong sides together.

Next Row (WS): P1 from front needle, *p1 from back needle, k1 from front needle; repeat from * to last 2 stitches, p1 from back needle, p1 from front needle. [345 (387, 433, 463, 499, 535), {559, 577, 601, 625} stitches on the needle]

Ribbing Row 1 (RS): K1, *k1, p1; repeat from * to last 2 stitches, k2.
Ribbing Row 2 (WS): P2, *k1, p1; repeat from * to last stitch, p1.

Repeat last 2 rows until piece measures 2"/5 cm from cast on, ending with a RS row.

Decrease Row (WS): Purl approximately half the number of stitches, P2TOG, purl to end. [344 (386, 432, 462, 498, 534), {558, 576, 600, 624} stitches]

Change to US 5/3.75 mm 32"/80 cm circular needle.

NOTE: Work Cable Chart for your size. The Cable Chart for the first 2 sizes is the same as the Sleeve Chart.

Pattern Set-Up Row 1 (RS): K3, p2, place marker, work Row 1 of Honeycomb Chart over 6 (12, 12, 18, 18, 24), {24, 30, 24, 30} stitches, working 6-stitch chart repeat 1 (2, 2, 3, 3, 4), {4, 5, 4, 5} time(s), place marker, work Row 1 of Cable Chart over the next 28 (28, 32, 32, 32), {32, 32, 32, 32} stitches, place marker, work Row 1 of Honeycomb Chart over 6 (12, 18, 18, 24, 24), {30, 30, 36, 36} stitches, working 6-stitch chart repeat 1 (2, 3, 3, 4, 4), {5, 5, 6, 6} time(s), place marker, p2, k2, place 1st side wedge marker, p2, work Row 1 of Honeycomb Chart over 66 (66, 72, 72, 78, 84), {84, 84, 90, 90} stitches, working 6-stitch chart repeat 11 (11, 12, 12, 13, 14), {14, 14, 15, 15} times, p2, place 2nd side wedge marker, k2, p2, place marker, work Row 1 of Honeycomb Chart over 6 (12, 18, 18, 24, 24), {30, 30, 36, 36} stitches, working 6-stitch chart repeat 1 (2, 3, 3, 4, 4), {5, 5, 6, 6} time(s), place marker, work Row 1 of Cable Chart over the next 28 (28, 32, 32, 32, 32), {32, 32, 32, 32} stitches, place marker, work Row 1 of Honeycomb Chart over 30 (36, 30, 48, 48, 60), {60, 66, 66, 78} stitches, working 6-stitch chart repeat 5 (6, 5, 8, 8, 10), {10, 11, 11, 13} time(s), place marker, work Row 1 of Cable Chart over the next 28 (28, 32, 32, 32, 32), {32, 32, 32, 32} stitches, place marker, work Row 1 of Honeycomb Chart over 6 (12, 18, 18, 24, 24), {30, 30, 36, 36} stitches, working 6-stitch chart repeat 1 (2, 3, 3, 4, 4), {5, 5, 6, 6} time(s), place marker, p2, k2, place 3rd side wedge marker, p2, work Row 1 of Honeycomb Chart over 66 (66, 72, 72, 78, 84), {84, 84, 90, 90} stitches, working 6-stitch chart repeat 11 (11, 12, 12, 13, 14), {14, 14, 15, 15} times, p2, place 4th side wedge marker, k2, p2, place marker, work Row 1 of Honeycomb Chart over 6 (12, 18, 18, 24, 24), {30, 30, 36, 36} stitches, working 6-stitch chart repeat 1 (2, 3, 3, 4, 4), {5, 5, 6, 6} time(s), place marker, work Row 1 of Cable Chart over the next 28 (28, 32, 32, 32, 32), {32, 32, 32, 32} stitches, place marker, work Row 1 of Honeycomb Chart over 6 (12, 12, 18, 18, 24), {24, 30, 24, 30} stitches, working 6-stitch chart repeat 1 (2, 2, 3, 3, 4), {4, 5, 4, 5} time(s), place marker, p2, k3.

Pattern Set-Up Row 2 (WS): P3, k2, slip marker, work Row 2 of Honeycomb Chart to marker, slip marker, work Row 2 of Cable pattern to marker, slip marker, work Row 2 of Honeycomb Chart to marker, slip marker, k2, p2, slip side wedge marker, k2, work Row 2 of Honeycomb Chart to 2 stitches before marker, k2, slip side wedge marker, p2, k2, slip marker, work Row 2 of Honeycomb Chart to marker, slip marker, work Row 2 of Cable pattern to marker, slip marker, work Row 2 of Honeycomb Chart to marker, slip marker, work Row 2 of Cable pattern to marker, slip marker, work Row 2 of Honeycomb Chart to marker, slip marker, k2, p2, slip side wedge marker, k2, work Row 2 of Honeycomb Chart to 2 stitches before marker, k2, slip side wedge marker, p2, k2, slip marker, work Row 2 of Honeycomb Chart to marker, slip marker, work Row 2 of Cable pattern to marker, slip marker, work Row 2 of Honeycomb Chart to marker, slip marker, k2, p3.

NOTE: During shaping, if there are not enough stitches to work a complete cable, work the stitches of the partial cable in stockinette stitch.

Shape side wedges:
Decrease Row (RS): *Work in established pattern to side wedge marker, slip marker, p1, P2TOG, work to 3 stitches before the next side wedge marker, P2TOG, p1, slip marker; repeat from * once more, work in established pattern to end. [4 stitches decreased]

Continue working, following charts and repeat Decrease Row in every 4th row (or every other RS row) another 8 (8, 5, 5, 2, 0), {0, 0, 0, 0} times, then in every 2nd row (or every RS row) 24 (24, 30, 30, 36, 41), {41, 41, 44, 44} times. [212 (254, 288, 318, 342, 366), {390, 408, 420, 444} stitches total on the needle, 4 stitches between each 2 side wedge markers]

Next Row (WS): Work all stitches in established pattern.
Decrease Row (RS): *Work in established pattern to side wedge marker, slip marker, [P2TOG] 2 times, slip marker; repeat from * once more, work in established pattern to end. [4 stitches decreased]

Next Row (WS): Work all stitches in established pattern.

Decrease Row (RS): *Work in established pattern to 1 stitch before side wedge marker, SSK, removing side wedge marker, place side marker, K2TOG, removing side wedge marker; repeat from * once more, work in established pattern to end.

[204 (246, 280, 310, 334, 358), {382, 400, 412, 436} stitches; 49 (61, 71, 77, 83, 89), {95, 101, 101, 107} stitches for each Front, 106 (124, 138, 156, 168, 180), {192, 198, 210, 222} stitches for Back]

Approximate Body height: 13 (13, 13, 13, 13, 13¼), {13¼, 13¼, 14, 14}"/32.5 (32.5, 32.5, 32.5, 32.5, 33), {33, 33, 35, 35} cm.

Work even without decreases for 1"/2.5 cm more, ending with WS row.

Divide for Fronts and Back:
Division Row (RS): K3, place marker, p2, remove marker, work in established pattern to 4 (8, 10, 10, 12, 14), {14, 16, 16, 17} stitches before side marker, place previous 45 (53, 61, 67, 71, 75), {81, 85, 85, 90} stitches on holder for Right Front, bind off next 8 (16, 20, 20, 24, 28), {28, 32, 32, 34} stitches, removing markers, work in established pattern to 4 (8, 10, 10, 12, 14), {14, 16, 16, 17} stitches before next side marker, place previous 98 (108, 118, 136, 144, 152), {164, 166, 178, 188} stitches on holder for Back, bind off next 8 (16, 20, 20, 24, 28), {28, 32, 32, 34} stitches, removing markers, work in established pattern to last marker, remove marker, p2, place marker, k3. [45 (53, 61, 67, 71, 75), {81, 85, 85, 90} stitches on the needle for Left Front]

02 LEFT FRONT

Continue working on the Left Front, shaping armhole and neckline:
Next Row (WS): P3, slip marker, k1, work in established pattern.

NOTE: The Sloped Bind Off for armhole and shoulder shaping is recommended (see Special Techniques, page 226).

Armhole Decrease and Neck Decrease Row (RS): Bind off 2 (2, 2, 3, 3, 4), {4, 4, 5, 5} stitches, work to 2 stitches before last marker, P2TOG, slip marker, k3.
Next Row (WS): P3, slip marker, k1, work in established pattern.

NOTE: Please read the following section through before proceeding. The armhole and neckline shaping is happening at the same time.

At the beginning of following RS rows, bind off 2 (1, 1, 2, 2, 2), {2, 2, 3, 3} stitch(es) once, then 1 (1, 1, 2, 2, 2), {2, 2, 3, 3} stitch(es) once, then 0 (1, 1, 1, 2, 2), {2, 2, 2, 2} stitch(es) once, then 1 stitch 0 (0, 5, 6, 7, 9), {13, 12, 12, 15} times.

AT THE SAME TIME, work neck decreases every 4th row (or every other RS row) another 8 (6, 6, 6, 8, 9), {11, 8, 14, 16} times, then in every 2nd row (or every RS row) 7 (12, 16, 16, 14, 14), {12, 20, 9, 7} times. [24 (29, 28, 30, 32, 32), {34, 34, 36, 38} stitches]

Work 3 rows even without decreases, ending with WS row.

Shape shoulder:
Bind off 6 (7, 7, 7, 8, 8), {8, 8, 9, 9} stitches at the beginning of next 3 RS rows. Bind off remaining 6 (8, 7, 9, 8, 8), {10, 10, 9, 11} stitches on the last RS row.

03 RIGHT FRONT

Place held 45 (53, 61, 67, 71, 75), {81, 85, 85, 90} Right Front stitches onto US 5/3.75 mm 32"/80 cm circular needle. Join yarn at the armhole, ready to work WS row.

Next Row (WS): Work in established pattern.

NOTE: The Sloped Bind Off for armhole and shoulder shaping is recommended.

Neck Decrease Row (RS): K3, slip marker, P2TOG, work to end. [1 stitch decreased]

Armhole Decrease Row (WS): Bind off 2 (2, 2, 3, 3, 4), {4, 4, 5, 5} stitches, work to 1 stitch before last marker, k1, slip marker, p3.

NOTE: Please read the following section through before proceeding. The armhole and neckline shaping is happening at the same time.

At the beginning of following WS rows, bind off 2 (1, 1, 2, 2, 2), {2, 2, 3, 3} stitches once, then 1 (1, 1, 2, 2, 2), {2, 2, 3, 3} stitches once, then 0 (1, 1, 1, 2, 2), {2, 2, 2, 2} stitches once, then 1 stitch 0 (0, 5, 6, 7, 9), {13, 12, 12, 15} times.

AT THE SAME TIME, repeat Neck Decrease Row in every 4th row (or every other RS row) another 8 (6, 6, 6, 8, 9), {11, 8, 14, 16} times, then in every 2nd row (or every RS row) 7 (12, 16, 16, 14, 14), {12, 20, 9, 7} times. [24 (29, 28, 30, 32, 32), {34, 34, 36, 38} stitches]
Work 4 rows even without decreases, ending with RS row.

Shape shoulder
Bind off 6 (7, 7, 7, 8, 8), {8, 8, 9, 9} stitches at the beginning of next 3 WS rows, then bind off remaining 6 (8, 7, 9, 8, 8), {10, 10, 9, 11} stitches on the last WS row.

04 BACK

Place held 98 (108, 118, 136, 144, 152), {164, 166, 178, 188} Back stitches onto US 5/3.75 mm 32"/80 cm circular needle. Join yarn at the armhole, ready to work WS row.

Next Row (WS): Work in in established pattern.

NOTE: Use the Sloped Bind Off for armhole and shoulder shaping.

At the beginning of the next 2 rows, bind off 2 (2, 2, 3, 3, 4), {4, 4, 5, 5} stitches at each side.
At the beginning of the next 2 rows, bind off 2 (1, 1, 2, 2, 2), {2, 2, 3, 3} stitch(es) at each side.
At the beginning of the next 2 rows, bind off 1 (1, 1, 2, 2, 2), {2, 2, 3, 3} stitch(es) at each side.

At the beginning of the next 2 rows, bind off 0 (1, 1, 1, 2, 2), {2, 2, 2, 2} stitch(es) at each side.
Bind off 1 stitch at the beginning of following 0 (0, 10, 12, 14, 18), {26, 24, 24, 30} rows.
[88 (98, 98, 108, 112, 114), {118, 122, 128, 132} stitches]

Continue working without decreases until armhole measure 6¾ (7, 8, 8, 8½, 9), {9½, 10, 10¼, 10¾}"/ 17 (17.5, 20, 20, 21.5, 22.5), {24, 25, 25.5, 27} cm from division row, ending with WS row.

Bind off 6 (7, 7, 7, 8, 8), {8, 8, 9, 9} stitches at the beginning of next 6 rows, then bind off 6 (8, 7, 9, 8, 8), {10, 10, 9, 11} stitches at the beginning of next 2 rows.

Bind off remaining 40 (40, 42, 48, 48, 50), {50, 54, 56, 56} back neck stitches.

Seam the shoulders.

05 SLEEVES (make 2)

Note: If you do not wish to work a Tubular Cast On, cast on with 54 (60, 60, 68, 68, 68), {78, 78, 82, 82} stitches, using US 4/3.5 mm double-pointed needle, working yarn, and your preferred method for a stretchy cast on. Join for working in the round, being careful not to twist stitches, then proceed to the Ribbing Round.

Tubular Cast On
With waste yarn, US 4/3.5 mm double-pointed needle and using your preferred method, cast on 27 (30, 30, 34, 34, 34), {39, 39, 41, 41} stitches. Do not join in the round.

Foundation Row (RS): Knit all stitches in row. This row is worked directly into your waste yarn stitches.

Row 1 (WS): Purl to end.
Row 2 (RS): Knit to end.
Row 3 (WS): Purl to end.

Carefully snip and remove the waste yarn from the cast-on edge, placing the stitches onto the second US 4/3.5 mm double-pointed needle as you go. Place the last half-loop at the edge of the fabric. Now we nave 27 (30, 30, 34, 34, 34), {39, 39, 41, 41} stitches on each needle. Bring the needle with the cast-on stitches up behind the working needle, wrong sides together.

Next Row (WS): *K1 from front needle, p1 from back needle; repeat from * to end. [54 (60, 60, 68, 68, 68), {78, 78, 82, 82} stitches on needle]
Place marker for the Beginning of the Round (BOR) and join in the round.

Continue working in the round with a set of double-pointed needles or any circular knitting method of your choice.

Ribbing Round: *K1, p1; repeat from * to end.
Repeat Ribbing Round until Sleeve measures 2½"/6.5 cm from ribbing edge.

Change to US 5/3.75 mm double-pointed needles.

Next Round: Knit.

Pattern Set-Up Round 1: K1, p1, place marker, k5 (2, 2, 0, 0, 0), {5, 5, 1, 1}, work Row 1 of Honeycomb Chart over the next 6 (12, 12, 18, 18, 18), {18, 18, 24, 24} stitches, place marker, work Row 1 of Sleeve Cable Chart over 28 stitches, place marker, work Row 1 of Honeycomb Chart over the next 6 (12, 12, 18, 18, 18), {18, 18, 24, 24} stitches, k5 (2, 2, 0, 0, 0), {5, 5, 1, 1}, place marker, p1, k1.

Pattern Set-Up Row 2: K1, p1, slip marker, k5 (2, 2, 0, 0, 0), {5, 5, 1, 1}, work Row 2 of Honeycomb Chart over the next 6 (12, 12, 18, 18, 18), {18, 18, 24, 24} stitches, working 6-stitch chart repeat 1 (2, 2, 3, 3, 3), {3, 3, 4, 4} time(s), place marker, work Row 2 of Sleeve Cable Chart over 28 stitches, place marker, work Row 1 of Honeycomb Chart over the next 6 (12, 12, 18, 18, 18), {18, 18, 24, 24} stitches, k5 (2, 2, 0, 0, 0), {5, 5, 1, 1}, slip marker, p1, k1.

Work in established pattern for 1"/2.5 cm.

NOTE: During shaping, if there are not enough stitches to work a complete cable, work the stitches of the partial cable in stockinette stitch.

Increase Round: K1, p1, slip marker, M1R, work in established pattern to last marker, M1L, slip marker, p1, k1.

Continue following the established pattern and repeat Increase Round another 15 (16, 23, 22, 26, 29), {28, 31, 32, 36} times in every 6th (6th, 4th, 4th, 4th, 4th), {4th, 3rd, 3rd, 3rd} round, including new stitches into Honeycomb Chart. [86 (94, 108, 114, 122, 128), {136, 142, 148, 156} stitches]

Continue working in established pattern without increases until Sleeve measures 18"/45 cm, ending with odd-numbered round of charts.

Next Round: Work in established pattern, working next (even-numbered) rond of charts to 4 (8, 10, 10, 12, 14), {14, 16, 16, 17} stitches before BOR.

Next Round: Bind off next 8 (16, 20, 20, 24, 28), {28, 32, 32, 34} stitches, removing BOR and 2 markers before and after BOR, work to end. [78 (78, 88, 94, 98, 100), {108, 110, 116, 122} stitches]

Shape sleeve cap
Continue working back and forth in rows.

Next Row (WS): Work in established pattern to end.

NOTE: When binding off stitches, use Sloped method.

At the beginning of the next 2 rows, bind off 2 (2, 2, 3, 3, 4), {4, 4, 5, 5} stitches at each side.
At the beginning of the next 2 rows, bind off 1 (1, 1, 2, 2, 2), {2, 2, 3, 3} stitch(es) at each side.
At the beginning of the next 2 rows, bind off 1 (1, 1, 2, 2, 2), {2, 2, 3, 3} stitch(es) at each side.
At the beginning of the next 2 rows, bind off 1 (1, 1, 1, 2, 2), {2, 2, 2, 2} stitch(es) at each side.

Stitch count: 68 (68, 78, 78, 80, 80), {88, 90, 90, 96} stitches on the needle.

Decrease Row (RS): K2, K2TOG, work in established pattern to last 4 stitches, SSK, k2. [2 stitches decreased]

Next Row (WS): P3, work in established pattern to last 3 stitches, p3.

Repeat last 2 rows another 9 (8, 8, 8, 6, 6), {6, 6, 6, 6} times. [48 (50, 60, 60, 66, 66), {74, 76, 76, 82} stitches]

Next Row (RS): K2, work in established pattern to last 2 stitches, k2.

Next Row (WS): P3, work in established pattern to last 3 stitches, p3.

Decrease Row (RS): K2, K2TOG, work in charted pattern to last 4 stitches, SSK, k2. [46 stitches]

Next Row (WS): P3, work in established pattern to last 3 stitches, p3.

Next Row (RS): K2, work in established pattern to last 2 stitches, k2.

Next Row (WS): P3, work in established pattern to last 3 stitches, p3.

Repeat last 4 rows 0 (1, 2, 2, 4, 4), {5, 5, 5, 5} more time(s). [46 (46, 54, 54, 56, 56), {62, 64, 64, 70} stitches]

Size XS only:

Decrease Row (RS): K2, K2TOG, work in established pattern to last 4 stitches, SSK, k2. [44 stitches]

Next Row (WS): P3, work in established pattern to last 3 stitches, p3.

Repeat last 2 rows once. [42 stitches]

Bind off 3 stitches at the beginning of next 2 rows. [36 stitches]
Bind off 4 stitches at the beginning of next 2 rows. [28 stitches]
Bind off 5 stitches at the beginning of next 2 rows. [18 stitches]

Size S only:

Decrease Row (RS): K2, K2TOG, work in established pattern to last 4 stitches, SSK, k2. [44 stitches]

Next Row (WS): P3, work in established pattern to last 3 stitches, p3.

Bind off 3 stitches at the beginning of next 2 rows. [38 stitches]
Bind off 4 stitches at the beginning of next 2 rows. [30 stitches]
Bind off 6 stitches at the beginning of next 2 rows. [18 stitches]

Size M only:

Bind off 4 stitches at the beginning of next 2 rows. [46 stitches]
Bind off 6 stitches at the beginning of next 2 rows. [34 stitches]
Bind off 7 stitches at the beginning of next 2 rows. [20 stitches]

Size L only:

Bind off 2 stitches at the beginning of next 2 rows. [50 stitches]
Bind off 5 stitches at the beginning of next 2 rows. [40 stitches]
Bind off 9 stitches at the beginning of next 2 rows. [22 stitches]

Size XL only:

Bind off 3 stitches at the beginning of next 2 rows. [50 stitches]
Bind off 5 stitches at the beginning of next 2 rows. [40 stitches]
Bind off 9 stitches at the beginning of next 2 rows. [22 stitches]

Size 2XL only:

Bind off 2 stitches at the beginning of next 4 rows. [48 stitches]
Bind off 3 stitches at the beginning of next 2 rows. [42 stitches]
Bind off 4 stitches at the beginning of next 2 rows. [34 stitches]
Bind off 6 stitches at the beginning of next 2 rows. [22 stitches]

Size 3XL only:

Bind off 2 stitches at the beginning of next 2 rows. [58 stitches]
Work next 2 rows even without decreases.
Bind off 3 stitches at the beginning of next 2 rows. [52 stitches]

Bind off 6 stitches at the beginning of next 2 rows. [40 stitches]
Bind off 9 stitches at the beginning of next 2 rows. [22 stitches]

Size 4XL only:
Bind off 2 stitches at the beginning of next 2 rows. [60 stitches]
Work next 2 rows even without decreases.

Repeat last 4 rows once more. [56 stitches]

Bind off 2 stitches at the beginning of next 2 rows. [52 stitches]
Bind off 4 stitches at the beginning of next 2 rows. [44 stitches]
Bind off 10 stitches at the beginning of next 2 rows. [24 stitches]

Size 5XL only:
Bind off 2 stitches at the beginning of next 2 rows. [60 stitches]
Work next 2 rows even without decreases.

Repeat last 4 rows once more. [56 stitches]

Bind off 2 stitches at the beginning of next 2 rows. [52 stitches]
Bind off 4 stitches at the beginning of next 2 rows. [44 stitches]
Bind off 9 stitches at the beginning of next 2 rows. [26 stitches]

Size 6XL only:
Bind off 2 stitches at the beginning of next 2 rows. [66 stitches]
Work next 2 rows even without decreases.

Repeat last 4 rows 2 more times. [58 stitches]

Bind off 3 stitches at the beginning of next 2 rows. [52 stitches]
Bind off 4 stitches at the beginning of next 2 rows. [44 stitches]
Bind off 9 stitches at the beginning of next 2 rows. [26 stitches]

All sizes:
Bind off all stitches.
Sew sleeves into armholes.

06 FINISHING

Collar and Front Bands
NOTE: The ribbing pick-up ratio is approx. 5 stitches per 6 rows. If you're changing the number of pick-up stitches, make sure that the total number of stitches is an odd number.

On both Fronts, mark the beginning of the V-neck decreases with removable markers.

With US 4/3.5 mm 32"/80 cm circular needle, RS facing and beginning at the bottom of right front, pick up and knit 88 (88, 88, 88, 88, 96), {96, 96, 96, 96} stitches up the right front edge to the first removable marker, 50 (52, 54, 58, 60, 64), {66, 70, 72, 76} stitches along the right neckline slope to shoulder seam, 37 (37, 39, 45, 45, 47), {47, 49, 53, 53} stitches along back neck, 50 (52, 54, 58, 60, 64), {66, 70, 72, 76} stitches along the left neckline slope to removable marker, and 88 (88, 88, 88, 88, 96), {96, 96, 96, 96} stitches down the left front edge to the bottom. [313 (317, 323, 337, 341, 367), {371, 381, 389, 397} stitches].

Ribbing Row 1 (WS): P1, *p1, k1; repeat from * to last 2 stitches, p2.
Ribbing Row 2 (RS): K1, *k1, p1; repeat from * to last 2 stitches, k2.
Work Ribbing Row 1 once more.
Buttonhole Row (RS): K2, p1, k1, *YO, K2TOG, [p1, k1] 7 (7, 7, 7, 7), {8, 8, 8, 8} times; repeat from * another 4 times, YO, K2TOG, [p1, k1] to the last stitch, k1.

Repeat Ribbing Rows 1 and 2 another 2 times.

Decrease Row (WS): Work in established pattern to the end of the row, P2TOG. [312 (316, 322, 336, 340, 366), {370, 380, 388, 396} stitches]
Bind off all stitches in pattern or using Tubular Bind Off method (see Special Techniques, page 226). Weave in ends. Block to measurements. Sew on buttons.

CHARTS

HONEYCOMB CHART

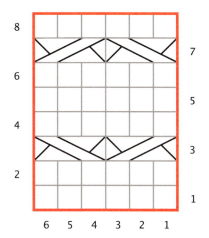

LEGEND

☐ **K**: Knit stitch on RS rows and all rounds; purl stitch on WS rows

⊡ **P**: Purl stitch on RS rows and all rounds; knit stitch on WS rows

2/1 RC: Slip 1 stitch to cable needle, hold in back, k2, k1 from cable needle

2/1 LC: Slip 2 stitches to cable needle, hold in front, k1, k2 from cable needle

2/1 RPC: Slip 1 stitch to cable needle, hold in back, k2, p1 from cable needle

2/1 LPC: Slip 2 stitches to cable needle, hold in front, p1, k2 from cable needle

2/2 RC: Slip 2 stitches to cable needle, hold in back, knit 2, knit 2 from cable needle

2/2 LC: Slip 2 stitches to cable needle, hold in front, knit 2, knit 2 from cable needle

2/2 RPC: Slip 2 stitches to cable needle, hold in back, k2, p2 from cable needle

2/2 LPC: Slip 2 stitches to cable needle, hold in front, p2, k2 from cable needle

☐ Pattern repeat

CABLE CHART (FOR SIZES XS (S, _, _, _, _), {_, _, _, _} ONLY)

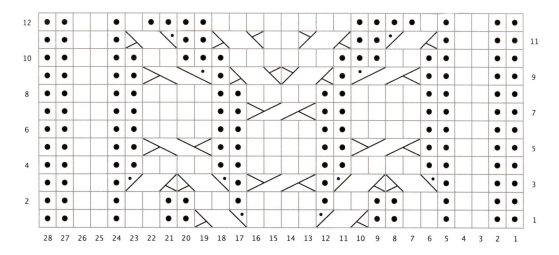

CABLE CHART (FOR SIZES _ (_, M, L, XL, 2XL), {3XL, 4XL, 5XL, 6XL} ONLY)

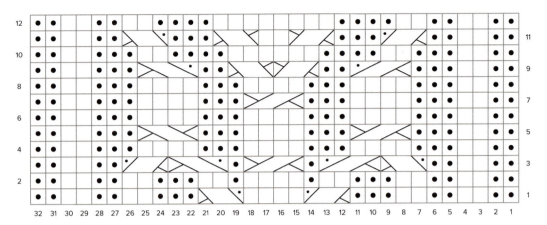

SLEEVE CHART

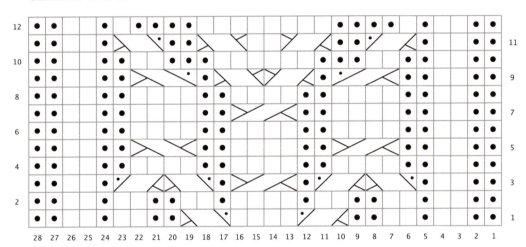

LEGEND

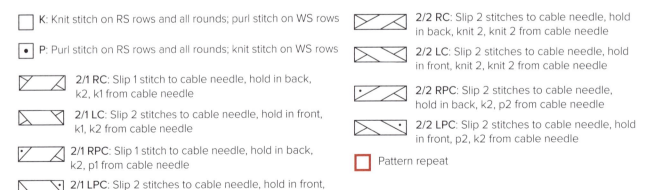

K: Knit stitch on RS rows and all rounds; purl stitch on WS rows

P: Purl stitch on RS rows and all rounds; knit stitch on WS rows

2/1 RC: Slip 1 stitch to cable needle, hold in back, k2, k1 from cable needle

2/1 LC: Slip 2 stitches to cable needle, hold in front, k1, k2 from cable needle

2/1 RPC: Slip 1 stitch to cable needle, hold in back, k2, p1 from cable needle

2/1 LPC: Slip 2 stitches to cable needle, hold in front, p1, k2 from cable needle

2/2 RC: Slip 2 stitches to cable needle, hold in back, knit 2, knit 2 from cable needle

2/2 LC: Slip 2 stitches to cable needle, hold in front, knit 2, knit 2 from cable needle

2/2 RPC: Slip 2 stitches to cable needle, hold in back, k2, p2 from cable needle

2/2 LPC: Slip 2 stitches to cable needle, hold in front, p2, k2 from cable needle

Pattern repeat

Written instructions for Honeycomb Chart (worked in rows)

Note: See Chart Legend for special abbreviations.
"..." - pattern repeat

Row 1 (RS): Knit.
Row 2 and all WS rows: Purl.
Row 3 (RS): *1/2 RC, 1/2 LC*
Row 5 (WS): Knit.
Row 7 (RS): *1/2 LC, 1/2 RC*
Row 8 (WS): Purl.

Written instructions for Honeycomb Chart (worked in the round)

Note: See Chart Legend for special abbreviations.
"..." - pattern repeat

Round 1: Knit.
Round 2 and all even-numbered rounds: Knit.
Round 3: *1/2 RC, 1/2 LC*
Round 5: Knit.
Round 7: *1/2 LC, 1/2 RC*
Round 8: Knit.

Written instructions for Cable Chart
(for sizes XS (S, _, _, _, _), {_, _, _, _} only) (worked in rows)

Row 1 (RS): P2, k2, p1, k2, p2, 2/1 RPC, k4, 2/1 LPC, p2, k2, p1, k2, p2.
Row 2 (WS): K2, p2, k1, p2, k2, p2, k1, p4, k1, p2, k2, p2, k1, p2, k2.
Row 3 (RS): P2, k2, p1, 2/1 LPC, 2/1 RPC, p1, 2/2 RC, p1, 2/1 LPC, 2/1 RPC, p1, k2, p2.
Row 4 (WS): K2, p2, [k2, p4] 3 times, k2, p2, k2.
Row 5 (RS): P2, k2, p2, 2/2 RC, p2, k4, p2, 2/2 LC, p2, k2, p2.
Row 6 (WS): K2, p2, [k2, p4] 3 times, k2, p2, k2.
Row 7 (RS): P2, k2, p2, k4, p2, 2/2 RC, p2, k4, p2, k2, p2.
Row 8 (WS): K2, p2, [k2, p4] 3 times, k2, p2, k2.
Row 9 (RS): P2, k2, p2, 2/2 RPC, p1, 2/1 RC, 2/1 LC, p1, 2/2 LPC, p2, k2, p2.
Row 10 (WS): [K2, p2] 2 times, k3, p6, k3, [p2, k2] 2 times.

Row 11 (RS): P2, k2, p1, 2/1 RPC, p2, 2/1 RC, k2, 2/1 LC, p2, 2/1 LPC, p1, k2, p2.
Row 12 (WS): K2, p2, k1, p1, k4, p8, k4, p1, k1, p2, k2.

Written instructions for Cable Chart
(for sizes XS (S, _, _, _, _), {_, _, _, _} only) (worked in the round)

Round 1: P2, k2, p1, k2, p2, 2/1 RPC, k4, 2/1 LPC, p2, k2, p1, k2, p2.
Round 2: P2, k2, p1, k2, p2, k2, p1, k4, p1, k2, p2, k2, p1, k2, p2.
Round 3: P2, k2, p1, 2/1 LPC, 2/1 RPC, p1, 2/2 RC, p1, 2/1 LPC, 2/1 RPC, p1, k2, p2.
Round 4: P2, k2, [p2, k4] 3 times, p2, k2, p2.
Round 5: P2, k2, p2, 2/2 RC, p2, k4, p2, 2/2 LC, p2, k2, p2.
Round 6: P2, k2, [p2, k4] 3 times, p2, k2, p2.
Round 7: P2, k2, p2, k4, p2, 2/2 RC, p2, k4, p2, k2, p2.
Round 8: P2, k2, [p2, k4] 3 times, p2, k2, p2.
Round 9: P2, k2, p2, 2/2 RPC, p1, 2/1 RC, 2/1 LC, p1, 2/2 LPC, p2, k2, p2.
Round 10: [P2, k2] 2 times, p3, k6, p3, [k2, p2] 2 times.
Round 11: P2, k2, p1, 2/1 RPC, p2, 2/1 RC, k2, 2/1 LC, p2, 2/1 LPC, p1, k2, p2.
Round 12: P2, k2, p1, k1, p4, k8, p4, k1, p1, k2, p2.

Written instructions for Cable Chart
(for sizes _ (_, M, L, XL, 2XL), {3XL, 4XL, 5XL, 6XL} only) (worked in rows)

Row 1 (RS): [P2, k2] 2 times, p3, 2/1 RPC, k4, 2/1 LPC, p3, [k2, p2] 2 times.
Row 2 (WS): [K2, p2] 2 times, k3, p2, k1, p4, k1, p2, k3, [p2, k2] 2 times.
Row 3 (RS): P2, k2, p2, 2/1 LPC, 2/2 RPC, p1, 2/2 RC, p1, 2/2 LPC, 2/1 RPC, p2, k2, p2.
Row 4 (WS): K2, p2, [k3, p4] 3 times, k3, p2, k2.
Row 5 (RS): P2, k2, p3, 2/2 RC, p3, k4, p3, 2/2 LC, p3, k2, p2.
Row 6 (WS): K2, p2, [k3, p4] 3 times, k3, p2, k2.
Row 7 (RS): P2, k2, p3, k4, p3, 2/2 RC, p3, k4, p3, k2, p2.
Row 8 (WS): K2, p2, [k3, p4] 3 times, k3, p2, k2.

Row 9 (RS): P2, k2, p3, 2/2 RPC, p2, 2/1 RC, 2/1 LC, p2, 2/2 LPC, p3, k2, p2.
Row 10 (WS): K2, p2, k3, p2, k4, p6, k4, p2, k3, p2, k2.
Row 11 (RS): P2, k2, p2, 2/1 RPC, p3, 2/1 RC, k2, 2/1 LC, p3, 2/1 LPC, p2, k2, p2.
Row 12 (WS): [K2, p2] 2 times, k4, p8, k4, [p2, k2] 2 times.

Written instructions for Cable Chart
(for sizes _ (_, M, L, XL, 2XL), {3XL, 4XL, 5XL, 6XL} only) (worked in the round)

Round 1: [P2, k2] 2 times, p3, 2/1 RPC, k4, 2/1 LPC, p3, [k2, p2] 2 times.
Round 2: [P2, k2] 2 times, p3, k2, p1, k4, p1, k2, p3, [k2, p2] 2 times.
Round 3: P2, k2, p2, 2/1 LPC, 2/2 RPC, p1, 2/2 RC, p1, 2/2 LPC, 2/1 RPC, p2, k2, p2.
Round 4: P2, k2, [p3, k4] 3 times, p3, k2, p2.
Round 5: P2, k2, p3, 2/2 RC, p3, k4, p3, 2/2 LC, p3, k2, p2.
Round 6: P2, k2, [p3, k4] 3 times, p3, k2, p2.
Round 7: P2, k2, p3, k4, p3, 2/2 RC, p3, k4, p3, k2, p2.
Round 8: P2, k2, [p3, k4] 3 times, p3, k2, p2.
Round 9: P2, k2, p3, 2/2 RPC, p2, 2/1 RC, 2/1 LC, p2, 2/2 LPC, p3, k2, p2.
Round 10: P2, k2, p3, k2, p4, k6, p4, k2, p3, k2, p2.
Round 11: P2, k2, p2, 2/1 RPC, p3, 2/1 RC, k2, 2/1 LC, p3, 2/1 LPC, p2, k2, p2.
Round 12: [P2, k2] 2 times, p4, k8, p4, [k2, p2] 2 times.

Written instructions for Sleeve Chart (worked in the round)

Round 1: P2, k2, p1, k2, p2, 2/1 RPC, k4, 2/1 LPC, p2, k2, p1, k2, p2.
Round 2: P2, k2, p1, k2, p2, k2, p1, k4, p1, k2, p2, k2, p1, k2, p2.
Round 3: P2, k2, p1, 2/1 LPC, 2/1 RPC, p1, 2/2 RC, p1, 2/1 LPC, 2/1 RPC, p1, k2, p2.
Round 4: P2, k2, [p2, k4] 3 times, p2, k2, p2.
Round 5: P2, k2, p2, 2/2 RC, p2, k4, p2, 2/2 LC, p2, k2, p2.
Round 6: P2, k2, [p2, k4] 3 times, p2, k2, p2.
Round 7: P2, k2, p2, k4, p2, 2/2 RC, p2, k4, p2, k2, p2.
Round 8: P2, k2, [p2, k4] 3 times, p2, k2, p2.

Round 9: P2, k2, p2, 2/2 RPC, p1, 2/1 RC, 2/1 LC, p1, 2/2 LPC, p2, k2, p2.
Round 10: [P2, k2] 2 times, p3, k6, p3, [k2, p2] 2 times.
Round 11: P2, k2, p1, 2/1 RPC, p2, 2/1 RC, k2, 2/1 LC, p2, 2/1 LPC, p1, k2, p2.
Round 12: P2, k2, p1, k1, p4, k8, p4, k1, p1, k2, p2.

Written instructions for Sleeve Chart (worked in rows)

Row 1 (RS): P2, k2, p1, k2, p2, 2/1 RPC, k4, 2/1 LPC, p2, k2, p1, k2, p2.
Row 2 (WS): K2, p2, k1, p2, k2, p2, k1, p4, k1, p2, k2, p2, k1, p2, k2.
Row 3 (RS): P2, k2, p1, 2/1 LPC, 2/1 RPC, p1, 2/2 RC, p1, 2/1 LPC, 2/1 RPC, p1, k2, p2.
Row 4 (WS): K2, p2, [k2, p4] 3 times, k2, p2, k2.
Row 5 (RS): P2, k2, p2, 2/2 RC, p2, k4, p2, 2/2 LC, p2, k2, p2.
Row 6 (WS): K2, p2, [k2, p4] 3 times, k2, p2, k2.
Row 7 (RS): P2, k2, p2, k4, p2, 2/2 RC, p2, k4, p2, k2, p2.
Row 8 (WS): K2, p2, [k2, p4] 3 times, k2, p2, k2.
Row 9 (RS): P2, k2, p2, 2/2 RPC, p1, 2/1 RC, 2/1 LC, p1, 2/2 LPC, p2, k2, p2.
Row 10 (WS): [K2, p2] 2 times, k3, p6, k3, [p2, k2] 2 times.
Row 11 (RS): P2, k2, p1, 2/1 RPC, p2, 2/1 RC, k2, 2/1 LC, p2, 2/1 LPC, p1, k2, p2.
Row 12 (WS): K2, p2, k1, p1, k4, p8, k4, p1, k1, p2, k2.

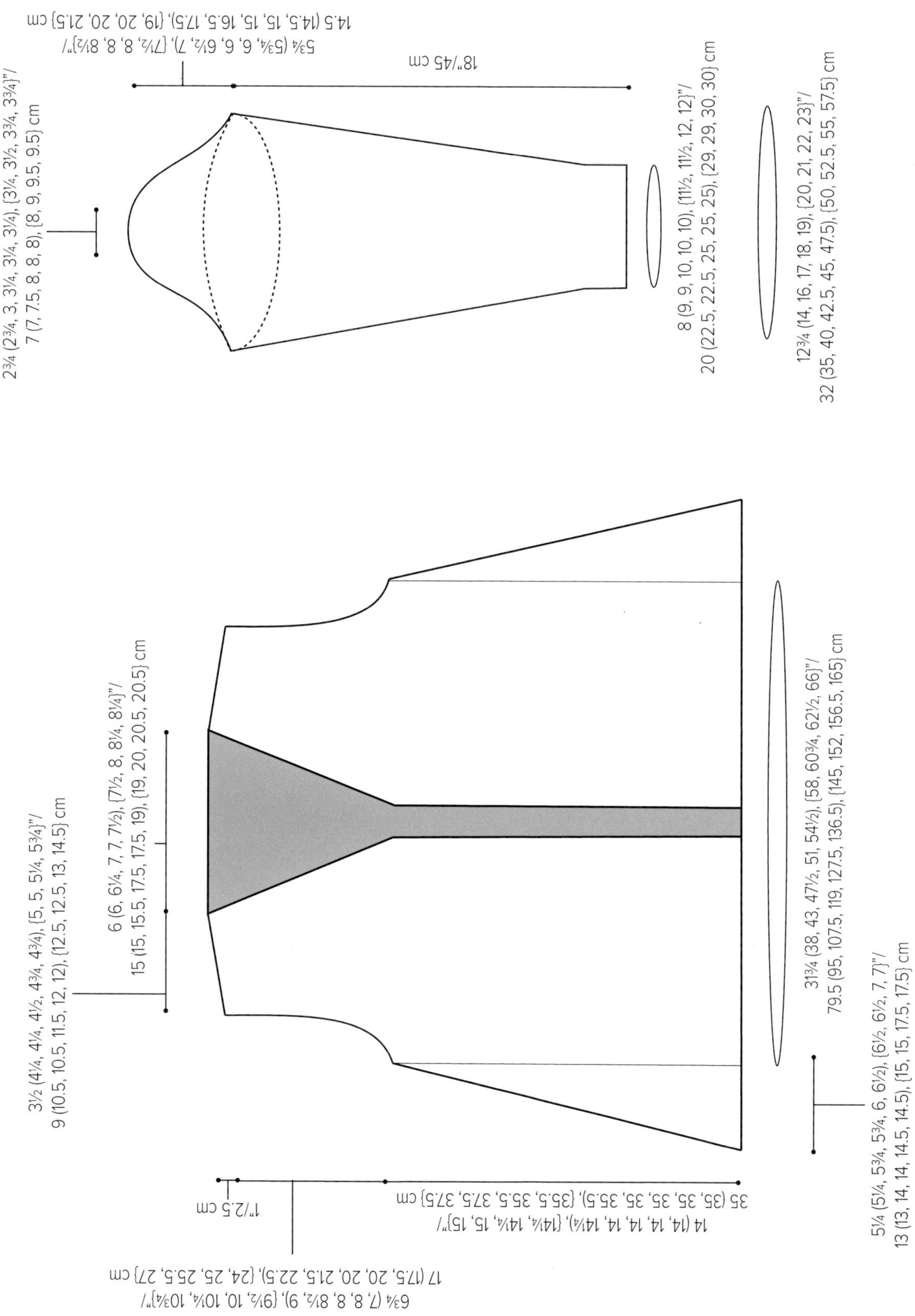
2¾ (2¾, 3, 3¼, 3¼, 3¼), {3¼, 3½, 3¾, 3¾}"/
7 (7, 7.5, 8, 8, 8), {8, 9, 9.5, 9.5} cm
5¾ (5¾, 6, 6, 6½, 7), {7½, 8, 8, 8½}"/
14.5 (14.5, 15, 15, 16.5, 17.5), {19, 20, 20, 21.5} cm
18"/45 cm
8 (9, 9, 10, 10, 10), {11½, 11½, 12, 12}"/
20 (22.5, 22.5, 25, 25, 25), {29, 29, 30, 30} cm
12¾ (14, 16, 17, 18, 19), {20, 21, 22, 23}"/
32 (35, 40, 42.5, 45, 47.5), {50, 52.5, 55, 57.5} cm
3½ (4¼, 4¼, 4½, 4¾, 4¾), {5, 5, 5¼, 5¾}"/
9 (10.5, 10.5, 11.5, 12, 12), {12.5, 12.5, 13, 14.5} cm
6 (6, 6¼, 7, 7, 7½), {7½, 8, 8¼, 8¼}"/
15 (15, 15.5, 17.5, 17.5, 19), {19, 20, 20.5, 20.5} cm
31¾ (38, 43, 47½, 51, 54½), {58, 60¾, 62½, 66}"/
79.5 (95, 107.5, 119, 127.5, 136.5), {145, 152, 156.5, 165} cm
5¼ (5¼, 5¾, 5¾, 6, 6½), {6½, 6½, 7, 7}"/
13 (13, 14, 14.5, 14.5, 14.5), {15, 15, 17.5, 17.5} cm
14 (14, 14, 14, 14¼), {14¼, 14¼, 15, 15}"/
35 (35, 35, 35, 35.5), {35.5, 35.5, 37.5, 37.5} cm
1"/2.5 cm
6¾ (7, 8, 8, 8½, 9), {9½, 10, 10¼, 10¾}"/
17 (17.5, 20, 20, 21.5, 22.5), {24, 25, 25.5, 27} cm

Arad

A round yoke of bold, interlocking cables makes this pullover stand out with sculptural detail. The motifs form diamond and chevron shapes that flow into the smooth stockinette of the body and sleeves, creating a striking contrast between texture and simplicity. Worked seamlessly from the top down, the sweater features a classic crew neckline, long sleeves, and ribbed edges for a polished finish. Arad offers both visual drama in the yoke and easy wearability in the body, making it a versatile piece for everyday layering.

Sizes

XS (S, M, L, XL, 2XL), {3XL, 4XL, 5XL, 6XL}: to fit bust 28-30 (32-34, 36-38, 40-42, 44-46, 48-50), {52-54, 56-58, 60-62, 64-66}"/70-75 (80-85, 90-95, 100-105, 110-115, 120-125), {130-135, 140-145, 150-155, 160-165} cm.

Finished Measurements

38 (41, 44¼, 52, 55, 61), {64, 69½, 72½, 75½}"/ 95 (102.5, 110.5, 130, 137.5, 152.5), {160, 174, 181.5, 189} cm bust circumference.
Shown in size M (44¼"/110.5 cm) on 38"/95 cm bust with 6¼"/15.5 cm of positive ease.

Yarn

DK weight yarn (approximate amounts): 945 (1020, 1095, 1280, 1360, 1510), {1590, 1720, 1800, 1870} yds/860 (928, 997, 1165, 1238, 1374), {1447, 1565, 1638, 1702} m.

Miss Babs Killington (85% Polwarth wool, 15% Silk; 350 yards/320 m in 120 g), Tasman:
945 (1020, 1095, 1280, 1360, 1510), {1590, 1720, 1800, 1870} yards/860 (928, 997, 1165, 1238, 1374), {1447, 1565, 1638, 1702} m or 3 (3, 4, 4, 4, 4), {5, 5, 6, 6} skeins.

Needles

Size US 6/4 mm: 24-32"/60-80 cm circular, 16"/40 cm circular and set of double-pointed.
Size US 5/3.75 mm: 24-32"/60-80 cm circular, 16"/40 cm circular and set of double-pointed.
Optional: spare size US 5/3.75 mm 24-32"/60-80 cm circular.
Adjust needle size if necessary to obtain gauge.

Notions

Stitch markers, waste yarn, tapestry needle, stitch holders, cable needle.

Gauge

21 stitches and 28 rows = 4"/10 cm Stockinette stitch on size US 6/4 mm needle, after blocking.

Notes

- This pullover is worked in the round from the top down with round yoke shaping.

DIRECTIONS

01 YOKE

With US 5/3.75 mm 16"/40 cm circular needle, cast on 96 (96, 96, 100, 104, 116), {116, 116, 120, 120} stitches. Place marker for the beginning of the round (BOR) and join for working in the round.
Knit all stitches for the next 4 (4, 4, 3, 3, 3), {3, 3, 3, 3} rounds.

Sizes L and XL only:
Increase Round: K4 (0), [M1L, k8 (13)] 12 (8) times. [112 stitches]

Sizes 2XL, 3XL and 4XL only:
Increase Round: K2, [M1L, k5] 2 times, [M1L, k4] 23 times, [M1L, k5] 2 times], k2. [144 stitches]

Size 5XL only:
Increase Round: *M1L, k5; repeat from * to end. [144 stitches]

Size 6XL only:
Increase Round: *M1L, k3; repeat from * to end. [160] stitches]

All sizes:
Total number of stitches on the needle: 96 (96, 96, 112, 112, 144), {144, 144, 144, 160} stitches.

Ribbing Round: *K1, p2, k1; repeat from * to end.
Repeat Ribbing Round 3 more times.

Shape raised back neck with German Short-Rows (see Special Techniques, page 226):
Short-Row 1 (RS): Work in established pattern for 31 (31, 31, 33, 33, 35), {35, 35, 51, 51} stitches, turn work.
Short-Row 2 (WS): Make double stitch, work to BOR, work for 31 (31, 31, 33, 33, 35), {35, 35, 51, 51} stitches, turn work.
Short-Row 3 (RS): Make double stitch, work to double stitch of previous row, work double stitch, work 4 (4, 4, 4, 4, 4), {6, 6, 6, 6} stitches, turn work.

Short-Row 4 (WS): Make double stitch, work to double stitch of previous row, work double stitch, work 4 (4, 4, 4, 4, 4), {6, 6, 6, 6} stitches, turn work.

Short-Rows 5-6: Repeat Rows 3 and 4 once more.

Next Row (RS): Make double stitch, work to BOR.

Begin working in the round again.

Next Round: Work to BOR, working double stitches as single stitches.

Change to to US 6/4 mm 16"/40 cm circular needle .

Chart A Set-Up Round: Work Row 1 of Chart A. Continue following Chart A until Row 48 is complete.

Chart B Set-Up Round: Work Row 1 of Chart B. Continue following Chart B for your size, until Row 7 (7, 9, 9, 17, 17), {19, 19, 23, 23} is complete, changing to size US 6/4 mm 24-32"/60-80 cm circular needle when needed. [312 (336, 360, 392, 420, 468), {468, 504, 540, 560} stitches]

NOTE: Working the next row, work Row 8 (8, 10, 10, 18, 18), {20, 20, 24, 24} of Chart B for your size.

Division Round: Work 48 (52, 54, 62, 66, 74), {76, 82, 86, 90} stitches, place next 60 (64, 72, 72, 78, 86), {82, 74, 98, 100} stitches on hold for right sleeve, place marker, cast on 4 (4, 8, 12, 12, 12), {16, 18, 18, 18} stitches for right underarm, place marker; work 96 (104, 108, 124, 132, 148), {152, 164, 172, 180} stitches, place 60 (64, 72, 72, 78, 86), {82, 88, 98, 100} stitches on hold for left sleeve, place marker, cast on 4 (4, 8, 12, 12, 12), {16, 18, 18, 18} stitches for left underarm, place marker, work 48 (52, 54, 62, 66, 74), {76, 82, 86, 90} stitches to end.

Continue working in the round on 200 (216, 232, 272, 288, 320), {336, 364, 380, 396} Body stitches.

02 BODY

NOTE: Working the next row, work Row 9 (9, 11, 11, 19, 19), {21, 21, 25, 25} of Chart B for your size.

Size XS only:
Next Round: Work 26-stitch pattern repeat once, then work stitches 1-22 of chart, slip marker, k4, slip marker, work stitches 5-26 of chart, then work 26-stitch pattern repeat 2 times, then work stitches 1-22 of chart, slip marker, k4, slip marker, work stitches 5-26 of chart, then work 26-stitch pattern repeat once.

Size S only:
Next Round: Work 28-stitch pattern repeat once, then work stitches 1-24 of chart, slip marker, k4, slip marker, work stitches 5-28 of chart, then work 28-stitch pattern repeat 2 times, then work stitches 1-24 of chart, slip marker, k4, slip marker, work stitches 5-28 of chart, then work 28-stitch pattern repeat once.

Size M only:
Next Round: Work 30-stitch pattern repeat once, then work stitches 1-24 of chart, slip marker, k8, slip marker, work stitches 7-30 of chart, then work 30-stitch pattern repeat 2 times, then work stitches 1-24 of chart, slip marker, k8, slip marker, work stitches 7-30 of chart, then work 30-stitch pattern repeat once.

Size L only:
Next Round: Work 28-stitch pattern repeat 2 times, then work stitches 1-6 of chart, slip marker, k12, slip marker, work stitches 23-28 of chart, then work 28-stitch pattern repeat 4 times, then work stitches 1-6 of chart, slip marker, k12, slip marker, work stitches 23-28 of chart, then work 28-stitch pattern 2 times.

Size XL only:
Next Round: Work 30-stitch pattern repeat 2 times, then work stitches 1-6 of chart, slip marker, k12, slip marker, work stitches 25-30 of chart, then work 30-stitch pattern repeat 4 times, then work stitches 1-6 of chart, slip marker, k12, slip marker, work stitches 25-30 of chart, then work 30-stitch pattern 2 times.

Size 2XL only:
Next Round: Work 26-stitch pattern repeat 2 times, then work stitches 1-22 of chart, slip marker, k12, slip marker, work stitches 5-26 of chart, then work 26-stitch pattern repeat 4 times, then work stitches 5-26 of chart, slip marker, k12, slip marker, work stitches 5-26 of chart, then work 26-stitch pattern 2 times.

Size 3XL only:
Next Round: Work 26-stitch pattern repeat 2 times, then work stitches 1-24 of chart, slip marker, k16, slip marker, work stitches 3-26 of chart, then work 26-stitch pattern repeat 4 times, then work stitches 1-24 of chart, slip marker, k16, slip marker, work stitches 3-26 of chart, then work 26-stitch pattern 2 times.

Size 4XL only:
Next Round: Work 28-stitch pattern repeat 2 times, then work stitches 1-26 of chart, slip marker, k18, slip marker, work stitches 3-28 of chart, then work 28-stitch pattern repeat 4 times, then work stitches 1-26 of chart, slip marker, k18, slip marker, work stitches 3-28 of chart, then work 28-stitch pattern 2 times.

Size 5XL only:
Next Round: Work 30-stitch pattern repeat 2 times, then work stitches 1-26 of chart, slip marker, k18, slip marker, work stitches 5-30 of chart, then work 30-stitch pattern repeat 4 times, then work stitches 1-26 of chart, slip marker, k18, slip marker, work stitches 5-30 of chart, then work 30-stitch pattern 2 times.

Size 6XL only:
Next Round: Work 28-stitch pattern repeat 3 times, then work stitches 1-6 of chart, slip marker, k18, slip marker, work stitches 23-28 of chart, then work 28-stitch pattern repeat 6 times, then work stitches 1-6 of chart, slip marker, k18, slip marker, work stitches 23-28 of chart, then work 28-stitch pattern 3 times.

All sizes:

Work in established pattern, slipping markers and working underarm stitches in Stockinette stitch, through Row 32 of Chart B, then work all stitches in Stockinette stitch until Body measures 11"/27.5 cm from underarms or 2"/5 cm less than desired Body length.

Change to US 5/3.75 mm 24-32"/60-80 cm circular needles.

Ribbing Round: *K1, p2, k1; repeat from * to end.

Repeat Ribbing Round until ribbing measures 2"/5 cm.

Bind off all stitches in pattern or using Tubular method for k2, p2 rib in the round (see Special Techniques, page 226).

03 SLEEVES

Place 60 (64, 72, 72, 78, 86), {82, 88, 98, 100} held Sleeve stitches onto US 6/4 mm double-pointed needles.

NOTE: Working the next row, work Row 9 (9, 11, 11, 19, 19), {21, 21, 25, 25} of Chart B for your size.

With RS facing, join yarn at the center of the underarm and pick up and knit 2 (2, 4, 6, 6, 6), {8, 9, 9, 9} stitches directly into the underarm stitches, place marker, work Chart B for your size as follows: work stitches 23-26 (25-28, 25-30, 7-28, 7-30, 23-26), {25-26, 27-28, 27-30, 7-28}, then work 26 (28, 30, 28, 30, 26), {26, 28, 30, 28}-stitch chart repeat 2 (2, 2, 1, 1, 3), {3, 3, 3, 2} times, then work stitches 1-4 (1-4, 1-6, 1-22, 1-24, 1-4), {1-2, 1-2, 1-4, 1-22}; place marker, pick up and knit 2 (2, 4, 6, 6, 6), {8, 9, 9, 9} stitches directly into remaining underarm stitches. [64 (68, 80, 84, 90, 98), {98, 106, 116, 118} stitches]

Place marker for the beginning of the round and join for working in the round.

Next Round: K1, purl to marker, slip marker, work next row of Chart B as established, slip marker, purl to last stitch, k1.
Work in established pattern for 2 more rounds.

Shape sleeve
Decrease Round: K1, K2TOG, purl to marker, slip marker, work next row of Chart B, slip marker, purl to last 3 stitches, SSK, k1.

Continue following the Chart B through Row 32 of Cable Chart, then work all stitches in Stockinette stitch, AT THE SAME TIME repeat Decrease Round in every 10 (9, 6, 6, 5, 4), {4, 4, 4, 4}th round another 9 (11, 17, 17, 20, 22), {22, 24, 25, 27} times. [44 (44, 44, 48, 48, 52), {52, 56, 64, 64} stitches]

Continue working without decreases until Sleeve measures 15½"/39 cm from underarm.

Change to US 5/3.75 mm double-pointed needles.

Ribbing Round: *K1, p2, k1; repeat from * to end.
Repeat Ribbing Round until ribbing measures 2"/5 cm.
Bind off all stitches in pattern or using Tubular method for k2, p2 rib in the round (see Special Techniques, page 226).

04 FINISHING

Block to measurements. Weave in ends.

CHARTS

CHART A

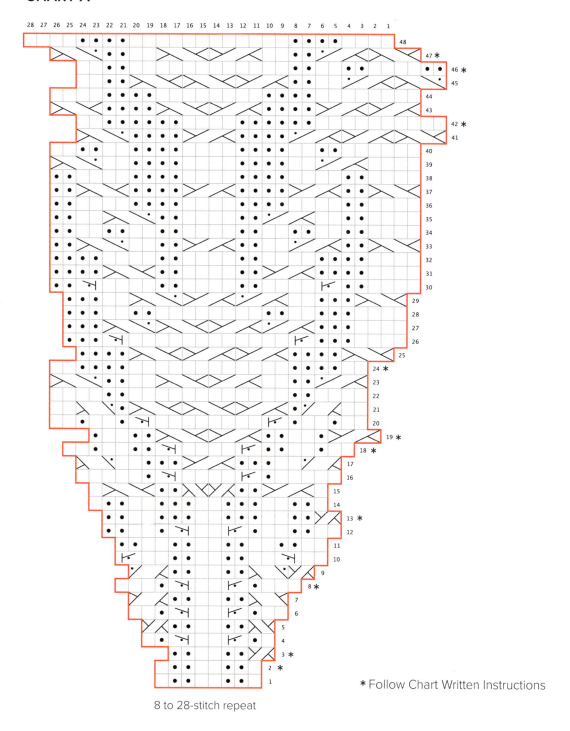

8 to 28-stitch repeat

*Follow Chart Written Instructions

CHART B (FOR SIZES XS (_, _, _, _, 2XL), {3XL, _, _, _} ONLY)

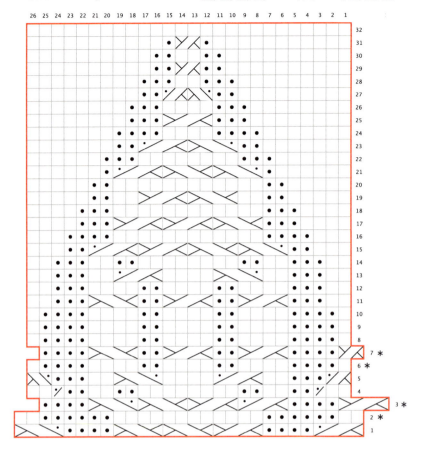

LEGEND

☐ **K**: Knit stitch

⊡ **P**: Purl stitch

▱ **P2TOG**: Purl 2 stitches together – 1 stitch decreased

▱ **RLIP**: Purl into back of the stitch in the row directly below the first stitch on the left needle, then purl the first stitch – 1 stitch increased

▱ **LLIP**: Purl 1, insert the left needle into the back of the first stitch on the right needle just below the stitch just purled, and purl it – 1 stitch increased

▱ **1/1 RC**: Slip 1 stitch to cable needle, hold in back, k1, k1 from cable needle

▱ **1/1 LC**: Slip 1 stitch to cable needle, hold in front, k1, k1 from cable needle

▱ **1/1 RPC**: Slip 1 stitch to cable needle, hold in back, k1, p1 from cable needle

▱ **1/1 LPC**: Slip 1 stitch to cable needle, hold in front, p1, k1 from cable needle

▱ **2/1 RC**: Slip 1 stitch to cable needle, hold in back, k2, k1 from cable needle

▱ **2/1 LC**: Slip 2 stitches to cable needle, hold in front, k1, k2 from cable needle

▱ **2/1 RPC**: Slip 1 stitch to cable needle, hold in back, k2, p1 from cable needle

▱ **2/1 LPC**: Slip 2 stitches to cable needle, hold in front, p1, k2 from cable needle

▱ **2/2 RC**: Slip 2 stitches to cable needle, hold in back, knit 2, knit 2 from cable needle

▱ **2/2 LC**: Slip 2 stitches to cable needle, hold in front, knit 2, knit 2 from cable needle

▱ **2/2 RPC**: Slip 2 stitches to cable needle, hold in back, k2, p2 from cable needle

▱ **2/2 LPC**: Slip 2 stitches to cable needle, hold in front, p2, k2 from cable needle

☐ Pattern repeat

* Follow Chart Written Instructions

CHART B (FOR SIZES _ (S, _, L, _, _), {_, 4XL _, 6XL} ONLY)

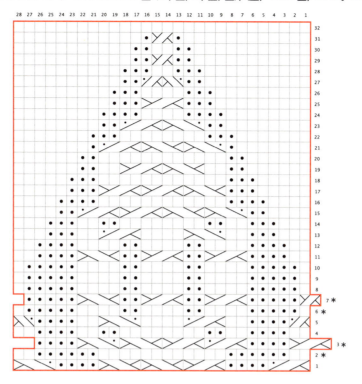

CHART B (FOR SIZES _ (M, _, _, XL, _), {_, _ 5XL, _} ONLY)

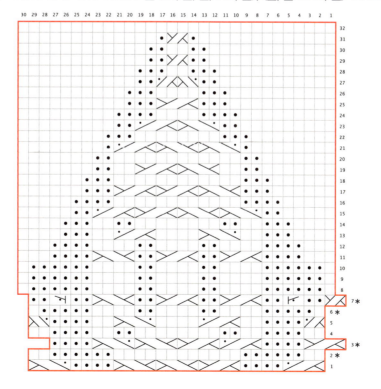

Written instructions for Chart A

... – *pattern repeat*

Note: See Chart Legend for special abbreviations.

Round 1: K1, p2, k2, p2, k1.

* Round 2 (Shift marker): *K1, p2, k2, p2, k1; repeat from * to last stitch of the round, slip 1 stitch purlwise to right needle, remove marker, slip 1 stitch back to left needle, replace marker.

* Round 3 (Shift marker): *1/1 RC, p2, k2, p2; repeat from * around. Remove marker, k1, replace marker.

Round 4: *K1, p1, RLIP, k2, LLIP, p1, k1*

Round 5: *1/1 LC, p2, k2, p2, 1/1 RC*

Round 6: *K2, p1, RLIP, k2, LLIP, p1, k2*

Round 7: *2/1 LC, p2, k2, p2, 2/1 RC*

* Round 8 (Shift marker): *K3, p1, RLIP, k2, LLIP, p1, k3; repeat from * to last stitch of the round, slip 1 stitch purlwise to right needle, remove marker, slip 1 stitch back to left needle, replace marker.

Round 9: *1/1 RC, 2/1 LPC, p2, k2, p2, 2/1 RPC*

Round 10: *K2, LLIP, [k2, p2] 2 times, k2, RLIP*

Round 11: *[K2, p2] 4 times*

Round 12: *K2, p2, k2, p1, RLIP, k2, LLIP, p1, k2, p2*

* Round 13 (Shift marker): *1/1 RC, p2, [k2, p3] 2 times, k2, p2; repeat from * around. Remove marker, k1, replace marker.

Round 14: *K1, p2, [k2, p3] 2 times, k2, p2, k1*

Round 15: *K1, 2/2 RC, p2, 1/1 RC, 1/1 LC, p2, 2/2 LC, k1*

Round 16: *K5, p1, RLIP, k4, LLIP, p1, k5*

Round 17: *2/1 RPC, k2, p3, 2/2 RC, p3, k2, 2/1 LPC*

* Round 18 (Shift marker): *K2, p1, k2, p2, RLIP, k4, LLIP, p2, k2, p1, k2; repeat from * to last 2 stitches of the round, slip 2 stitches purlwise to right needle, remove marker, slip 2 stitches back to left needle, replace marker.

* Round 19 (Shift marker): *2/2 RC, p1, k2, p2, 2/2 RC, 2/2 LC, p2, k2, p1; repeat from * around. Remove marker, k2, replace marker.

Round 20: *[K2, p1] 2 times, RLIP, k8, LLIP, [p1, k2] 2 times*

Round 21: *K2, 2/1 RPC, p1, 2/2 RC, [2/2 LC] 2 times, p1, 2/1 LPC, k2*

Round 22: *K4, p2, k12, p2, k4*

Round 23: *2/2 RPC, p2, k2, 2/2 RC, 2/2 LC, k2, p2, 2/2 LPC*

* Round 24 (Shift marker): *K2, p4, k12, p4, k2; repeat from * to last 2 stitches of the round, slip 2 stitches purlwise to right needle, remove marker, slip 2 stitches back to left needle, replace marker.

Round 25: *2/2 LC, p4, [2/2 RC] 2 times, 2/2 LC, p4*

Round 26: *K4, p3, RLIP, k12, LLIP, p3*

Round 27: *K4, p3, 2/2 RPC, 2/2 RC, 2/2 LC, 2/2 LPC, p3*

Round 28: *K4, p3, k2, p2, k8, p2, k2, p3*

Round 29: *2/2 LC, p3, k2, 2/2 RPC, 2/2 RC, 2/2 LPC, k2, p3*

Round 30: *K4, p2, RLIP, [k4, p2] 2 times, k4, LLIP, p2*

Round 31: *K4, p4, 2/2 RC, p2, k4, p2, 2/2 LC, p4*

Round 32: *K4, p4, [k4, p2] 2 times, k4, p4*

Round 33: *2/2 LC, p2, 2/2 RPC, k2, p2, 2/2 RC, p2, k2, 2/2 LPC, p2*

Round 34: *[K4, (p2, k2) 2 times, p2] 2 times*

Round 35: *K4, p2, k2, 2/2 RPC, p2, k4, p2, 2/2 LPC, k2, p2*

Round 36: *K4, p2, [k4, p4] 2 times, k4, p2*

Round 37: *2/2 LC, p2, [2/2 RC, p4] 2 times, 2/2 LC, p2*

Round 38: *K4, p2, [k4, p4] 2 times, k4, p2*

Round 39: *K4, 2/2 RPC, k2, p4, k4, p4, k2, 2/2 LPC*

* Round 40 (Shift marker): *K6, p2, k2, p4, k4, p4, k2, p2, k2; repeat from * to last 2 stitches of the round, slip 2 stitches purlwise to right needle, remove marker, slip 2 stitches back to left needle, replace marker.

Round 41: *2/2 LC, 2/2 RC, 2/2 RPC, p4, 2/2 RC, p4, 2/2 LPC*

* Round 42 (Shift marker): *K10, p6, k4, p6, k2; repeat from * around. Remove marker, k2, replace marker.

Round 43: *[2/2 RC] 2 times, p4, 2/2 RC, 2/2 LC, p4, 2/2 LC*

* Round 44 (Shift marker): *[K8, p4] 2 times, k4; repeat from * to last 2 stitches of the round, slip 2 stitches purlwise to right needle, remove marker, slip 2 stitches back to left needle, replace marker.

Round 45: *2/2 LPC, 2/2 RPC, k2, p2, 2/2 RC, [2/2 LC] 2 times, p2, k2*

* Round 46 (Shift marker): *P2, k4, p2, k2, p2, k12, p2, k2; repeat from * around. Remove marker, p2, replace marker.

* Round 47 (Shift marker): *2/2 LC, 2/2 RPC, p2, k2, 2/2 RC, 2/2 LC, k2, p2, 2/2 LPC ; repeat from * around. Remove marker, k2, replace marker.

Round 48: *K4, p4, k12, p4, k4*

Written instructions for Chart B
(sizes XS (_, _, _, _, 2XL), {3XL, _, _, _} only)
... – pattern repeat

Round 1: *2/2 RPC, p4, 2/2 RC, [2/2 LC] 2 times, p4, 2/2 LPC*
* Round 2 (Shift Marker): *K2, p6, k12, p6, k2; repeat from * to last 2 stitches of the round, slip 2 stitches purlwise to right needle, remove marker, slip 2 stitches back to left needle, replace marker.
* Round 3 (Shift Marker): *2/2 RC, p4, 2/2 RPC, 2/2 RC, 2/2 LC, 2/2 LPC, p4; repeat from * around. Remove marker, k2, replace marker.
Round 4: *K2, P2TOG, p2, k2, p2, k8, p2, k2, p2, P2TOG, k2*
Round 5: *1/1 RPC, p3, k2, 2/2 RPC, k4, 2/2 LPC, k2, p3, 1/1 LPC*
* Round 6 (Shift Marker): *K1, p4, [k4, p2] 2 times, k4, p4, k1; repeat from * to last stitch of the round, slip 1 stitch purlwise to right needle, remove marker, slip 1 stitch back to left needle, replace marker.
* Round 7 (Shift Marker): *1/1 RC, p4, [2/2 RC, p2] 2 times, 2/2 LC, p4; repeat from * around. Remove marker, k1, replace marker.
Rounds 8 - 10: *K1, p4, [k4, p2] 2 times, k4, p4, k1*
Round 11: *K2, p3, [2/2 RC, p2] 2 times, 2/2 LC, p3, k2*
Round 12: *K2, p3, [k4, p2] 2 times, k4, p3, k2*
Round 13: *K2, p3, k2, 2/2 LPC, k4, 2/2 RPC, k2, p3, k2*
Round 14: *K2, p3, k2, p2, k8, p2, k2, p3, k2*
Round 15: *K3, p2, 2/2 LPC, 2/2 LC, 2/2 RC, 2/2 RPC, p2, k3*
Round 16: *K3, p4, k12, p4, k3*
Round 17: *K4, p3, 2/2 LC, [2/2 RC] 2 times, p3, k4*
Round 18: *K4, p3, k12, p3, k4*
Round 19: *K5, p2, k2, 2/2 LC, 2/2 RC, k2, p2, k5*
Round 20: *K5, p2, k12, p2, k5*
Round 21: *K6, p1, 2/2 LPC, 2/2 LC, 2/2 RPC, p1, k6*
Round 22: *K6, p3, k8, p3, k6*
Round 23: *K7, p2, 2/2 LPC, 2/2 RPC, p2, k7*
Round 24: *K7, p4, k4, p4, k7*
Round 25: *K8, p3, 2/2 RC, p3, k8*
Round 26: *K8, p3, k4, p3, k8*
Round 27: *K9, p2, 1/1 LPC, 1/1 RPC, p2, k9*
Round 28: *K9, p3, k2, p3, k9*
Round 29: *K10, p2, 1/1 RC, p2, k10*

Round 30: *K10, p2, k2, p2, k10*
Round 31: *K11, p1, 1/1 RC, p1, k11*
Round 32: Knit.

Written instructions for Chart B
(sizes _ (S, _, L, _, _), {_, 4XL _, 6XL} only)
... – pattern repeat

Round 1: *2/2 RPC, p4, 2/2 RC, [2/2 LC] 2 times, p4, 2/2 LPC*
* Round 2 (Shift Marker): *K2, p6, k12, p6, k2; repeat from * to last 2 stitches of the round, slip 2 stitches purlwise to right needle, remove marker, slip 2 stitches back to left needle, replace marker.
* Round 3 (Shift Marker): *2/2 RC, p4, 2/2 RPC, 2/2 RC, 2/2 LC, 2/2 LPC, p4; repeat from * around. Remove marker, k2, replace marker.
Round 4: *K2, p4, k2, p2, k8, p2, k2, p4, k2*
Round 5: *1/1 RPC, p4, k2, 2/2 RPC, k4, 2/2 LPC, k2, p4, 1/1 LPC*
* Round 6 (Shift Marker): *K1, p5, (k4, p2) 2 times, k4, p5, k1; repeat from * to last stitch of the round, slip 1 stitch purlwise to right needle, remove marker, slip 1 stitch back to left needle, replace marker.
* Round 7 (Shift Marker): *1/1 RC, p5, (2/2 RC, p2) 2 times, 2/2 LC, p5; repeat from * around. Remove marker, k1, replace marker.
Rounds 8 - 10: *K1, p5, [k4, p2] 2 times, k4, p5, k1*
Round 11: *K2, p4, [2/2 RC, p2] 2 times, 2/2 LC, p4, k2*
Round 12: *K2, p4, [k4, p2] 2 times, k4, p4, k2*
Round 13: *K3, p3, k2, 2/2 LPC, k4, 2/2 RPC, k2, p3, k3*
Round 14: *K3, p3, k2, p2, k8, p2, k2, p3, k3*
Round 15: *K4, p2, 2/2 LPC, 2/2 LC, 2/2 RC, 2/2 RPC, p2, k4*
Round 16: *K4, p4, k12, p4, k4*
Round 17: *K5, p3, 2/2 LC, [2/2 RC] 2 times, p3, k5*
Round 18: *K5, p3, k12, p3, k5*
Round 19: *K6, p2, k2, 2/2 LC, 2/2 RC, k2, p2, k6*
Round 20: *K6, p2, k12, p2, k6*
Round 21: *K7, p1, 2/2 LPC, 2/2 LC, 2/2 RPC, p1, k7*
Round 22: *K7, p3, k8, p3, k7*
Round 23: *K8, p2, 2/2 LPC, 2/2 RPC, p2, k8*
Round 24: *K8, p4, k4, p4, k8*
Round 25: *K9, p3, 2/2 RC, p3, k9*
Round 26: *K9, p3, k4, p3, k9*

Round 27: *K10, p2, 1/1 LPC, 1/1 RPC, p2, k10*
Round 28: *K10, p3, k2, p3, k10*
Round 29: *K11, p2, 1/1 RC, p2, k11*
Round 30: *K11, p2, k2, p2, k11*
Round 31: *K12, p1, 1/1 RC, p1, k12*
Round 32: Knit.

Written instructions for Chart B
(sizes _ (M, _, _, XL, _), {_, _ 5XL, _} only)
... – pattern repeat

Round 1: *2/2 RPC, p4, 2/2 RC, [2/2 LC] 2 times, p4, 2/2 LPC*
* Round 2 (Shift Marker): *K2, p6, k12, p6, k2; repeat from * to last 2 stitches of the round, slip 2 stitches purlwise to right needle, remove marker, slip 2 stitches back to left needle, replace marker.
* Round 3 (Shift Marker): *2/2 RC, p4, 2/2 RPC, 2/2 RC, 2/2 LC, 2/2 LPC, p4; repeat from * around. Remove marker, k2, replace marker.
Round 4: *K2, p4, k2, p2, k8, p2, k2, p4, k2*
Round 5: *1/1 RPC, p4, k2, 2/2 RPC, k4, 2/2 LPC, k2, p4, 1/1 LPC*
* Round 6 (Shift Marker): *K1, p5, (k4, p2) 2 times, k4, p5, k1; repeat from * to last stitch of the round, slip 1 stitch purlwise to right needle, remove marker, slip 1 stitch back to left needle, replace marker.
* Round 7 (Shift Marker): *1/1 RC, p2, RLIP, [p2, 2/2 RC] 2 times, p2, 2/2 LC, p2, LLIP, p2; repeat from * around. Remove marker, k1, replace marker.

Rounds 8 - 10: *K1, p6, [k4, p2] 2 times, k4, p6, k1*
Round 11: *K3, p4, [2/2 RC, p2] 2 times, 2/2 LC, p4, k3*
Round 12: *K3, p4, [k4, p2] 2 times, k4, p4, k3*
Round 13: *K4, p3, k2, 2/2 LPC, k4, 2/2 RPC, k2, p3, k4*
Round 14: *K4, p3, k2, p2, k8, p2, k2, p3, k4*
Round 15: *K5, p2, 2/2 LPC, 2/2 LC, 2/2 RC, 2/2 RPC, p2, k5*
Round 16: *K5, p4, k12, p4, k5*
Round 17: *K6, p3, 2/2 LC, [2/2 RC] 2 times, p3, k6*
Round 18: *K6, p3, k12, p3, k6*
Round 19: *K7, p2, k2, 2/2 LC, 2/2 RC, k2, p2, k7*
Round 20: *K7, p2, k12, p2, k7*
Round 21: *K8, p1, 2/2 LPC, 2/2 LC, 2/2 RPC, p1, k8*
Round 22: *[K8, p3] 2 times, k8*
Round 23: *K9, p2, 2/2 LPC, 2/2 RPC, p2, k9*
Round 24: *K9, p4, k4, p4, k9*
Round 25: *K10, p3, 2/2 RC, p3, k10*
Round 26: *K10, p3, k4, p3, k10*
Round 27: *K11, p2, 1/1 LPC, 1/1 RPC, p2, k11*
Round 28: *K11, p3, k2, p3, k11*
Round 29: *K12, p2, 1/1 RC, p2, k12*
Round 30: *K12, p2, k2, p2, k12*
Round 31: *K13, p1, 1/1 RC, p1, k13*
Round 32: Knit.

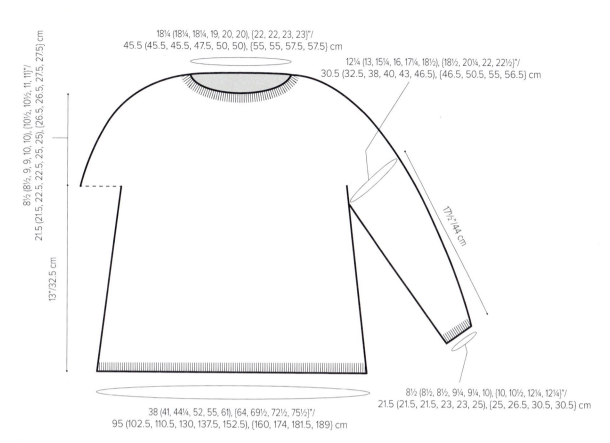

18¼ (18¼, 18¼, 19, 20, 20), {22, 22, 23, 23}"/
45.5 (45.5, 45.5, 47.5, 50, 50), {55, 55, 57.5, 57.5} cm

12¼ (13, 15¼, 16, 17¼, 18½), {18½, 20¼, 22, 22½}"/
30.5 (32.5, 38, 40, 43, 46.5), {46.5, 50.5, 55, 56.5} cm

8½ (8½, 9, 9, 10, 10), {10½, 10½, 11, 11}"/
21.5 (21.5, 22.5, 22.5, 25, 25), {26.5, 26.5, 27.5, 27.5} cm

13"/32.5 cm

17½"/44 cm

8½ (8½, 8½, 9¼, 9¼, 10), {10, 10½, 12¼, 12¼}"/
21.5 (21.5, 21.5, 23, 23, 25), {25, 26.5, 30.5, 30.5} cm

38 (41, 44¼, 52, 55, 61), {64, 69½, 72½, 75½}"/
95 (102.5, 110.5, 130, 137.5, 152.5), {160, 174, 181.5, 189} cm

Maximalist

Bold colorwork and playful geometry define this short-sleeved pullover. The round yoke features striking bands of stripes, scallops, and polka-dot motifs that flow together in an eye-catching palette. Below the yoke, the body transitions into smooth stockinette with subtle textured accents, letting the vibrant upper section instantly catch attention.

Sizes

XS (S, M, L, XL, 2XL), {3XL, 4XL, 5XL, 6XL}: to fit bust 28-30 (32-34, 36-38, 40-42, 44-46, 48-50), {52-54, 56-58, 60-62, 64-66}"/70-75 (80-85, 90-95, 100-105, 110-115, 120-125), {130-135, 140-145, 150-155, 160-165} cm.

Finished Measurements

35 (40¾, 43½, 48, 51, 56¾), {59, 62½, 67, 71¼}"/ 87.5 (102, 109, 120, 127.5, 142), {147.5, 156.5, 167.5, 178} cm bust circumference.
Intended ease: +3-8"/7.5-20 cm.
Shown in size M (43½"/109 cm) on 38"/95 cm bust with 5½"/14 cm of positive ease.

Yarn

DK weight yarn (approximate amounts): 880 (970, 1070, 1190, 1230, 1330), {1445, 1475, 1575, 1735} yds/805 (887, 978, 1088, 1124, 1216), {1320, 1348, 1440, 1586} m.

Miss Babs Yowza (100% Superwash Merino Wool; 560 yards/512 m in 225 g),
A: Antique Brass (mustard) – 2 (2, 2, 2, 2, 2), {2, 3, 3, 3} skeins.

Miss Babs Yowza Mini (100% Superwash Merino Wool; 200 yards/182 m in 80 g), 1 skein each:
B: Sable (black)
C: Santa Fe (brick)
D: Dark Adobe (dark pink)
E: White Peppercorn (off-white)
F: Sugar (light pink)

Needles

Size US 6/4 mm: 24-32"/60-80 cm circular, 16"/40 cm circular and set of double-pointed.
Size US 5/3.75 mm: 24-32"/60-80 cm circular, 16"/40 cm circular and set of double-pointed.
Optional: spare size US 5/3.75 mm 24-32"/60-80 cm circular.
Adjust needle size if necessary to obtain gauge.

Notions

Stitch markers, waste yarn, tapestry needle.

Gauge

22 stitches and 30 rounds = 4"/10 cm in Stockinette stitch or Textured Pattern (see Stitch Guide below) on size US 5/3.75 mm needle, after blocking.

Notes

- This pullover is worked in one piece from the top down with round yoke shaping.
- Knitters may consider placing stitch markers between chart repeats.
- Due to significant variance between knitters, I recommend colorwork swatching in advance to determine whether the needle size for colorwork should be larger, smaller or equal to the needle size used for main fabric (US 5/3.75 mm). It is helpful to work a few rows in plain stockinette and at least 20 rows of colorwork.

Stitch Guide

Textured Pattern in the round (4-stitches repeat):
Round 1: *K2, p1, k1; repeat from * to end.
Rounds 2-4: Knit.
Round 5: *P1, k3; repeat from * to end.
Rounds 6-8: Knit.
Repeat Rounds 1-8 for pattern.

DIRECTIONS

01 YOKE

With B and US 4/3.5 mm 16"/40 cm circular needle, cast on 100 (104, 104, 108, 108, 116), {116, 120, 120, 128} stitches.
Join for working in the round, being careful not to twist stitches, place beginning-of-the round marker (BOR).
Knit all stitches in the next 2 rounds.

Break B and join C.
Next Round: With C, knit.
Ribbing Round: *K2, p2; repeat from * to BOR.
Repeat Ribbing Round 3 more times.

Change to US 5/3.75 mm 16"/40 cm circular needle.
Next Round: With C, knit.

Work 1ˢᵗ set of increases:
Increase Round: *K2, M1L; repeat from * to BOR. [150 (156, 156, 162, 162, 174), {174, 180, 180, 192} stitches]

Change to US 5/3.75 mm 24-32"/60-80 cm circular needle.

Work 1ˢᵗ set of Short-Rows (see Special Techniques, page 226) to shape the back neck:
Short-Row 1 (RS): K50 (50, 50, 54, 54, 58), {58, 60, 60, 64}, turn work.
Short-Row 2 (WS): Make double stitch, purl to BOR, slip BOR, p50 (50, 50, 54, 54, 58), {58, 60, 60, 64}, turn work.
Short-Row 3 (RS): Make double stitch, knit to next double stitch, work double stitch as a single stitch, k5, turn work.

Short-Row 4 (WS): Make double stitch, purl to next double stitch, work double stitch as a single stitch, p5, turn work.
Short-Row 5 (RS): Make double stitch, knit to BOR. Resume working in the round.

Next Round: Knit all stitches, working double stitch as single stitches.
Knit all stitches in the next 5 rounds.

Work 2ⁿᵈ set of Increase Rounds:
Size XS: [M1L, k12] 3 times, [M1L, k13] 3 times, [M1L, k12] 3 times, [M1L, k13] 3 times. [162 stitches]
Size S: [M1L, k7] 2 times, [M1L, k8] 8 times, [M1L, k7] 2 times, [M1L, k8] 8 times. [176 stitches]
Size M: [M1L, k4] 2 times, [M1L, k5] 14 times, [M1L, k4] 2 times, [M1L, k5] 14 times. [188 stitches]
Size L: [M1L, k4] 4 times, [M1L, k5] 13 times, [M1L, k4] 4 times, [M1L, k5] 13 times. [196 stitches]
Size XL: [M1L, k4] 19 times, [M1L, k5] 1 time, [M1L, k4] 19 times, [M1L, k5] 1 time. [202 stitches]
Size 2XL: [M1L, k3] 5 times, [M1L, k4] 18 times, [M1L, k3] 5 times, [M1L, k4] 18 times. [220 stitches]
Size 3XL: [M1L, k3] 58 times. [232 stitches]
Size 4XL: [M1L, k2] 18 times, [M1L, k3] 18 times, [M1L, k2] 18 times, [M1L, k3] 18 times. [252 stitches]
Size 5XL: [M1L, k2] 27 times, [M1L, k3] 12 times, [M1L, k2] 27 times, [M1L, k3] 12 times. [258 stitches]
Size 6XL: [M1L, k2] 21 times, [M1L, k3] 18 times, [M1L, k2] 21 times, [M1L, k3] 18 times. [270 stitches]

Total number of stitches at the end of Increase Round: 162 [176, 188, 196, 202, 220], {232, 252, 258, 270} stitches.

Break C and join D.
With D, knit all stitches in the next 2 (2, 3, 3, 3, 3), {5, 5, 5, 5} rounds.

Work 3rd set of Increase Rounds:
Size XS: [M1L, k20] 3 times, [M1L, k21] 1 time, [M1, k20] 3 times, [M1, k21] 1 time. [170 stitches]
Size S: [M1L, k12] 3 times, [M1L, k13] 4 times, [M1, k12] 3 times, [M1, k13] 4 times. [190 stitches]
Size M: [M1L, k8] 5 times, [M1L, k9] 6 times, [M1, k8] 5 times, [M1, k9] 6 times. [210 stitches]
Size L: [M1L, k8] 10 times, [M1L, k9] 2 times, [M1, k8] 10 times, [M1, k9] 2 times. [220 stitches]
Size XL: [M1L, k7] 11 times, [M1L, k8] 3 times, [M1, k7] 11 times, [M1, k8] 3 times. [230 stitches]
Size 2XL: [M1L, k7] 10 times, [M1L, k8] 5 times, [M1, k7] 10 times, [M1, k8] 5 times. [250 stitches]
Size 3XL: [M1L, k6] 17 times, [M1L, k7] 2 times, [M1, k6] 17 times, [M1, k7] 2 times. [270 stitches]
Size 4XL: [M1L, k6] 7 times, [M1L, k7] 12 times, [M1, k6] 7 times, [M1, k7] 12 times. [290 stitches]
Size 5XL: [M1L, k4] 1 time, [M1L, k5] 25 times, [M1, k4] 1 time, [M1, k5] 25 times. [310 stitches]
Size 6XL: [M1L, k5] 15 times, [M1L, k6] 10 times, [M1, k5] 15 times, [M1, k6] 10 times. [320 stitches]

Total number of stitches at the end of Increase Round: 170 [190, 210, 220, 230, 250], {270, 290, 310, 320} stitches.

Work 39 (39, 47, 47, 47, 47), {54, 54, 54, 54} Rounds of Yoke Chart for your size. [272 (304, 336, 352, 368, 400), {432, 464, 496, 512} stitches]

Continue working with A.

Work 2nd set of Short-Rows to shape the back neck:
Short-Row 1 (RS): K86 (96, 106, 112, 122, 128), {138, 154, 160, 168}, turn work.
Short-Row 2 (WS): Make double stitch, purl to BOR, slip BOR, p86 (96, 106, 112, 122, 128), {138, 154, 160, 168}, turn work.
Short-Row 3 (RS): Make double stitch, knit to next double stitch, work double stitch as a single stitch, k6, turn work.
Short-Row 4 (WS): Make double stitch, purl to next double stitch, work double stitch as a single stitch, p6, turn work.
Short-Rows 5-8: Repeat Short-Rows 3 and 4 another 2 times.
Short-Row 9 (RS): Make double stitch, knit to BOR. Resume working in the round.

Knit all stitches for 1 (1, 1, 2, 4, 4), {1, 1, 8, 8} round(s).

Divide for Body and Sleeves
Division Round: Remove BOR, k41 (48, 52, 57, 60, 67), {69, 74, 79, 84}, place next 54 (56, 64, 62, 64, 66), {78, 84, 90, 88} stitches on hold for Right Sleeve, with Backward-Loop method (see Special Techniques, page 226), cast on 7 (8, 8, 9, 10, 11), {12, 12, 13, 14} stitches, place marker for right side (new BOR), cast on 7 (8, 8, 9, 10, 11), {12, 12, 13, 14} stitches, k82 (96, 104, 114, 120, 134), {138, 148, 158, 168}, place next 54 (56, 64, 62, 64, 66), {78, 84, 90, 88} stitches on hold for Left Sleeve, cast on 7 (8, 8, 9, 10, 11), {12, 12, 13, 14} stitches, place marker for left side, cast on 7 (8, 8, 9, 10, 11), {12, 12, 13, 14} stitches, k41 (48, 52, 57, 60, 67), {69, 84, 79, 84} to the end of the round.
[192 (224, 240, 264, 280, 312), {324, 344, 368, 392} stitches on the needle for Body]

02 BODY

Continue working with A on Body stitches in the round and knit all stitches until Body measures 1"/2.5 cm from the Division Round.
Work in Textured pattern (see Stitch Guide) for 16 rounds.

Increase Round: K1, M1L, work to last stitch before side marker, M1R, k1, slip marker, k1, M1L, knit to last stitch of the round, M1R, k1. [196 (228, 244, 268, 284, 316), {328, 348, 372, 396} stitches]

Work even in Stockinette stitch in the round for 10 rounds.

Repeat Increase Round. [200 (232, 248, 272, 288, 320), {332, 352, 376, 400} stitches]

Work in Textured pattern for 16 rounds.

Repeat Increase Round. [204 (236, 252, 276, 292, 324), {336, 356, 380, 404} stitches]

Work even in Stockinette stitch in the round for 10 rounds.

Repeat Increase Round. [208 (240, 256, 280, 296, 328), {340, 360, 384, 408} stitches]

Work in Textured pattern for 16 rounds.

Repeat Increase Round. [212 (244, 260, 284, 300, 332), {344, 364, 388, 412} stitches]

Continue working in Stockinette stitch in the round until Body measures 12"/30 cm from underarm.

Change to US 4/3.5 mm 24-32"/60-80 cm circular needle.

Ribbing Round: K1, *p2, k2; repeat from * to last 3 stitches, p2, k1.
Work ribbing for 2"/5 cm.

Bind off all stitches in pattern or using Tubular method for k2, p2 rib in the round (see Special Techniques, page 226).

03 SLEEVES

With A, US 5/3.75 mm double-pointed needles and RS facing, beginning at the center of underarm, pick up and knit 7 (8, 8, 9, 10, 11), {12, 12, 13, 14} stitches from the underarm, knit 54 (56, 64, 62, 64, 66), {78, 84, 90, 88} held Sleeve stitches, pick up and knit 7 (8, 8, 9, 10, 11), {12, 12, 13, 14} stitches from the underarm.
[68 (72, 80, 80, 84, 88), {100, 108, 116, 116} stitches]
Place BOR and join in the round.

Work even in Stockinette stitch in the round until Sleeve measures 1"/2.5 cm from underarm.

Work in Textured pattern for 16 rounds.

Continue working in Stockinette stitch in the round for 6 rounds.

Decrease Round:
Size XS: [K2TOG, k6] 2 times, [K2TOG, k7] 2 times, [K2TOG, k6] 2 times, [K2TOG, k7] 2 times.
[60 stitches]
Size S: [K2TOG, k7] 2 times, [K2TOG, k7] 2 times, [K2TOG, k7] 2 times, [K2TOG, k7] 2 times.
[64 stitches]
Size M: [K2TOG, k5] 4 times, [K2TOG, k4] 2 times, [K2TOG, k5] 4 times, [K2TOG, k4] 2 times.
[68 stitches]
Size L: [K2TOG, k8] 8 times. [72 stitches]
Size XL: [K2TOG, k8] 2 times, [K2TOG, k9] 2 times, [K2TOG, k8] 2 times, [K2TOG, k9] 2 times.
[76 stitches]
Size 2XL: [K2TOG, k20] 4 times. [84 stitches]
Size 3XL: [K2TOG, k10] 2 times, [K2TOG, k11] 2 times, [K2TOG, k10] 2 times, [K2TOG, k11] 2 times.
[92 stitches]
Size 4XL: [K2TOG, k7] 12 times. [96 stitches]
Size 5XL: [K2TOG, k5] 6 times, [K2TOG, k6] 2 times, [K2TOG, k5] 6 times, [K2TOG, k6] 2 times.
[100 stitches]
Sizes 6XL: [K2TOG, k7] 2 times, [K2TOG, k8] 4 times, [K2TOG, k7] 2 times, [K2TOG, k8] 4 times.
[104 stitches]

Change to US 4/3.5 mm double-pointed needles.

Ribbing Round: *K2, p2; repeat from * to BOR.
Work ribbing for 1¾"/4.5 cm.

Change to C. With C, knit all stitches for 3 rounds.
Bind off all stitches.

04 FINISHING

Weave in ends. Block to measurements.

CHARTS

YOKE CHART FOR SIZES XS AND S

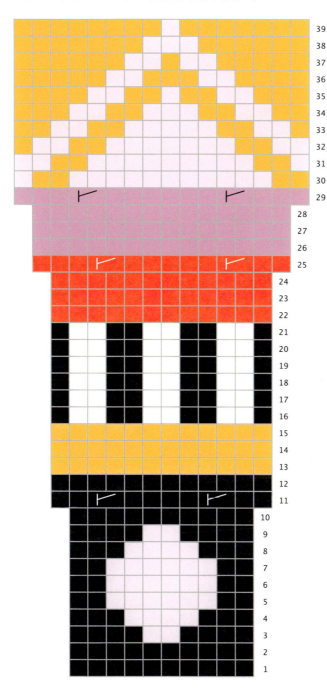

10-stitch repeat, increased to 16-stitch repeat

LEGEND

■ Knit with A (mustard)

■ Knit with B (black)

■ Knit with C (brick)

■ Knit with D (dark pink)

□ Knit with E (off-white)

□ Knit with F (light pink)

⊦ **RLI**: Insert tip of right needle into right leg of stitch below first stitch on left needle from back to front, lifting this stitch up onto left needle tip. Knit the lifted stitch, then slip the original stitch purlwise with yarn in back. [1 stitch increased]

Tip: How to avoid the jog when changing the color

1. Knit one full round of the new color.
2. After working the last stitch of the round, slip BOR, lift the old color stitch of the round below the first stitch of the round and put it on your left needle tip.
3. Knit the first stitch of the round together with the round below (as K2TOG).

YOKE CHART FOR SIZES M, L, XL, 2XL

YOKE CHART FOR SIZES 3XL, 4XL, 5XL, 6XL

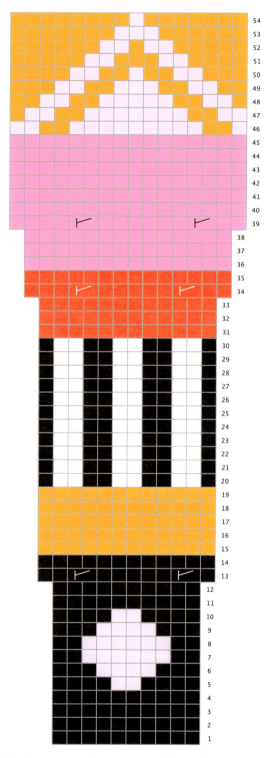

10-stitch repeat, increased to 16-stitch repeat

10-stitch repeat, increased to 16-stitch repeat

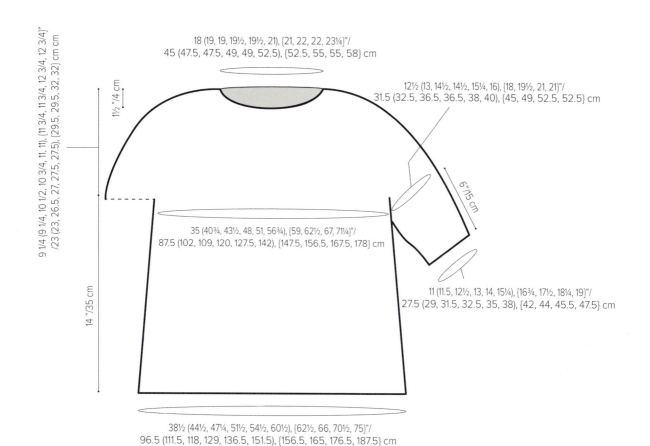

18 (19, 19, 19½, 19½, 21), {21, 22, 22, 23¼}"/
45 (47.5, 47.5, 49, 49, 52.5), {52.5, 55, 55, 58} cm

1½ "/4 cm

9 1/4 (9 1/4, 10 1/2, 10 3/4, 11, 11), {11 3/4, 11 3/4, 12 3/4, 12 3/4}"/
{23 (23, 26.5, 27, 27.5, 27.5), {29.5, 29.5, 32, 32} cm

12½ (13, 14½, 14½, 15¼, 16), {18, 19½, 21, 21}"/
31.5 (32.5, 36.5, 36.5, 38, 40), {45, 49, 52.5, 52.5} cm

6"/15 cm

35 (40¾, 43½, 48, 51, 56¾), {59, 62½, 67, 71¼}"/
87.5 (102, 109, 120, 127.5, 142), {147.5, 156.5, 167.5, 178} cm

11 (11.5, 12½, 13, 14, 15¼), {16¾, 17½, 18¼, 19}"/
27.5 (29, 31.5, 32.5, 35, 38), {42, 44, 45.5, 47.5} cm

14 "/35 cm

38½ (44½, 47¼, 51½, 54½, 60½), {62½, 66, 70½, 75}"/
96.5 (111.5, 118, 129, 136.5, 151.5), {156.5, 165, 176.5, 187.5} cm

Wavey Hat

A tangle of intertwining cables gives this hat both texture and elegance. The design features vertical columns of asymmetric cables that flow seamlessly from the ribbed brim to the crown, creating a fluid, architectural look. The rhythmic cable pattern makes for an engaging knit with satisfying results.
Worked in the round from the bottom up, the hat combines warmth, structure, and stretch, ensuring a comfortable fit.

Finished Measurements
18"/45 cm brim circumference.
8"/20 cm height.
Measurements are taken after blocking.
Fits average adult head sizes 20-21"/51-53 cm.

Yarn
Worsted weight yarn (approximate amount):
158 yards/144 m.

Miss Babs Intrepid (100% Targhee Wool; 280 yards/
255 m in 4 oz/115 gr): Lace Murex - 1 skein.

Note: For Wavey Cowl and Wavey Hat total of 2 skeins of Miss Babs Intrepid is needed.

Needles
Size US 8/5 mm 16"/40 cm circular and set of double-pointed.
Size US 7/4.5 mm: 16"/40 cm circular.
Adjust needle size if necessary to obtain gauge.

Notions
Stitch markers, tapestry needle.
Optional: waste yarn and crochet hook US 7/4.5 mm.

Gauge
26 stitches and 28 rounds = 4"/10 cm on size US 8/5 mm needles in Cable Chart after blocking.

Notes
- This hat is worked from brim to crown in the round.
- All rounds on the chart are read from right to left.
- Knitters may consider placing markers between the chart repetitions.

DIRECTIONS

01 BRIM

NOTE: If you do not wish to work a Tubular Cast On, cast on 100 stitches using size US 7/4.5 mm circular needle, working yarn, and your preferred method for a stretchy cast on. Place marker for beginning of the round and join for working in the round, being careful not to twist stitches, then proceed to the "Work Ribbing" section.

Tubular Cast On (see Special Techniques, page 226)

With US 7/4.5 mm 16"/40 cm circular needle, waste yarn, and using your prefered method, cast on 50 stitches. Do not join in the round.

Switch to working yarn.

Foundation Row (RS): Knit all stitches in row. This row is worked directly into your waste yarn stitches.
Next Row (WS): Purl all stitches.
Next Row (RS): Knit all stitches.
Next Row (WS): Purl all stitches.

Carefully remove the waste yarn and place the cast-on stitches onto a second, smaller needle, ending with the half loop at the edge of the fabric. Make sure you have the same number of stitches on each needle.

Next Row (RS): Knit 1 from front needle, *purl 2 from back needle, knit 2 from front needle; repeat from * to last 3 stitches, purl 2 from back needle, knit 1 from front needle. [100 stitches on the needle]

Next Round: Join in the round, knit 1, purl 1, place marker for beginning of the round, *purl 1, knit 2, purl 1; repeat from * to the end of the round.

Work Ribbing
Ribbing Round: *Purl 1, knit 2, purl 1; repeat from * to the end of the round.
Repeat Ribbing Round until brim measures 1½"/4 cm in height.

02 BODY

Increase Round: Work Increase Round of the Body Chart. [120 stitches]

Change to US 8/5 mm 16"/40 cm circular needle as you work the next round.

Work Rounds 1-43 of Body Chart. [10 stitches]

03 FINISHING

Cut yarn, leaving an 8"/20 cm tail.

Using a tapestry needle, thread yarn tail through remaining stitches two times, then pull tightly.

Weave in yarn ends. Block to measurements.

CHARTS

BODY CHART

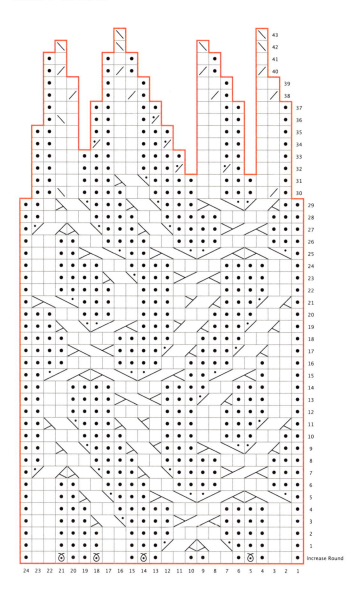

LEGEND

☐ **K:** Knit stitch

⊡ **P:** Purl stitch

⊙ **M1P:** With left needle tip, pick up the thread between stitches from back to front. Purl lifted loop through the front loop – 1 stitch increased

◹ **K2TOG:** Knit 2 stitches together – 1 stitch decreased with right slant.

◸ **SSK:** Slip 1 stitch knitwise, slip 1 stitch knitwise, return 2 slipped stitches back to left needle and knit them together through back loops – 1 stitch decreased with left slant

◹ **P2TOG:** Purl 2 stitches together – 1 stitch decreased

2/1 RC: Slip 1 stitch to cable needle, hold in back, k2, k1 from cable needle

2/1 LC: Slip 2 stitches to cable needle, hold in front, k1, k2 from cable needle

2/1 RPC: Slip 1 stitch to cable needle, hold in back, k2, p1 from cable needle

2/1 LPC: Slip 2 stitches to cable needle, hold in front, p1, k2 from cable needle

2/2 RC: Slip 2 stitches to cable needle, hold in back, knit 2, knit 2 from cable needle

2/2 LC: Slip 2 stitches to cable needle, hold in front, knit 2, knit 2 from cable needle

2/2 RPC: Slip 2 stitches to cable needle, hold in back, k2, p2 from cable needle

2/2 LPC: Slip 2 stitches to cable needle, hold in front, p2, k2 from cable needle

☐ Pattern repeat

Written instructions for Body Chart
Note: See Chart Legend for special abbreviations.
... - chart repeat

Increase Round: *P1, k2, p1, M1P, p1, k2, p2, k2, p1, M1P, p1, k2, M1P, p2, M1P, k2, p1*. [120 stitches]

Round 1: *P1, k2, p3, 2/1 LPC, 2/1 RPC, p3, k2, p4, k2, p1*.

Round 2: *P1, k2, p4, k4, [p4, k2] 2 times, p1*.

Round 3: *P1, k2, p4, 2/2 RC, p4, 2/1 LPC, p3, k2, p1*.

Round 4: *P1, k2, p4, k4, p5, k2, p3, k2, p1*.

Round 5: *P1, 2/2 LPC, 2/2 RPC, 2/2 LPC, p3, 2/1 LPC, p2, k2, p1*.

Round 6: *P3, k4, [p4, k2] 2 times, p2, k2, p1*.

Round 7: *P3, 2/2 RC, p4, 2/1 LPC, p3, 2/1 LPC, 2/1 RPC, p1*.

Round 8: *P3, k4, p5, k2, p4, k4, p2*.

Round 9: *P2, 2/1 RPC, 2/2 LPC, p3, 2/1 LC, p3, 2/1 LPC, k1, p2*.

Round 10: *P2, [k2, p3] 2 times, k3, p4, k3, p2*.

Round 11: *P1, 2/1 RPC, p3, k2, p3, k1, 2/1 LC, p3, 2/1 LPC, p2*.

Round 12: *P1, k2, p4, k2, p3, k4, p4, k2, p2*.

Round 13: *P1, k2, p3, 2/1 RPC, p3, 2/2 LC, p4, k2, p2*.

Round 14: *P1, k2, p3, k2, p4, k4, p4, k2, p2*.

Round 15: *P1, k2, p1, 2/2 RPC, p2, 2/2 RPC, 2/2 LPC, 2/2 RPC, p2*.

Round 16: *[P1, k2] 2 times, p4, k2, p4, k4, p4*.

Round 17: *P1, k2, 2/1 RPC, p3, 2/1 RPC, p4, 2/2 LC, p4*.

Round 18: *P1, k4, p4, k2, p5, k4, p4*.

Round 19: *P1, k1, 2/1 RPC, p3, 2/1 RC, p3, 2/2 RPC, 2/1 LPC, p3*.

Round 20: *P1, k3, p4, k3, [p3, k2] 2 times, p3*.

Round 21: *P1, 2/1 RPC, p3, 2/1 RC, k1, p3, k2, p3, 2/2 LPC, p1*.

Round 22: *P1, k2, p4, k4, p3, k2, p5, k2, p1*.

Round 23: *P1, k2, p4, 2/2 RC, p3, 2/1 LPC, p4, k2, p1*.

Round 24: *P1, k2, p4, k4, [p4, k2] 2 times, p1*.

Round 25: *P1, 2/2 LPC, 2/2 RPC, [2/2 LPC, p2] 2 times, k2, p1*.

Round 26: *P3, k4, [p4, k2] 2 times, p2, k2, p1*.

Round 27: *P3, 2/2 RC, p4, 2/1 LPC, p3, 2/1 LPC, 2/1 RPC, p1*.

Round 28: *P3, k4, p5, k2, p4, k4, p2*.

Round 29: *P2, 2/1 RPC, 2/2 LPC, [p3, 2/1 LPC] 2 times, k1, p2*.

Round 30: *P1, K2TOG, k1, p3, [k2, p4] 2 times, k1, SSK, p2*. [110 stitches]

Round 31: *P1, k2, p3, k2, p4, 2/1 LPC, p3, k2, p2*.

Round 32: *P1, k2, p1, P2TOG, k2, P2TOG, [p3, k2] 2 times, p2*. [100 stitches]

Round 33: *P1, k2, p2, k2, p4, k2, p3, k2, p2*.

Round 34: *P1, k2, p2, k2, P2TOG, p2, k2, p1, P2TOG, k2, p2*. [90 stitches]

Round 35: *P1, k2, p2, k2, p3, [k2, p2] 2 times*.

Round 36: *P1, k2, p2, k2, P2TOG, p1, k2, p2, k1, SSK, p1*. [80 stitches]

Round 37: *P1, [k2, p2] 3 times, k2, p1*.

Round 38: *[K2TOG, k1, p1] 4 times*. [60 stitches]

Round 39: [K2, p1] to the end of the round.

Round 40: [K2TOG, p1] to the end of the round. [40 stitches]

Round 41: [K1, p1] to the end of the round.

Round 42: [SSK] to the end of the round. [20 stitches]

Round 43: [SSK] to the end of the round. [10 stitches]

Wavey Cowl

The Wavey Cowl is designed as a companion to the matching Wavey Hat, with both patterns showcasing the same flowing cable motifs. Worked from the pointed edge upward, the cowl grows into a generous shape that sits neatly across the chest while transitioning into a deep ribbed collar. The design combines the coverage of a kerchief with the practicality of a cowl, making it easy to layer under a jacket or wear as a textured statement piece. Paired with the Wavey Hat, it creates a beautifully coordinated set.

Finished Measurements
23"/57.5 cm neck opening circumference.
25"/62.5 cm depth at deepest point.
Measurements are taken after blocking.

Yarn
Worsted weight yarn (approximate amount): 365 yards/332 m.

Miss Babs Intrepid (100% Targhee Wool; 280 yards/255 m in 4 oz/115 gr): Lace Murex - 2 skeins.

NOTE: For Wavey Cowl and Wavey Hat total of 2 skeins of Miss Babs Intrepid is needed.

Needles
Size US 8/5 mm 24-32"/60-80 cm circular or straight and set of double-pointed needles.
Adjust needle size if necessary to obtain gauge.

Notions
Stitch markers, stitch holders, waste yarn, cable needle, tapestry needle.

Gauge
18 stitches and 30 rows = 4"/10 cm in k2, p2 rib, after blocking.
31-stitch of Charts B1 or B2 = 5"/12.5 cm, after blocking.

Notes
- The cowl is worked flat in one piece from the pointed end up to the neck opening.
- On charts, read RS (odd-numbered) chart rows from right to left; read WS (even-numbered) chart rows from left to right.
- On right side, slip stitches purlwise with yarn in back, on wrong side, slip stitches purlwise with yarn in front.

DIRECTIONS

01 COWL

Cast on 4 stitches.

Chart Set-Up Row 1 (Right Side): Work Row 1 of Chart A.
Chart Set-Up Row 2 (Wrong Side): Work Row 2 of Chart A.

Continue following the Chart A until the Row 62 is worked. [64 stitches]

Next Row (Right Side): Work Row 1 of Chart B1, place marker, work Row 1 of Chart C, place marker, work Row 1 of Chart B2. [66 stitches]

Next Row (Wrong Side): Work Row 2 of Chart B2, slip marker, work Row 2 of Chart C, slip marker, work Row 2 of Chart B1.

Continue working in established pattern, following Charts B1, B2 and C through Row 8. [72 stitches]
After that, continue following the charts as follows:
- Charts B1 and B2: work Rows 9-20, then work Rows 1-20 another 4 times.
- Chart C: work Rows 9-16 total of 11 times, then work Rows 9-12 once.

[164 stitches on the needle]

Next Row (Right Side): Knit 4, work to marker stitches as they appear (knit the knit stitches and purl the purl stitches), place just worked 31 stitches on hold, remove marker, bind off next 102 stitches in pattern, removing marker, work stitches as they appear to last 4 stitches, knit 4, place just worked 31 stitches on hold.

02 FINISHING

Block cowl to measurements.

Fold work in half lengthwise with WS facing out. Hold spare and working needles parallel. Use 3-Needle Bind Off (see Special Techniques, page 226) to join all stitches and create neck opening.

I-cord at neck opening edge
With double-pointed needle, waste yarn, and using a provisional method of your choice, cast on 3 stitches. 3 stitches of working yarn on the needle.
With Right Side facing and beginning at the seam, work applied I-cord as follows: *Knit 2, slip 1 purlwise with yarn in back, yarn over, pick up and knit 1 stitch from the neck opening edge, pass yarn over and slipped stitch over picked up stitch, slide stitches to opposite end of double-pointed needle; repeat from *, picking up 1 stitch in every bind-off stitch around neck opening edge. Remove waste yarn from provisional cast on and place stitches onto the other double-pointed needle.
With tail threaded on a tapestry needle, graft stitches together using Kitchener Stitch (see Special Techniques, page 226).

Weave in ends.

CHARTS

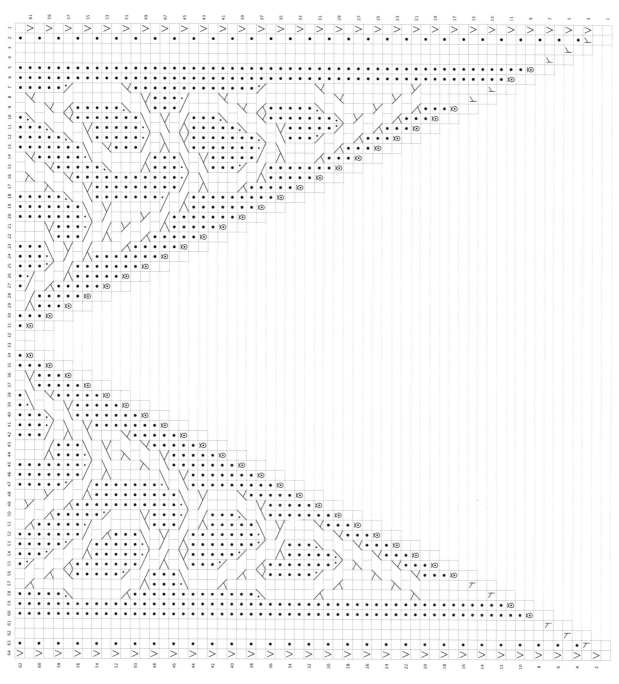

CHART A

CHART B1

CHART C

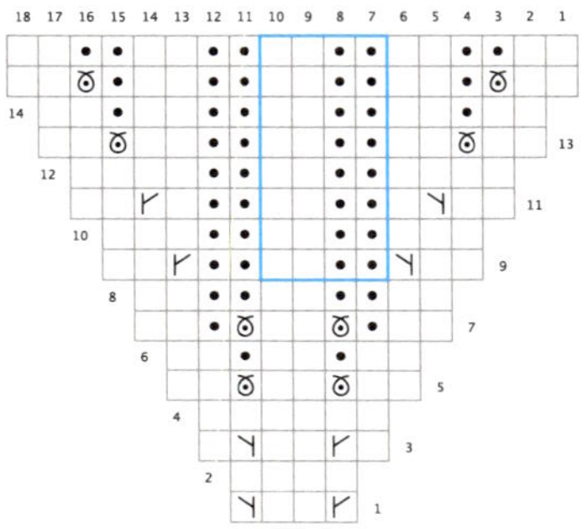

CHART B2

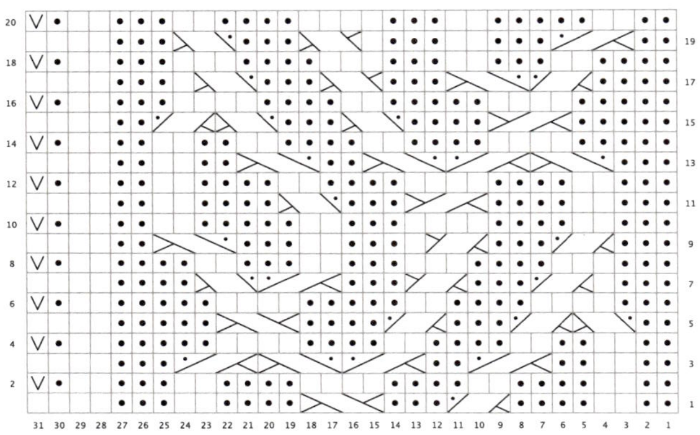

Wavey Cowl

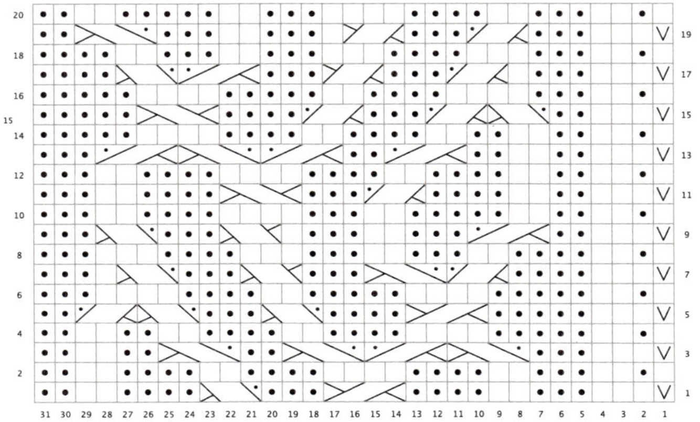

LEGEND

K: Knit stitch on RS; purl stitch on WS

P: Purl stitch on RS; knit stitch on WS

M1R: With left needle tip, pick up the thread between stitches from back to front. Knit lifted loop through the front loop – 1 stitch increased

M1L: With left needle tip, pick up the thread between stitches from front to back. Knit lifted loop through the backloop – 1 stitch increased

M1P: With left needle tip, pick up the thread between stitches from back to front. Purl lifted loop through the front loop – 1 stitch increased

Slip 1 stitch purlwise with yarn in back on RS
Slip 1 stitch purlwise with yarn in front on WS

2/1 RC: Slip 1 stitch to cable needle, hold in back, k2, k1 from cable needle

2/1 LC: Slip 2 stitches to cable needle, hold in front, k1, k2 from cable needle

2/1 RPC: Slip 1 stitch to cable needle, hold in back, k2, p1 from cable needle

2/1 LPC: Slip 2 stitches to cable needle, hold in front, p1, k2 from cable needle

2/2 RC: Slip 2 stitches to cable needle, hold in back, knit 2, knit 2 from cable needle

2/2 LC: Slip 2 stitches to cable needle, hold in front, knit 2, knit 2 from cable needle

2/2 RPC: Slip 2 stitches to cable needle, hold in back, k2, p2 from cable needle

2/2 LPC: Slip 2 stitches to cable needle, hold in front, p2, k2 from cable needle

Pattern repeat

Written instructions for Chart A

Note: See Chart Legend for special abbreviations.

Row 1 (RS): Knit. [4 stitches]
Row 2 (WS): Slip 1, p3.
Row 3 (RS): Slip 1, M1R, k2, M1L, k1. [6 stitches]
Row 4 (WS): Slip 1, k1, p2, k1, p1.
Row 5 (RS): Slip 1, k1, M1R, k2, M1L, k2. [8 stitches]
Row 6 (WS): Slip 1, k1, p4, k1, p1.
Row 7 (RS): Slip 1, k2, M1R, k2, M1L, k3. [10 stitches]
Row 8 (WS): Slip 1, k1, p6, k1, p1.
Row 9 (RS): Slip 1, k3, M1P, k2, M1P, k4. [12 stitches]
Row 10 (WS): Slip 1, [k1, p2] 3 times, k1, p1.
Row 11 (RS): Slip 1, k3, p1, M1P, k2, M1P, p1, k4.
 [14 stitches]
Row 12 (WS): Slip 1, k1, [p2, k2] 2 times, p2, k1, p1.
Row 13 (RS): Slip 1, k3, p2, M1R, k2, M1L, p2, k4.
[16 stitches]
Row 14 (WS): Slip 1, k1, p2, k2, p4, k2, p2, k1, p1.
Row 15 (RS): Slip 1, k3, p2, k1, M1R, k2, M1L, k1, p2, k4.
[18 stitches]
Row 16 (WS): Slip 1, k1, p2, k2, p6, k2, p2, k1, p1.
Row 17 (RS): Slip 1, k3, p2, [k2, M1P] 2 times, k2, p2, k4.
[20 stitches]
Row 18 (WS): Slip 1, k1, p2, k2, [p2, k1] 2 times, p2, k2,
p2, k1, p1.
Row 19 (RS): Slip 1, k3, p2, k2, p1, M1P, k2, M1P, p1, k2,
p2, k4. [22 stitches]
Row 20 (WS): Slip 1, k1, [p2, k2] 4 times, p2, k1, p1.
Row 21 (RS): Slip 1, k3, p2, 2/1 LC, p1, M1P, k2, M1P, p1,
2/1 RC, p2, k4. [24 stitches]
Row 22 (WS): Slip 1, k1, [p2, k2, p3, k2] 2 times, p2, k1,
p1.
Row 23 (RS): Slip 1, k3, p2, k1, 2/1 LC, p1, M1P, k2, M1P,
p1, 2/1 RC, k1, p2, k4. [26 stitches]
Row 24 (WS): Slip 1, k1, [p2, k2, p4, k2] 2 times, p2, k1,
p1.
Row 25 (RS): Slip 1, k3, p2, k2, 2/1 LC, p1, M1P, k2, M1P,
p1, 2/1 RC, k2, p2, k4. [28 stitches]
Row 26 (WS): Slip 1, k1, [p2, k2, p5, k2] 2 times, p2, k1,
p1.
Row 27 (RS): Slip 1, k3, p2, k3, 2/1 LC, p1, M1P, k2, M1P,
p1, 2/1 RC, k3, p2, k4. [30 stitches]
Row 28 (WS): Slip 1, k1, [p2, k2, p6, k2] 2 times, p2,
k1, p1.

Row 29 (RS): Slip 1, k3, p2, k1, 2/1 RPC, 2/1 LPC, p1,
M1P, k2, M1P, p1, 2/1 RPC, 2/1 LPC, k1, p2, k4.
[32 stitches]
Row 30 (WS): Slip 1, k1, p2, k2, p3, [k2, p2] 3 times, k2,
p3, k2, p2, k1, p1.
Row 31 (RS): Slip 1, k3, p2, 2/1 RPC, p2, 2/1 LPC, p1,
M1P, k2, M1P, p1, 2/1 RPC, p2, 2/1 LPC, p2, k4.
[34 stitches]
Row 32 (WS): Slip 1, k1, [p2, k2, p2, k4, p2, k2] 2 times,
p2, k1, p1.
Row 33 (RS): Slip 1, k3, p2, k2, p4, k2, p2, M1P, k2, M1P,
p2, k2, p4, k2, p2, k4. [36 stitches]
Row 34 (WS): Slip 1, k1, p2, k2, p2, k4, [p2, k3] 2 times,
p2, k4, p2, k2, p2, k1, p1.
Row 35 (RS): Slip 1, k3, p2, k2, p2, 2/2 RC, p3, M1P, k2,
M1P, p3, 2/2 LC, p2, k2, p2, k4. [38 stitches]
Row 36 (WS): Slip 1, k1, [p2, k2] 2 times, p4, k4, p2, k4,
p4, [k2, p2] 2 times, k1, p1.
Row 37 (RS): Slip 1, k3, p2, 2/1 LPC, 2/1 RPC, 2/2 LPC,
p2, M1P, k2, M1P, p2, 2/2 RPC, 2/1 LPC, 2/1 RPC, p2, k4.
[40 stitches]
Row 38 (WS): Slip 1, k1, p2, k3, p4, [k3, p2] 3 times, k3,
p4, k3, p2, k1, p1.
Row 39 (RS): Slip 1, k3, p3, k1, 2/1 RPC, p3, 2/1 LPC, p2,
M1P, k2, M1P, p2, 2/1 RPC, p3, 2/1 LPC, k1, p3, k4.
[42 stitches]
Row 40 (WS): Slip 1, k1, p2, k3, p3, k5, [p2, k3] 2 times,
p2, k5, p3, k3, p2, k1, p1.
Row 41 (RS): Slip 1, k3, p3, 2/1 RPC, p5, k2, p3, M1P, k2,
M1P, p3, k2, p5, 2/1 LPC, p3, k4. [44 stitches]
Row 42 (WS): Slip 1, k1, p2, k3, p2, k6, [p2, k4] 2 times,
p2, k6, p2, k3, p2, k1, p1.
Row 43 (RS): Slip 1, k3, p3, k2, p4, 2/2 RC, p4, M1P, k2,
M1P, p4, 2/2 LC, p4, k2, p3, k4. [46 stitches]
Row 44 (WS): Slip 1, k1, p2, k3, p2, k4, p4, k5, p2, k5,
p4, k4, p2, k3, p2, k1, p1.
Row 45 (RS): Slip 1, k3, p3, 2/2 LPC, 2/2 RPC, 2/2 LPC,
p3, M1P, k2, M1P, p3, 2/2 RPC, 2/2 LPC, 2/2 RPC, p3,
k4. [48 stitches]
Row 46 (WS): Slip 1, k1, p2, k5, p4, [k4, p2] 3 times, k4,
p4, k5, p2, k1, p1.
Row 47 (RS): Slip 1, k3, p5, 2/2 RC, p4, 2/2 LPC, p2,
M1P, k2, M1P, p2, 2/2 RPC, p4, 2/2 LC, p5, k4.
[50 stitches]

Row 48 (WS): Slip 1, k1, p2, k5, p4, k5, p3, k3, p2, k3, p3, k5, p4, k5, p2, k1, p1.

Row 49 (RS): Slip 1, k3, p3, 2/2 RPC, 2/2 LPC, p3, k1, 2/1 LC, p2, M1P, k2, M1P, p2, 2/1 RC, k1, p3, 2/2 RPC, 2/2 LPC, p3, k4. [52 stitches]

Row 50 (WS): Slip 1, k1, p2, k3, p2, k4, [p2, k3, p4, k3] 2 times, p2, k4, p2, k3, p2, k1, p1.

Row 51 (RS): Slip 1, k3, p2, 2/1 RPC, p4, k2, p3, k2, 2/1 LC, p2, M1P, k2, M1P, p2, 2/1 RC, k2, p3, k2, p4, 2/1 LPC, p2, k4. [54 stitches]

Row 52 (WS): Slip 1, k1, p2, k2, p2, k5, [p2, k3, p5, k3] 2 times, p2, k5, p2, k2, p2, k1, p1.

Row 53 (RS): Slip 1, k3, p2, k2, p4, 2/1 RPC, p3, 2/2 LC, k1, p3, M1P, k2, M1P, p3, k1, 2/2 RC, p3, 2/1 LPC, p4, k2, p2, k4. [56 stitches]

Row 54 (WS): Slip 1, k1, p2, k2, p2, [k4, p2, k4, p5] 2 times, [k4, p2] 2 times, k2, p2, k1, p1.

Row 55 (RS): Slip 1, k3, p2, k2, [p2, 2/2 RPC] 2 times, 2/2 LPC, p3, M1P, k2, M1P, p3, 2/2 RPC, [2/2 LPC, p2] 2 times, k2, p2, k4. [58 stitches]

Row 56 (WS): Slip 1, k1, [p2, k2] 2 times, [p2, k4] 6 times, [p2, k2] 2 times, p2, k1, p1.

Row 57 (RS): Slip 1, k3, p2, 2/1 LPC, 2/1 RPC, p3, 2/1 RPC, p4, 2/2 LC, p2, M1P, k2, M1P, p2, 2/2 RC, p4, 2/1 LPC, p3, 2/1 LPC, 2/1 RPC, p2, k4. [60 stitches]

Row 58 (WS): Slip 1, k1, p2, k3, p4, k4, p2, k5, p4, k3, p2, k3, p4, k5, p2, k4, p4, k3, p2, k1, p1.

Row 59 (RS): Slip 1, k3, p3, k1, 2/1 RPC, p3, 2/1 RC, p3, 2/2 RPC, 2/1 LPC, p2, M1P, k2, M1P, p2, 2/1 RPC, 2/2 LPC, p3, 2/1 LC, p3, 2/1 LPC, k1, p3, k4. [62 stitches]

Row 60 (WS): Slip 1, k1, p2, k3, p3, k4, p3, [k3, p2] 5 times, k3, p3, k4, p3, k3, p2, k1, p1.

Row 61 (RS): Slip 1, k3, p3, 2/1 RPC, p3, 2/1 RC, k1, p3, k2, p3, 2/2 LPC, p1, M1P, k2, M1P, p1, 2/2 RPC, p3, k2, p3, k1, 2/1 LC, p3, 2/1 LPC, p3, k4. [64 stitches]

Row 62 (WS): Slip 1, k1, p2, k3, p2, k4, p4, k3, p2, k5, [p2, k2] 2 times, p2, k5, p2, k3, p4, k4, p2, k3, p2, k1, p1.

Written instructions for Chart B1

Row 1 (RS): Slip 1, k3, p3, k2, p4, 2/2 RC, p3, 2/1 LPC, p4, k2, p2.

Row 2 (WS): K2, [p2, k4] 2 times, p4, k4, p2, k3, p2, k1, p1.

Row 3 (RS): Slip 1, k3, p3, 2/2 LPC, 2/2 RPC, [2/2 LPC, p2] 2 times, k2, p2.

Row 4 (WS): [K2, p2] 2 times, k4, p2, k4, p4, k5, p2, k1, p1.

Row 5 (RS): Slip 1, k3, p5, 2/2 RC, p4, 2/1 LPC, p3, 2/1 LPC, 2/1 RPC, p2.

Row 6 (WS): K3, p4, k4, p2, k5, p4, k5, p2, k1, p1.

Row 7 (RS): Slip 1, k3, p4, 2/1 RPC, 2/2 LPC, p3, 2/1 LC, p3, 2/1 LPC, k1, p3.

Row 8 (WS): K3, p3, k4, p3, [k3, p2] 2 times, k4, p2, k1, p1.

Row 9 (RS): Slip 1, k3, p2, 2/2 RPC, p3, k2, p3, k1, 2/1 LC, p3, 2/1 LPC, p3.

Row 10 (WS): K3, p2, k4, p4, k3, p2, k5, p2, k2, p2, k1, p1.

Row 11 (RS): Slip 1, k3, p2, k2, p4, 2/1 RPC, p3, 2/2 LC, p4, k2, p3.

Row 12 (WS): K3, p2, k4, p4, [k4, p2] 2 times, k2, p2, k1, p1.

Row 13 (RS): Slip 1, k3, p2, k2, [p2, 2/2 RPC] 2 times, 2/2 LPC, 2/2 RPC, p3.

Row 14 (WS): K5, p4, [k4, p2] 2 times, [k2, p2] 2 times, k1, p1.

Row 15 (RS): Slip 1, k3, p2, 2/1 LPC, 2/1 RPC, p3, 2/1 RPC, p4, 2/2 LC, p5.

Row 16 (WS): K5, p4, k5, p2, k4, p4, k3, p2, k1, p1.

Row 17 (RS): Slip 1, k3, p3, k1, 2/1 RPC, p3, 2/1 RC, p3, 2/2 RPC, 2/1 LPC, p4.

Row 18 (WS): K4, [p2, k3] 2 times, p3, k4, p3, k3, p2, k1, p1.

Row 19 (RS): Slip 1, k3, p3, 2/1 RPC, p3, 2/1 RC, k1, p3, k2, p3, 2/2 LPC, p2.

Row 20 (WS): K2, p2, k5, p2, k3, p4, k4, p2, k3, p2, k1, p1.

Written instructions for Chart B2

Row 1 (RS): P2, k2, p4, 2/1 RPC, p3, 2/2 LC, p4, k2, p3, k4.

Row 2 (WS): Slip 1, k1, p2, k3, p2, k4, p4, [k4, p2] 2 times, k2.

Row 3 (RS): P2, k2, [p2, 2/2 RPC] 2 times, 2/2 LPC, 2/2 RPC, p3, k4.

Row 4 (WS): Slip 1, k1, p2, k5, p4, [k4, p2] 2 times, k2, p2, k2.

Row 5 (RS): P2, 2/1 LPC, 2/1 RPC, p3, 2/1 RPC, p4, 2/2 LC, p5, k4.

Row 6 (WS): Slip 1, k1, p2, k5, p4, k5, p2, k4, p4, k3.

Row 7 (RS): P3, k1, 2/1 RPC, p3, 2/1 RC, p3, 2/2 RPC, 2/1 LPC, p4, k4.

Row 8 (WS): Slip 1, k1, p2, k4, [p2, k3] 2 times, p3, k4, p3, k3.

Row 9 (RS): P3, 2/1 RPC, p3, 2/1 RC, k1, p3, k2, p3, 2/2 LPC, p2, k4.

Row 10 (WS): Slip 1, k1, p2, k2, p2, k5, p2, k3, p4, k4, p2, k3.

Row 11 (RS): P3, k2, p4, 2/2 RC, p3, 2/1 LPC, p4, k2, p2, k4.

Row 12 (WS): Slip 1, k1, p2, k2, [p2, k4] 2 times, p4, k4, p2, k3.

Row 13 (RS): P3, 2/2 LPC, 2/2 RPC, [2/2 LPC, p2] 2 times, k2, p2, k4.

Row 14 (WS): Slip 1, k1, [p2, k2] 2 times, [p2, k4] 2 times, p4, k5.

Row 15 (RS): P5, 2/2 RC, p4, 2/1 LPC, p3, 2/1 LPC, 2/1 RPC, p2, k4.

Row 16 (WS): Slip 1, k1, p2, k3, p4, k4, p2, k5, p4, k5.

Row 17 (RS): P4, 2/1 RPC, 2/2 LPC, p3, 2/1 LC, p3, 2/1 LPC, k1, p3, k4.

Row 18 (WS): Slip 1, k1, p2, k3, p3, k4, p3, [k3, p2] 2 times, k4.

Row 19 (RS): P2, 2/2 RPC, p3, k2, p3, k1, 2/1 LC, p3, 2/1 LPC, p3, k4.

Row 20 (WS): Slip 1, k1, p2, k3, p2, k4, p4, k3, p2, k5, p2, k2.

Written instructions for Chart C
... - chart repeat

Row 1 (RS): M1R, k2, M1L.

Row 2 (WS): Purl.

Row 3 (RS): K1, M1R, k2, M1L, k1.

Row 4 (WS): Purl.

Row 5 (RS): [K2, M1P] 2 times, k2.

Row 6 (WS): [P2, k1] 2 times, p2.

Row 7 (RS): K2, p1, M1P, k2, M1P, p1, k2.

Row 8 (WS): [P2, k2] 2 times, p2.

Row 9 (RS): K2, M1L, *p2, k2*, p2, M1R, k2.

Row 10 (WS): P3, k2, *p2, k2*, p3.

Row 11 (RS): K2, M1L, k1, *p2, k2*, p2, k1, M1R, k2.

Row 12 (WS): P4, k2, *p2, k2*, p4.

Row 13 (RS): K2, M1P, k2, *p2, k2*, p2, k2, M1P, k2.

Row 14 (WS): P2, k1, p2, k2, *p2, k2*, p2, k1, p2.

Row 15 (RS): K2, M1P, p1, k2, *p2, k2*, p2, k2, p1, M1P, k2.

Row 16 (WS): [P2, k2] 2 times, *p2, k2*, p2, k2, p2.

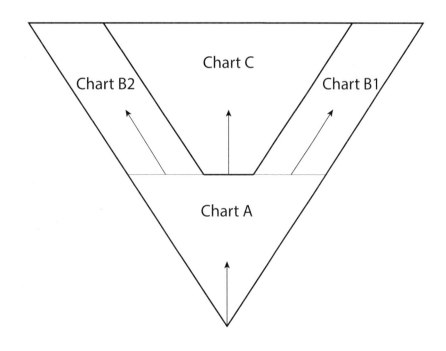

Isidora

This cardigan channels a distinctly preppy look with its neat round neckline and polished button band. The cropped silhouette feels crisp and versatile, perfect for pairing with dresses, skirts, or high-waisted trousers. What sets it apart is the unusual stitch pattern: classic cables intertwined with airy eyelets, creating a fabric that is both refined and full of character. The result is a cardigan that nods to tradition while offering something unexpected, making it an engaging knit and a stylish addition to any wardrobe. Equal parts classic and playful, it's a piece you'll wear on repeat.

Sizes
XS (S, M, L, XL, 2XL), {3XL, 4XL, 5XL, 6XL}: to fit bust 28-30 (32-34, 36-38, 40-42, 44-46, 48-50), {52-54, 56-58, 60-62, 64-66}"/70-75 (80-85, 90-95, 100-105, 110-115, 120-125), {130-135, 140-145, 150-155, 160-165} cm.

Finished Measurements
38 (41½, 45½, 49½, 52½, 59), {61½, 65½, 69½, 73½}"/ 95 (104, 114, 124, 131.5, 147.5), {154, 164, 174, 184} cm bust circumference, buttoned.
Cardigan shown measures 45½"/114 cm with 7½"/19 cm of positive ease.

Yarn
DK weight yarn (approx. amount): 1425 (1540, 1690, 1840, 1960, 2200), {2290, 2440, 2590, 2740} yards/1297 (1401, 1538, 1674, 1784, 2002), {2084, 2220, 2357, 2493} m.

Miss Babs Killington (85% Polwarth Wool, 15% Tussah Silk; 350 yds/320 m in 4.2 oz/120 gr), Moss: 4 (5, 5, 6, 6, 7), {7, 7, 8, 8} skeins.

Needles
Size US 6/4 mm: 24"-32"/60-80 cm circular and set of double-pointed needles.
Size US 5/3.75 mm: 24"-32"/60-80 cm circular, 16"/40 cm circular, and set of double-pointed needles.
Optional: spare US 5/3.75 mm 32"/80 cm long circular for Tubular Cast On.

Adjust needle size if necessary to obtain gauge.

Notions
Stitch markers, stitch holders, cable needle, 7 buttons ¾"/17 mm in diameter, tapestry needle.

Gauge
21 stitches and 32 rows = 4"/10 cm in Stockinette stitch on US 6/4 mm after blocking.
20 stitches and 32 rows = 4"/10 cm in Moss stitch on US 6/4 mm after blocking.
30 stitches and 32 rows = 4"/10 cm in Lattice pattern on US 6/4 mm after blocking.
26 stitches and 32 rows = 4"/10 cm in Cable pattern on US 6/4 mm after blocking.

Notes
- The cardigan is worked in one piece from the bottom up to underarms; then divided for fronts and back and worked separately to shoulders. Stitches for sleeves are picked up around the armholes and sleeves are worked in the round from the top down.
- During shaping, if there are not enough stitches to work a complete cable, work the stitches of the partial cable in stockinette stitch.
- While working on the Lattice Chart, we decrease the number of stitches by 2 stitches for each 6-stitch repeat on Rows 1 and 5 and increase the number of stitches back to the initial number on Rows 3 and 7. To make the neckline and shoulder shaping easier, the switch to the Mock Lattice Chart is recommended at the beginning of neckline shaping (see the Left Front, Right Front, and Back instructions). The Mock Lattice Chart has the same number of stitches in every row, which makes the stitch count easier to manage.

Stitch Guide

Moss stitch in rows: (even number of stitches):
Row 1 (RS): *K1, p1; repeat from * to end.
Row 2 (WS): Repeat Row 1.
Row 3 (RS): *P1, k1; repeat from * to end.
Row 4 (WS): Repeat Row 3.
Repeat Rows 1–4 for pattern.

Moss stitch in rounds (even number of stitches):
Rounds 1 and 2: *K1, p1; repeat from * to end.
Rounds 3 and 4: *P1, k1; repeat from * to end.
Repeat Rounds 1–4 for pattern.

Moss stitch in rounds (odd number of stitches):
Rounds 1 and 2: *K1, p1; repeat from * to last stitch, k1.
Rounds 3 and 4: *P1, k1; repeat from * to last stitch, p1.
Repeat Rounds 1–4 for pattern.

DIRECTIONS

01 BODY

NOTE: If you do not wish to work a Tubular Cast On, cast on with 245 (261, 289, 317, 341, 389), {409, 437, 457, 477} stitches, using size US 5/3.75 mm 32"/80 cm circular needle, working yarn, and your preferred method for a stretchy cast on. Proceed to the Ribbing Row 1.

With waste yarn, size US 5/3.75 mm 32"/80 cm circular needle and using your preferred method, cast on 123 (131, 145, 159, 171, 195), {205, 219, 229, 239} stitches. Do not join in the round.

Foundation Row (RS): Knit all stitches in row. This row is worked directly into your waste yarn stitches.
Row 1 (WS): Purl to end.
Row 2 (RS): Knit to end.
Row 3 (WS): Purl to end.

Carefully snip and remove the waste yarn from the cast-on edge, placing the stitches onto the second US 5/3.75 mm 32"/80 cm circular needle as you go. Don't place the last half-loop at the edge of the fabric.

Now we have 123 (131, 145, 159, 171, 195), {205, 219, 229, 239} stitches on first needle and 122 (130, 144, 158, 170, 194), {204, 218, 228, 238} cast-on stitches on the spare needle. Bring the needle with the cast-on stitches up behind the working needle, wrong sides together.

Next Row (WS): *K1 from front needle, p1 from back needle; repeat from * to last stitch, k1 from front needle. [245 (261, 289, 317, 341, 389), {409, 437, 457, 477} stitches on the needle]

Ribbing Row 1 (RS): K1, *k1, p1; repeat from * to last 2 stitches, k2.
Ribbing Row 2 (WS): P2, *k1, p1; repeat from * to last stitch, p1.
Repeat last 2 rows until piece measures 2"/5 cm from cast on, ending with a RS row.

Decrease Row (WS): Work in pattern approximately half the number of stitches, K2TOG, work in pattern to end. [244 (260, 288, 316, 340, 388), {408, 436, 456, 476} stitches]

Change to US 6/4 mm circular needle.

Chart Set-Up Row 1 (RS): K2, place marker, work Foundation Row 1 of Chart A over 12 stitches, place marker, work Foundation Row 1 of Lattice Chart over 26 (26, 32, 38, 44, 56), {62, 68, 68, 68} stitches, place marker, work Foundation Row 1 of Chart A over 12 stitches, place marker, work Row 1 of Moss stitch in rows (see Stitch Guide) over 16 (24, 26, 28, 28, 28), {26, 28, 38, 48} stitches, place marker, work Foundation Row 1 of Chart B over 12 stitches, place marker, work Foundation Row 1 of Lattice Chart over 26 (26, 32, 38, 44, 56), {62, 68, 68, 68} stitches, place marker, work Foundation Row 1 of Chart C over 32 stitches, place marker, work Foundation Row 1 of Lattice Chart over 26 (26, 32, 38, 44, 56), {62, 68, 68, 68} stitches, place marker, work Foundation Row 1 of Chart A over 12 stitches, place marker, work Row 1 of Moss stitch in rows over 16 (24, 26, 28, 28, 28), {26, 28, 38, 48}, place marker, work Foundation Row 1 of Chart B over 12 stitches, place marker, work Foundation Row 1 of Lattice Chart over 26 (26, 32, 38, 44, 56), {62, 68, 68, 68} stitches, place marker, work Foundation Row 1 of Chart B over 12 stitches, place marker, k2.

Chart Set-Up Row 2 (WS): P2, slip marker, work Foundation Row 2 of Chart B to marker, slip marker, work Foundation Row 2 of Lattice Chart to marker, slip marker, work Foundation Row 2 of Chart B to marker, slip marker, work Row 2 of Moss stitch to marker, slip marker, work Foundation Row 2 of Chart A to marker, slip marker, work Foundation Row 2 of Lattice Chart to marker, slip marker, work Foundation Row 2 of Chart C to marker, slip marker, work Foundation Row 2 of Lattice Chart to marker, slip marker, work Foundation Row 2 of Chart B to marker, slip marker, work Row 2 of Moss stitch to marker, slip marker, work Foundation Row 2 of Chart A to marker, slip marker, work Foundation Row 2 of Lattice Chart to marker, slip marker, work Foundation Row 2 of Chart A to marker, slip marker, p2.

Chart Set-Up Row 3 (RS): K2, slip marker, work Row 1 of Chart A to marker, slip marker, work Row 1 of Lattice Chart to marker, working 6-stitch repeat 3 (3, 4, 5, 6, 8), {9, 10, 10, 10} times, slip marker, work Row 1 of Chart A to marker, slip marker, work Row 3 of Moss stitch to marker, slip marker, work Row 1 of Chart B to marker, slip marker, work Row 1 of Lattice Chart to marker, working 6-stitch repeat 3 (3, 4, 5, 6, 8), {9, 10, 10, 10} times, slip marker, work Row 1 of Chart C to marker, slip marker, work Row 1 of Lattice Chart to marker, working 6-stitch repeat 3 (3, 4, 5, 6, 8), {9, 10, 10, 10} times, slip marker, work Row 1 of Chart A to marker, slip marker, work Row 3 of Moss stitch to marker, slip marker, work Row 1 of

Chart B to marker, slip marker, work Row 1 of Lattice Chart to marker, working 6-stitch repeat 3 (3, 4, 5, 6, 8), {9, 10, 10, 10} times, slip marker, work Row 1 of Chart B to marker, slip marker, k2.

Chart Set-Up Row 4 (WS): P2, slip marker, work Row 2 of Chart B to marker, slip marker, work Row 2 of Lattice Chart to marker, slip marker, work Row 2 of Chart B to marker, slip marker, work Row 4 of Moss stitch to marker, slip marker, work Row 2 of Chart A to marker, slip marker, work Row 2 of Lattice Chart to marker, slip marker, work Row 2 of Chart C to marker, slip marker, work Row 2 of Lattice Chart to marker, slip marker, work Row 2 of Chart B to marker, slip marker, work Row 4 of Moss stitch to marker, slip marker, work Row 2 of Chart A to marker, slip marker, work Row 2 of Lattice Chart to marker, slip marker, work Row 2 of Chart A to marker, slip marker, p2.

NOTE: Continue to work in established pattern, working first and last 2 stitches in Stockinette stitch and follow the Moss stitch pattern according to Stitch Guide.
While following charts, repeat:
Charts A and B – Rows 1-6
Chart C – Rows 1-24
Lattice Chart – Rows 1-8 (remember that on Rows 3 and 7 you decrease 2 stitches for each repeat, then return to the original number of stitches appear again with yarn over increases on Rows 5 and 9).

Continue following charts as described in NOTE above until Body measures 11"/27.5 cm from cast-on edge, ending with Row 2 or 6 of Lattice Chart.

Divide for fronts and back
Division Row (RS): [Work in pattern to marker, slip marker] 4 times, work next row of Moss stitch over 8 (12, 13, 14, 14, 14), {13, 14, 19, 24} stitches, place just worked 60 (64, 71, 78, 84, 96), {101, 108, 113, 118} stitches on hold for Right Front, work next row of Moss stitch over 8 (12, 13, 14, 14, 14), {13, 14, 19, 24} stitches, slip marker, [work in pattern to marker, slip marker] 4 times, work next row of Chart A, to marker slip marker, work next row of Moss over 8 (12, 13, 14, 14, 14), {13, 14, 19, 24} stitches, place just worked 124 (132, 146, 160, 172, 196), {206, 220, 230, 240} stitches on hold for Back, work next row of Moss stitch over 8 (12, 13, 14, 14, 14), {13, 14, 19, 24} stitches, slip marker, [work in pattern to marker, slip marker] 3 times, k2 – 60 (64, 71, 78, 84, 96), {101, 108, 113, 118} stitches on the needle for Left Front.
Continue working on left front stitches.

02 LEFT FRONT

Next Row (WS): Work in established pattern to last 2 stitches, place marker, p2.
Next Row (RS): K2, slip marker, work to end.

Work in established pattern on Left Front stitches until it measures approximately 4 (5¼, 6, 6½, 7, 7½), {7¾, 8, 8½, 9}"/10 (13, 15, 16.5, 17.5, 19), {19.5, 20, 21.5, 22.5} cm from Division Row, ending with WS row (recommended last row – Lattice Row 8).

Mock Lattice Chart Set-Up Row (RS): K2, slip marker, work next row of Moss stitch to marker, slip marker, work next row of Chart B to marker, slip marker, work Row 1 of Mock Lattice Chart to marker, slip marker, work next row of Chart B to marker, slip marker, k2.

NOTE: Continue working in Mock Lattice Chart instead of Lattice Chart (see Notes).

Shape neckline

NOTE: While shaping the neckline and working on Mock Lattice Chart, make sure that the number of increases in pattern correlate with the number of decreases to keep the stitch count accurate.
If there are not enough stitches for cable crossing, work these stitches in Stockinette stitch.

Next Row (WS): Bind off 13 (15, 15, 17, 17, 17), {18, 18, 20, 20} stitches, work remaining stitches of Row 2 of Mock Lattice Chart to marker, slip marker, work next row of Chart B to marker, slip marker, work next row of Moss stitch to marker, slip marker, p2. [47 (49, 56, 61, 67, 79), {83, 90, 93, 98} stitches on the needle]

Next Row (RS): K2, slip marker, work next row of Moss stitch to marker, slip marker, work next row of Chart B, slip marker, work remaining stitches of Row 3 of Mock Lattice Chart.

At the beginning of following 5 WS rows, bind off 3 stitches once, 2 stitches once and 1 stitch 3 times. [39 (41, 48, 53, 59, 71), {75, 82, 85, 90} stitches on the needle]

Next Row (RS): K2, slip marker, work next row of Moss stitch to marker, slip marker, work next row of Chart B, slip marker, work remaining stitches of Row 5 of Mock Lattice Chart.

Shape left shoulder, using the German Short-Rows
Short-Row 1 (WS): Work in pattern to last 4 (4, 4, 5, 6, 6), {7, 8, 8, 9} stitches, turn work.
Short-Row 2 (RS): Make double stitch, work in pattern to end.
Short-Row 3 (WS): Work in pattern to 3 (3, 3, 4, 5, 5), {6, 7, 7, 8} stitches before double stitch, turn work.
Short-Row 4 (RS): Make double stitch, work in pattern to end.
Short-Rows 5-14: Repeat last 2 rows 5 more times.

Next Row (WS): Work all left shoulder stitches in pattern (knit the knit stitches and purl the purls) to end, working double stitches as single stitches. Place all stitches on hold. Break yarn, leaving long tail for 3-Needle Bind Off.

03 BACK

Place held 124 (132, 146, 160, 172, 196), [206, 220, 230, 240] Back stitches onto US 6/4 mm circular needle. Join yarn, ready to work WS row.
Work in rows in established pattern until Back measures 5¼, (6½, 7¼, 7¾, 8¼, 8¾), [9, 9¼, 9¾, 10¼]"/13 (16.5, 18, 19.5, 20.5, 22), {22.5, 23, 24.5, 25.5} cm from Division Row, ending with WS row (recommended last row – Lattice Row 8).

Shape shoulders
Short-Row 1 (RS): Work, following Moss stitch and charts, and substituting Lattice Chart with Mock Lattice Chart (see Notes) to last 4 (4, 4, 5, 6, 6), {7, 8, 8, 9} stitches, turn work.
Short-Row 2 (WS): Make double stitch, work in established pattern to last 4 (4, 4, 5, 6, 6), {7, 8, 8, 9} stitches, turn work.
Short-Row 3 (RS): Work to 3 (3, 3, 4, 5, 5), {6, 7, 7, 8} stitches before double stitch, turn work.
Short-Row 4 (WS): Work to 3 (3, 3, 4, 5, 5), {6, 7, 7, 8} stitches before double stitch, turn work.

Short-Rows 5-14: Repeat last 2 rows 5 more times.
Next Row (RS): Work all stitches in pattern (knit the knit stitches and purl the purls) to end, working double stitches as single stitches.
Next Row (WS): Work 39 (41, 48, 53, 59, 71), {75, 82, 85, 90} left shoulder stitches in pattern and place them on hold, bind off next 46 (50, 50, 54, 54, 54), {56, 56, 60, 60} stitches for back neck, work last 39 (41, 48, 53, 59, 71), {75, 82, 85, 90} right shoulder stitches in pattern, working double stitches as single stitches. Place right shoulder stitches on hold.

04 RIGHT FRONT

Place held 60 (64, 71, 78, 84, 96), [101, 108, 113, 118] right front stitches onto US 6/4 mm circular needle. Join yarn at the beginning of WS row.

Next Row (WS): P2, place marker, work in established pattern to end.
Next Row (RS): Work to marker, slip marker, k2.

Work in rows in established pattern until front measures approximately 4 (5¼, 6, 6½, 7, 7½), {7¾, 8, 8½, 9}"/10 (13, 15, 16.5, 17.5, 19), {19.5, 20, 21.5, 22.5} cm from Division Row, ending with WS row.

Mock Lattice Chart Set-Up Row (RS): K2, slip marker, work next row of Chart A to marker, slip marker, work Row 1 of Mock Lattice Chart to marker, slip marker, work next row of Chart A to marker, slip marker, work next row of Moss stitch to marker, slip marker, k2.

NOTE: Continue working in Mock Lattice Chart instead of Lattice Chart (see Notes).

Shape neckline
*NOTE: While shaping the neckline and working on Mock Lattice Chart, make sure that the number of increases in pattern correlate with the number of decreases to keep the stitch count accurate.
If there are not enough stitches for cable crossing, work these stitches in Stockinette stitch.*

At the beginning of next 6 RS rows, bind off 13 (15, 15, 17, 17, 17), {18, 18, 20, 20} stitches once, 3 stitches once, 2 stitches once and 1 stitch 3 times. [39 (41, 48, 53, 59, 71), {75, 82, 85, 90} stitches on the needle]

Next Row (WS): Work all stitches in established pattern.

Shape right shoulder
Short-Row 1 (RS): Work to last 4 (4, 4, 5, 6, 6), {7, 8, 8, 9} stitches, turn work.
Short-Row 2 (WS): Make double stitch, work to end.
Short-Row 3 (RS): Work to 3 (3, 3, 4, 5, 5), {6, 7, 7, 8} stitches before double stitch, turn work.
Short-Row 4 (WS): Make double stitch, work to end.
Short-Rows 5-14: Repeat last 2 rows 5 more times.

Next Row (RS): Work all right shoulder stitches in pattern (knit the knit stitches and purl the purls) to end, working double stitches as single stitches. Place all stitches on hold.
Do not break yarn.

Place right back shoulder stitches onto needles and, with RS together, join them with right front shoulder stitches, using 3-Needle Bind Off method (see Special Techniques, page 226).
Repeat for left shoulder.

05 SLEEVES

With US 6/4 mm double-pointed needles, beginning at underarm, pick up and knit 64 (78, 84, 90, 94, 100), {102, 104, 110, 114} stitches along the armhole.
Join for working in the round.

Chart Set-Up Round 1: K1, place marker, work Round 1 of Moss pattern in the round (see Stitch Guide) over 15 (22, 25, 28, 30, 33), {34, 35, 38, 40} stitches, place marker, work Round 1 of Sleeve Chart over 32 stitches, place marker, work Round 1 of Moss pattern in the round (see Stitch Guide) over 15 (22, 25, 28, 30, 33), {34, 35, 38, 40} stitches, slip marker, k1.
Chart Set-Up Row 2: K1, slip marker, work Round 2 of Moss pattern to marker, slip marker, work Round 2 of Sleeve Chart to marker, slip marker, work Round 2 of Moss pattern to marker, slip marker, k1.

Decrease Round: K1, slip marker, P2TOG, work in established pattern to last 2 stitches, P2TOG, k1.

Repeat Decrease Round 4 (11, 14, 15, 17, 19), {20, 19, 22, 24} more times on every 28 (10, 8, 7, 6, 6), {5, 6, 5, 4}th round. [54 (54, 54, 58, 58, 60), {60, 64, 64, 64} stitches]

Continue working in pattern until sleeve measures 15"/37.5 cm from underarm.
Change to US 5/3.25 mm double-pointed needles.

Work the cuff
Ribbing Round: *K1, p1; repeat from * to end.

Repeat Ribbing Round until cuff measures 2"/5 cm.

Bind off all stitches in pattern or using Tubular Bind Off for k1, p1 rib (see Special Techniques, page 226).

06 FINISHING

06a. Collar
With US 5/3.75 mm circular needle, RS facing, and starting at the open edge of Right Front, pick up and knit 105 (111, 111, 119, 121, 121), {123, 125, 131, 133} stitches along the neck opening.
Next Row (WS): P2, *k1, p1; repeat from * to last stitch, p1.
Next Row (RS): K2, *p1, k1; repeat from * to last stitch, k1.
Repeat last 2 rows until collar measures 1¼"/3.5 cm.

Bind off all stitches in pattern or use the Tubular method for k1, p1 rib in rows:
Decrease Row (WS): Work to last 2 stitches, P2TOG. [1 stitch decreased]

Bind off all stitches, using Tubular method (see Special Techniques, page 226).

06b. Button Band
NOTE: The pick-up ratio on bands is 5 stitches per 6 rows. The number of picked up stitches for each band should be an odd number.

With US 5/3.75 mm circular needle and RS facing, starting at the top of the collar, pick up and knit 107 (117, 119, 119, 129, 131), {131, 131, 141, 143} stitches along left front edge, including collar. Do not join in the round.

Next Row (WS): P2, *k1, p1; repeat from * to last stitch, p1.
Next Row (RS): K2, *p1, k1; repeat from * to last stitch, k1.
Next Row (WS): Slip 1 stitch with yarn in front, p1, *k1, p1; repeat from * to last stitch, slip 1 stitch with yarn in front.
Repeat last 2 rows until piece measures 1½"/4 cm, ending with a RS row.

Bind off all stitches in pattern or use the Tubular method for k1, p1 rib in rows:
Decrease Row (WS): Work to last 2 stitches, P2TOG. [1 stitch decreased]

Bind off all stitches, using Tubular method (see Special Techniques, page 226).

06c. Buttonhole Band

NOTE: If you vary the spacing of your buttonholes, make sure you have an even number of stitches between them.

With US 5/3.75 mm circular needle and RS facing, starting at the lower edge of the right front, pick up and knit 107 (117, 119, 119, 129, 131), {131, 131, 141, 143} stitches along the right front. Work as for button band until piece measures ¾"/2 cm from pick-up row, ending with a WS row.

Buttonhole row (RS): Work 6 (4, 6, 6, 4, 6), {6, 6, 4, 6} stitches in pattern, *YO, K2TOG, work 14 (16, 16, 16, 18, 18), {18, 18, 20, 20} stitches in pattern; repeat from * 5 more times, YO, K2TOG, work 3 stitches to end.

Next Row (WS): Work in rib pattern, working each YO as k1.

Work even in established rib pattern until piece measures 1½"/4 cm from pick-up row, ending with a RS row.

Bind off all stitches in pattern or use the Tubular method for k1, p1 rib in rows:
Decrease Row (WS): Work to last 2 stitches, P2TOG. [1 stitch decreased]

Bind off all stitches, using Tubular method (see Special Techniques, page 226).

Block to measurements.
Weave in ends. Sew on buttons.

CHARTS

CHART A

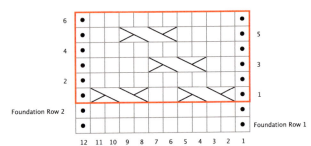

CHART B

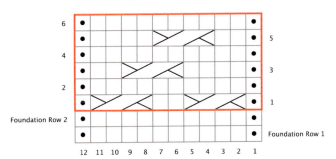

LATTICE CHART

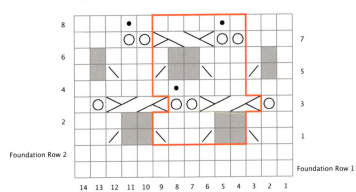

MOCK LATTICE CHART

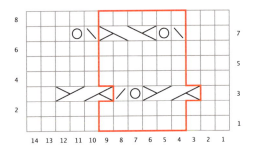

CHART C

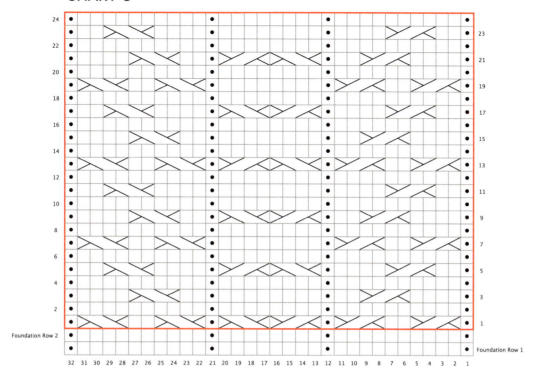

Foundation Row 2

Foundation Row 1

SLEEVE CHART

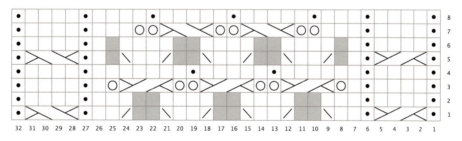

LEGEND

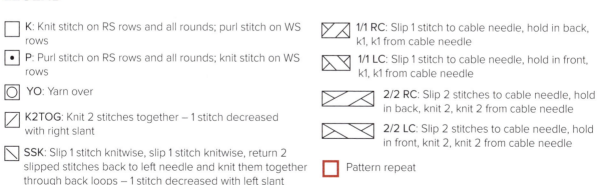

K: Knit stitch on RS rows and all rounds; purl stitch on WS rows

P: Purl stitch on RS rows and all rounds; knit stitch on WS rows

YO: Yarn over

K2TOG: Knit 2 stitches together – 1 stitch decreased with right slant

SSK: Slip 1 stitch knitwise, slip 1 stitch knitwise, return 2 slipped stitches back to left needle and knit them together through back loops – 1 stitch decreased with left slant

1/1 RC: Slip 1 stitch to cable needle, hold in back, k1, k1 from cable needle

1/1 LC: Slip 1 stitch to cable needle, hold in front, k1, k1 from cable needle

2/2 RC: Slip 2 stitches to cable needle, hold in back, knit 2, knit 2 from cable needle

2/2 LC: Slip 2 stitches to cable needle, hold in front, knit 2, knit 2 from cable needle

Pattern repeat

Written instructions for Chart A

Note: See Chart Legend for special abbreviations.

Foundation Row 1 (RS): P1, k10, p1.
Foundation Row 2 (WS): K1, p10, k1.
Row 1 (RS): P1, 2/2 LC, k2, 2/2 LC, p1.
Row 2 and all WS rows: K1, p10, k1.
Row 3 (RS): P1, k2, 2/2 LC, k4, p1.
Row 5 (RS): P1, k4, 2/2 LC, k2, p1.
Row 6 (WS): K1, p10, k1.

Written instructions for Chart B

Foundation Row 1 (RS): P1, k10, p1.
Foundation Row 2 (WS): K1, p10, k1.
Row 1 (RS): P1, 2/2 RC, k2, 2/2 RC, p1.
Row 2 and all WS rows: K1, p10, k1.
Row 3 (RS): P1, k4, 2/2 RC, k2, p1.
Row 5 (RS): P1, k2, 2/2 RC, k4, p1.
Row 6 (WS): K1, p10, k1.

Written instructions for Chart C

Foundation Row 1 (RS): P1, k10, p1, k8, p1, k10, p1.
Foundation Row 2 (WS): K1, p10, k1, p8, k1, p10, k1.
Row 1 (RS): P1, 2/2 RC, k2, 2/2 RC, p1, 2/2 RC, 2/2 LC, p1, 2/2 LC, k2, 2/2 LC, p1.
Row 2 and all WS rows: K1, p10, k1, p8, k1, p10, k1.
Row 3 (RS): P1, k4, 2/2 RC, k2, p1, k8, p1, k2, 2/2 LC, k4, p1.
Row 5 (RS): P1, k2, 2/2 RC, k4, p1, 2/2 LC, 2/2 RC, p1, k4, 2/2 LC, k2, p1.
Row 7 (RS): P1, 2/2 RC, k2, 2/2 RC, p1, k8, p1, 2/2 LC, k2, 2/2 LC, p1.
Row 9 (RS): P1, k4, 2/2 RC, k2, p1, 2/2 RC, 2/2 LC, p1, k2, 2/2 LC, k4, p1.
Row 11 (RS): P1, k2, 2/2 RC, k4, p1, k8, p1, k4, 2/2 LC, k2, p1.
Row 13 (RS): P1, 2/2 RC, k2, [2/2 RC, p1, 2/2 LC] 2 times, k2, 2/2 LC, p1.
Row 15 (RS): P1, k4, 2/2 RC, k2, p1, k8, p1, k2, 2/2 LC, k4, p1.
Row 17 (RS): P1, k2, 2/2 RC, k4, p1, 2/2 RC, 2/2 LC, p1, k4, 2/2 LC, k2, p1.
Row 19 (RS): P1, 2/2 RC, k2, 2/2 RC, p1, k8, p1, 2/2 LC, k2, 2/2 LC, p1.
Row 21 (RS): P1, k4, 2/2 RC, k2, p1, 2/2 LC, 2/2 RC, p1, k2, 2/2 LC, k4, p1.

Row 23 (RS): P1, k2, 2/2 RC, k4, p1, k8, p1, k4, 2/2 LC, k2, p1.
Row 24 (WS): K1, p10, k1, p8, k1, p10, k1.

Written instructions for Lattice Chart
.. – pattern repeat

Foundation Row 1 (RS): Knit.
Foundation Row 2 (WS): Purl.
Row 1 (RS): K2, SSK, *k2 K2TOG, k2, SSK*, K2TOG, k2.
Row 2 (WS): Purl.
Row 3 (RS): K1, YO, 2/2 RC, [YO] 2 times, *2/2 RC, [YO] 2 times*, 2/2 RC, YO, k1.
Row 4 (WS): P6, *(k1, p1) into double YO, p4*, p2.
Row 5 (RS): K1, K2TOG, *k2, SSK, K2TOG*, k2, SSK, k1.
Row 6 (WS): Purl.
Row 7 (RS): K3, *[YO] 2 times, 2/2 LC*, [YO] 2 times, k3.
Row 8 (WS): P3, *(k1, p1) into double YO, p4*, (k1, p1) in double YO, p3.

Written instructions for Mock Lattice Chart
.. – pattern repeat

Row 1 (RS): Knit.
Row 2 and all WS rows: Purl.
Row 3 (RS): K2, *2/2 RC, YO, K2TOG*, 2/2 RC, k2.
Row 5 (RS): Knit.
Row 7 (RS): K3, *SSK, YO, 2/2 LC*, SSK, YO, k3.
Row 8 (WS): Purl.

Written instructions for Sleeve Chart
.. – pattern repeat

Round 1: P1, 2/2 RC, p1, [k2, SSK, K2TOG] 3 times, k2, p1, 2/2 LC, p1.
Round 2: P1, k4, p1, k14, p1, k4, p1.
Round 3: P1, k4, p1, k1, YO, [2/2 RC, [YO] 2 times] 2 times, 2/2 RC, YO, k1, p1, k4, p1.
Round 4: P1, k4, p1, k6, (p1, k1) into double YO, k4, (p1, k1) into double YO, k6, p1, k4, p1.
Round 5: P1, 2/2 RC, p1, k1, [K2TOG, k2, SSK] 3 times, k1, p1, 2/2 LC, p1.
Round 6: P1, k4, p1, k14, p1, k4, p1.
Round 7: P1, k4, p1, k3, [YO] 2 times, [2/2 LC, *[YO] 2 times] 2 times, k3, p1, k4, p1.
Round 8: P1, k4, p1, k3, [(p1, k1) into double YO, k4] 3 times, p1, k4, p1.

6½ (7¼, 8¼, 9, 9½, 11¼), {11½, 12½, 13½, 14½}"/
16.5 (18, 20.5, 22.5, 24, 28), {29, 31.5, 34, 36.5} cm

6 (6½, 6½, 7, 7, 7), {7½, 7½, 8, 8}"/
15 (16.5, 16.5, 17.5, 17.5, 17.5), {19, 19, 20, 20} cm

17"/42.5 cm

5½ (6¾, 7½, 8, 8½, 9), {9¼, 9½, 10, 10½}"/
14 (17, 19, 20, 21.5, 22.5), {23, 24, 25, 26.5} cm

11"/ 27.5 cm

9 (9, 9, 9½, 9½, 10), {10, 11, 11, 11}"/
22.5 (22.5, 22.5, 24, 24, 25), {25, 27.5, 27.5, 27.5} cm

11 (13½, 15, 16¼, 17, 18), {18½, 19, 20, 21}"/
27.5 (34, 37.5, 40.5, 42.5, 45), {46.5, 47.5, 50, 52.5} cm

38 (41½, 45½, 49½, 52½, 59), {61½, 65½, 69½, 73½}"/
95 (104, 114, 124, 131.5, 147.5), {154, 164, 174, 184} cm

Rock Cress

Rock Cress combines elegance with a touch of whimsy, worked in a lace-and-eyelet motif that creates an intricate, almost botanical texture. Its triangular shape begins from a single point and expands outward, letting the pattern unfold with graceful repetition. Draped loosely or wrapped snugly, it lends an air of sophistication while remaining easy to wear.

Finished Measurements
54"/135 cm long.
39.5"/99 cm wide.
Measurements are taken after blocking.

Yarn
Fingering weight yarn (approximate amount): 760 yards/695 m.

Miss Babs Yummy 2-ply (100% Superwash Merino Wool; 400 yards/365 m in 110 g); Gold Leaf - 2 skeins.

Needles
Size US 4/3.5 mm circular needle 24-32"/60-80 cm long, or size to obtain gauge.
While gauge is not critical for this project, the different gauge can affect the size and overall yardage.

Notions
Stitch markers, tapestry needle.

Gauge
21 stitches and 30 rows = 4"/10 cm in Cable pattern, blocked.

Notes
- This shawl is worked flat from the lower left point to the top edge with increases along the right side edge.
- All slipped stitches are slipped purlwise with yarn in front on WS rows.
- Read odd-numbered chart rows from right to left, and even-numbered rows from left to right.

DIRECTIONS

01 BEGINNING

With US 4/3.5 mm circular needle, cast on 1 stitch.
Work Rows 1-72 of Point Chart [38 stitches]

02 BODY

Work Rows 1-24 of Body Chart 12 times total. [182 stitches]

On the needles:

24-Row Body Chart Repeat	1	2	3	4	5	6	7	8	9	10	11	12
Number of stitches at the end of the repeat	50	62	74	86	98	110	122	134	146	158	170	182

03 BORDER

Work Rows 1-14 of Border Chart once. [189 stitches]

Work Rows 15-26 of Border Chart 3 times total. [207 stitches]

Bind Off Row (RS): Slip the first stitch, knit 1 into next stitch, * knit last 2 stitches together through back loop, knit next stitch; repeat from * to end, knit last 2 stitches together through back loop.

04 FINISHING

Weave in ends. Block to measurements.

CHARTS

POINT CHART

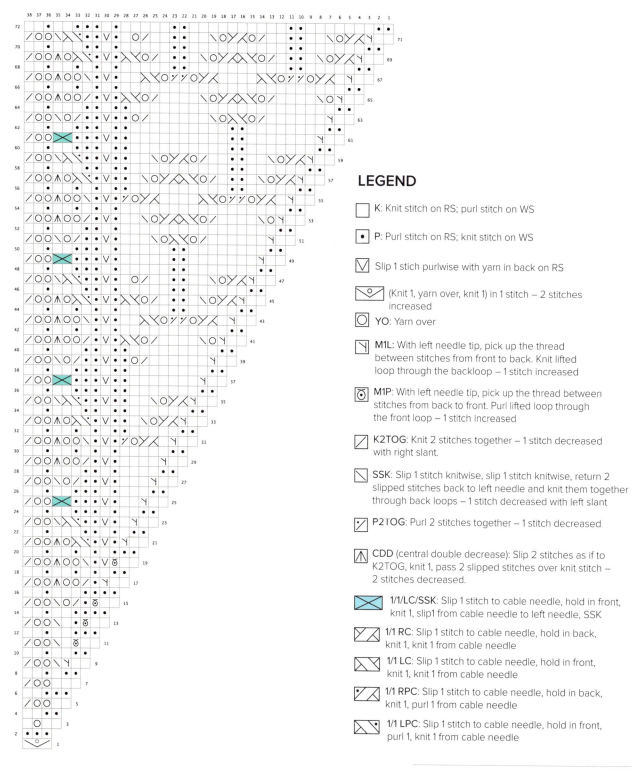

LEGEND

☐ **K**: Knit stitch on RS; purl stitch on WS

⊡ **P**: Purl stitch on RS; knit stitch on WS

▽ **Slip 1 stitch purlwise with yarn in back on RS**

▱ **(Knit 1, yarn over, knit 1) in 1 stitch – 2 stitches increased**

◯ **YO**: Yarn over

⊼ **M1L**: With left needle tip, pick up the thread between stitches from front to back. Knit lifted loop through the backloop – 1 stitch increased

⊙ **M1P**: With left needle tip, pick up the thread between stitches from back to front. Purl lifted loop through the front loop – 1 stitch increased

⟋ **K2TOG**: Knit 2 stitches together – 1 stitch decreased with right slant.

⟍ **SSK**: Slip 1 stitch knitwise, slip 1 stitch knitwise, return 2 slipped stitches back to left needle and knit them together through back loops – 1 stitch decreased with left slant

⟋ **P2TOG**: Purl 2 stitches together – 1 stitch decreased

⋀ **CDD (central double decrease)**: Slip 2 stitches as if to K2TOG, knit 1, pass 2 slipped stitches over knit stitch – 2 stitches decreased.

⊠ **1/1/LC/SSK**: Slip 1 stitch to cable needle, hold in front, knit 1, slip1 from cable needle to left needle, SSK

⟋⟍ **1/1 RC**: Slip 1 stitch to cable needle, hold in back, knit 1, knit 1 from cable needle

⟍⟋ **1/1 LC**: Slip 1 stitch to cable needle, hold in front, knit 1, knit 1 from cable needle

⟋⟍ **1/1 RPC**: Slip 1 stitch to cable needle, hold in back, knit 1, purl 1 from cable needle

⟍⟋ **1/1 LPC**: Slip 1 stitch to cable needle, hold in front, purl 1, knit 1 from cable needle

BODY CHART

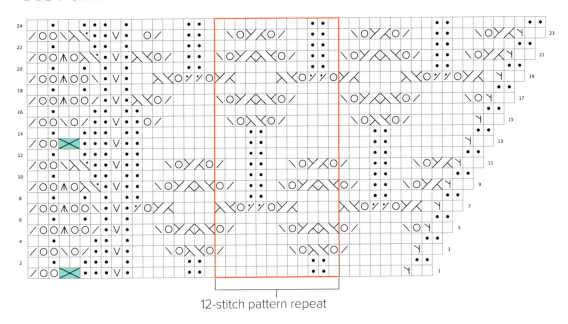

12-stitch pattern repeat

LEGEND

☐ **K**: Knit stitch on RS; purl stitch on WS

• **P**: Purl stitch on RS; knit stitch on WS

Ⅴ Slip 1 stich purlwise with yarn in back on RS

〰 (Knit 1, yarn over, knit 1) in 1 stitch – 2 stitches increased

O **YO**: Yarn over

Ⅵ **M1L**: With left needle tip, pick up the thread between stitches from front to back. Knit lifted loop through the backloop – 1 stitch increased

⊙ **M1P**: With left needle tip, pick up the thread between stitches from back to front. Purl lifted loop through the front loop – 1 stitch increased

╱ **K2TOG**: Knit 2 stitches together – 1 stitch decreased with right slant.

╲ **SSK**: Slip 1 stitch knitwise, slip 1 stitch knitwise, return 2 slipped stitches back to left needle and knit them together through back loops – 1 stitch decreased with left slant.

╱• **P2TOG**: Purl 2 stitches together – 1 stitch decreased

╱⊼ **CDD** (central double decrease): Slip 2 stitches as if to K2TOG, knit 1, pass 2 slipped stitches over knit stitch – 2 stitches decreased.

⧅ **1/1/LC/SSK**: Slip 1 stitch to cable needle, hold in front, knit 1, slip1 from cable needle to left needle, SSK

⧄ **1/1 RC**: Slip 1 stitch to cable needle, hold in back, knit 1, knit 1 from cable needle

⧅ **1/1 LC**: Slip 1 stitch to cable needle, hold in front, knit 1, knit 1 from cable needle

⧄ **1/1 RPC**: Slip 1 stitch to cable needle, hold in back, knit 1, purl 1 from cable needle

⧅ **1/1 LPC**: Slip 1 stitch to cable needle, hold in front, purl 1, knit 1 from cable needle

O Ⅰ Ⅼ O **YO/2KS/YO**: Insert tip of right needle into 3rd and 4th stitches on left needle purlwise, lift over stitches 1 and 2 and let it drop. Yarn over, knit 2, yarn over.

☐ Pattern repeat

BORDER CHART

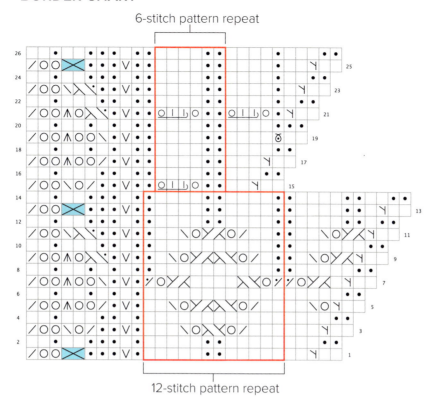

6-stitch pattern repeat

12-stitch pattern repeat

$\boxed{O\ |\ \mathsf{b}\ O}$ **YO/2KS/YO**

 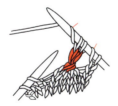  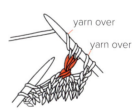

yarn over

yarn over

1. Insert tip of right needle into 3rd and 4th stitches on left needle purlwise, lift over stitches 1 and 2 **and let it drop.**

2. Yarn over, knit 2, yarn over.

Written instructions for Point Chart

1 stitch increased on every RS row.

Note: See Chart Legend for special abbreviations.

Row 1 (RS): [K1, YO, k1] in 1 stitch. [3 stitches]
Row 2 (WS): Knit.
Row 3 (RS): K2, YO, k1. [4 stitches]
Row 4 (WS): P2, k2.
Row 5 (RS): K2, [YO] 2 times, K2TOG. [5 stitches]
Row 6 (WS): P2, k3.
Row 7 (RS): K3, [YO] 2 times, K2TOG. [6 stitches]
Row 8 (WS): P2, k1, p1, k2.
Row 9 (RS): K2, M1L, SSK, [YO] 2 times, K2TOG.
[7 stitches]
Row 10 (WS): P2, k1, p2, k2.
Row 11 (RS): K2, M1P, k1, SSK, [YO] 2 times, K2TOG.
[8 stitches]
Row 12 (WS): P2, k1, p2, k3.
Row 13 (RS): K2, M1P, p1, k1, SSK, [YO] 2 times, K2TOG.
[9 stitches]
Row 14 (WS): P2, k1, p2, k4.
Row 15 (RS): K2, M1P, p1, K2TOG, YO, SSK, [YO] 2 times, K2TOG. [10 stitches]
Row 16 (WS): P2, k1, p3, k4.
Row 17 (RS): K2, M1L, p1, K2TOG, [YO] 2 times, CCD, [YO] 2 times, K2TOG. [11 stitches]
Row 18 (WS): [P2, k1] 2 times, p1, k1, p1, k2.
Row 19 (RS): K2, M1P, slip 1, p1, SSK, [YO] 2 times, CCD, [YO] 2 times, K2TOG. [12 stitches]
Row 20 (WS): [P2, k1] 2 times, p1, k1, p1, k3.
Row 21 (RS): K2, M1L, p1, slip 1, p1, 1/1 LPC, YO, CCD, [YO] 2 times, K2TOG. [13 stitches]
Row 22 (WS): P2, k1, p3, k2, p1, k1, p1, k2.
Row 23 (RS): K2, M1L, k1, p1, slip 1, p2, 1/1 LPC, SSK, [YO] 2 times, K2TOG. [14 stitches]
Row 24 (WS): P2, k1, p2, k3, p1, k1, p2, k2.
Row 25 (RS): K2, M1L, k2, p1, slip 1, p3, 1/1/LC/SSK, [YO] 2 times, K2TOG. [15 stitches]
Row 26 (WS): P2, k1, p2, k3, p1, k1, p3, k2.
Row 27 (RS): K2, M1L, k3, p1, slip 1, p2, K2TOG, YO, SSK, [YO] 2 times, K2TOG. [16 stitches]
Row 28 (WS): P2, k1, p3, k2, p1, k1, p4, k2.
Row 29 (RS): K2, M1L, k4, p1, slip 1, p1, K2TOG, [YO] 2 times, CCD, [YO] 2 times, K2TOG. [17 stitches]
Row 30 (WS): [P2, k1] 2 times, [p1, k1] 2 times, p5, k2.

Row 31 (RS): K2, M1L, k1, 1/1 RC, YO, P2TOG, p1, slip 1, p1, SSK, [YO] 2 times, CCD, [YO] 2 times, K2TOG. [18 stitches]
Row 32 (WS): [P2, k1] 2 times, p1, k1, p1, k2, p5, k2.
Row 33 (RS): K2, M1L, 1/1 RC, YO, SSK, k1, p2, slip 1, p1, 1/1 LPC, YO, CCD, [YO] 2 times, K2TOG. [19 stitches]
Row 34 (WS): P2, k1, p3, k2, p1, k2, p6, k2.
Row 35 (RS): K2, M1L, 1/1 RC, YO, SSK, k2, p2, slip 1, p2, 1/1 LPC, SSK, [YO] 2 times, K2TOG. [20 stitches]
Row 36 (WS): P2, k1, p2, k3, p1, k2, p7, k2.
Row 37 (RS): K2, M1L, k7, p2, slip 1, p3, 1/1/LC/SSK, [YO] 2 times, K2TOG. [21 stitches]
Row 38 (WS): P2, k1, p3, k2, p1, k2, p8, k2.
Row 39 (RS): K2, M1L, k6, K2TOG, YO, p2, slip 1, p2, K2TOG, YO, SSK, [YO] 2 times, K2TOG. [22 stitches]
Row 40 (WS): P2, k1, p3, k2, p1, k2, p9, k2.
Row 41 (RS): K2, M1L, YO, SSK, k4, K2TOG, YO, 1/1 LC, p1, slip 1, p1, K2TOG, [YO] 2 times, CCD, [YO] 2 times, K2TOG. [23 stitches]
Row 42 (WS): [P2, k1] 2 times, [p1, k1] 2 times, p11, k2.
Row 43 (RS): K2, M1L, k1, 1/1 RC, YO, [P2TOG] 2 times, YO, 1/1 LC, k2, p1, slip 1, p1, SSK, [YO] 2 times, CCD, [YO] 2 times, K2TOG. [24 stitches]
Row 44 (WS): [P2, k1] 2 times, [p1, k1] 2 times, [p5, k2] 2 times.
Row 45 (RS): K2, M1L, 1/1 RC, YO, SSK, k1, p2, k1, K2TOG, YO, 1/1 LC, p1, slip 1, p1, 1/1 LPC, YO, CCD, [YO] 2 times, K2TOG. [25 stitches]
Row 46 (WS): P2, k1, p3, k2, p1, k1, p5, k2, p6, k2.
Row 47 (RS): K2, M1L, 1/1 RC, YO, SSK, k2, p2, k2, K2TOG, YO, k1, p1, slip 1, p2, 1/1 LPC, SSK, [YO] 2 times, K2TOG. [26 stitches]
Row 48 (WS): P2, k1, p2, k3, p1, k1, p5, k2, p7, k2.
Row 49 (RS): K2, M1L, k7, p2, k5, p1, slip 1, p3, 1/1/LC/SSK, [YO] 2 times, K2TOG. [27 stitches]
Row 50 (WS): P2, k1, p2, k3, p1, k1, p5, k2, p8, k2.
Row 51 (RS): K2, M1L, k6, K2TOG, YO, 1/1 LC, YO, SSK, k3, p1, slip 1, p2, K2TOG, YO, SSK, [YO] 2 times, K2TOG. [28 stitches]
Row 52 (WS): P2, k1, p3, k2, p1, k1, p16, k2.
Row 53 (RS): K2, M1L, YO, SSK, k4, K2TOG, YO, 1/1 LC, 1/1 RC, YO, SSK, k2, p1, slip 1, p1, K2TOG, [YO] 2 times, CCD, [YO] 2 times, K2TOG. [29 stitches]
Row 54 (WS): [P2, k1] 2 times, [p1, k1] 2 times, p17, k2.

Row 55 (RS): K2, M1L, k1, 1/1 RC, YO, [P2TOG] 2 times, YO, 1/1 LC, k4, 1/1 RC, YO, P2TOG, p1, slip 1, p1, SSK, [YO] 2 times, CCD, [YO] 2 times, K2TOG. [30 stitches]
Row 56 (WS): [P2, k1] 2 times, p1, k1, p1, k2, p10, k2, p5, k2.
Row 57 (RS): K2, M1L, 1/1 RC, YO, SSK, k1, p2, k1, K2TOG, YO, 1/1 LC, 1/1 RC, YO, SSK, k1, p2, slip 1, p1, 1/1 LPC, YO, CCD, [YO] 2 times, K2TOG. [31 stitches]
Row 58 (WS): P2, k1, p3, k2, p1, k2, p10, k2, p6, k2.
Row 59 (RS): K2, M1L, 1/1 RC, YO, SSK, k2, p2, k2, K2TOG, YO, 1/1 RC, YO, SSK, k2, p2, slip 1, p2, 1/1 LPC, SSK, [YO] 2 times, K2TOG. [32 stitches]
Row 60 (WS): P2, k1, p2, k3, p1, k2, p10, k2, p7, k2.
Row 61 (RS): K2, M1L, k7, p2, k10, p2, slip 1, p3, 1/1/LC/SSK, [YO] 2 times, K2TOG. [33 stitches]
Row 62 (WS): P2, k1, p2, k3, p1, k2, p10, k2, p8, k2.
Row 63 (RS): K2, M1L, k6, K2TOG, YO, 1/1 LC, YO, SSK, k6, K2TOG, YO, p2, slip 1, p2, K2TOG, YO, SSK, [YO] 2 times, K2TOG. [34 stitches]
Row 64 (WS): P2, k1, p3, k2, p1, k2, p21, k2.
Row 65 (RS): K2, M1L, YO, SSK, k4, K2TOG, YO, 1/1 LC, 1/1 RC, YO, SSK, k4, K2TOG, YO, 1/1 LC, p1, slip 1, p1, K2TOG, [YO] 2 times, CCD, [YO] 2 times, K2TOG. [35 stitches]
Row 66 (WS): [P2, k1] 2 times, [p1, k1] 2 times, p23, k2.
Row 67 (RS): K2, M1L, k1, 1/1 RC, YO, [P2TOG] 2 times, YO, 1/1 LC, k4, 1/1 RC, YO, [P2TOG] 2 times, YO, 1/1 LC, k2, p1, slip 1, p1, SSK, [YO] 2 times, CCD, [YO] 2 times, K2TOG. [36 stitches]
Row 68 (WS): [P2, k1] 2 times, [p1, k1] 2 times, p5, k2, p10, k2, p5, k2.
Row 69 (RS): K2, M1L, [1/1 RC, YO, SSK, k1, p2, k1, K2TOG, YO, 1/1 LC] 2 times, p1, slip 1, p1, 1/1 LPC, YO, CCD, [YO] 2 times, K2TOG. [37 stitches]
Row 70 (WS): P2, k1, p3, k2, p1, k1, p5, k2, p10, k2, p6, k2.
Row 71 (RS): K2, M1L, [1/1 RC, YO, SSK, k2, p2, k2, K2TOG, YO] 2 times, k1, p1, slip 1, p2, 1/1 LPC, SSK, [YO] 2 times, K2TOG. [38 stitches]
Row 72 (WS): P2, k1, p2, k3, p1, k1, p5, k2, p10, k2, p7, k2.

Written instructions for Body Chart
1 stitch increased on every RS row.
... - chart repeat

Row 1 (RS): K2, M1L, k6, *k1, p2, k9*, k1, p2, k5, p1, slip 1, p3, 1/1/LC/SSK, [YO] 2 times, K2TOG.
Row 2 (WS): P2, k1, p2, k3, p1, k1, p5, k2, p1, *p9, k2, p1*, p7, k2.
Row 3 (RS): K2, M1L, k6, K2TOG, *YO, 1/1 LC, YO, SSK, k6, K2TOG*, YO, 1/1 LC, YO, SSK, k3, p1, slip 1, p2, K2TOG, YO, SSK, [YO] 2 times, K2TOG.
Row 4 (WS): P2, k1, p3, k2, p1, k1, purl to last 2 stitches, k2.
Row 5 (RS): K2, M1L, YO, SSK, k4, K2TOG, YO, *1/1 LC, 1/1 RC, YO, SSK, k4, K2TOG, YO*, 1/1 LC, 1/1 RC, YO, SSK, k2, p1, slip 1, p1, K2TOG, [YO] 2 times, CCD, [YO] 2 times, K2TOG.
Row 6 (WS): [P2, k1] 2 times, [p1, k1] 2 times, purl to last 2 stitches k2.
Row 7 (RS): K2, M1L, k1, 1/1 RC, YO, [P2TOG] 2 times, YO, 1/1 LC, *k4, 1/1 RC, YO, [P2TOG] 2 times, YO, 1/1 LC*, k4, 1/1 RC, YO, P2TOG, p1, slip 1, p1, SSK, [YO] 2 times, CCD, [YO] 2 times, K2TOG.
Row 8 (WS): [P2, k1] 2 times, p1, k1, p1, k2, p7, *p3, k2, p7*, p3, k2, p5, k2.
Row 9 (RS): K2, M1L, 1/1 RC, YO, SSK, k1, p2, k1, K2TOG, YO, *1/1 LC, 1/1 RC, YO, SSK, k1, p2, k1, K2TOG, YO*, 1/1 LC, 1/1 RC, YO, SSK, k1, p2, slip 1, p1, 1/1 LPC, YO, CCD, [YO] 2 times, K2TOG.
Row 10 (WS): P2, k1, p3, k2, p1, k2, p7, *p3, k2, p7*, p3, k2, p6, k2.
Row 11 (RS): K2, M1L, 1/1 RC, YO, SSK, k2, p2, k2, K2TOG, *YO, 1/1 RC, YO, SSK, k2, p2, k2, K2TOG*, YO, 1/1 RC, YO, SSK, k2, p2, slip 1, p2, 1/1 LPC, SSK, [YO] 2 times, K2TOG.
Row 12 (WS): P2, k1, p2, k3, p1, k2, p7, *p3, k2, p7*, p3, k2, p7, k2.
Row 13 (RS): K2, M1L, k7, p2, k3, *k7, p2, k3*, k7, p2, slip 1, p3, 1/1/LC/SSK, [YO] 2 times, K2TOG.
Row 14 (WS): P2, k1, p2, k3, p1, k2, p7, *p3, k2, p7*, p3, k2, p8, k2.
Row 15 (RS): K2, M1L, k6, K2TOG, YO, 1/1 LC, YO, SSK, k1, *k5, K2TOG, YO, 1/1 LC, YO, SSK, k1*, k5, K2TOG, YO, p2, slip 1, p2, K2TOG, YO, SSK, [YO] 2 times, K2TOG.
Row 16 (WS): P2, k1, p3, k2, p1, k2, purl to last 2 stitches, k2.

Row 17 (RS): K2, M1L, YO, SSK, k4, K2TOG, YO, 1/1 LC, 1/1 RC, YO, SSK, *k4, K2TOG, YO, 1/1 LC, 1/1 RC, YO, SSK*, k4, K2TOG, YO, 1/1 LC, p1, slip 1, p1, K2TOG, [YO] 2 times, CCD, [YO] 2 times, K2TOG.

Row 18 (WS): [P2, k1] 2 times, [p1, k1] 2 times, purl to last 2 stitches, k2.

Row 19 (RS): K2, M1L, k1, 1/1 RC, YO, [P2TOG] 2 times, YO, 1/1 LC, k4, 1/1 RC, *YO, [P2TOG] 2 times, YO, 1/1 LC, k4, 1/1 RC*, YO, [P2TOG] 2 times, YO, 1/1 LC, k2, p1, slip 1, p1, SSK, [YO] 2 times, CCD, [YO] 2 times, K2TOG.

Row 20 (WS): [P2, k1] 2 times, [p1, k1] 2 times, p5, k2, p1, *p9, k2, p1*, p9, k2, p5, k2.

Row 21 (RS): K2, M1L, 1/1 RC, YO, SSK, k1, p2, k1, K2TOG, YO, 1/1 LC, 1/1 RC, YO, SSK, *k1, p2, k1, K2TOG, YO, 1/1 LC, 1/1 RC, YO, SSK*, k1, p2, k1, K2TOG, YO, 1/1 LC, p1, slip 1, p1, 1/1 LPC, YO, CCD, [YO] 2 times, K2TOG.

Row 22 (WS): P2, k1, p3, k2, p1, k1, p5, k2, p1, *p9, k2, p1*, p9, k2, p6, k2.

Row 23 (RS): K2, M1L, 1/1 RC, YO, SSK, k2, p2, k2, K2TOG, YO, 1/1 RC, YO, SSK, k1, *k1, p2, k2, K2TOG, YO, 1/1 RC, YO, SSK, k1*, k1, p2, k2, K2TOG, YO, k1, p1, slip 1, p2, 1/1 LPC, SSK, [YO] 2 times, K2TOG.

Row 24 (WS): P2, k1, p2, k3, p1, k1, p5, k2, p1, *p9, k2, p1*, p9, k2, p7, k2.

Written instructions for Border Chart

1 stitch increased on every RS row.

... - chart repeat

Row 1 (RS): K2, M1L, k2, *k5, p2, k5*, p1, slip 1, p3, 1/1/LC/SSK, [YO] 2 times, K2TOG.

Row 2 (WS): P2, k1, p2, k3, p1, k1, *p5, k2, p5*, p3, k2.

Row 3 (RS): K2, M1L, k3, *k3, K2TOG, YO, 1/1 LC, YO, SSK, k3*, p1, slip 1, p2, K2TOG, YO, SSK, [YO] 2 times, K2TOG.

Row 4 (WS): P2, k1, p3, k2, p1, k1, purl to last 2 stitches, k2.

Row 5 (RS): K2, M1L, YO, SSK, k2, *k2, K2TOG, YO, 1/1 LC, 1/1 RC, YO, SSK, k2*, p1, slip 1, p1, K2TOG, [YO] 2 times, CCD, [YO] 2 times, K2TOG.

Row 6 (WS): [P2, k1] 2 times, [p1, k1] 2 times, purl to last 2 stitches, k2.

Row 7 (RS): K2, M1L, k1, 1/1 RC, YO, P2TOG, *P2TOG, YO, 1/1 LC, k4, 1/1 RC, YO, P2TOG*, p1, slip 1, p1, SSK, [YO] 2 times, CCD, [YO] 2 times, K2TOG.

Row 8 (WS): [P2, k1] 2 times, [p1, k1] 2 times, *k1, p10, k1*, k1, p5, k2.

Row 9 (RS): K2, M1L, 1/1 RC, YO, SSK, k1, p1, *p1, k1, K2TOG, YO, 1/1 LC, 1/1 RC, YO, SSK, k1, p1*, p1, slip 1, p1, 1/1 LPC, YO, CCD, [YO] 2 times, K2TOG.

Row 10 (WS): P2, k1, p3, k2, p1, k1, *k1, p10, k1*, k1, p6, k2.

Row 11 (RS): K2, M1L, 1/1 RC, YO, SSK, k2, p1, *p1, k2, K2TOG, YO, 1/1 RC, YO, SSK, k2, p1*, p1, slip 1, p2, 1/1 LPC, SSK, [YO] 2 times, K2TOG.

Row 12 (WS): P2, k1, p2, k3, p1, k1, *k1, p4, k2, p4, k1*, k1, p4, k2, p1, k2.

Row 13 (RS): K2, M1L, k1, p2, k4, p1, *p1, k4, p2, k4, p1*, p1, slip 1, p3, 1/1/LC/SSK, [YO] 2 times, K2TOG.

Row 14 (WS): P2, k1, p2, k3, p1, k1, *k1, p4, k2, p4, k1*, k1, p4, k2, p2, k2.

Row 15 (RS): K2, M1L, k2, *p2, YO/2KS/YO*, p2, slip 1, p2, K2TOG, YO, SSK, [YO] 2 times, K2TOG.

Row 16 (WS): P2, k1, p3, k2, p1, k2, *p4, k2*, p3, k2.

Row 17 (RS): K2, M1L, k3, *p2, k4*, p2, slip 1, p1, K2TOG, [YO] 2 times, CCD, [YO] 2 times, K2TOG.

Row 18 (WS): [P2, k1] 2 times, p1, k1, p1, k2, *p4, k2*, p4, k2.

Row 19 (RS): K2, M1P, k4, *p2, k4*, p2, slip 1, p1, SSK, [YO] 2 times, CCD, [YO] 2 times, K2TOG.

Row 20 (WS): [P2, k1] 2 times, p1, k1, p1, k2, *p4, k2*, p4, k3.

Row 21 (RS): K2, M1P, p1, YO/2KS/YO, *p2, YO/2KS/YO*, p2, slip 1, p1, 1/1 LPC, YO, CCD, [YO] 2 times, K2TOG.

Row 22 (WS): P2, k1, p3, k2, p1, k2, *p4, k2*, p4, k4.

Row 23 (RS): K2, M1L, p2, k4, *p2, k4*, p2, slip 1, p2, 1/1 LPC, SSK, [YO] 2 times, K2TOG.

Row 24 (WS): P2, k1, p2, k3, p1, k2, *p4, k2*, p4, k2, p1, k2.

Row 25 (RS): K2, M1L, k1, p2, k4, *p2, k4*, p2, slip 1, p3, 1/1/LC/SSK, [YO] 2 times, K2TOG.

Row 26 (WS): P2, k1, p2, k3, p1, k2, *p4, k2*, p4, k2, p2, k2.

Annemarie

The Annemarie Cardigan is a modern classic with just the right balance of simplicity and detail. Knit from the top down in smooth Stockinette, it features textured sleeves and deep patch pockets adorned with bold cables. The clean V-neck and ribbed button bands give it a cozy, wearable look, while the buttons add a touch of character. Designed for worsted-weight yarn, Annemarie is a soothing knit that flows easily on the needles and results in a cardigan you'll reach for every season.

Sizes
XS (S, M, L, XL, 2XL), {3XL, 4XL, 5XL, 6XL}: to fit bust 28-30 (32-34, 36-38, 40-42, 44-46, 48-50), {52-54, 56-58, 60-62, 64-66}"/70-75 (80-85, 90-95, 100-105, 110-115, 120-125), {130-135, 140-145, 150-155, 160-165} cm.

Finished Measurements
38½ (42¾, 46, 50½, 54½, 58¾), {62, 66½, 70½, 74¾}"/96.5 (107, 115, 126.5, 136.5, 147), {155, 166.5, 176.5, 187} cm bust circumference.
Intended Ease: +8–10"/20–25 cm.
Sample shown in size M and measures 46"/115 cm on 38"/95 cm bust with 8"/20 cm of positive ease.

Yarn
Worsted weight yarn (approximate amounts): 1220 (1350, 1460, 1600, 1730, 1860), {1970, 2100, 2240, 2370} yds/1110 (1230, 1330, 1456, 1574, 1695), {1795, 1910, 2040, 2160} m.

Miss Babs Intrepid (100% Targhee Wool; 280 yards/255 m in 4 oz/115 g), Black Salt: 5 (5, 6, 6, 7, 7), {8, 8, 8, 9} skeins.

Needles
Size US 8/5 mm: 24-32"/60-80 cm circular.
Size US 7/4.5 mm: 24-32"/60-80 cm circular and set of double-pointed. Optional: spare US 7/4.5 mm 24-32"/60-80 cm circular for the Tubular Bind Off.
Adjust needle size if necessary to obtain gauge.

Notions
Stitch markers, cable needle, stitch holders or waste yarn, tapestry needle, 5 buttons 3/4"/20 mm in diameter.

Gauge
19 stitches and 28 rows = 4"/10 cm in Stockinette Stitch on size US 8/5 mm needle, after blocking.
22 stitches and 28 rows = 4"/10 cm in charted pattern on size US 8/5 mm needle, after blocking.

Notes
- This cardigan is worked from the top down in one piece. The back and the fronts are worked separately down to the armholes and then joined.
- Sleeves are worked separately and sewn into armholes.
- Read RS (odd-numbered) chart rows from right to left; read WS (even-numbered) chart rows from left to right.
- The German Short-Row method is used in this pattern. Knitters may substitute their preferred short-row method.

Stitch Guide

Stockinette stitch
RS rows and all rounds: Knit.
WS rows: Purl.

Inv-R (Invisible Increase Right): Insert tip of right needle into right leg of stitch below first stitch on left needle from back to front, lifting this stitch up onto left needle tip. Knit the lifted stitch, then slip the original stitch purlwise with yarn in back — 1 right-leaning stitch increased.

Inv-L (Invisible Increase Left): Slip stitch purlwise with yarn in back, insert tip of left needle into the left leg of stitch in the row below the stitch just slipped to right needle, from back to front, lifting this stitch up onto left needle tip (the lifted stitch will sit on left needle in the wrong orientation). Knit the lifted stitch through the back loop — 1 left-leaning stitch increased.

DIRECTIONS

01 BACK

With US 8/5 mm circular needle cast on 34 (38, 42, 46, 50, 55), {58, 63, 67, 72} stitches for left shoulder, place marker, cast on 30 (32, 32, 34, 36, 36), {38, 38, 40, 40} stitches for back neck, place marker, cast on 34 (38, 42, 46, 50, 55), {58, 63, 67, 72} stitches for right shoulder. [98 (108, 116, 126, 136, 146), {154, 164, 174, 184} stitches total]

Short-Row 1 (RS): [Knit to marker, slip marker] twice, k3 (4, 4, 5, 5, 6), {6, 7, 7, 8}, turn work.
Short-Row 2 (WS): Make double stitch, [purl to marker, slip marker] 2 times, p3 (4, 4, 5, 5, 6), {6, 7, 7, 8}, turn work.
Short-Row 3 (RS): Make double stitch, knit to double stitch and work it as a knit stitch, k3 (4, 4, 5, 5, 6), {6, 7, 7, 8}, turn work.
Short-Row 4 (WS): Make double stitch, purl to double stitch and work it as a purl stitch, p3 (4, 4, 5, 5, 6), {6, 7, 7, 8}, turn work.

Short-Rows 5-14: Repeat Short-Rows 3 and 4 another 5 times.
Next Row (RS): Make double stitch, knit to double stitch and work it as a knit stitch, knit to the end of row.

Next Row (WS): Purl to the end of row, working double stitch as a purl stitch.

Work 2 rows even in Stockinette Stitch.

Shape armhole
Armhole Decrease Row (RS): K2, K2TOG, knit to last 4 stitches, SSK, k2. [2 stitches decreased]
Work next 9 (9, 11, 11, 11, 13), {13, 13, 13, 13} rows even in Stockinette Stitch, ending with WS row.

Repeat last 10 (10, 12, 12, 12, 14), {14, 14, 14, 14} rows another 3 times.
Work Armhole Decrease Row once more.
[88 (98, 106, 116, 126, 136), {144, 154, 164, 174} stitches]

Continue working in Stockinette stitch even until Back measures 8 (8¼, 8½, 8¾, 9¼, 9½), {9¾, 10, 10¼, 10½}"/ 20 (20.5, 21.5, 22, 23, 24), {24.5, 25, 25.5, 26.5} cm from cast-on edge, measured along the armhole edge, ending with WS row.

Break yarn and place stitches on hold.

02 RIGHT FRONT

With US 8/5 mm circular needle, starting at the right armhole edge, with the RS facing, pick up and knit first 34 (38, 42, 46, 50, 55), {58, 63, 67, 72} stitches along the cast on edge of right shoulder.

Shape shoulder
Short-Row 1 (WS): P3 (4, 4, 5, 5, 6), {6, 7, 7, 8}, turn work.
Short-Row 2 (RS): Make double stitch, knit to end.
Short-Row 3 (WS): Purl to double stitch and work it as a purl stitch, p3 (4, 4, 5, 5, 6), {6, 7, 7, 8}, turn work.
Short-Row 4 (RS): Make double stitch, knit to end.

Short-Rows 5-14: Repeat Short-Rows 3 and 4 another 5 times.
Next Row (WS): Purl to the end of row, working double stitch as a purl stitch.

Start shaping neckline and armhole
NOTE: Neck and armhole shaping are worked at the same time; read following section through before proceeding.

Neck Increase Row (RS): Knit to last 3 stitches, Inv-R (see Stitch Guide), k2. [1 stitch increased]
Work 1 WS row.

Armhole Decrease Row (RS): K2, K2TOG, knit to end. [1 stitch decreased]
Work 1 WS row.

Repeat Neck Increase Row in every other RS row another 9 (9, 9, 9, 10, 11), {11, 12, 11, 12} times, then in every RS row 5 (6, 6, 7, 7, 6), {7, 6, 8, 7} times and AT THE SAME TIME work Armhole Decrease Row in every 10 (10, 12, 12, 12, 14), {14, 14, 14, 14}th row 4 times more.
[44 (49, 53, 58, 63, 68), {72, 77, 82, 87} stitches]

NOTE: When working some of the Armhole Decrease Rows, you will need to work the Neck Increase at the end of the same row.

Continue working in Stockinette stitch even until Right Front measures 8 (8¼, 8½, 8¾, 9¼, 9½), {9¾, 10, 10¼, 10½}"/ 20 (20.5, 21.5, 22, 23, 24), {24.5, 25, 25.5, 26.5} cm from cast-on edge, measured along the armhole edge, ending with WS row.

Break yarn and place stitches on hold.

03 LEFT FRONT

With US 8/5 mm circular needle, beginning at the neck edge, with the RS facing, pick up and knit 34 (38, 42, 46, 50, 55), {58, 63, 67, 72} stitches along the cast on edge of left shoulder.

Next Row (WS): Purl to end.

Shape shoulder
Short-Row 1 (RS): K3 (4, 4, 5, 5, 6), {6, 7, 7, 8}, turn work.
Short-Row 2 (WS): Make double stitch, purl to end.
Short-Row 3 (RS): Knit to double stitch and work it as a knit stitch, k3 (4, 4, 5, 5, 6), {6, 7, 7, 8}, turn work.
Short-Row 4 (WS): Make double stitch, purl to end.
Short-Rows 5-14: Repeat Short-Rows 3 and 4 another 5 times.
Next Row (RS): Knit to the end of row, working double stitch as a knit stitch.
Next Row (WS): Purl to the end of the row.

Start shaping neckline and armhole
NOTE: Neck and armhole shaping are worked at the same time; read following section through before proceeding.

Neck Increase Row (RS): K2, Inv-L (see Stitch Guide), knit to end. [1 stitch increased]
Work 1 WS row.
Armhole Decrease Row (RS): Knit to last 4 stitches, SSK, k2. [1 stitch decreased]
Work 1 WS row.

Repeat Neck Increase Row in every **other** RS row another 9 (9, 9, 9, 10, 11), {11, 12, 11, 12} times, then in every RS row 5 (6, 6, 7, 7, 6), {7, 6, 8, 7} times and AT THE SAME TIME work Armhole Decrease Row in every 10 (10, 12, 12, 12, 14), {14, 14, 14, 14}th row 4 times more.
[44 (49, 53, 58, 63, 68), {72, 77, 82, 87} stitches]

NOTE: When working some Armhole Decrease Rows, you will need to work the Neck Increase at the beginning of the same row.

Continue working in Stockinette stitch even until Left Front measures 8 (8¼, 8½, 8¾, 9¼, 9½), {9¾, 10, 10¼, 10½}"/ 20 (20.5, 21.5, 22, 23, 24), {24.5, 25, 25.5, 26.5} cm from cast-on edge, measured along the armhole edge, ending with WS row.

Do not break yarn.

Join Fronts and Back
Joining Row (RS): K44 (49, 53, 58, 63, 68), {72, 77, 82, 87} Left Front Stitches, k88 (98, 106, 116, 126, 136), {144, 154, 164, 174} held Back stitches, k44 (49, 53, 58, 63, 68), {72, 77, 82, 87} Right Front Stitches. [176 (196, 212, 232, 252, 272), {288, 308, 328, 348} stitches]

04 BODY

Work in Stockinette stitch on Body stitches, until piece measures 10 (10, 10, 11, 11, 11), {12, 12, 12, 12}"/ 25 (25, 25, 27.5, 27.5, 27.5), {30, 30, 30, 30} cm from the underarm, ending with WS row.

Change to US 7/4.5 mm circular needle.

Ribbing Row 1 (RS): K1, *k2, p2; repeat from * to last 3 stitches, k3.
Ribbing Row 2 (WS): P3, *k2, p2; repeat from * to last stitch, p1.
Repeat last 2 rows until ribbing measures 2"/5 cm, ending with RS row.

Bind off all stitches in pattern or using Tubular Bind Off method for k2, p2 ribbing in rows (see Special Techniques, page 226).

05 SLEEVES (make 2)

With US 8/5 mm circular needle and your preferred Provisional method, cast on 60 stitches.

Chart Set-Up Row (WS): Work Row 22 (20, 38, 38, 32, 32), {30, 28, 26, 24} of Sleeve Chart.

Continue following the Sleeve Chart and work Rows 23-40 (21-40, 39-40, 39-40, 33-40, 33-40), {31-40, 29-40, 27-40, 25-40} once, then work Rows 1-40 two (2, 2, 2, 3, 3), {3, 3, 3, 3} time(s), then work Rows 1-14 (1-16, 1-40, 1-40, 1-4, 1-4), {1-6, 1-8, 1-10, 1-12} once.

Place live stitches of the last row on hold.
Block sleeve to measurements.

Transfer live stitches from cast on to circular needle and live held stitches to the second circular needle. With right side held together and wrong side out, join the cast on with held stitches, using 3-Needle Bind Off (see Special Techniques, page 226) to create the tube. Turn the tube out, so the RS is outside.

05a. Cuff
With RS facing and US 7/4.5 mm double-pointed needles, beginning at the seam, pick up and knit 75 (75, 80, 85, 90, 90), {90, 95, 100, 100} stitches evenly along the right sleeve opening. Place marker and join in the round.

Next Round: K1, *p3, k2; repeat from * to last 4 stitches, p3, k1.
Decrease Round: K1, *P2TOG, p1, k2; repeat from * to last 4 stitches, P2TOG, p1, k1. [60 (60, 64, 68, 72, 72), {72, 76, 80, 80} stitches]
Next Round: K1, *p2, k2; repeat from * to last 3 stitches, p1, k1.
Repeat last round until cuff measures 6 (6, 6, 6, 6, 5½), {5½, 5, 5, 4½}"/15 (15, 15, 15, 15, 14), {14, 12.5, 12.5, 11.5} cm.

Bind off all stitches in pattern or using the Tubular Bind Off for k2, p2 ribbing in rounds (see Special Techniques, page 226).

06 FINISHING

Sew both sleeves in armholes.

06a. Pockets (make 2)
With US 8/5 mm circular needle cast on 34 stitches.

Next Row (WS): Purl.
Work Rows 1-26 of Pocket Chart.

Increase Row (RS): K2, [p1, k1] 7 times, p1, M1L, [p1, k1] 7 times, p1, k2. [35 stitches]

Change to US 7/4.5 mm circular needles.

Ribbing Row 1 (RS): K2, *p1, k1; repeat from * to last stitch, k1.
Ribbing Row 2 (WS): P2, *k1, p1; repeat from * to last stitch, p1.
Repeat last 2 rows 2 more times, then work 1 RS row. Bind off all stitches in pattern.

If you prefer using the Tubular method, work as follows:

Decrease Row (WS): Work to last 2 stitches, P2TOG. [31 stitch]
Work the Tubular Bind Off for k1, p1 rib (see Special Techniques, page 226),

06b. Collar and Front Bands
NOTE: The ribbing pick-up ratio is approx. 5 stitches per 6 rows. If you're changing the number of pick-up stitches, make sure that the total number of stitches is divisible by 4.

With US 7/4.5 mm 32"/80 cm circular needle and RS facing, beginning at hem edge, pick up and knit 72 (72, 72, 76, 76, 76), {84, 84, 84, 84} stitches to the beginning of the neckline increases, place marker, pick up and knit 58 (60, 62, 62, 64, 66), {68, 68, 70, 72} stitches along the neckline to the shoulder seam, 28 (32, 32, 32, 36, 36), {36, 36, 40, 40} stitches across back neck, 58 (60, 62, 62, 64, 66), {68, 68, 70, 72} stitches down the neckline to the beginning of the neckline increases, place marker, pick up and knit 72 (72, 72, 76, 76, 76), {84, 84, 84, 84} stitches down the left front edge.
[288 (296, 300, 308, 316, 320), {340, 340, 348, 352} stitches]
Next Row (WS): P3, *k2, p2; repeat from * to last stitch, p1.

Next Row (RS): K3, *p2, k2; repeat from * to last stitch, k1.
Next Row (WS): Slip 1 purlwise wyif, p2, *k2, p2; repeat from * to last stitch, slip 1 purlwise wyif.

Repeat last two rows one more time.

Buttonhole Row (RS): Work 6 stitches as established, SSK, [YO] 2 times, *work 14 (14, 14, 14, 14, 14), {18, 18, 18, 18} stitches as established, SSK, [YO] 2 times; repeat from * 3 more times, work in pattern to end.
Next Row (WS): [Work to double YO, knit 1 dropping extra wrap] 5 times, work to end.

Work 4 rows even.

If you do not wish to work a Tubular Bind Off, bind off all stitches in pattern now using your preferred stretchy bind off method.
Bind off all stitches in pattern or using the Tubular Bind Off for k2, p2 ribbing in rows.

Block to measurements, blocking the pockets separately.
Sew pockets to fronts, centering them on each front and aligning cast-on edge of pocket with top of ribbing.
Weave in ends. Sew on buttons.

CHARTS

SLEEVE CHART

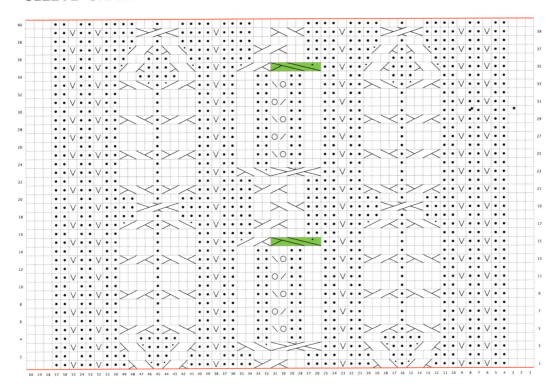

LEGEND

□ **K**: Knit stitch on RS; purl stitch on WS

⊡ **P**: Purl stitch on RS; knit stitch on WS

▣ **YO**: Yarn over

▽ Slip 1 stitch purlwise with yarn in back on RS

◿ **K2TOG**: Knit 2 stitches together – 1 stitch decreased with right slant.

◺ **SSK**: Slip 1 stitch knitwise, slip 1 stitch knitwise, return 2 slipped stitches back to left needle and knit them together through back loops – 1 stitch decreased with left slant

 2/1 RPC: Slip 1 stitch to cable needle, hold in back, k2, p1 from cable needle

 2/1 LPC: Slip 2 stitches to cable needle, hold in front, p1, k2 from cable needle

 2/2 RC: Slip 2 stitches to cable needle, hold in back, knit 2, knit 2 from cable needle

 2/2 LC: Slip 2 stitches to cable needle, hold in front, knit 2, knit 2 from cable needle

2/2 RPC: Slip 2 stitches to cable needle, hold in back, k2, p2 from cable needle

2/2 LPC: Slip 2 stitches to cable needle, hold in front, p2, k2 from cable needle

2/1/2 RPC: Slip next 3 stitches to cable needle and hold in back, k2 from left needle. Slip the purl stitch from cable needle to the left needle, holding the 2 knit stitches on cable needle in back, p1 from the left needle, k2 from cable needle

2/2/2 RPC: Slip next 4 stitches to cable needle and hold in back, k2 from left needle. Slip the 2 purl stitches from cable needle to the left needle, holding the 2 knit stitches on cable needle in back, p2 from the left needle, k2 from cable needle

2/4 LPC: Slip 2 stitches onto cable needle, hold in front, p2, k2, then knit 2 stitches from cable needle.

□ Pattern repeat

POCKET CHART

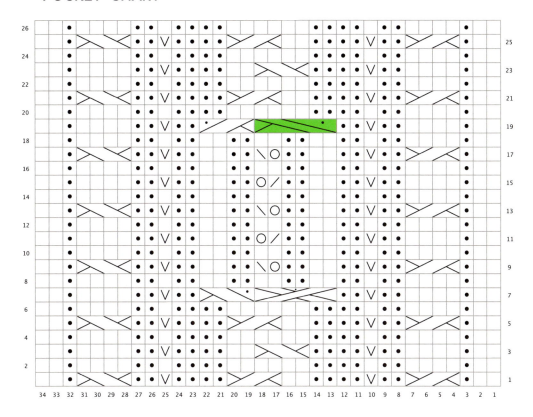

Written instructions for Sleeve Chart

Note: See Chart Legend for special abbreviations. Slip all slipped stitches with yarn in back.

Row 1 (RS): K3, [p2, slip 1] 2 times, p3, 2/1 RPC, p1, 2/1 LPC, p3, slip 1, p4, k2, 2/2 RC, p4, slip 1, p3, 2/1 RPC, p1, 2/1 LPC, p3, [slip 1, p2] 2 times, k3.

Row 2 (WS): P3, [k2, p1] 2 times, [k3, p2] 2 times, k3, p1, k4, p6, k4, p1, [k3, p2] 2 times, k3, [p1, k2] 2 times, p3.

Row 3 (RS): K3, [p2, slip 1] 2 times, p2, 2/1 RPC, p3, 2/1 LPC, p2, slip 1, p2, 2/2/2 RPC, 2/2 LPC, p2, slip 1, p2, 2/1 RPC, p3, 2/1 LPC, [p2, slip 1] 2 times, p2, k3.

Row 4 (WS): P3, [k2, p1] 2 times, k2, p2, k5, p2, k2, p1, [k2, p2] 3 times, k2, p1, k2, p2, k5, p2, k2, [p1, k2] 2 times, p3.

Row 5 (RS): K3, [p2, slip 1] 2 times, p2, 2/2 LC, p1, 2/2 RC, p2, slip 1, p2, k2, p2, YO, SSK, p2, k2, p2, slip 1, p2, 2/2 LC, p1, 2/2 RC, [p2, slip 1] 2 times, p2, k3.

Row 6 (WS): P3, [k2, p1] 2 times, k2, p4, k1, p4, k2, p1, [k2, p2] 3 times, k2, p1, k2, p4, k1, p4, k2, [p1, k2] 2 times, p3.

Row 7 (RS): K3, [p2, slip 1] 2 times, p2, k4, p1, k4, p2, slip 1, p2, k2, p2, K2TOG, YO, p2, k2, p2, slip 1, p2, k4, p1, k4, [p2, slip 1] 2 times, p2, k3.

Row 8 (WS): P3, [k2, p1] 2 times, k2, p4, k1, p4, k2, p1, [k2, p2] 3 times, k2, p1, k2, p4, k1, p4, k2, [p1, k2] 2 times, p3.

Row 9 (RS): K3, [p2, slip 1] 2 times, p2, 2/2 LC, p1, 2/2 RC, p2, slip 1, p2, k2, p2, YO, SSK, p2, k2, p2, slip 1, p2, 2/2 LC, p1, 2/2 RC, [p2, slip 1] 2 times, p2, k3.

Rows 10 - 13: Repeat rows 6 - 9.

Row 14 (WS): P3, [k2, p1] 2 times, k2, p4, k1, p4, k2, p1, [k2, p2] 3 times, k2, p1, k2, p4, k1, p4, k2, [p1, k2] 2 times, p3.

Row 15 (RS): K3, [p2, slip 1] 2 times, p2, k4, p1, k4, p2, slip 1, p2, 2/4 LPC, 2/2 RPC, p2, slip 1, p2, k4, p1, k4, [p2, slip 1] 2 times, p2, k3.

Row 16 (WS): P3, [k2, p1] 2 times, k2, p4, k1, p4, k2, p1, k4, p6, k4, p1, k2, p4, k1, p4, k2, [p1, k2] 2 times, p3.
Row 17 (RS): K3, [p2, slip 1] 2 times, p2, 2/2 LPC, p1, 2/2 RPC, p2, slip 1, p4, k2, 2/2 RC, p4, slip 1, p2, 2/2 LPC, p1, 2/2 RPC, [p2, slip 1] 2 times, p2, k3.
Row 18 (WS): P3, [k2, p1] 2 times, k4, p2, k1, p2, k4, p1, k4, p6, k4, p1, k4, p2, k1, p2, k4, [p1, k2] 2 times, p3.

Row 19 (RS): K3, [p2, slip 1] 2 times, p4, 2/1/2 RPC, p4, slip 1, p4, 2/2 LC, k2, p4, slip 1, p4, 2/1/2 RPC, p4, [slip 1, p2] 2 times, k3.
Row 20 (WS): P3, [k2, p1] 2 times, k4, p2, k1, p2, k4, p1, k4, p6, k4, p1, k4, p2, k1, p2, k4, [p1, k2] 2 times, p3.
Row 21 (RS): K3, [p2, slip 1] 2 times, p2, 2/2 RC, p1, 2/2 LC, p2, slip 1, p4, k2, 2/2 RC, p4, slip 1, p2, 2/2 RC, p1, 2/2 LC, [p2, slip 1] 2 times, p2, k3.
Row 22 (WS): P3, [k2, p1] 2 times, k2, p4, k1, p4, k2, p1, k4, p6, k4, p1, k2, p4, k1, p4, k2, [p1, k2] 2 times, p3.
Row 23 (RS): K3, [p2, slip 1] 2 times, p2, k4, p1, k4, p2, slip 1, p2, 2/2/2 RPC, 2/2 LPC, p2, slip 1, p2, k4, p1, k4, [p2, slip 1] 2 times, p2, k3.
Row 24 (WS): P3, [k2, p1] 2 times, k2, p4, k1, p4, k2, p1, [k2, p2] 3 times, k2, p1, k2, p4, k1, p4, k2, [p1, k2] 2 times, p3.
Row 25 (RS): K3, [p2, slip 1] 2 times, p2, 2/2 RC, p1, 2/2 LC, p2, slip 1, p2, k2, p2, YO, SSK, p2, k2, p2, slip 1, p2, 2/2 RC, p1, 2/2 LC, [p2, slip 1] 2 times, p2, k3.
Row 26 (WS): P3, [k2, p1] 2 times, k2, p4, k1, p4, k2, p1, [k2, p2] 3 times, k2, p1, k2, p4, k1, p4, k2, [p1, k2] 2 times, p3.
Row 27 (RS): K3, [p2, slip 1] 2 times, p2, k4, p1, k4, p2, slip 1, p2, k2, p2, K2TOG, YO, p2, k2, p2, slip 1, p2, k4, p1, k4, [p2, slip 1] 2 times, p2, k3.
Rows 28 - 31: Repeat rows 24 - 27.
Row 32 (WS): P3, [k2, p1] 2 times, k2, p4, k1, p4, k2, p1, [k2, p2] 3 times, k2, p1, k2, p4, k1, p4, k2, [p1, k2] 2 times, p3.
Row 33 (RS): K3, [p2, slip 1] 2 times, p2, 2/2 RPC, p1, 2/2 LPC, p2, slip 1, p2, k2, p2, YO, SSK, p2, k2, p2, slip 1, p2, 2/2 RPC, p1, 2/2 LPC, [p2, slip 1] 2 times, p2, k3.
Row 34 (WS): P3, [k2, p1] 2 times, k2, p2, k5, p2, k2, p1, [k2, p2] 3 times, k2, p1, k2, p2, k5, p2, k2, [p1, k2] 2 times, p3.
Row 35 (RS): K3, [p2, slip 1] 2 times, p2, 2/1 LPC, p3, 2/1 RPC, p2, slip 1, p2, 2/4 LPC, 2/2 RPC, p2, slip 1, p2, 2/1 LPC, p3, 2/1 RPC, [p2, slip 1] 2 times, p2, k3.

Row 36 (WS): P3, [k2, p1] 2 times, [k3, p2] 2 times, k3, p1, k4, p6, k4, p1, [k3, p2] 2 times, k3, [p1, k2] 2 times, p3.
Row 37 (RS): K3, [p2, slip 1] 2 times, p3, 2/1 LPC, p1, 2/1 RPC, p3, slip 1, p4, k2, 2/2 RC, p4, slip 1, p3, 2/1 LPC, p1, 2/1 RPC, p3, [slip 1, p2] 2 times, k3.
Row 38 (WS): P3, [k2, p1] 2 times, k4, p2, k1, p2, k4, p1, k4, p6, k4, p1, k4, p2, k1, p2, k4, [p1, k2] 2 times, p3.
Row 39 (RS): K3, [p2, slip 1] 2 times, p4, 2/1/2 RPC, p4, slip 1, p4, 2/2 LC, k2, p4, slip 1, p4, 2/1/2 RPC, p4, [slip 1, p2] 2 times, k3.
Row 40 (WS): P3, [k2, p1] 2 times, k4, p2, k1, p2, k4, p1, k4, p6, k4, p1, k4, p2, k1, p2, k4, [p1, k2] 2 times, p3.

Written instructions for Pocket Chart

Note: See Chart Legend for special abbreviations.
Slip all slipped stitches with yarn in back.

Row 1 (RS): K2, p1, 2/2 RC, p2, slip 1, p4, k2, 2/2 RC, p4, slip 1, p2, 2/2 LC, p1, k2.
Row 2 (WS): P2, k1, p4, k2, p1, k4, p6, k4, p1, k2, p4, k1, p2.
Row 3 (RS): K2, p1, k4, p2, slip 1, p4, 2/2 LC, k2, p4, slip 1, p2, k4, p1, k2.
Row 4 (WS): P2, k1, p4, k2, p1, k4, p6, k4, p1, k2, p4, k1, p2.
Row 5 (RS): K2, p1, 2/2 RC, p2, slip 1, p4, k2, 2/2 RC, p4, slip 1, p2, 2/2 LC, p1, k2.
Row 6 (WS): P2, k1, p4, k2, p1, k4, p6, k4, p1, k2, p4, k1, p2.
Row 7 (RS): K2, p1, k4, p2, slip 1, p2, 2/2/2 RPC, 2/2 LPC, p2, slip 1, p2, k4, p1, k2.
Row 8 (WS): P2, k1, p4, k2, p1, [k2, p2] 3 times, k2, p1, k2, p4, k1, p2.
Row 9 (RS): K2, p1, 2/2 RC, p2, slip 1, p2, k2, p2, YO, SSK, p2, k2, p2, slip 1, p2, 2/2 LC, p1, k2.
Row 10 (WS): P2, k1, p4, k2, p1, [k2, p2] 3 times, k2, p1, k2, p4, k1, p2.
Row 11 (RS): K2, p1, k4, p2, slip 1, p2, k2, p2, K2TOG, YO, p2, k2, p2, slip 1, p2, k4, p1, k2.
Row 12 (WS): P2, k1, p4, k2, p1, [k2, p2] 3 times, k2, p1, k2, p4, k1, p2.
Rows 13 - 16: Repeat rows 9 - 12.
Row 16 (WS): P2, k1, p4, k2, p1, [k2, p2] 3 times, k2, p1, k2, p4, k1, p2.

Row 17 (RS): K2, p1, 2/2 RC, p2, slip 1, p2, k2, p2, YO, SSK, p2, k2, p2, slip 1, p2, 2/2 LC, p1, k2.

Row 18 (WS): P2, k1, p4, k2, p1, [k2, p2] 3 times, k2, p1, k2, p4, k1, p2.

Row 19 (RS): K2, p1, k4, p2, slip 1, p2, 2/4 LPC, 2/2 RPC, p2, slip 1, p2, k4, p1, k2.

Row 20 (WS): P2, k1, p4, k2, p1, k4, p6, k4, p1, k2, p4, k1, p2.

Rows 21 - 26: Repeat rows 1 - 6.

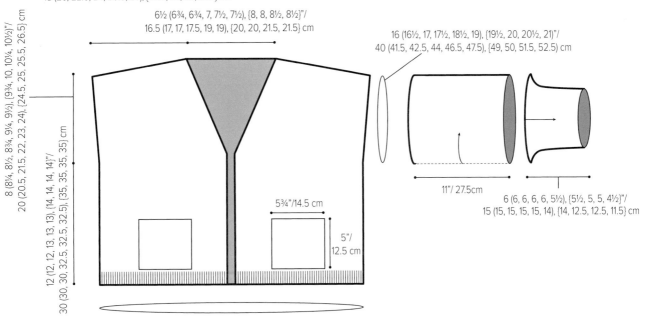

7¼ (8, 9, 9½, 10½, 11½), {12¼, 13¼, 14, 15}"/
18 (20, 22.5, 24, 26.5, 29), {30.5, 33, 35, 37.5} cm

6½ (6¾, 6¾, 7, 7½, 7½), {8, 8, 8½, 8½}"/
16.5 (17, 17, 17.5, 19, 19), {20, 20, 21.5, 21.5} cm

16 (16½, 17, 17½, 18½, 19), {19½, 20, 20½, 21}"/
40 (41.5, 42.5, 44, 46.5, 47.5), {49, 50, 51.5, 52.5} cm

8 (8¼, 8½, 8¾, 9¼, 9½), {9¾, 10, 10¼, 10½}"/
20 (20.5, 21.5, 22, 23, 24), {24.5, 25, 25.5, 26.5} cm

12 (12, 12, 13, 13, 13), {14, 14, 14, 14}"/
30 (30, 30, 32.5, 32.5, 32.5), {35, 35, 35, 35} cm

5¾"/14.5 cm

5"/
12.5 cm

11"/ 27.5cm

6 (6, 6, 6, 6, 5½), {5½, 5, 5, 4½}"/
15 (15, 15, 15, 15, 14), {14, 12.5, 12.5, 11.5} cm

38½ (42¾, 46, 50½, 54½, 58¾), {62, 66½, 70½, 74¾}"/
96.5 (107, 115, 126.5, 136.5, 147), {155, 166.5, 176.5, 187} cm

Holwick

This wrap is worked from the center outward, beginning with a provisional cast-on that allows the fabric to grow symmetrically toward both ends. The body is shaped in soothing, simple stitches that set the stage for the dramatic finishes: large, angular motifs of diamond lace that unfold at each end like facets of crystal.

The lace panels bring striking geometry and lightness to the design, their openwork contrasting beautifully with the solid center section. To complete the piece, the stitches are finished with a delicate picot bind-off, adding a refined edge that softens the boldness of the lace.

Finished Measurements
72"/180 cm length.
18¾"/47.5 cm width.
Measurements are taken after blocking.

Yarn
Fingering weight yarn (approximate amount): 1150 yds/1047 m.

Miss Babs Caroline (70% Superwash Merino Wool, 20% Cashmere, 10% Nylon; 400 yards/365 m in 3.3 oz/95 g); Provence: 3 skeins.

Needles
Size US 4/3.5 mm circular needle 24-32"/60-80 cm long, or size to obtain gauge.
While gauge is not critical for this project, the different gauge can affect the size and overall yardage.

Notions
Stitch markers, waste yarn, tapestry needle.

Gauge
25 stitches and 30 rows = 4"/10 cm in Stockinette stitch or charted pattern, blocked.

Notes
- The wrap is worked flat, back and forth in rows; a circular needle is used to accommodate the large number of stitches.
- Read odd-numbered chart rows from right to left, and even-numbered rows from left to right.

DIRECTIONS

01 FIRST HALF

With US 4/3.5 mm needles and waste yarn, cast on 117 stitches. Break waste yarn.

Next Row (RS): With working yarn, knit into cast-on 117 stitches.

Next Row (WS): K2, place marker, purl to last 2 stitches, place marker, k2.

Set-Up Row 1 (RS): K2, slip marker, *p1, k7; repeat from * to last 3 stitches, p1, slip marker, k2.

Set-Up Row 2 (WS): K2, slip marker, purl to last 2 stitches, slip marker, k2.

Repeat last 2 rows until piece measures 14"/35 cm from cast-on edge.

01a. Lace Section 1

NOTE: If following written instructions for charts, work as follows:

Chart 1 Set-Up Row 1 (RS): K2, slip marker, work Row 1 of written instructions to marker, slip marker, k2.

Continue following the written instructions throughout.

Chart 1 Set-Up Row 1 (RS): K2, slip marker, work Row 1 of Chart 1 as follows: repeat stitches 1-8 total of 5 times, work stitches 9-41, then repeat stitches 42-49 total of 5 times, slip marker, k2.

Continue following the Chart 1 through Row 26.

01b. Lace Section 2

Chart 2 Set-Up Row 1 (RS): K2, slip marker, work Row 1 of Chart 2 as follows: repeat stitches 1-8 total of 3 times, work stitches 9-24, repeat stitches 25-40 total of 2 times, then work stitches 41-57, repeat stitches 58-65 total of 3 times, slip marker, k2.

Continue following the Chart 2 through Row 28.

01c. Lace Section 3

Chart 3 Set-Up Row 1 (RS): K2, slip marker, work Row 1 of Chart 3 as follows: work stitches 1-24, repeat stitches 25-40 total of 4 times, then work stitches 41-65, slip marker, k2.

Continue following the Chart 3 through Row 28.

01d. Lace Section 4

Chart 4 Set-Up Row 1 (RS): K2, slip marker, work Row 1 of Chart 3 as follows: work stitches 1-8, repeat stitches 9-24 total of 6 times, then work stitches 25-33, slip marker, k2.

Continue following the Chart 4 through Row 26.

With Right Side facing, bind off all stitches, using Picot Bind Off as follows:

Step 1: Cast on 2 stitches, using Knitted method (*insert right needle into the 1st stitch on the left needle, yarn over, pull this loop through and slip it onto left needle without slipping off the 1st stitch; repeat from * once more).

Step 2: Bind off 4 stitches.

Step 3: Slide the stitch on the right needle to the left needle.

Repeat Steps 1-3 until 1 stitch remains. Bind off remaining stitch.

02 SECOND HALF

Carefully unravel waste yarn from the cast-on and place 117 live stitches onto US 4/3.5 mm needles. Join working yarn, ready to work RS row.

Set-Up Row 1 (RS): K2, place marker, *p1, k7; repeat from * to last 3 stitches, p1, place marker, k2.

Set-Up Row 2 (WS): K2, slip marker, purl to last 2 stitches, slip marker, k2.

Repeat last 2 rows until piece measures 14"/35 cm from cast-on edge.

Continue working on Lace pattern as for First Half.

03 FINISHING

Weave in ends. Block to measurements.

CHARTS

CHART 1

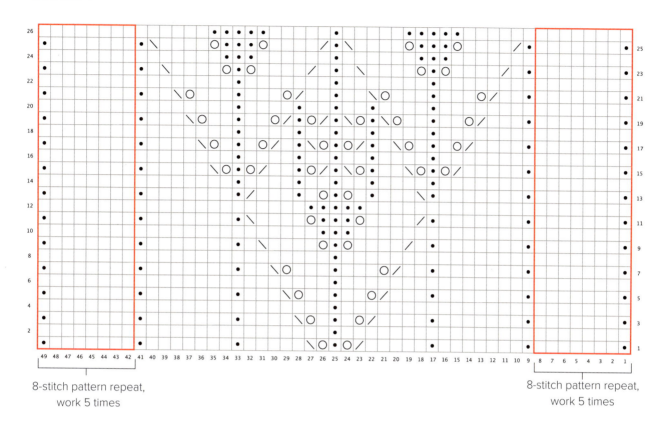

8-stitch pattern repeat,
work 5 times

8-stitch pattern repeat,
work 5 times

LEGEND

☐ **K**: Knit stitch on RS; purl stitch on WS

● **P**: Purl stitch on RS; knit stitch on WS

Ⓞ **YO**: Yarn over

◢ **K2TOG**: Knit 2 stitches together –
1 stitch decreased with right slant

◣ **SSK**: Slip 1 stitch knitwise, slip 1 stitch knitwise,
return 2 slipped stitches back to left needle
and knit them together through back loops –
1 stitch decreased with left slant

CHART 2

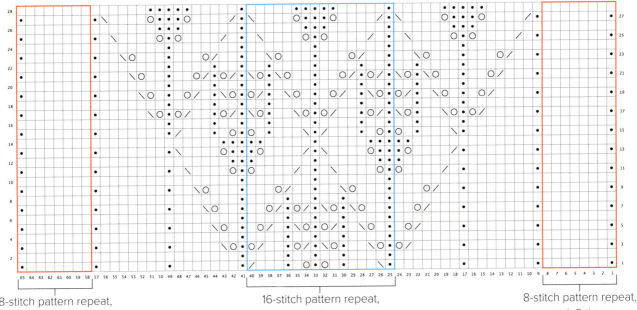

8-stitch pattern repeat,
work 3 times

16-stitch pattern repeat,
work 2 times

8-stitch pattern repeat,
work 3 times

CHART 3

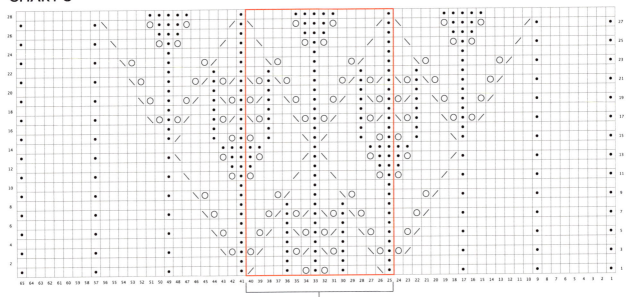

16-stitch pattern repeat,
work 4 times

LEGEND

☐ **K**: Knit stitch on RS; purl stitch on WS

• **P**: Purl stitch on RS; knit stitch on WS

Ⓞ **YO**: Yarn over

◪ **K2TOG**: Knit 2 stitches together –
1 stitch decreased with right slant

◩ **SSK**: Slip 1 stitch knitwise, slip 1 stitch knitwise,
return 2 slipped stitches back to left needle
and knit them together through back loops –
1 stitch decreased with left slant

CHART 4

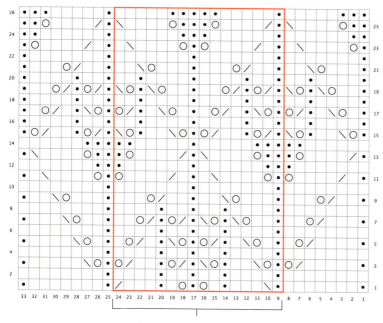

16-stitch pattern repeat,
work 6 times

Written instructions for Chart 1

Note: See Chart Legend for special abbreviations.

Row 1 (RS): [P1, k7] 6 times, p1, k5, K2TOG, YO, p1, YO, SSK, k5, p1, [k7, p1] 6 times.
Row 2 (WS): P56, k1, p56.
Row 3 (RS): [P1, k7] 6 times, p1, k4, K2TOG, YO, k1, p1, k1, YO, SSK, k4, p1, [k7, p1] 6 times.
Row 4 (WS): P56, k1, p56.
Row 5 (RS): [P1, k7] 6 times, p1, k3, K2TOG, YO, k2, p1, k2, YO, SSK, k3, p1, [k7, p1] 6 times.
Row 6 (WS): P56, k1, p56.
Row 7 (RS): [P1, k7] 6 times, p1, k2, K2TOG, YO, k3, p1, k3, YO, SSK, k2, p1, [k7, p1] 6 times.
Row 8 (WS): P56, k1, p56.
Row 9 (RS): [P1, k7] 6 times, p1, k1, K2TOG, k4, YO, p1, YO, k4, SSK, k1, p1, [k7, p1] 6 times.
Row 10 (WS): P55, k3, p55.
Row 11 (RS): [P1, k7] 6 times, p1, K2TOG, k4, YO, p3, YO, k4, SSK, p1, [k7, p1] 6 times.
Row 12 (WS): P54, k5, p54.
Row 13 (RS): [P1, k7] 6 times, p1, SSK, k3, p1, k1, YO, p1, YO, k1, p1, k3, K2TOG, p1, [k7, p1] 6 times.

Row 14 (WS): P48, k1, p4, [k1, p2] 2 times, k1, p4, k1, p48.
Row 15 (RS): [P1, k7] 5 times, p1, k5, K2TOG, YO, p1, YO, SSK, k2, p1, YO, SSK, p1, K2TOG, YO, p1, k2, K2TOG, YO, p1, YO, SSK, k5, p1, [k7, p1] 5 times.
Row 16 (WS): P48, k1, p4, [k1, p2] 2 times, k1, p4, k1, p48.
Row 17 (RS): [P1, k7] 5 times, p1, k4, K2TOG, YO, k1, p1, k1, YO, SSK, k1, p1, K2TOG, YO, p1, YO, SSK, p1, k1, K2TOG, YO, k1, p1, k1, YO, SSK, k4, p1, [k7, p1] 5 times.
Row 18 (WS): P48, k1, p4, [k1, p2] 2 times, k1, p4, k1, p48.
Row 19 (RS): [P1, k7] 5 times, p1, k3, K2TOG, YO, k2, p1, k2, [YO, SSK, p1] 2 times, K2TOG, YO, p1, K2TOG, YO, k2, p1, k2, YO, SSK, k3, p1, [k7, p1] 5 times.
Row 20 (WS): P48, k1, p4, [k1, p2] 2 times, k1, p4, k1, p48.
Row 21 (RS): [P1, k7] 5 times, [p1, k2, K2TOG, YO, k3, p1, k3, YO, SSK, k2] 2 times, p1, [k7, p1] 5 times.
Row 22 (WS): P48, [k1, p7] 2 times, k1, p48.
Row 23 (RS): [P1, k7] 5 times, [p1, k1, K2TOG, k4, YO, p1, YO, k4, SSK, k1] 2 times, p1, [k7, p1] 5 times.
Row 24 (WS): P47, k3, p6, k1, p6, k3, p47.

Row 25 (RS): [P1, k7] 5 times, [p1, K2TOG, k4, YO, p3, YO, k4, SSK] 2 times, p1, [k7, p1] 5 times.
Row 26 (WS): P46, k5, p5, k1, p5, k5, p46.

Written instructions for Chart 2

Row 1 (RS): [P1, k7] 5 times, *p1, SSK, k3, p1, k1, yo, p1, YO, k1, p1, k3, K2TOG; repeat from * once, p1, [k7, p1] 5 times.
Row 2 (WS): P40, k1, *p4, [k1, p2] 2 times, k1, p4, k1; repeat from * once, p40.
Row 3 (RS): [P1, k7] 4 times, p1, k5, K2TOG, YO, *p1, yo, SSK, k2, p1, YO, SSK, p1, K2TOG, YO, p1, k2, K2TOG, YO; repeat from * once, p1, YO, SSK, k5, p1, [k7, p1] 4 times.
Row 4 (WS): P40, k1, *p4, [k1, p2] 2 times, k1, p4, k1; repeat from * once, p40.
Row 5 (RS): [P1, k7] 4 times, p1, k7, p1, k4, K2TOG, YO, k1, *p1, k1, YO, SSK, k1, p1, K2TOG, YO, p1, YO, SSK, p1, k1, K2TOG, YO, k1; repeat from * once, p1, k1, YO, SSK, k4, p1, [k7, p1] 4 times.
Row 6 (WS): P40, k1, *p4, [k1, p2] 2 times, k1, p4, k1; repeat from * once, p40.
Row 7 (RS): [P1, k7] 4 times, p1, k3, K2TOG, YO, k2, *p1, k2, [YO, SSK, p1] 2 times, K2TOG, YO, p1, K2TOG, YO, k2; repeat from * once, p1, k2, YO, SSK, k3, p1, [k7, p1] 4 times.
Row 8 (WS): P40, k1, *p4, [k1, p2] 2 times, k1, p4, k1; repeat from * once, p40.
Row 9 (RS): [P1, k7] 4 times, p1, k7, p1, k2, K2TOG, YO, k3, *p1, k3, YO, SSK, k2, p1, k2, K2TOG, YO, k3; repeat from * once, p1, k3, YO, SSK, k2, p1, [k7, p1] 4 times.
Row 10 (WS): P40, k1, [p7, k1] 4 times, p40.
Row 11 (RS): [P1, k7] 4 times, p1, k1, K2TOG, k4, YO, *p1, YO, k4, SSK, k1, p1, k1, K2TOG, k4, YO; repeat from * once, p1, YO, k4, SSK, k1, p1, [k7, p1] 4 times.
Row 12 (WS): P39, k2, *[k1, p6] 2 times, k2; repeat from * once, k1, p39.
Row 13 (RS): [P1, k7] 4 times, p1, k7, p1, K2TOG, k4, YO, p1, *p2, YO, k4, SSK, p1, K2TOG, k4, YO, p1; repeat from * once, p2, YO, k4, SSK, p1, [k7, p1] 4 times.
Row 14 (WS): P38, k3, *k2, p5, k1, p5, k3; repeat from * once, k2, p38.
Row 15 (RS): [P1, k7] 4 times, p1, SSK, k3, p1, k1, YO, *p1, YO, k1, p1, k3, K2TOG, p1, SSK, k3, p1, k1, YO; repeat from * once, p1, YO, k1, p1, k3, K2TOG, p1, [k7, p1] 4 times.

Row 16 (WS): P32, k1, p4, k1, p2, k1, *p2, [k1, p4] 2 times, k1, p2, k1; repeat from * once, p2, k1, p4, k1, p32.
Row 17 (RS): [P1, k7] 3 times, p1, k5, K2TOG, YO, p1, YO, SSK, k2, p1, YO, SSK, *p1, K2TOG, YO, p1, k2, K2TOG, YO, p1, YO, SSK, k2, p1, YO, SSK; repeat from * once, p1, K2TOG, YO, p1, k2, K2TOG, YO, p1, YO, SSK, k5, p1, [k7, p1] 3 times.
Row 18 (WS): P32, k1, p4, k1, p2, k1, *p2, [k1, p4] 2 times, k1, p2, k1; repeat from * once, p2, k1, p4, k1, p32.
Row 19 (RS): [P1, k7] 3 times, p1, k4, K2TOG, YO, k1, p1, k1, YO, SSK, k1, p1, K2TOG, YO, *p1, YO, SSK, p1, k1, K2TOG, YO, k1, p1, k1, YO, SSK, k1, p1, K2TOG, YO; repeat from * once, p1, YO, SSK, p1, k1, K2TOG, YO, k1, p1, k1, YO, SSK, k4, p1, [k7, p1] 3 times.
Row 20 (WS): P32, k1, p4, k1, p2, k1, *p2, [k1, p4] 2 times, k1, p2, k1; repeat from * once, p2, k1, p4, k1, p32.
Row 21 (RS): [P1, k7] 3 times, p1, k3, K2TOG, YO, k2, p1, k2, YO, SSK, p1, YO, SSK, *[p1, K2TOG, YO] 2 times, k2, p1, k2, YO, SSK, p1, YO, SSK; repeat from * once, [p1, K2TOG, YO] 2 times, k2, p1, k2, YO, SSK, k3, p1, [k7, p1] 3 times.
Row 22 (WS): P32, k1, p4, k1, p2, k1, *p2, [k1, p4] 2 times, k1, p2, k1; repeat from * once, p2, k1, p4, k1, p32.
Row 23 (RS): [P1, k7] 3 times, p1, k2, K2TOG, YO, k3, p1, k3, YO, SSK, k2, *p1, k2, K2TOG, YO, k3, p1, k3, YO, SSK, k2; repeat from * once, p1, k2, K2TOG, YO, k3, p1, k3, YO, SSK, k2, p1, [k7, p1] 3 times.
Row 24 (WS): P32, k1, [p7, k1] 6 times, p32.
Row 25 (RS): [P1, k7] 3 times, p1, k1, K2TOG, k4, YO, p1, YO, k4, SSK, k1, *p1, k1, K2TOG, k4, YO, p1, YO, k4, SSK, k1; repeat from * once, p1, k1, K2TOG, k4, YO, p1, YO, k4, SSK, k1, p1, [k7, p1] 3 times.
Row 26 (WS): P31, k3, p6, k1, *p6, k3, p6, k1; repeat from * once, p6, k3, p31.
Row 27 (RS): [P1, k7] 3 times, p1, K2TOG, k4, YO, p3, YO, k4, SSK, *p1, K2TOG, k4, YO, p3, YO, k4, SSK; repeat from * once, p1, K2TOG, k4, YO, p3, YO, k4, SSK, p1, [k7, p1] 3 times.
Row 28 (WS): P30, k5, p5, k1, *p5, k5, p5, k1; repeat from * once, p5, k5, p30.

Written instructions for Chart 3

Row 1 (RS): [P1, k7] 3 times, *p1, SSK, k3, p1, k1, YO, p1, YO, k1, p1, k3, K2TOG; repeat from * 3 times, [p1, k7] 3 times, p1.
Row 2 (WS): P24, k1, *p4, [k1, p2] 2 times, k1, p4, k1; repeat from * 3 times, p24.
Row 3 (RS): [P1, k7] 2 times, p1, k5, K2TOG, YO, *p1, YO, SSK, k2, p1, YO, SSK, p1, K2TOG, YO, p1, k2, K2TOG, YO; repeat from * 3 times, p1, YO, SSK, k5, [p1, k7] 2 times, p1.
Row 4 (WS): P24, k1, *p4, [k1, p2] 2 times, k1, p4, k1; repeat from * 3 times, p24.
Row 5 (RS): [P1, k7] 2 times, p1, k4, K2TOG, YO, k1, *p1, k1, YO, SSK, k1, p1, K2TOG, YO, p1, YO, SSK, p1, k1, K2TOG, YO, k1; repeat from * 3 times, p1, k1, YO, SSK, k4, [p1, k7] 2 times, p1.
Row 6 (WS): P24, k1, *p4, [k1, p2] 2 times, k1, p4, k1; repeat from * 3 times, p24.
Row 7 (RS): [P1, k7] 2 times, p1, k3, K2TOG, YO, k2, *p1, k2, [YO, SSK, p1] 2 times, K2TOG, YO, p1, K2TOG, YO, k2; repeat from * 3 times, p1, k2, YO, SSK, k3, [p1, k7] 2 times, p1.
Row 8 (WS): P24, k1, *p4, [k1, p2] 2 times, k1, p4, k1; repeat from * 3 times, p24.
Row 9 (RS): [P1, k7] 2 times, p1, k2, K2TOG, YO, k3, *p1, k3, YO, SSK, k2, p1, k2, K2TOG, YO, k3; repeat from * 3 times, p1, k3, YO, SSK, k2, [p1, k7] 2 times, p1.
Row 10 (WS): P24, k1, [p1, k7] 8 times, p24.
Row 11 (RS): [P1, k7] 2 times, p1, k1, K2TOG, k4, YO, *p1, YO, k4, SSK, k1, p1, k1, K2TOG, k4, YO; repeat from * 3 times, p1, YO, k4, SSK, k1, [p1, k7] 2 times, p1.
Row 12 (WS): P23, k2, *[k1, p6] 2 times, k2; repeat from * 3 times, k1, p23.
Row 13 (RS): [P1, k7] 2 times, p1, K2TOG, k4, YO, p1, *p2, YO, k4, SSK, p1, K2TOG, k4, YO, p1; repeat from * 3 times, p2, YO, k4, SSK, [p1, k7] 2 times, p1.
Row 14 (WS): P22, k3, *k2, p5, k1, p5, k3; repeat from * 3 times, k2, p22.
Row 15 (RS): [P1, k7] 2 times, p1, SSK, k3, p1, k1, YO, *p1, YO, k1, p1, k3, K2TOG, p1, SSK, k3, p1, k1, YO; repeat from * 3 times, p1, YO, k1, p1, k3, K2TOG, [p1, k7] 2 times, p1.
Row 16 (WS): P16, k1, p4, k1, p2, k1, *p2, [k1, p4] 2 times, k1, p2, k1; repeat from * 3 times, p2, k1, p4, k1, p16.

Row 17 (RS): P1, k7, p1, k5, K2TOG, YO, p1, YO, SSK, k2, p1, YO, SSK, *p1, K2TOG, YO, p1, k2, K2TOG, YO, p1, YO, SSK, k2, p1, YO, SSK; repeat from * 3 times, p1, K2TOG, YO, p1, k2, K2TOG, YO, p1, YO, SSK, k5, p1, k7, p1.
Row 18 (WS): P16, k1, p4, k1, p2, k1, *p2, [k1, p4] 2 times, k1, p2, k1; repeat from * 3 times, p2, k1, p4, k1, p16.
Row 19 (RS): P1, k7, p1, k4, K2TOG, YO, k1, p1, k1, YO, SSK, k1, p1, K2TOG, YO, *p1, YO, SSK, p1, k1, K2TOG, YO, k1, p1, k1, yo, SSK, k1, p1, K2TOG, YO; repeat from * 3 times, p1, YO, SSK, p1, k1, K2TOG, YO, k1, p1, k1, YO, SSK, k4, p1, k7, p1.
Row 20 (WS): P16, k1, p4, k1, p2, k1, *p2, [k1, p4] 2 times, k1, p2, k1; repeat from * 3 times, p2, k1, p4, k1, p16.
Row 21 (RS): P1, k7, p1, k3, K2TOG, YO, k2, p1, k2, YO, SSK, p1, YO, SSK, *[p1, k2tog, YO] 2 times, k2, p1, k2, YO, SSK, p1, YO, SSK; repeat from * 3 times, [p1, K2TOG, YO] 2 times, k2, p1, k2, YO, SSK, k3, p1, k7, p1.
Row 22 (WS): P16, k1, p4, k1, p2, k1, *p2, [k1, p4] 2 times, k1, p2, k1; repeat from * 3 times, p2, k1, p4, k1, p16.
Row 23 (RS): P1, k7, *p1, k2, K2TOG, YO, k3, p1, k3, YO, SSK, k2; repeat from * 5 times, p1, k7, p1.
Row 24 (WS): P16, k1, [p7, k1] 10 times, p16.
Row 25 (RS): P1, k7, *p1, k1, K2TOG, k4, YO, p1, YO, k4, SSK, k1; repeat from * 5 times, p1, k7, p1.
Row 26 (WS): P15, k3, p6, k1, *p6, k3, p6, k1; repeat from * 3 times, p6, k3, p15.
Row 27 (RS): P1, k7, *p1, K2TOG, k4, YO, p3, YO, k4, SSK; repeat from * 5 times, p1, k7, p1.
Row 28 (WS): P14, k5, p5, k1, *p5, k5, p5, k1; repeat from * 3 times, p5, k5, p14.

Written instructions for Chart 4

Row 1 (RS): P1, k7, *p1, SSK, k3, p1, k1, YO, p1, YO, k1, p1, k3, K2TOG; repeat from * 5 times, p1, k7, p1.
Row 2 (WS): P8, k1, *p4, [k1, p2] 2 times, k1, p4, k1; repeat from * 5 times, p8.
Row 3 (RS): P1, k5, K2TOG, YO, *p1, YO, SSK, k2, p1, YO, SSK, p1, K2TOG, YO, p1, k2, K2TOG, YO; repeat from * 5 times, p1, YO, SSK, k5, p1.
Row 4 (WS): P8, k1, *p4, [k1, p2] 2 times, k1, p4, k1; repeat from * 5 times, p8.

Row 5 (RS): P1, k4, K2TOG, YO, k1, *p1, k1, YO, SSK, k1, p1, K2TOG, YO, p1, YO, SSK, p1, k1, K2TOG, YO, k1; repeat from * 5 times, p1, k1, YO, SSK, k4, p1.

Row 6 (WS): P8, k1, *p4, [k1, p2] 2 times, k1, p4, k1; repeat from * 5 times, p8.

Row 7 (RS): P1, k3, K2TOG, YO, k2, *p1, k2, [YO, SSK, p1] 2 times, K2TOG, YO, p1, K2TOG, YO, k2; repeat from * 5 times, p1, k2, YO, SSK, k3, p1.

Row 8 (WS): P8, k1, *p4, [k1, p2] 2 times, k1, p4, k1; repeat from * 5 times, p8.

Row 9 (RS): P1, k2, K2TOG, YO, k3, *p1, k3, YO, SSK, k2, p1, k2, K2TOG, YO, k3; repeat from * 5 times, p1, k3, YO, SSK, k2, p1.

Row 10 (WS): P8, k1, [p7, k1] 12 times, p8.

Row 11 (RS): P1, k1, K2TOG, k4, YO, *p1, YO, k4, SSK, k1, p1, k1, K2TOG, k4, YO; repeat from * 5 times, p1, YO, k4, SSK, k1, p1.

Row 12 (WS): P7, k2, *[k1, p6] 2 times, k2 ; repeat from * 5 times, k1, p7.

Row 13 (RS): P1, K2TOG, k4, YO, p1, *p2, YO, k4, SSK, p1, K2TOG, k4, YO, p1; repeat from * 5 times, p2, YO, k4, SSK, p1.

Row 14 (WS): P6, k3, *k2, p5, k1, p5, k3; repeat from * 5 times, k2, p6.

Row 15 (RS): P1, YO, SSK, k2, p1, YO, SSK, *p1, K2TOG, YO, p1, k2, K2TOG, YO, p1, YO, SSK, k2, p1, YO, SSK; repeat from * 5 times, p1, K2TOG, YO, p1, k2, K2TOG, YO, p1.

Row 16 (WS): K1, p4, k1, p2, k1, *p2, [k1, p4] 2 times, k1, p2, k1; repeat from * 5 times, p2, k1, p4, k1.

Row 17 (RS): P1, k1, YO, SSK, k1, p1, K2TOG, YO, *p1, YO, SSK, p1, k1, K2TOG, YO, k1, p1, k1, YO, SSK, k1, p1, K2TOG, YO; repeat from * 5 times, p1, YO, SSK, p1, k1, K2TOG, YO, k1, p1.

Row 18 (WS): K1, p4, k1, p2, k1, *p2, [k1, p4] 2 times, k1, p2, k1; repeat from * 5 times, p2, k1, p4, k1.

Row 19 (RS): P1, k2, YO, SSK, p1, YO, SSK, *[p1, K2TOG, YO] 2 times, k2, p1, k2, YO, SSK, p1, YO, SSK; repeat from * 5 times, [p1, K2TOG, YO] 2 times, k2, p1.

Row 20 (WS): K1, p4, k1, p2, k1, *p2, [k1, p4] 2 times, k1, p2, k1; repeat from * 5 times, p2, k1, p4, k1.

Row 21 (RS): P1, k3, YO, SSK, k2, *p1, k2, K2TOG, YO, k3, p1, k3, YO, SSK, k2; repeat from * 5 times, p1, k2, K2TOG, YO, k3, p1.

Row 22 (WS): [K1, p7] 14 times, k1.

Row 23 (RS): P1, YO, k4, SSK, k1, *p1, k1, K2TOG, k4, YO, p1, YO, k4, SSK, k1; repeat from * 5 times, p1, k1, K2TOG, k4, YO, p1.

Row 24 (WS): K2, p6, k1, *p6, k3, p6, k1; repeat from * 5 times, p6, k2.

Row 25 (RS): P2, YO, k4, SSK, *p1, K2TOG, k4, YO, p3, YO, k4, SSK; repeat from * 5 times, p1, K2TOG, k4, YO, p2.

Row 26 (WS): K3, p5, k1, *p5, k5, p5, k1; repeat from * 5 times, p5, k3.

ABBREVIATIONS

BOR   Beginning of the round

g   grams

K   Knit

K2TOG   Knit 2 together - 1 stitch decreased with right slant

M1L   Make 1 knit stitch with left slant

M1R   Make 1 knit stitch with right slant

M1P   Make 1 purl stitch

P   Purl stitch

P2TOG   Purl 2 stitches together

RS   Right Side

SSK   Slip 1 stitch knitwise, slip 1 stitch knitwise, return 2 slipped stitches back to left needle and knit them through back loops – 1 stitch decreased with left slant

Tbl   Through back loop

Wyib   With yarn in back

Wyif   With yarn in front

WS   Wrong Side

yds   yards

YO   Yarn over

Special Techniques

CAST-ONS

Backward Loop Cast-on

1. Position the working yarn so that it comes from the needle in between your fingers and thumb, and then outside and around your thumb (fig. 1)
2. Insert the needle tip under the loop of yarn on the outside of your thumb (fig. 2).
3. Let the loop slide off your thumb and gently tighten. Repeat steps 1-3 for the desired number of stitches.

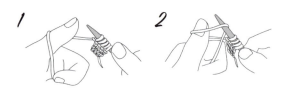

Long tail Cast-On

1. Make a slip knot, place it on the needle.
2. Hold the needle in your right hand. Create a V with the tail end of the yarn over your thumb and the working yarn over your index finger (fig 1).
3. Reach with needle under and into the loop on the left thumb (fig 2).
4. Go over the yarn on your left index finger and bring that yarn through the thumb loop (fig 3).
5. Drop the yarn off your left thumb and gently tighten the loop on the needle.
Repeat steps 2-5 for the desired number of stitches.

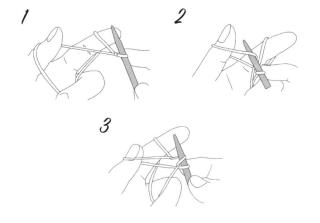

Old Norwegian Cast-On (Twisted German)

1. Leaving a long tail, make a slipknot (this counts as the first stitch.) Place your thumb and index finger between the yarn ends so that the working yarn is around your index finger and the tail end is around your thumb. Secure the ends with your other fingers and hold your palm upward, making a V of yarn (fig 1).
2. Bring the needle in front of the thumb, under both strands around the thumb, down into the center of the thumb loop, then forward toward you (fig 2).
3. Now bring the needle over the strand going to the index finger to grab it (fig.3).
4. Bring the needle back through the loop on the thumb, turning the thumb slightly to make room for the needle to pass through (fig. 4).
5. Drop the loop off the thumb and, placing the thumb back in the V configuration, tighten up the resulting stitch on the needle.
Repeat steps 2-5 for the desired number of stitches.

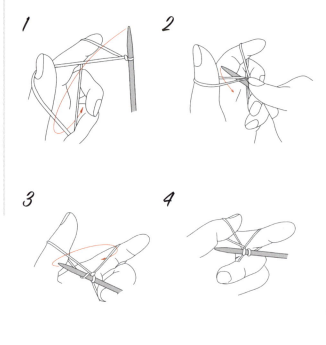

Tubular Cast-on *(folded method)*

With waste yarn, cast on needed number of stitches Do not join in the round.

Foundation Row (RS): With working yarn, knit all stitches in row. This row is worked directly into your waste yarn stitches.

Purl 1 row. Knit 1 row. Purl 1 row (fig. 1).

Carefully remove the waste yarn and place the cast-on stitches onto a spare needle (fig. 2) Make sure you have the same number of stitches on each needle. Now bring the needle with the cast-on stitches up behind the working needle, with wrong sides together and work rib as instructed by the pattern (fig. 3).

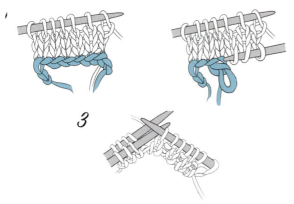

SHORT-ROWS

German Short-rows

Work to the stitch specified in your pattern. Turn the work so the opposite side is facing.

With yarn in front, slip 1 stitch purlwise from left needle to right needle. Pull yarn to back of work over needle until both legs of the stitch in row below are on top of needle, creating a "double stitch" on both sides of needle (fig. 1).

Continue to work in pattern as established.

When working the double stitch, work it as a single stitch (fig. 2).

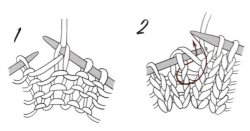

INCREASES

M1L *(Left Slant)*

With left-hand needle tip, pick up the thread between stitches from front to back (fig. 1). Knit lifted loop through the back loop (fig. 2).

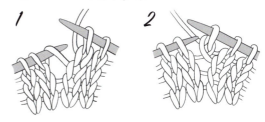

M1R *(Right Slant)*

With left-hand needle tip, pick up the thread between stitches from back to front (fig. 1). Knit lifted loop through the front loop (fig. 2).

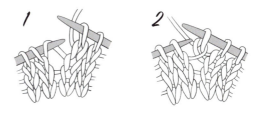

M1P *(Make one purl)*

With left-hand needle tip, pick up the thread between stitches from back to front (fig. 1). Purl lifted loop through the front loop (fig. 2).

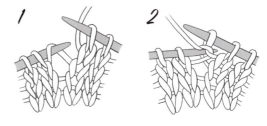

BIND · OFFS

3-Needle Bind-off

With the wrong side of each knitted piece facing out, and the needles parallel, slip a third (working) needle into the first stitch on each of the two needles (fig. 1).

Wrap yarn around working needle as if to knit and pull a loop through. Allow the first stitch from each of the parallel needles to fall from the needles (fig. 2).

*Knit together the new first stitch on both parallel needles in the same way as above.

There will be two stitches on the working needle (fig. 3).

Using one of the two parallel needles, pass the first stitch on the working needle over the second stitch and off the needle as you normally would when binding off (fig. 4).

Repeat from * until only one stitch remains on the working needle.

Break yarn and pull the tail through the last stitch to fasten off.

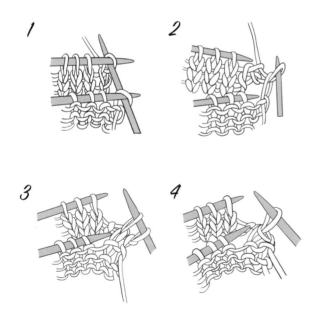

Sloped Bind Off

Step 1: Work the first bind off row at the garment edges as usual.

Step 2: One row before the next bind off row, work to the last stitch of the row, turn.

Step 3: Slip the first stitch from the left needle purlwise, pass the unworked stitch of the previous row over the slipped stitch (the first stitch is bound off).

Bind off the remaining stitches as usual.

Tubular Bind-off for k1, p1 rib

With 2 smaller circular needles held parallel, work as follows: *Slip 1 stitch to front needle, slip 1 stitch to back needle; repeat from * to end. Break yarn, leaving a tail 4 times the length of the finished edge. With tail threaded on a tapestry needle, graft stitches together using Kitchener stitch.

Tubular Bind Off for k2, p2 rib in the round

Using the two Size B circular needles, divide the knit and purl stitches as follows: Slip first stitch onto first (front) needle, *slip the next 2 (purl) stitches to back needle, slip the next 2 (knit) stitches to front needle; repeat from * to last 3 stitches, slip the next 2 purl stitches to back needle, slip the final stitch to front needle. With tail threaded on a tapestry needle, graft stitches together using Kitchener stitch.

Tubular Bind Off for k2, p2 rib in rows (starts and ends with 3 knit stitches)

Using the circular needles, divide the knit and purl stitches as follows: Slip first (knit) stitch onto back needle, *slip the next 2 (knit) stitches to front needle, slip the next 2 (purl) stitches to back needle; repeat from * to last 3 stitches, slip the next 2 knit stitches to front needle, slip the final (knit) stitch to back needle.

With tail threaded on a tapestry needle, graft stitches together using Kitchener stitch.

Kitchener Stitch (grafting)

Hold your two needles parallel to each other with wrong sides together. Use a length of yarn approximately 4 times the length of the finished seam, attached to the right edge of the Back knitted piece. Thread the yarn onto a blunt tapestry needle and follow the instructions below, working from right to left:

Set-Up Step 1: Go into first stitch on front needle as if to purl, pull yarn up and leave stitch on needle (fig. 1).

Set-Up Step 2: Go into first stitch on back needle as if to knit, pull yarn up and leave stitch on needle (fig. 2).

Proceed to grafting:

Step 1: Go into first stitch on front needle as if to knit, pull yarn up and drop stitch off the needle (fig. 3).

Step 2: Go into next stitch on front needle as if to purl, pull yarn up and leave stitch on needle (fig. 4).

Step 3: Go into first stitch on back needle as if to purl, pull yarn up and drop stitch off the needle (fig. 5).

Step 4: Go into next stitch on back needle as if to knit, pull yarn up and leave stitch on needle (fig. 6).

Repeat steps 1 – 4 until all the stitches have been worked, try to control the tension you use when pulling the yarn up through the stitches.

You want to have enough tension so that the stitch being created isn't saggy, but not so much that it's tight and distorts the line of stitches you are creating.

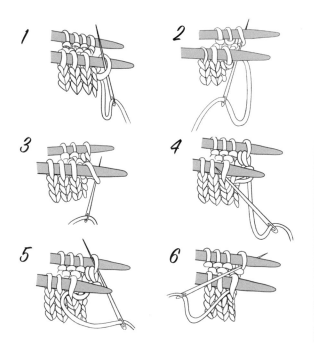

DECREASES

CDD

Slip 2 stitches at the same time from left to right needle (fig. 1), knit next stitch (fig. 2), pass 2 slipped stitches over knit stitch – 2 stitches decreased.

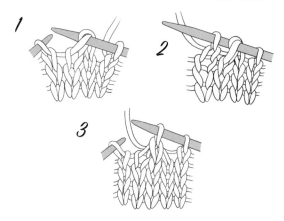

K2TOG (Right slant)

Knit 2 stitches together.

SSK (Left slant)

Slip 1 stitch knitwise (fig. 1), slip 1 stitch knitwise (fig. 2), knit 2 slipped stitches together through back loop (1 stitch decreased with left slant) (fig. 3)

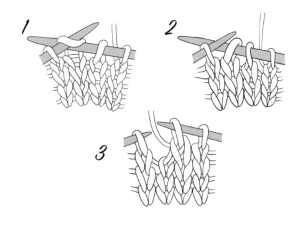

Acknowledgments

I am deeply grateful to everyone who supported me throughout the journey of creating this book. To the incredible Miss Babs team, thank you for generously providing your beautiful yarns and for your flexibility, care, and encouragement along the way.

My sincere thanks to my wonderful editor, Sue McCain, whose sharp eyes, dedication, and professionalism elevated my patterns in every way.

To my test knitters, thank you for your keen observations and thoughtful suggestions, which made these patterns stronger and more accessible.

And to my dear Monday Knitting Group, your friendship, encouragement, and shared meals have nourished both my work and my spirit.

Finally, my deepest gratitude goes to my husband, Oleg — my steadfast source of support. Thank you for your patience behind the camera, your unwavering belief in me, and for always being by my side.

About the author

Before she became a full-time knitwear designer, Irina Anikeeva had a career in fashion retail management. She loves the achievement she gets from working with yarn, learning new techniques, and enhancing her fiber knowledge.

Since 2014 she began designing as Irmian Design full-time and has contributed work to many yarn company collections, magazines, books, including Interweave Knits, Brooklyn Tweed Wool People, Woolfolk, Quince & Co and many more. She released number of books including Nautical Accessories Collection and Vernal. Collection of Warm Weather knitwear.

Solace
Published in 2025 by IrmianDesign
Text © 2025 Irina Anikeeva
Pattern photography © 2025 Irina Anikeeva,
Oleg Todorenko
Illustrations © 2025 Irina Anikeeva

ISBN-13: 978-0-9996990-4-1
Design, layout and illustrations: Irina Anikeeva

Contact Us
www.irmiandesign.com
Instagram: @irmiandesign
Twitter: @irmiandesign
Email: irmiandesign@gmail.com

For pattern corrections, please visit
www.irmiandesign.com/errata

Made in United States
Troutdale, OR
11/12/2025